GAME DEVELOPMENT WITH UNITY®, SECOND EDITION

MICHELLE MENARD
AND
BRYAN WAGSTAFF

Cengage Learning PTR

CENGAGE
Learning®

Professional • Technical • Reference

Australia • Brazil • Japan • Korea • Mexic ed States

D0490535

Game Development with Unity®, Second Edition
Michelle Menard and Bryan Wagstaff

Publisher and General Manager, Cengage Learning PTR: Stacy L. Hiquet

Associate Director of Marketing: Sarah Panella

Manager of Editorial Services: Heather Talbot

Senior Marketing Manager: Mark Hughes

Senior Product Manager: Emi Smith

Project Editor: Kate Shoup

Technical Reviewer: Michael Duggan

Copy Editor: Kate Shoup

Interior Layout Tech: MPS Limited

Cover Designer: Mike Tanamachi

Indexer: Larry Sweazy

Proofreader: Sam Garvey

For product information and technology assistance, contact us at **Cengage Learning Customer & Sales Support, 1-800-354-9706.**

For permission to use material from this text or product, submit all requests online at **cengage.com/permissions.**

Further permissions questions can be emailed to **permissionrequest@cengage.com.**

Unity is a registered trademark of Unity Technologies. All other trademarks are the property of their respective owners.

All images © Cengage Learning unless otherwise noted.

Library of Congress Control Number: 2014939188

ISBN-13: 978-1-305-11054-0

ISBN-10: 1-305-11054-4

Cengage Learning PTR

20 Channel Center Street

Boston, MA 02210

USA

Cengage Learning is a leading provider of customized learning solutions with office locations around the globe, including Singapore, the United Kingdom, Australia, Mexico, Brazil, and Japan. Locate your local office at: **international.cengage.com/region.**

Cengage Learning products are represented in Canada by Nelson Education, Ltd.

For your lifelong learning solutions, visit **cengageptr.com.**

Visit our corporate website at **cengage.com.**

Printed in the United States of America
1 2 3 4 5 6 7 16 15 14

Acknowledgments

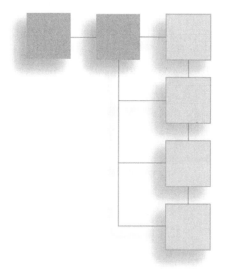

Revising this book has been quite an adventure. When Emi Smith of Cengage Learning contacted me about this project, I felt I could do the job easily. After all, I was comfortable with Unity, had a list of game credits, and had helped edit books in the past. It certainly loomed larger as time passed. The months revising this book and bringing it up to date have been an enjoyable challenge, and I could not have done it alone.

I need to thank the Unity team for their steady stream of updates and providing such a great engine. Unity is updated frequently. The first edition was written against early editions of the 3.x Unity series. Revising it meant every sentence needed to be verified against the current version, every screenshot updated, and every line of code validated. On finding any place that Unity's behavior had changed, sections needed to be rewritten. Unity's animation engine and particle system had been completely replaced, so the book required effort there. The number of supported platforms had grown from three in the first edition to over 15 potential platforms today. Even so, the book is already out of date. As this revision nears completion, the 5.x series is nearly here and will probably be released before this book. Thanks to all of you who continue to improve the tools.

I also need to thank Emi for putting up with me. Michael Duggan, Kate Shoup, Karen Gill, and the rest of the team have done an amazing job, and I have been impressed by their speed and professional skills. Then there are the people I've never met but still work hard to bring the book into reality; thank you to those behind the scenes at Cengage Learning. Next, my wife Sarah also deserves thanks for pushing through the days of writer's block while putting her own book writing aside. Even though it was annoying at times, it could not have been finished without her reminders, "Turn that game off and go work on the book." And perhaps most importantly, thank you to the readers who will use this book. I hope you take what you learn, continue to grow, and develop the next generation of awe-inspiring entertainment.

—Bryan Wagstaff

ABOUT THE AUTHORS

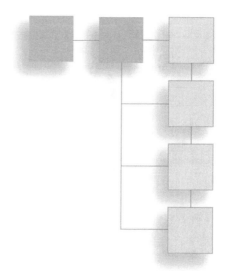

Michelle Menard is a freelance writer and a game producer. After receiving a double bachelor of arts in applied mathematics and music from Brown University, she decided to jump into the games industry by getting a master of fine arts in game design from the Savannah College of Art and Design. She lives in Baltimore, MD, with her husband, two plants, and 3,000 pounds of yarn.

Bryan Wagstaff is a game programmer. He discovered his passion for programming in elementary school with "guess the number" style games and advanced from there. After earning a bachelor of science in computer science from Weber State University, and graduate studies in the 3D Graphics Lab at Brigham Young University, his professional career has included programming for video games, broadcast television, interactive meeting systems, and more. He currently lives in Salt Lake City, UT, with his wife, three daughters, and a flock of birds.

CONTENTS

Introduction

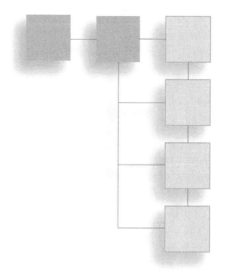

First things first, welcome to the Unity Engine! Whether you're new to game development or a seasoned pro looking into new technology, the Unity Engine has a lot to offer. Available for Mac, Linux, and Windows, the engine can create games that can be deployed on just about any platform available, from the Web, to the Xbox and PlayStation (if you are a licensed developer), to mobile devices like smart phones and tablets. The easy interface, friendly development environment, and wide-ranging support of all popular gaming platforms make it a great choice for the student, indie, and larger developer team.

Unity's clients include such names as Ubisoft, Disney, and Electronic Arts, but the engine is also highly utilized by small independent studios, hobbyists, students, and even companies outside of the gaming industry for medical simulations and architectural walkthroughs. Whatever the end goal, Unity allows anyone, regardless of background, to create fun, interesting, and interactive content. Let's get started.

What Will Be Covered (And What Won't)

This book is an introductory look into the engine. It explains what Unity has to offer and gives a few pointers on how to best use its capabilities for whatever it is you want to do. If you're a hobbyist or student, you'll probably want to start reading from the beginning and follow along with the example project. If you're using this book as a tool to evaluate whether the engine is right for you, you're probably best skipping around to the relevant chapters.

If you start from the beginning, you'll learn all the important interface commands, how to set up and organize your project, and all the basics of getting a 3D game up and running, from character importation to scripting to audio. After completing the sample project, you'll have all the skills necessary to go out and make your own games.

What this book *isn't* is a crash course in the Unified Theory of Game Development and Design. By that, I mean you won't be granted some mystical information or mad skills for everything there is to know in design, programming, art, or sound. Each topic covered (such as game design) does include some basic theory and information—enough to get you going on a working vocabulary and introductory concepts. This book won't make you a star designer or a world-class programmer, however. That requires years of study and practice.

If, after reading, you do find yourself interested in a particular field, check out Appendix D, "Resources and References," for pointers on where to get more information. Think of this as a sampler course stretching across multiple cuisines, not an in-depth exploration of one particular food type. More advanced and singular topics such as network integration and discussions on Unity's shader language are also not covered.

Intended Audience

So, who exactly is this book for, anyway? If you fall into any of the following categories, you've come to the right place:

- A solo developer or generalist looking for some well-rounded information on utilizing the engine
- A developer looking to evaluate the engine for use in future projects
- A hobbyist needing a how-to guide about some specific areas
- A student (or prospective student) wanting to know whether game development is right for you
- Anyone looking to build a game portfolio using an affordable (or in some cases free) professional engine

As stated, all the game development sections cover some basic background knowledge and go over a few key terms. However, the text does assume some knowledge or skills in a few areas if you plan to work away from the sample project. For example, creation of 3D art assets and how to use a 3D modeling package are not covered. All the required models used in the text (and then some) are included on the companion website (more on that in a moment), but their creation is not described. If you stick to the sample project while reading the book, you won't really need any outside knowledge or skills (although any game development information is a plus). If you plan to work on your own project from the start using this book as a guide, then you'll need to educate yourself in the other areas of development or find other places and people to provide art and code. If creating models and animations isn't your thing, the Unity Store has a wide range of assets for free and for sale, and there are many communities out there who can help you develop your own.

THE BOOK'S STRUCTURE

The information in the book is organized into five parts, each covering a general aspect of game development. Within each part, chapters are devoted to each single concept, such as one chapter for AI development and another for particle effects. If you need help on a specific area of Unity, go to the corresponding chapter or use the handy index. The appendixes include a list of common and helpful shortcut keys, a rundown of the most-used classes, and exercises for you to complete if you want a few pointers on what to do once you finish reading. A compiled glossary for all keywords introduced in the text is also contained there.

I've tried to make learning the engine a little more straightforward by using some general formatting guidelines. Steps for you to complete in the engine always appear in numbered lists. If you see such lists coming up on the page, you should open Unity to follow along.

Links between steps in a folder chain or nested menu are marked with the > symbol. So the line "My Documents > My Unity Project" would mean to open the My Documents folder and then open the folder My Unity Project contained within it. Pretty straightforward. Code to write in the engine is blocked off in its own formatting, as shown here:

```
//I'm a comment
Update()
  {
    print("Hello World");
  }
```

Finally, some extra information is included in the form of sidebars. These mostly cover more advanced technical data or engine specs and aren't required knowledge for using the engine on a day-to-day basis. They do tend to be helpful, however. Also be mindful of tips, notes, and warnings scattered throughout the text. These are often important, containing information about common pitfalls and helping to stave off potentially hard-to-fix disasters. If time was taken to graphically embellish something, it's probably worth a second look.

INSTALLATION INSTRUCTIONS

Installing Unity is quick and painless and technically requires an Internet connection. Unity comes in two flavors, Unity Basic, which is free, and Unity Pro. Both are regularly updated by developers. Although you won't need the Internet again after activation, it is advisable to have a connection if only for the patch updates and fixes.

The Unity Engine

First up, install Unity. You can download Unity from the Unity Technologies website: unity3d.com/. From the Download menu, click on either the Mac or Windows version button, whichever is right for you. (This book uses the Windows version for all its examples.) You can choose to download the free Unity Basic version directly or get a Unity Pro license trial version, which is free for 30 days. It doesn't really matter as far as the book is concerned, but it can be fun to see what goodies the Pro version includes.

Note that Unity has grown to include many features and these features require space. The installer is about 1 GB. The download time will depend on your Internet connection. A fast broadband connection can usually handle the transfer in a few minutes.

Once the download is complete, run the UnitySetup-###.exe file, accept the terms of agreement, and follow the onscreen command prompts. When you get to the Choose Components screen, shown in Figure I.1, make sure the Example Project checkbox is selected. You'll probably also want to select the Unity Development Web Player checkbox as well, in case you ever want to publish your games to the Internet. In addition, consider selecting the MonoDevelop checkbox even if you have your own development environment because the bundled version of the MonoDevelop editor has some specialized features that are hard to get in other editors. If you change your mind later you can re-run the installer to add or remove components. Then click Next and finish the installation.

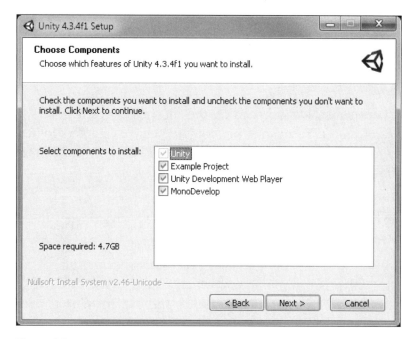

Figure I.1
All components are selected by default, requiring nearly 5 GB of space.
Source: Unity Technologies.

Use the default install path or select your own, and then click Install. Unity takes nearly 5 GB of install space, so make sure your selected destination can handle this plus any other add-ons or projects you want to use later. Follow the other onscreen instructions to complete the install.

After the install has finished, Unity will prompt you to register your copy. For the free version and trial Pro, this is easy. Select the Internet registration version (if available) and fill out the form on the website the engine takes you to—usually it's just your name and email address. After this, Unity is yours to use.

Once the engine has finished installing, it's time to move on to the contents of the companion website.

Using the Companion Website

To access the book's companion website, visit www.cengageptr.com/downloads, and type the name of this book in the Search field. The companion website is divided into a few main sections:

- **Chapters:** This folder contains subfolders for each chapter in the book, whenever they require the use of files or assets. You can either copy the entire Chapters folder to your hard drive now or just grab the individual files when you need them. The text always specifies when a file is needed and where to grab it.

- **Design Documents:** This folder houses all the basic information for the sample project discussed in the text, a game called *Widget*. When the text says to view the Design Docs, they're located in here.

- **Shader Test:** A sample project detailing and comparing the basic shaders side-by-side that are available in Unity. If you're not sure which shader to use or how some shaders may interact in a specific lighting rig, modify and use this file as needed.

- **Final Project Files:** Unlike the Chapters folder, which houses all the individual files as they come up in the text, the Final Project Files folder is a complete Unity project for the *Widget* game. If you ever get stuck or want to see how something fits together later, you can always check out the game here. Extra assets such as more models, textures, and UI elements are also included here for any further expansion you may want to pursue.

Optional Installs

Between Unity and the contents of the companion website, you can complete every exercise in this book and get the sample project up and running. However, you may find yourself wanting to tweak a graphic or texture here or there, or maybe even sculpt a new model to import. Many free software packages are described both in the text where appropriate and in Appendix D. If you don't already have something installed on your computer, check the appendix for information and a link.

Unity includes MonoDevelop, a free code editor to use for scripting, but you can use your own favorite coding environment if desired. Chapter 6, "Scripting in Unity," covers compatible ones in more detail, and Appendix D also provides links where appropriate.

Parting Words of Wisdom

You probably have tons of great game ideas floating around in your head. Maybe you've even started working on one, the big one that'll net you that dream job or needed raise. Maybe you have built some small projects in the past and want to use a comprehensive engine rather than doing everything yourself. Or perhaps you've started two games, or three, or…you get the picture. Working on making your snippets of ideas and musings into playable games is great—but how many have you actually finished? Making a game is a huge commitment, fraught with tons of unforeseen setbacks, design changes, and software explosions, all for a tiny little bundle of ideas that you hope others will love as much as you do. It's far too easy once the first dragon rears its head to stop working, take an extended break, and never return to the field to try again. It's not procrastination, you tell others, it's just a short time away to rest your eyes, to let your ideas simmer free of worry. The short break becomes a week, and then a month, and years roll by as your little unfinished game collects dust in the corner.

Tackling the problems in game development is hard work. Sometimes you follow a trail of ideas and discover barriers that need to be climbed, worked around, or pushed through. Other times you need to admit that the idea was wrong, it didn't work out as expected, or it's just plain un-fun. Don't walk away from the whole project and leave the game unfinished. Try something else, even if you're unsure where this new path will take you. Maybe it won't work out, but maybe it'll be the solution to a whole host of problems. Try, make mistakes, learn, and try again. Be willing to make mistakes and learn from them, and keep fighting your way through until the game is complete. No game is perfect and defect-free, but you can reach the point where you can say it is complete.

Finish that game, and then finish another. It doesn't matter if you think they're horrible, terrible piles of swill you'd be embarrassed to show your own mother. Show her anyway. They may suck, or they may not. Either way, analyze what you did that worked and didn't work. The process is as much about learning as it is about creating, and no one ever excelled by stopping halfway. If you get discouraged, it is okay to take a break, but always, always come back to it in the end. Support from friends can help greatly in this—involve some of your buddies in rounds of routine play tests. Make a party of it. Celebrate what you do and remember to have fun. If you're not having fun, you're probably not making fun!

One late night, as we were pushing to finish a game, I was sitting in the cafeteria, dining with co-workers on a large tray of studio-provided "mystery nuggets" for dinner. Someone said, "It is eight o'clock at night and I'm still at work on this crazy project that never seems to end. I could be spending time on so many other things. Will you remind me why we are still here?" Another co-worker spoke up, and his reply was heartfelt: "Because we love it. No matter how many problems we encounter and difficulties we overcome, we love it. We love creating these amazing games that entertain millions of people. We are artisans, passionate about doing our best on every task. We are not just working late and eating deep-fried mystery nuggets; we are building a game to inspire, to entertain, and to give the world something that they may savor and enjoy. Just like the mystery nuggets, most people will have no idea what is inside, but when they play the game they can be entertained and enjoy a moment of life. That makes the difficulties worthwhile."

Be passionate. Development is work and sometimes it is difficult. Sometimes it is painful. Sometimes you will be disappointed and unsatisfied with the results. Just keep pushing, sharing your passion, and doing your best work. Game development is a powerful career. We create new worlds, teach, entertain, and inspire. We start with a blank file and finish with a product that can change the world. Be a game developer.

Part I

In the Beginning ...

As with any new endeavor, it's usually best to start somewhere in the beginning. And before you even start, it's best to lay out your tools and get your ideas in order. You wouldn't attempt (I hope) to build a house without a blueprint, and games are no different. The best game ideas in the world won't get you very far unless you have the knowledge, skills, and discipline to see them fully realized and implemented.

Before Unity, making a game from scratch for the newbie game designer was a rather daunting process. Engines, especially free ones, weren't terribly easy to come across, and those that were often suffered from poor execution or lack of documentation. Now with Unity, you can quickly get your ideas in motion, even if you lack a strong art or programming background.

In this part, you'll learn the basics of the engine and its interface, as well as how to refine your game idea from the get-go, hopefully saving you some time and energy later in the process.

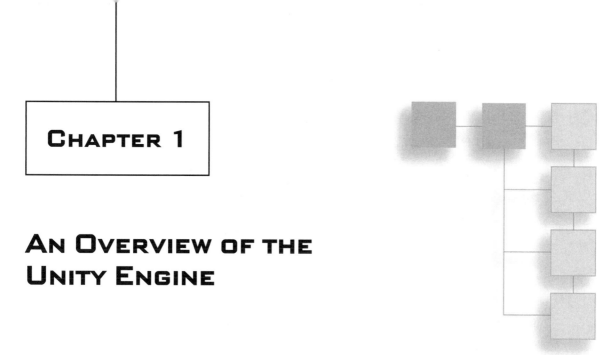

CHAPTER 1

AN OVERVIEW OF THE UNITY ENGINE

Unity is a powerful integrated game engine and editor, enabling you to quickly and efficiently create objects, import external assets, and link them all together with code. The editor is visually driven and built around the principles that you can do everything with a simple drag-and-drop motion—even connect scripts, assign variables, or create complicated multi-part assets. Unity also boasts an integrated scripting environment, built-in networking capabilities, and the ability to build and deploy for multiple platforms. All of this is wrapped up in a simple, intuitive, and customizable workspace.

GETTING ACQUAINTED WITH THE INTERFACE

Before diving headfirst into making your first game with Unity, it's worth the time to first take a quick look at how to get around in the editor. Unity may look a bit daunting when you first open it, but you'll find that you can easily master its basics in a day.

If you haven't done so already, open Unity. Choose Start > Programs > Unity (C:\Program Files\Unity\Editor\Unity.exe) or click the desktop icon if you created one. Then load the Ch1_TestFile.unity file located on this book's companion website to follow along. Figure 1.1 shows the Unity environment.

3

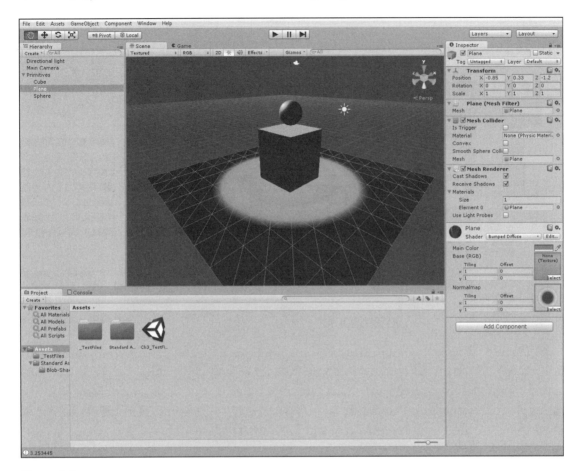

Figure 1.1
The Unity environment after you load the Chapter 1 sample. By the end of the chapter, you will understand all the parts you see on the screen.
Source: Unity Technologies.

Note

If you installed one of the demos with the engine, a scene from the demo will load by default until you either load a different scene or create a new one.

The editor's default layout is broken into a series of different panes and tabbed windows called views. Each view details a specific aspect of the editor and allows you to perform different functions when working on your game. If you've used a 3D modeling program or other game editor in the past, you may find some of this familiar.

You can rearrange the views to suit your preferences. Views can be repositioned, resized, and even broken off to their own separate windows. Several presets can be found in the menu under Window > Layouts. Depending on the size of your monitor, you might prefer the Wide layout or the Tall layout, or you might decide to create your own. Don't worry about getting the settings wrong; you can always reset the Unity views back to the default layout by selecting Window > Layouts > Revert Factory Settings.

The Project View

All of a game's files—scripts, objects, scenes, anything and everything—are organized into a Project folder, each of which contains an Assets folder. The Assets folder houses *everything* you've created or imported to include in your game—meshes, textures, scripts, cameras, levels…everything. (See Figure 1.2.) The Project View panel displays this Project folder and the incorporated Assets folder.

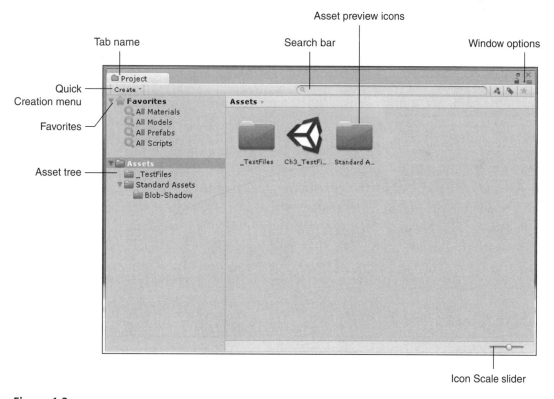

Figure 1.2
The Project view.
Source: Unity Technologies.

The Project view displays everything included in the game's Assets directly, exactly how they are organized and arranged on your computer's hard drive. If you are unsure, however, of where these files are located (or if you ever forget), you can simply right-click any selected asset in the Project view and select Show in Explorer.

Arrows next to folders indicate nested layers. Clicking any one of these will expand that folder's contents. You can also Shift-click an arrow to fully expand or contract its contents. Moving and organizing files into different folders can be achieved in the Project view with a simple click and drag.

Caution

Be careful about moving your asset files around outside the Unity Editor. In fact, avoid it at all costs. If you need to reorganize or move an asset, do it from within the Project view. Not doing so could break or remove any metadata or links associated with that asset, possibly breaking your game in the process.

When you select an asset folder or a Favorites folder, the preview icons update to show you the folder's contents. Use the Icon Scale slider to change the size of the icons. If you slide the Icon Scale slider all the way to the left, the display will change from icons to a list.

Each type of object listed also has its own descriptive icon or thumbnail, making it easy to quickly scan the contents. Many assets, like directories, source code, and general data files, use a standard icon. Other assets, like Photoshop images, 3D models, textures, and materials, display a thumbnail preview of the asset in the file.

The Search bar enables you to quickly find assets directly by name. The three buttons on the right side of the Search bar let you search by type, search by tag, and save the search as a favorite. On a small project, you can usually remember where all your assets are located. But when a project contains hundreds or even thousands of assets, using the search tool is the easiest way to find what you need. The Project view's list will dynamically update after each letter you type, allowing for easier browsing if you don't quite remember the asset's exact name.

You can open and edit files directly from within the Project view. If you find you need to tweak or correct something in any file (like a Photoshop file), simply double-click the file to open it in its default editor. Save the file normally to have Unity import it back into your project.

Sometimes you'll find it necessary to make new assets or objects that aren't contained already in your Project view. Unity makes this easy from within this view—simply click the Quick Creation menu to bring up the available options. This shortcut menu is located right beneath the Project tab. From here, you can make new folders, empty script files, or other game-specific objects without having to leave the editor. Right-clicking in the Project view itself will also give you a link to the Quick Creation menu and its options, placing the new file at your current location in the file tree.

Tip

To rename any file or folder, you can click twice slowly on the name (not a normal fast double-click) or select the desired file and press the F2 key. Then start typing. Press Enter when you are done renaming your file.

Right-clicking in the Project view will bring up a few advanced options, including asset importation, syncing with external project controllers, and asset package manipulation. See Figure 1.3. These are covered in more depth in later chapters.

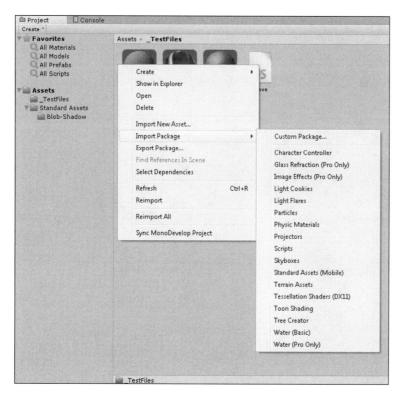

Figure 1.3
The right-click menu and Import Package menu options.
Source: Unity Technologies.

All tabbed windows have a Windows Options drop-down list, allowing you to maximize the selected view, close the viewed tab, or add another tab view to the window. Click the icon to bring up the available options.

The Hierarchy View

Whereas the Project view lists all the objects and files available in your game, the Hierarchy view lists just the ones you're actually using in the current scene. The objects in the scene are listed alphabetically. As you add or remove objects from your game, the Hierarchy view will update with each change. Selecting an object in the Hierarchy view and pressing the Delete key (or right-clicking and selecting Delete) will remove the object from your current scene in the game, but not from the project's Assets folder. Figure 1.4 shows the game's current contents as an example.

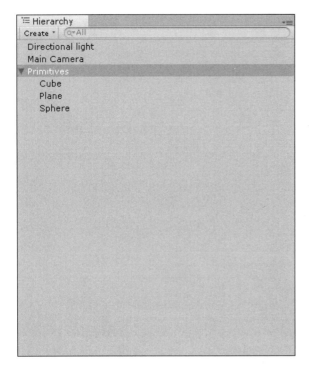

Figure 1.4
The Hierarchy view, showing the game scene's current contents.
Source: Unity Technologies.

Each *instance* (a copy or occurrence) of an asset will be listed individually, so good naming conventions are especially important. If you have 30 instances of an object all named Cube, you may have trouble finding the one you want later. You can rename any object in the Hierarchy view independently of its actual filename in the Project view. A simple mesh named Cube in your Project view can then be instanced and renamed in the Hierarchy view to anything you want, like Crate, Box, or Mystery Pickup23, making it easier to find and use later. Note that this will not update the filename of the actual object in the Project view or on your computer. To do that, you must change the name from within the Project view.

Parenting objects together in the Hierarchy view can also help with organization and make editing your game easier. When you parent objects together, you are basically linking a collection of unrelated objects together in a group under a single object, the parent. All the objects under this parent are called its children, or child objects. See Figure 1.5.

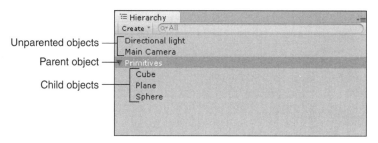

Figure 1.5
Parented and unparented objects.
Source: Unity Technologies.

In the example, the parent object is an asset called Primitives, under which three child objects are located: Sphere, Cube, and Plane. Clicking the arrow next to Primitives will expand or collapse the group, much like with the folders in the Project view. However, parenting gives you one other important benefit besides a speedy way to group like objects together: Moving or manipulating the parent object will in turn do the same to all the children underneath it. They are said to inherit the parent's data. The child objects can still be edited independently of each other and the parent object, giving you more control.

If you're still uncertain about parenting, think of a normal person's body. An arm is parented to the torso, and a hand is parented to the end of the arm. Moving the torso forward (the parent) will move the arm with it, which will in turn move the hand (the two children). However, you can move and rotate the hand around without moving the torso or the arm.

Using parented objects can make moving large numbers of objects around much easier and more precise, and should be used whenever possible. A few more advanced concepts of parenting will be covered in Chapter 4, "Building Your Environment: Importing Basic Custom Assets" and Chapter 6, "Scripting in Unity."

The Inspector

The Inspector, as its name suggests, displays the detailed information contained in each object in your game (see Figure 1.6). Click the Sphere object (you may need to expand Primitives to see it) to bring up its details in the Inspector view.

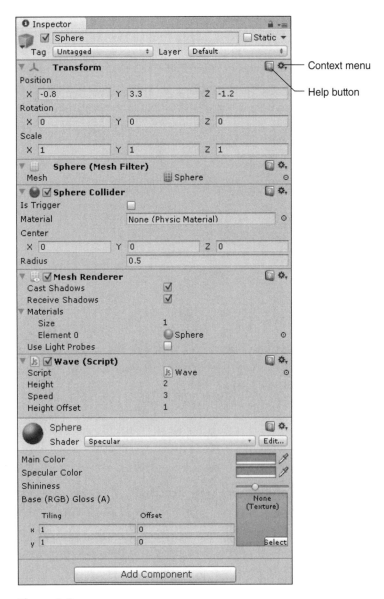

Figure 1.6
The Inspector view for the Sphere object.

Source: Unity Technologies.

On first glance, this may seem overwhelming, but all Inspector views follow the same basic principle for each object. At the top of the Inspector is the object's name, followed by a list of the different properties of the object, such as Transform and Sphere Collider. Each of these different kinds of properties will be discussed in greater detail later. For now, just know that this is where you come to edit any piece of information about your object.

Each property in the Inspector has a Help button and a Context menu attached to it. Clicking the Help button will bring up the related document for the property in the reference manual. Try it with any one of the properties. Clicking the Context menu will give you specific options related to just that property, as well as a way to reset the property back to its default values.

Note

You will need an active Internet connection to view the reference manual when you click the Help button, because it is hosted online at Unity's website.

The Toolbar

The Toolbar, shown in Figure 1.7, consists of the available menus and five basic control groups for your game. The menus along the top of the editor contain the basic generic options available to you and are grouped by function. They are as follows:

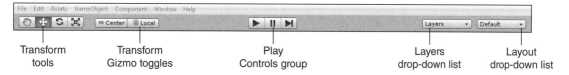

Figure 1.7
The Toolbar.
Source: Unity Technologies.

- **File menu:** Use this menu to open and save scenes and projects and to create builds of your game.

- **Edit menu:** This menu contains the normal copy and paste functions, as well as selection setups and settings.

- **Assets menu:** Everything having to do with creating, importing, exporting, and syncing assets can be found in this menu.

■ **GameObject menu:** This menu is for creating, viewing, and parenting GameObjects.

■ **Component menu:** This menu is for creating new components or properties for GameObjects.

■ **Window menu:** Use this menu to bring up specific views (such as the Project or Hierarchy view) and to switch to saved window layouts.

■ **Help menu:** This menu links to the manuals, community forums, and a page where you can activate your license.

Sometimes Unity will add menus for you to access functions when editing terrains, animations, or other items. For now, just be aware of the general functionality contained in each menu. The individual aspects will be discussed in detail as they're needed.

The control tools are also grouped by function, and serve primarily to assist with editing and movement in the Scene and Game views, discussed more fully next. These tools are as follows:

■ **Transform tools:** These are used in the Scene view to control and manipulate objects. In order from left to right, they are the Hand tool, Translate tool, Rotate tool, and Scale tool.

■ **Transform Gizmo toggles:** These change how the Transform tools work in the Scene view.

■ **Play Controls group:** You use these to start and stop testing a game from within the editor.

■ **Layers drop-down list:** This controls which specific objects are displayed in the Scene view at any given time.

■ **Layout drop-down list:** This changes the layout of your windows and views and saves any custom layouts you create. It also serves as a shortcut to the Window > Layouts list.

The Scene View

One of the most important windows in the editor is the Scene view—a visual representation of your game world or level (see Figure 1.8). This is where you'll maneuver, manipulate, and position all your objects and assets listed in the Hierarchy view, creating the physical space that your players will explore and interact with.

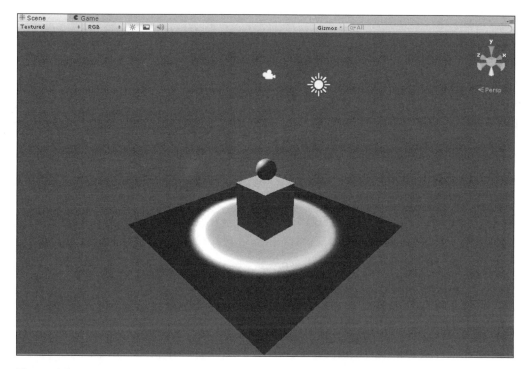

Figure 1.8
A simple Scene view.
Source: Unity Technologies.

As you can see, the objects listed within the Hierarchy view are displayed in all their brilliance in the Scene view. You can click the object's name in the Hierarchy view to select it or just manually click it in the Scene view. Clicking the different objects in the Scene view or Hierarchy view will update the Inspector with the object's appropriate data.

Note

If you see lists of items populating your Hierarchy view but the Scene view appears to be empty, your view may be zoomed out too much to view the individual assets. To fix this, select an item in the Hierarchy view, move and hover your mouse over the Scene view, and press the F key to zoom in to the object.

Note that by clicking the Primitives object in the Hierarchy view, you actually select all the child objects in the Scene view. There isn't a separate Primitives object displayed in the Scene view. If you want to select an entire parented group of objects, you must do so through the Hierarchy view.

Camera Navigation

Learning to move around quickly in the Scene is one of the most important aspects of the editor to master. (If you're an Autodesk Maya user, you'll be right at home with these controls.) You can think of the Scene as the output or focus of a virtual camera. To move around the scene, you move your camera's view around as you look at different objects. The controls are as follows:

- **Tumble (Alt-click):** The camera will pivot around all axes, thus "tumbling" the view.

- **Track (Alt–middle mouse button click):** Moves the camera left, right, up, and down in the scene.

- **Zoom (Alt–right click or mouse scroll wheel):** Zooms the camera in and out of the scene.

- **Flythrough mode (press the W, A, S, or D key while pressing the right-mouse button):** The camera will enter a "first-person" mode, allowing you to quickly move and zoom around the scene.

- **Center (click the desired GameObject and press the F key):** The camera will zoom in and center on the selected object in the view. Your mouse cursor must be located in the Scene view, not over the object in the Hierarchy view.

- **Full Screen Mode (spacebar):** Press the spacebar to make the active view take up all available space in the editor. Press it again to return to your previous layout. The active view is whichever one your mouse is hovering over.

If your mouse has only one button (or if you only want to use your left mouse button), you're not at a complete loss. Select the Hand tool from the Toolbar (or press the Q key on your keyboard) to put your mouse in Move mode. Then use the following commands:

- **Tumble (Alt-click):** The camera will pivot around all axes, thus "tumbling" the view.

- **Track (click and drag):** Click and drag to move the camera left, right, up, and down in the scene.

- **Zoom (Ctrl-click):** Zoom the camera in and out of the scene.

Try the different movement controls until they become comfortable and second nature. Being able to quickly move around your game scene with precision will make your development time much faster and more enjoyable.

The Scene view also contains a special tool called the Scene gizmo, shown in Figure 1.9. This special tool gives you fast access to the scene camera's orientation, allowing you to quickly change the view to premade selections.

Figure 1.9
The Scene gizmo.
Source: Unity Technologies.

Buzzword

A *gizmo* is an icon or symbol often used for something that doesn't have a visual representation in the real world. In 3D programs like Unity, gizmos are often used to represent movement and camera controls.

Try clicking the different arrows on the Scene gizmo and watch how the Scene view updates. Each arrow changes the camera's view to one of the different orthogonal, or 2D, directions, like Top, Back, Front, or Right (see Figure 1.10). Sometimes you'll need to change to one of these views to properly line up an object in the scene.

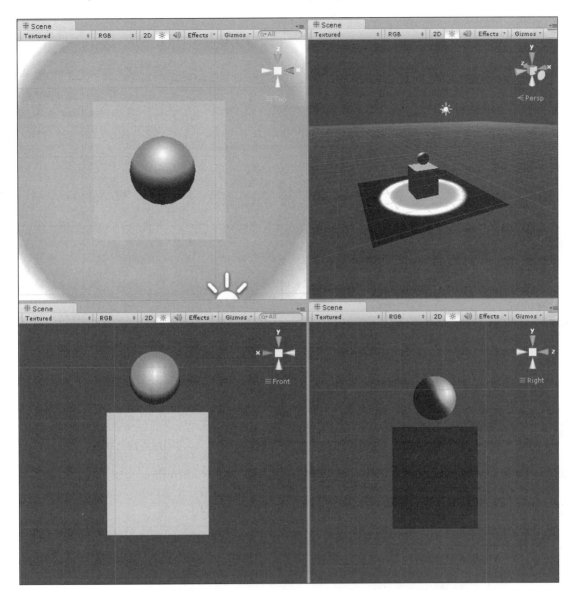

Figure 1.10
The four main orientation views.
Source: Unity Technologies.

Note

The Plane object seems to disappear in some of the side views because it is a 2D object. That is, planes are defined only along two axes and don't have height. If ever your 2D objects seem to disappear, switch to a different orthogonal view.

Click the center cube icon on the gizmo to switch between Perspective and Isometric views. If you Shift-click the center cube of the gizmo, you'll enter a Perspective view. The gizmo uses three diverging lines to indicate Perspective mode and three parallel lines to indicate Isometric mode. Perspective view emulates real-world perspective sight, where objects get smaller as they become farther away. Notice that in Isometric view, the objects do not change size or shape as they become farther away. They remain the same uniform size. This camera view lacks the emulation of perspective. You may recognize this look from many older games. See Figure 1.11.

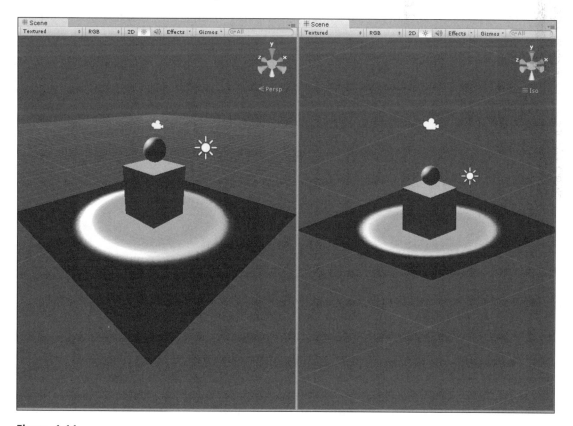

Figure 1.11
Isometric versus Perspective view.
Source: Unity Technologies.

Each of the arrows is color-coordinated to match one of the axes of the game world: red for the X axis, green for the Y axis, and blue for the Z axis. Unity's world space is set up in a Cartesian coordinate system—the X and Z axes form the ground plane, and the Y axis defines the height of the world. The center of the world is located where these three axes intersect at the origin, the point (0,0,0). This is common vector notation for X = 0, Y = 0, Z = 0, or more generally, (X, Y, Z).

Note

If you're more comfortable using different colors than the defaults to denote the world axes, you can change them to anything you like by choosing Edit > Preferences > Colors.

Scene View Controls

The Scene view's Control Bar, shown in Figure 1.12, changes the way you view the scene. The default values give a good approximation of what your scene would look like rendered in game, as well as displaying a handy grid to help position and move objects.

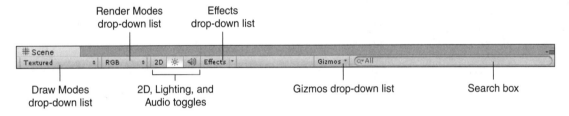

Figure 1.12
The Scene view's Control Bar.
Source: Unity Technologies.

While the default view is very useful, sometimes you will want to change what you see during development. The Control Bar lets you change many different options. The settings do not affect the built game, so switch them around as much as you need to help you with your project.

The first drop-down list, Draw Modes, controls how the objects are drawn in your scene. The default value is Textured—the objects are drawn using the colors and texture maps assigned to them. Click the menu to change the draw mode. You have the following options:

- **Wireframe.** Wireframe mode shows the objects' meshes without textures attached.

- **Textured Wire.** Textured Wire mode shows the textures with their wireframes overlaid.

- **Render Paths.** This mode allows you to see objects assigned to deferred lighting or forward rendering. (Both of these are advanced settings.)
- **Lightmap Resolution.** This mode is a tool for artists to preview how lighting will appear.

None of these selections change the way your game will display, only how the Scene view's camera views the objects.

The Render Modes drop-down list is useful for optimizing your game scene by fine-tuning your objects. The options are as follows:

- **RGB.** The default value, RGB shows all the objects colored as normal.
- **Alpha.** Selecting Alpha will show all the objects in the scene by their alpha values. Fully opaque objects will render as white, fully transparent objects will render as black, and objects that are partly translucent will render in different shades of gray.
- **Overdraw.** Overdraw shows how much of the screen is being overdrawn—in other words, it shows you objects being drawn behind others.
- **Mipmaps.** This is a tool to help you find the ideal texture sizes for your objects. Objects drawn in blue have textures that are too small and objects drawn in red have ones that are too large.

Just like the draw modes, none of these selections change the game will display, but only change that Scene view's content.

The Lighting button toggles whether the Scene view uses the default built-in lighting or your own implemented lighting. If you haven't placed a light source in the scene yet, using the built-in lighting setup can be useful. The 2D button switches between 2D and 3D in the Scene view window. If you are building a 2D game scene, you can still manipulate objects in 3D space to order their visual depth, so toggling between 2D and 3D is very useful. The Audio button toggles whether audio effects should be played for the view.

The Effects drop-down list allows you to show or hide certain visual effects. Sometimes it is difficult to see objects in the scene when you have fog, flares, or other effects visible. Changing the visibility of the effects in the Scene view can be useful in complex scenes.

The Gizmos drop-down list is similar to the Effects drop-down list, enabling you to show or hide items in the Scene view. Inside the drop-down list are several adjustments you can make to the gizmos. The 3D Gizmos checkbox toggles between using the real 3D position of the object versus drawing the gizmo as an overlay on top. The slider will adjust the size of gizmo icons. You can adjust the gizmo icons and colors, hide them, hide the ground plane grid, and also toggle the gizmos in controls you make yourself.

Finally, the Search box lets you filter items in the scene. Objects that don't match the search will turn gray in the Scene view and be filtered from the Hierarchy view. Objects that do match the filter will remain in color in the Scene view and remain visible on the Hierarchy view.

Manipulating Objects

Besides moving your camera view around, you'll also need to reposition and move objects within the scene. These manipulations are called *object transforms*. They handle the position, rotation, and scale (relative size) of any selected object. You can adjust object transforms by typing in new values for the transforms in the Inspector or by manipulating the object with gizmos.

Click the Sphere object in the Hierarchy view or Scene view to bring up its information in the Inspector, as shown in Figure 1.13. The first property listed for each object is Transform, which stores the object's current position, rotation, and scale. Click and type in any of the boxes to change the numbers. Unity's base units are in meters, so making Y = 2 will move the sphere 2 meters into the air. Making Y = −2 will move the sphere beneath the plane.

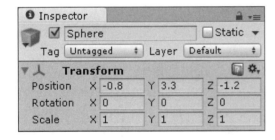

Figure 1.13
The Transform property.
Source: Unity Technologies.

Besides typing values directly, you can also scrub the value in any of the boxes. Click any one of the axis labels in the Transform box (X, Y, or Z) and drag your mouse left or right. The object will move or deform with your changes. This isn't a very precise way to position or manipulate an object, but it can be a quick and dirty way to get your objects basically where you want them before fine-tuning.

Another option for transforming objects is to use the Transform tools—Translate, Rotate, and Scale. (See Figure 1.14.) You can manually select a tool from the Toolbar or use the hotkeys provided in the following sections to switch between them more quickly (definitely recommended).

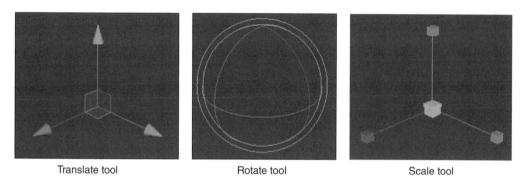

Translate tool   Rotate tool   Scale tool

Figure 1.14
From left to right: the Translate, Rotate, and Scale tools.
Source: Unity Technologies.

The Translate tool moves the selected object's position around the scene, either along one of the three axes or freely in space. Click the Sphere object in the Hierarchy view and press the W key to activate the Translate tool. Grab one of the handles, or arrows, to move the object along that axis in the game world (again, red for along the X axis, green for along the Y axis, and blue for along the Z axis). Notice that the values in the Inspector update based on your changes. You can also scrub using the Translate tool—simply select a handle with the mouse and then click and drag the middle mouse button to move the asset along the chosen axis. Finally, you can click in the center of the tool (or on the object itself) and drag around the scene to freely move the object along all three axes. This usually isn't the best method, as you don't have the finest of control over placement.

Tip

You'll find that switching between the orthographic views (like Front and Right) via the Scene gizmo can help greatly in the precise placement of objects.

The Rotate tool rotates the object around any one of the given axes. Click the Cube object and press the E key to activate the tool. The handles for this tool resemble three colored rings wrapped around a center sphere. Drag the handles or scrub around to rotate the object. Note that the colors for these rings don't line up with the world axes colors—they instead indicate around which axis the object will rotate. If you grab the blue handle, for instance, the cube will rotate around the Z axis. The tool also has a simple yellow ring encompassing the other three. You can click and drag this ring to rotate the object in all three axes.

The final Transform tool is the Scale tool, which you can access by pressing the R key on your keyboard. This tool works similarly to the Translate tool: You grab one of the handles to scale the object only in that axis or use the center yellow square to scale the object uniformly in all three dimensions. Try this out with any of the three objects in the scene. Scaling your mesh using this tool comes with its own risks. While it does seem like a great way to quickly resize any of your assets, you may slow the performance of your game if you use too many scaled objects or stretch your textures completely out of whack. The best way to adjust scale is to ensure that the mesh in your 3D application is the right size to begin with.

Note

You can change the default keys for any of these tools from Edit > Preferences > Keys.

Moving Multiple and Parented Objects

Up to this point, you've only been moving single objects around—the child objects of the Primitives object. Now try selecting the Primitives object in the Hierarchy view and moving it to the point (0,−3.5,0). The entire Primitives group, including all its children, moves to the new location. Now click any one of the child objects and look at its information in the Inspector. Notice anything? The individual position transforms of the children did not update or change when you moved the Primitives object to its new location, even though you can clearly see they have changed. This is because child objects inherit all transform data from their parent object. The transform values of the children are actually relative to the parent object, not world values.

For example, examine the Cube's position data in the Inspector. The Y coordinate doesn't mean that it's located at position $Y = 1.5$ meters. Instead, it means that it is located 1.5 meters above the location of the parent object. Changing the parent object's location in the world won't change the fact that the Cube will remain 1.5 meters above it. The child's position is referred to as *local coordinates*, and the parent object houses the *global coordinates*.

For this reason, it is often good practice to manually place an object you plan to make a parent at the origin before applying its child. This will make it easier in the long run when you need to start placing hundreds of assets relative to each other.

You can also select multiple objects in a scene by holding down the Shift key as you click different items with the left mouse button. If you accidentally select an item you didn't mean to, hold down the Ctrl key and click to remove it from the selection.

Transform Gizmo Toggles

Remember the Transform Gizmo toggles from the Toolbar? These dictate how the Transform tools behave and function. The first toggle button, Pivot/Center, changes where in space the tool is located. Select the Primitives object in the Hierarchy view and then activate the Rotate tool. The default value, Pivot, places the tool at the object's pivot point, or the point in space around which the object transforms. (Pivot points are generally predefined at the object's creation and can be easily moved from within your chosen 3D application.) Change the Scene view to an orthographic view like Front or Back and rotate the object around one of the axes. Note that the object always rotates the same relative distance from the pivot point.

Now click the Pivot toggle to change it to Center. The Rotate tool jumps to the local center of the selected object. Try rotating the object again. This time, the object rotates around its center instead of around the imaginary pivot point in space. Using both Pivot and Center to your advantage can greatly reduce headaches when trying to move assets into position.

Return to the Perspective view. This time, select the Plane object and rotate it 45 degrees around its Y axis. Activate the Translate tool. With the Local toggle active, the Translate tool's axes stay relative and local to the object's position. Click the Local toggle to change it to Global, and watch how the tool updates to realign itself with the world coordinate system. Being able to move an object in either its local space or global space is hugely beneficial, especially when objects become rotated at haywire angles.

The Game View

In the default Tall layout, the Game view is located on a tab next to the Scene tab. Here, your game is rendered exactly as it would be if you were to finalize your build and publish it. You can test and play your game at any time from within the editor using this view, never having to stop to build or cook anything. While this may not seem like the biggest deal to you right now, when you start to tweak and balance hundreds of little details, having the flexibility to switch between the editor and the game on the fly is priceless. See Figure 1.15.

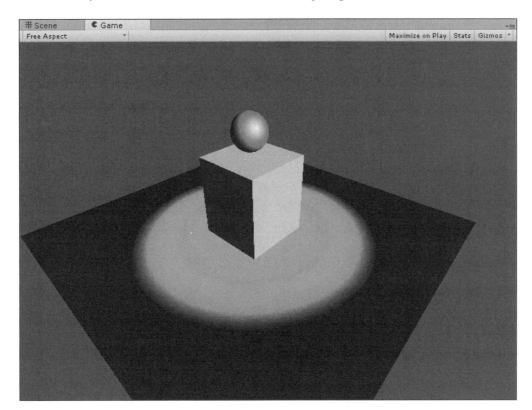

Figure 1.15
The rendered Game view.
Source: Unity Technologies.

To test the game, click the Play button (the one that looks like a right-facing arrow) in the Play Controls group on the Toolbar. The editor will activate the Game view, slightly darken the user interface (UI), and start your game. Test this now.

There is a small script attached to the Sphere object that is causing it to slowly move up and down. See Figure 1.16. While this isn't anything revolutionary (or even in the neighborhood of fun), it does serve to illustrate one very important feature of the Game view.

Figure 1.16
The Wave script component on the Sphere object.
Source: Unity Technologies.

While your game is playing, click the Sphere object in the Hierarchy view and take a look at the Wave script component in the Inspector. There are three variables defined in the script—values that dictate how the script behaves and affects the sphere: Height, Speed, and Height Offset. Notice that as the sphere moves, the Height variable updates on the fly to reflect the sphere's current position.

Now here's the fun part: Click the number next to Speed and change it to anything else, like 1 or 10. The script and sphere both update in real time with your new change! Try playing with the Height Offset number, too, to see how it affects the game.

Note

If you want to see the few lines used in the code script to make the sphere move, you can either click the Wave file in the Project view (under _TestFiles) or double-click the Wave script in the Component field in the Inspector (the actual icon to the right of the Script field, not the title).

Being able to change any variable or value of any asset while you actively test your game will become your new best friend. Think your character is moving too slow? Try a faster Speed value. Too fast? Scale it down a bit. Industry veterans can share their war stories about games that required a build of 20 minutes or more to make small changes. Not having to rebuild your game after every small change is one of the highlights of Unity.

Caution

Any change you make while your game is playing won't be saved when you stop play. You must click the Pause button to pause the game, update the value field with your new permanent change, and click the Play button to jump back in. This is worth repeating: Any change made while playing won't be saved.

The other two buttons on the Play Controls group of the Toolbar help with debugging and testing your game. The middle button, Pause, obviously pauses the game. Click the Pause button again to start play back up from where you left off. The last button is the Step button. It allows you to move frame by frame through your game. This is especially useful when you need to debug a particularly bad patch of code and want to see where something starts to go wrong.

Like the Scene view, the Game view also has its own Control Bar, as shown in Figure 1.17. The first area, the Aspect drop-down list, lets you change the aspect ratio of the Game view on the fly, even while it is playing. The Free Aspect setting will allow the Game view to fill up all the available space of the current window size, whereas the other selections will emulate the resolutions and ratios of most common monitors. This is really handy when you need to start making your GUI conform to different size screens.

Stats toggle

Aspect drop-down list

Maximize
toggle

Gizmos
toggle

Figure 1.17
The Game view Control Bar.
Source: Unity Technologies.

Activating the Maximize on Play toggle button will expand your Game view to take up the entire editor window when you start playing. Note that you can't change this toggle when the game is playing; you need to stop first, make the change, and then restart.

If you click the Gizmos toggle button, you'll toggle all gizmos to be drawn and rendered in your game. Currently, you don't have any gizmos in the scene, so this doesn't do much right now. Later, though, you could have something like a custom gizmo denoting a special area of your game, and you may want to always see exactly where its boundaries are, even when playing.

The Stats toggle button displays the Rendering Statistics window. This is extremely useful when you start optimizing your game. This may look mostly like gibberish to you right now, but it will all be covered in greater detail in Chapter 15, "Basic Unity Debugging and Optimization." Know for now that this is a quick way to view your game's frames per second (FPS), a general indicator for how smooth or choppy your game is. Click the Stats toggle button again to hide the page.

The Animation and Animators Views

Unity includes animation views that enable you to view and tweak animation curves and connect animations together in sequence. These views are not displayed by default. Because the file for this chapter does not include animation clips, the views will be blank when you open them.

You can open the Animation view by choosing Window > Animation or pressing Ctrl+6. The Animation view will pop up in a separate floating window, which you can move, dock, or resize. You can open the Animator window by choosing Window > Animator. It will open up as a new tab by the Scene and Game views. The Animator view lets you manage transitions between animations. In Chapter 8, "Hooking Up the Animations," you'll see how you can use this view to watch clips and update data outside of a 3D animation application.

Two other useful debugging tools are the Console and the Status Bar, shown in Figure 1.18. The Status Bar is always visible along the bottom of the editor (usually it's a blank gray line), and you can display the Console by choosing Window > Console or by pressing Ctrl+Shift+C. You can also click the Status Bar to open the Console.

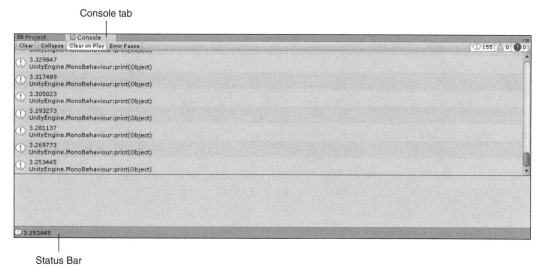

Figure 1.18
The Console and the Status Bar in action.
Source: Unity Technologies.

Click the Play button to begin testing the game and watch how the Console and the Status Bar both update with the sphere's height data. It's possible in your scripts to have the game spit out pieces of information to the Console and the Status Bar, which can help with debugging and fixing errors. Any errors, messages, or warnings your game comes across will also be displayed here, along with any details about the specific bug.

The Profiler and Version Control

You may have noticed two other options available under the Windows menu: Profiler and Version Control. If you are using Unity Basic, the free version of Unity, these two options will be grayed out and inaccessible. If you have a Pro license, you can open the Profiler by selecting the menu item or pressing Ctrl+7 on your keyboard. The Profiler is a very powerful integrated debugging and optimization tool that's covered more fully in Chapter 15.

The Pro license also allows the use of integrated version control systems. Version control allows you to track the history of your project and view older revisions of your changes, and allows teams to branch to a private copy of the project and merge the results back to the team. You can still use a version control system without the Pro license; you just need to manage the files with external tools instead of using the built-in interfaces.

Customizing the Editor

While the default layout of the editor is pretty good, you may find it not to your liking, or that you require a specific layout of windows for a task at hand. The Layout drop-down list on the Toolbar has a few common layouts available for you, as well as the ability to save custom layouts, delete layouts, or return to the default "factory" layout. You can also view the available saved layouts by choosing Window > Layouts.

Customizing your editor's layout is as simple as dragging and dropping. You can move any window or view by clicking and dragging on its tab. (You'll know you did it right when a small gray box attaches itself to your cursor.) You can dock tabs to any edge of the editor's window by dragging the tab to any of the edges. You can also make any tab a floating window by dragging it into the middle of the editor and releasing the mouse button. If you want to layer windows behind each other, drag a tab next to another to dock it to that same window.

Play around with the layout options until you find something that works for you. There isn't any right layout, and you probably have a personal workflow you like to follow. I find myself moving and resizing windows all the time to accommodate wide text, to see more content in a Scene view, or to see multiple views of something at once. When you find a layout that works for you, click the Layout drop-down list and click Save Layout. A small dialog box will open, allowing you to type a custom name for your new layout. Click the Save button when you're done.

Unity's Basic Concepts

Unity is a unique development tool—one that is very much different from other editors and engines on the market. As such, there are a few basic concepts to familiarize yourself with to make full use of its capabilities.

As mentioned, each game you create is organized into its own project. The project contains all the scenes, levels, assets, sounds, scripts, and anything else your game uses. Projects can be created, saved, and opened from the File menu.

Your game is made up of a series of connected Scene files. Often, each level in your game will be contained within its own Scene file. Scene files can also be used for full-screen GUI elements (like a main menu or game over screen), cut scenes, or anything else you want to load separately.

Buzzword

The basic building blocks within your Scene files are GameObjects (GOs). At its most basic form, a GameObject is a simple container for pieces called components. All GameObjects have at least one component (the Transform component) and often contain many more. In the test scene, the Sphere, Plane, and Cube objects are all GameObjects (as are Main Camera, Directional Light, and Primitives, as well as imported 3D models or texture files). GameObjects can also be nested within other GameObjects by parenting, as with the Primitives object. This is known as a GameObject hierarchy.

Note

If you use the GameObject > Create Empty menu option to create a new GameObject in the scene and select it, you'll notice that it's still not actually empty. Even this so-called "empty" object still contains a Transform component.

Click any one of the GameObjects in the Hierarchy view and look at the Inspector. Each division in the Inspector is a component. For example, the Cube object has Transform, Cube (Mesh Filter), Box Collider, Mesh Renderer, and Shader components. You can think of each component as being a different defining aspect or characteristic. When combined, they create the object you see in the game. There are no limits to the number of components you can place in a GameObject, and many kinds of components, like scripts, can be placed multiple times on the same GO. If you browse through the Component menu, you can see the different kinds of components available for use, all organized by base function.

Note

Components cannot be found or placed alone in your scene. They must be connected to a GameObject.

This helps to describe the major difference between Unity and other development tools: It is asset-centric at its core, not code-centric. Everything in your game has a visual representation and physical presence in the editor—even intangible things like scripts, cameras, and light sources. In this way, you'll find that working in Unity is more similar to working in a 3D modeling application than in a strict coding environment.

Available Unity Licenses

Unity comes in a variety of different flavors and natively supports multiple platforms. The free license gives you access to everything you need to make games on Windows, Mac, Linux, and the Web, plus allows you to target mobile devices that use iOS (such as iPhone, iPad, and iPod Touch), as well as BlackBerries, Android phones and tablets, and more.

The Pro license gives you access to several additional features, such as the Profiler and integrated version control mentioned earlier. The Pro license unlocks several tools that professional developers can use to help get the most out of hardware. Professional studios that have publishing agreements with Sony, Microsoft, or Nintendo can buy plug-ins that allow Unity to work with PS3, PS4, PS Vita, Xbox 360, Xbox One, Wii, Wii U, and 3DS.

A complete side-by-side comparison of all the licenses is kept up to date on Unity's website. Although all these optional features will make your game shinier and your development pipeline more customizable, they come with a price tag attached. If you're a solo or new developer, you may want to start with the free license before determining if you need, or want, to upgrade to the Pro license.

Note

> Be aware when shopping around that there are a few license restrictions currently in place for Unity Basic. If your "commercial entity" had gross revenues over U.S. $100,000 in its last fiscal year or you are part of an organization with a budget over U.S. $100,000 in its last fiscal year, you must license Unity Pro. Also, a development team cannot mix Unity Pro and Unity Basic licenses. The team must use the same type of license together.

Unity Technologies also offers gambling and non-game license options, add-ons for additional mobile device options, an integrated asset server and other team features, a license for the editor's source code, as well as educational licenses.

CHAPTER 2

YOUR FIRST GAME: WHERE TO START?

Designing and building your own game from the ground up may seem like a daunting or even impossible task, but it doesn't have to be. Much like any other large or lengthy undertaking, it can help to break your game up into manageable-sized chunks and approach the design one area at a time. A good place to start is to learn the basics behind game design theory and its terminology, which can help you organize your ideas on paper before bringing them to life on the computer. Planning some of your high-level ideas first can help make the first time you sit down at the computer to build your game a little less intimidating and a lot more fun.

BASIC DESIGN THEORY

If this is your first foray into making a game, you may find yourself lost for ideas or perhaps uncertain where to begin. Some fledgling designers have the uncanny ability to start making a game at a moment's notice, without any thought paid to structure or planning, and create something imaginative and fun on the first go round. Lucky them. For the rest of us, learning basic design theory can help organize a random collection of ideas into something that can later be turned into a playable and fun game.

The video game industry is a relatively young one, having only come into being in the latter half of the 20th century. The academic study and classification of video games is even newer. It's only fairly recently that a standardized set of theories and terminology has come into somewhat standard use.

The most basic building block of the game is a *mechanic*, a rule or description that governs a single, specific aspect of play. In a video game, pressing a certain sequence of buttons to make your character jump is a simple mechanic. Defeating an enemy onscreen when you hit him with a fireball is also a mechanic. Collecting colored bubbles for points is another mechanic. All games are built on a collection of mechanics that, when put together in a meaningful way, create a fun and interactive experience. Think of your favorite game and make a list of all the different things you as a player can do in the game world. Each item on this list is a mechanic of the game.

Similar and interrelated mechanics can be grouped into a larger set of rules known as a *system*. Well-designed and imaginative systems are at the heart of any fun game. This is often where the bulk of a designer's time is spent, polishing, balancing, and tweaking. You can identify systems in any given game by thinking of the high-level descriptions of what you can do as a player. For example, a sample game allows you to move a character around by tilting a joystick, to cause the character to jump into the air with the push of a button, and to have your character take flight by holding down two buttons at once. Each of these three mechanics can be grouped into a larger movement system—they all relate to how you as the player control your character. While many games have similar kinds of systems in place—movement, combat, leveling up—it is the individual mechanics in each system that make a game unique.

When you start designing a game, one of the first things you should identify is the core of your game. The *core* is basically one defining and unifying statement that describes your game. You can think of the core as being like a thesis statement for a research paper. Every paragraph in the paper should relate to and support the thesis, much like every part of the game should support and strengthen the core. Taking the time to define and develop a strong core statement can make your design process much easier and more efficient as your game begins to take shape.

Core statements are often composed as a "who-what-where" style of statement, describing who the characters are, where they are, and in very general terms what they'll be doing in the game.

Pretend a friend asks you about your game. Can you quickly strip down the game to its bare essence and answer in just one sentence? Your answer is your core game idea.

Tip

Besides defining your game's main idea, the core statement can also be used later to help solve dilemmas while designing. For example, suppose you have two fun vehicle ideas for your game, and you don't know which one to use. You only have time to implement one, so testing both isn't an option. Look at both objectively and determine which one relates more strongly to the core idea, in everything from gameplay functions to physical form. If you have to go with just one, pick the one that more strongly supports your core idea.

If the core is like the thesis statement of a research paper, the *feature set* is the collection of main ideas from each supporting paragraph. Each element in the feature set describes a main part of the play in your game, and each should definitively relate back to the core idea.

Let's say you're making a game about pirates. A possible core statement for a pirate game could be as follows:

> *Work, duel, and beguile your way up from a deck scrubber to the captain of your own ship as you become the most feared pirate on the Seven Seas.*

As it stands, this core idea could describe any number of pirate games, so you'll need to create a more defined list of features that will help develop your idea into something unique and more complex. One feature set for this game could be the following:

- Completely customize your own pirate ship with more than 100 unique parts.
- Sail around the game's open world and visit more than 50 different port towns, each with its own characters and culture.
- Find hidden treasure and bury your own goods with a detailed mapping system.
- Fight one-on-one sword and saber duels with other members of the ship to work your way up the pirate ranks.
- Defend your ship in epic sea battles against rival pirates and enemy vessels with upgradable cannons and more than 20 kinds of ammunition.

Note

A game that's said to be "open world" has no defined levels that the player must progress through in a set order. Players can roam around the world and visit any place whenever they want.

This isn't the only possible feature list you could make from this core idea. A second game could be as follows:

- Swindle your deck mates out of cash and treasure by mastering the in-game collectable card game.
- Promote your character through the pirate ranks by performing quests for the captain, combating other pirates in pirate competitions, or finding the most unusual treasure in city raids.
- Purchase unique and randomly generated islands to build your pirate fortress and store your most valuable finds.

- Seduce governors' daughters and ransom pompous politicians for fame or fortune.

- Assemble a pirate fleet from more than 30 kinds of ships.

- Unlock special ships, treasure, and upgrades as you play.

Both of these feature sets describe and support the core statement, but each details a completely different game experience. Neither is better than the other; they both equally describe a game about pirates.

If you find yourself stuck when trying to make a feature list, think of yourself as a new player placed into your world. What is it that you want to do? What seems fun or cool to you? Do you like collecting things? Racing? Customizing characters or vehicles? Researching and developing new items? Make a list of tasks that would interest you in the world. Then ask yourself how you could go about actually performing these actions. Each of these is a possible feature for you to use.

Tip
<hr>
Never throw away an unused game or feature idea, even if you think it's the silliest idea in the world. Keep a notebook or file with all your ideas and add any new ones you have to it. Even if an idea doesn't work for you at the moment, later on you may find it's the perfect solution to a different design problem.
<hr>

From the feature set, you can now begin to develop your systems and mechanics. Let's say you decided to go with your first pirate feature set. Just from quickly reading the entries, you know you'll need some sort of sailing system, a character customization system, a dueling system, a treasure-hunting and burying system, a combat system, and a research system to develop new cannons and ship parts. Now pick one of your systems and begin to flesh out the individual mechanics. For the ship-combat system, you know you'll need a cannon-firing mechanic, a loading- and mixing-ammunition mechanic, a mechanic to control how damage is applied to the ship, and perhaps a dodge or evasive-maneuvers mechanic.

At this stage, you don't need to know how every little mechanic works. In fact, sometimes it's better if you don't. Most of the best games are built using an iterative process—trying one idea, testing it, and tweaking it a few times until you're happy with the result. Often, you may not be sure if a mechanic is working well when you first implement it. It isn't until you begin to get more pieces into the game that certain flaws or merits in your mechanics become apparent. Don't be discouraged if things don't seem to work out right from the beginning. A game evolves and grows throughout the design process, and will invariably face a few hurdles along the way before it meshes into something fun and playable.

FINDING THE CORE IDEA

Ideas for new games can come from anything, anytime, anywhere. There's no one definitive or magical way a designer comes up with a game idea. Each designer has a process that works uniquely for himself and sometimes no one else.

You can get ideas from watching movies or television shows, reading books, playing other games, flipping through the newspaper, daydreaming, shopping, or taking a walk. Some lucky designers actually find they have too many ideas to ever have time to fully develop, and have to pick only one idea from a collection of hundreds. Others can wrestle with one idea for weeks or months at a time before they work out something they're happy to continue with.

Brainstorming

Designing is a different process for each person, but there are basic methods of brainstorming that can help if you find yourself staring at a blank screen.

- **Freewriting:** Get out a blank sheet of paper (or open a new computer file), set a timer for five minutes, and begin to list topics or ideas as they come to you. Simple, single nouns are fine at this point. Don't worry about whether the idea makes sense or if the noun is silly or doesn't mean anything. Just write down words as they pop into your head. Look around the room, glance out a window, or flip through a magazine and write down things that interest you. Don't think about what you're writing down— just write. At the end of five minutes, look through your list and see if one item or a collection of different listings catches your attention.

- **Random searches:** Go online to your favorite search engine, encyclopedia, or database and request a random page. (Wikipedia works well for this.) Keep refreshing and looking up random pages until something catches your eye. Then write it down. Just as with freewriting, don't think about what the idea could mean or what you could do with it; just write it down if it interests you. When you've compiled a sizable list, look it over and see if anything stands out. You can also open a volume of a physical encyclopedia to a random page or browse around the local library and pick up random books and jot down the title or subject matter.

- **Matching items:** Make a list of subjects or hobbies that interest you, such as "coffee," "cats," "murder mysteries," "the 100 Years War," "Irish history," "Barcelona," or "hiking." Place each of these subjects on a small slip of paper or index card and put them all in a box. Now make a second list of kinds of games you like to play, such as "puzzles," "platformer," "adventure," "card collecting," "flight simulator," or "racing." Put each of these game types on its own card, and put the cards in a separate box. Now mix up the cards. Pick one card from the "subject" box and one card from the "game type" box. Make a list of the combinations you draw. Does anything look interesting to you? You can also try drawing two or more subject cards for each game type card to make a more detailed list.

■ **Browse a bookstore:** Go to either a physical store or an online storefront and read the descriptions and summaries of books and movies that interest you. Find one that grabs your attention. Would it be fun for you to play a game with this or a similar description? Make a list of the basic descriptions and formulate a core idea from each summary. Do keep in mind, however, that you shouldn't blatantly copy an idea from an existing product. Rather, you should use it as a springboard for your own ideas.

■ **Consult your notebook:** If you've been keeping a design notebook with all your various ideas, take a moment to read it over. Does anything in it strike your fancy? Could a few of the items you wrote down be used for the basis of another brainstorming method, like creating a matched list? You should probably make it a habit to read through it on a regular basis. You never know when a random idea will come in handy!

Brainstorming shouldn't be a painful process. If you find you're getting frustrated, take a break and come back to it later. There's no rush to create that first game idea. Forcing an idea will pretty much guarantee it won't be something all that fun for you to work on. Remember, you'll be spending a large amount of time on your game—weeks or months, and maybe even years for larger projects—so make sure it's an idea that can interest you for that long.

Researching Other Games

Besides brainstorming, you should also actively research and document games that you enjoy playing. If it's a game you like to play for hours on end, it stands to reason that that particular style of game could also be fun for you to make. You don't have to write a lengthy, in-depth analysis of every game you play, but begin to notice certain features or kinds of gameplay that stand out as fun to you.

First, write down the basic core statement of a game you like. What's it about? What about it draws you to it? Is it the subject or theme material or the actual gameplay itself? Create a list of the features that appeal to you. Do you like driving different kinds of cars, picking out new armor for your warrior, or matching up colored stones into a defined pattern? What is it about the feature that makes it fun for you?

After you've broken down the game a bit, begin to question what you would do differently or what features you'd want to see added. Change the theme, modify one feature, delete another, or add a new gameplay element. Again, the object isn't to copy another game already on the market, but to identify common features and elements you think are fun and to use that as a starting point for your own game.

Rent or borrow games in other genres you don't usually play. If you've never tried a first-person shooter, pick one up from a friend, get a quick tutorial, and see how it works and what makes it fun for others. Even if it's a game you end up hating, there might be an idea floating around in it that you could incorporate into your own design. Constantly expand your game horizons, trying new genres and kinds of games. Not only might you find something new to play, but you'll also expand your design repertoire into a fuller and richer body of ideas.

Paper Prototyping: It's Not Just for Business Software

Another method for brainstorming video game ideas is to try similar ones in the non-digital realm—that is, to make a board or card game using similar mechanics. *Paper prototyping* is a term used in interactive markets, often in a business setting, when a new piece of software or website is being developed. It can be very expensive to hire a team of programmers to make a custom program, and businesses want to capitalize on the time they have without forgoing quality.

With paper prototyping, designers work out the software or website on paper first, creating sheet after sheet of the different screens a user would see. They then run tests with focus groups, using these sheets to determine if their basic ideas make sense. Even though it's not on a computer screen, users can still point out if a button placement doesn't make sense, if the wording is too vague, or if the layout of the program's interface is too hard to understand. That way, the designers can work out the kinks in their design and iterate as much as they want before spending thousands on actual implementation. It's a lot cheaper and faster to change something on paper than it is to recode a program!

Games aren't any different. While it takes time to create the art and to code up the game systems, it's a lot faster to write some quick notes on some cards and draw up a basic game board on a sheet of paper. Although not all video games can be easily turned into a board game, many of the underlying mechanics can. If you're unsure of an idea, try it on paper first and invite some friends over to play. You'll have the chance to quickly change rules to see how it affects play and discover new aspects of play you may not have thought of before. Perhaps a side mechanic that didn't mean much to you is an absolute hit with the play group. If so, you now know that it's something you could focus more on. Or maybe that movement system you designed made it way too easy to get across the world. In that case, you can probably scale it back some and make it more competitive.

You don't need to create fancy artwork or get specialized pieces for testing. Blank pieces of paper, pencils, and random bits found around the house all work to get a point across. There are, however, many stores that sell random game parts and pieces if you find it useful to have those on hand. While browsing around parts or craft stores, you may also come across pieces or items that intrigue you by their shape, color, texture, or other physical aspect. Just because it's physical doesn't mean it won't translate well to the digital realm. What about it do you find fun and interesting? Is it something you can incorporate into your larger design?

Planning It All Out

Once you have a basic core idea and feature set, it's time to begin to really plan your game design. Some designers can simply sit down at the computer and knock out their game piece by piece, but especially for first-time designers, it may be easier to take a more systematic approach. That way, you won't forget to add something and can set out a better schedule to get your game finished. Haphazardly designing and implementing features in your game can make the process more unwieldy and introduce problems or inconsistencies where none originally existed.

A Basic Outline

The first thing you might find useful is to flesh out a simple gameplay-oriented outline of your game. There's a sample blank outline template for you to use (if you want) on the companion website. (See Design Documents > Blank_Outline_Template.) This can help form a preliminary basis for you to get all your ideas in order. You can either use the provided template or think about the following questions as you compose your own outline:

- What is the name of your game? You don't need one right away, but it can help to set the tone and feel of your game as you go along.

- What is your game's core statement? Is it something that interests you?

- Describe the feature set. Is it a unique list? Does it fully describe and support the core statement?

- Provide a basic description of the game world. When and where does it take place? Are there any special features of note? Is it an open world or is it composed of many individual levels?

- What's the overall victory condition or goal in the game? Is the player trying to reach a certain space or collect a set number of a specific item? How does the player win? Does the game ever actually end?

- Where does the game start? What options are available to the players when they start the game?

- Who are the characters in the game? What do they look like? What do they do in the game? Do they provide any services to the player? Does the player control any of the characters?

- What are the main systems in your game? Which features do they support?

- What are the main gameplay mechanics in the game? To which system do they belong?

Figure 2.1 shows a sample outline page using the pirate game described earlier in the chapter.

Game Name:	High Seas

Core Theme/ Idea: In High Seas you work, duel, and beguile your way up from a lowly deck scrubber to the captain of your own ship as you become the most feared pirate on the seven seas.

Feature Set

1 Completely customize your own pirate ship with over 100 unique parts

2 Sail around the world and visit more than 50 different port towns, each with its own characters and culture

3 Find hidden treasure and bury your own with a detailed mapping system

4 Fight one-on-one sword and saber duels with other members of the ship to work your way up the pirate ranks

5 Defend your ships in epic sea battles against rival pirates and enemy vessels with upgradable cannons and over 20 kinds of ammunition

6 Seduce governor's daughters and ransom pompous politicians for fame or fortune.

7

8

9

10

World Description

High Seas takes place across the Atlantic, from the New World to the western coasts of Afria and Europe. Hundreds of islands dot the waves and players can freely navigate around the open world. Coastal port towns offer opportunity for looting and purchasing of goods, and each town is uniquely decorated with specific cultural items and flair.

Victory or Goals

Players attempt to promote their way up to the rank of pirate captain, and then have the option to complete online against other players for the top score. The game ends ten in-game years after the status of Captain is reached. A special New Game+ mode may be unlocked along the way.

Player Start

The player starts out in a random city with the rank of Deck Scrubber, no funds, and only the clothes on his back. He must find a crew in port to join to begin his journey.

Figure 2.1
High Seas' outline page, based on the template provided.

If you can answer most of these questions, you're at a great place to begin. Don't feel that your answers must be set in stone once you write them down, however. You may have a better idea later or need to tweak something if it's not turning out to be that fun. If you can't answer all these questions at the moment, that's also fine. Not everyone designs in the same manner or at the same pace, so don't feel the need to compare your process to someone else's. If what you're doing works for you, stick with it. If you're having problems keeping everything in order and coming up with new ideas, try a new approach.

A Simple Level Document

Creating a simple level design document can also help you get your game information in order. Level documents are compiled for many games and generally detail one individual level or section of the game world. If your game is small enough, it could even cover the entire game world.

The concept behind the level document is simple: You provide a map of your game world and add specific notes and map points detailing all the important aspects of your game. Important gameplay notes and descriptions accompany the map. The idea behind the document is that any person who saw it would have enough information to build your game exactly as you envisioned, down to each individual detail.

A sample blank level document template is provided on this book's companion website. (See Design Documents > Blank_Level_Template). Alternatively, you can think about the following questions and lines of direction to compile your own level document:

- What does your game map look like? Where and what are the important features?

- Where does the player start and finish? Are these places obvious in the game world?

- Who are the characters in the world and where are they located? Does the player need to do anything special to reach them? Do they do something for the player or say anything?

- Are there items located around the world to pick up or hidden items to find? What do they look like? What do they do?

- Are there enemies or obstacles in the world? Where and what are they?

- Do the enemies or obstacles have special abilities, or does the player need special items to overcome them?

- Do all the listed and mapped elements relate back to your core and feature set?

- Is there a specific path the player must follow through the world or a set sequence of actions he must take? Are there side paths with special rewards to find?

- Are there special abilities the player needs to acquire to reach certain areas of the map? Are there specific items he needs to complete the journey?

Figure 2.2 shows a sample level document and map for the pirate game described earlier in the chapter.

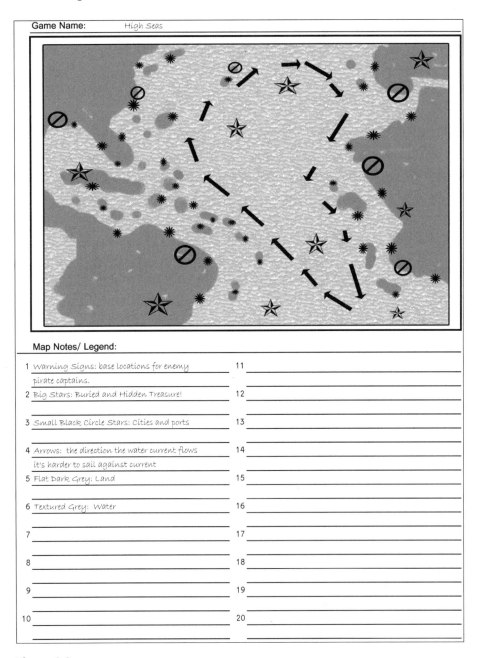

Figure 2.2
High Seas' map with points of interest marked.

Even if you decide not to write a full level document, you should at least draw up a simple map of your game world. Besides a sheet of paper or a computer drawing program, a good material to use for level designing is a plain whiteboard and set of markers. The whiteboard makes it easy to erase and redraw areas of your level as you see fit and to quickly use different colors to denote different areas of your map. You can also get color-coded or uniquely shaped magnets to place on your whiteboard. These can be used for specific gameplay notes, enemy positions, item pickup locations, or anything you want.

Have fun with your map, and don't hesitate to draw up a few different iterations of it. Look at maps for other games you enjoy playing and try to pick out specific features you thought were fun or interesting. Observe real-world maps of cities and land masses to get an idea of how real maps flow. If your game map is more 3D in nature, try physically building it out of wooden blocks or other children's toys.

Tip

> Much like your design ideas, save your map ideas even if you're not using them for this specific game. You never know when you might want to use one in the future.

Getting Started

Spend some time thinking about and planning what you'd like to make in Unity. At this point, shoot for the proverbial moon. Concentrate on what's fun, not on the actual logistics of making it. That'll come in time.

From this point forward, each chapter of the book will focus on implementing specific features using tools within Unity to create a simple sample game. All of the files and resources referenced are available for use on this book's companion website, split up by chapter as well as compiled into a final build. Of course, you also have the option of making your own idea from scratch and just following along for the process or using the provided assets as a springboard for your own unique creation.

The design files for the sample game, *Widget*, can be found on the companion website under "Design Documents." You should familiarize yourself with the basic idea if you plan to use the sample as a learning aid. Each chapter folder on the website contains the base files referenced in the text. You can download them to your computer as you need them. A final compiled project folder is also included, which you can download and view if you run into trouble.

PART II

ASSEMBLING THE GAME ASSETS

You now have a working knowledge of Unity's interface and at least the beginnings of a new idea to work with. In this part, you'll look at compiling and importing the different art assets the *Widget* game will require, from terrain sculpting to character setups. Unity has one of the slickest asset importers around, and with it you'll be creating your game worlds in no time.

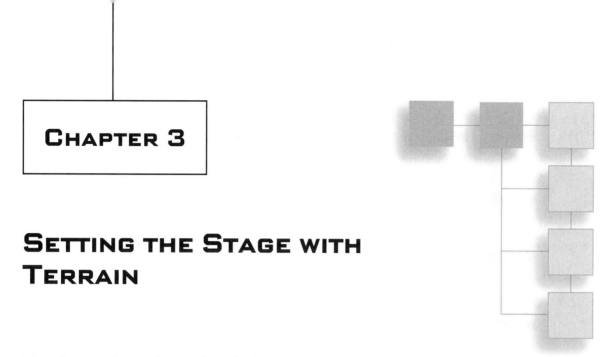

CHAPTER 3

SETTING THE STAGE WITH TERRAIN

Now that you have a basic idea of what you want to make, you need to start compiling the various pieces and parts needed to bring the game to life. You can create some of these items, such as terrain and simple primitive objects, directly within Unity. Others, like a main character and special pickup items, will need to be imported from other 3D modeling packages, such as Autodesk Maya or Blender.

One of the flashier and more rewarding parts to start with is fleshing out the world's environment—the physical space around which your character will run, jump, defeat enemies, and save the proverbial princess. Getting this laid out first will make placing your characters and items a bit easier and more straightforward.

In Unity, you can make game environments in three ways:

- Using only terrain generated from within the engine
- Importing a complete 3D mesh of the world
- Using a combination of terrain and meshes to carve out the world's space

Widget will use the last of these, but you may find it useful to make your entire game's environment in a 3D package and just import it all at once. You'll know that everything fits together and is exactly where you want it without having to reposition it. Unity's free "3D Platformer" tutorial, available for download from its website, uses this method. If you find that you want something organic or to simulate real-world landmasses, you should consider using terrain.

UNITY'S TERRAIN ENGINE

At this point, you should set up your project space on your computer. Follow these steps:

1. With Unity open, choose File > New Project.

2. Click the Create New Project tab.

3. Browse to the folder in which you'd like to save your files and decide what assets you want to include. If you're following along with *Widget*, select the packages for Character Controllers, Skyboxes, Terrain Assets, Toon Shading, and Water.

4. Click Create. This new project will be loaded by default until you open or create a new one.

5. When you create your new project, it automatically creates a new scene as well. Add a directional light (choose GameObject > Create Other > Directional Light) and rotate it so it doesn't point directly down. (To rotate it, select the Rotate tool and drag the handles.) This will act as the "sun." A directional light affects all objects regardless of location, so you can place the light anywhere in your scene.

6. A terrain is a specialized GameObject. To add one, choose GameObject > Create Other > Terrain. You'll be greeted with a large, gray, plane-like object, as shown in Figure 3.1.

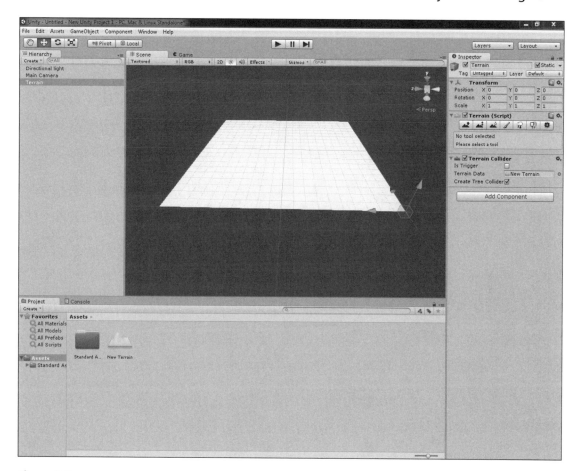

Figure 3.1
A default terrain.
Source: Unity Technologies.

As it stands, you could run this in the engine and have a little character run around it, but a flat terrain isn't terribly interesting to look at. Fortunately, you can change its settings. Make sure it is selected in the Hierarchy view. Then look at the Inspector. You will find several buttons, each representing a different tool. There are several families of terrain modification tools. (See Figure 3.2.)

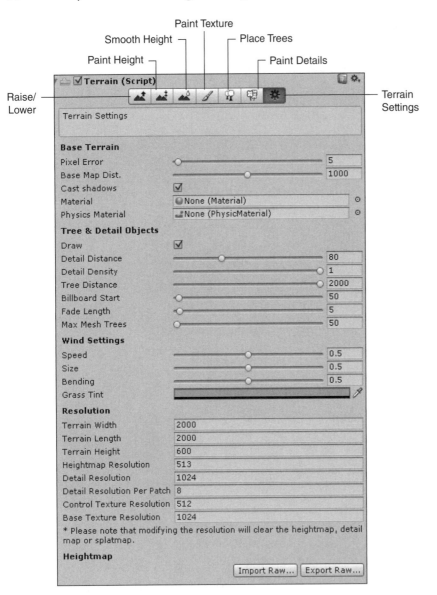

Figure 3.2
Terrain settings.
Source: Unity Technologies.

The tools are as follows:

■ **Raise/Lower Terrain:** Add or remove height by painting over the ground.

■ **Paint Height:** Set a specific height by painting over the ground.

- **Smooth Height:** Level out areas by painting over the ground.
- **Paint Texture:** Draw textures on the ground, such as sand or grass.
- **Place Trees:** Create and modify tree prototypes, add them to the terrain, or remove them.
- **Paint Details:** Paint grass, flowers, and other objects on the terrain.
- **Terrain Settings:** View details about how the terrain is drawn.

Let's begin by selecting the Terrain Settings tool. There are many settings available, but for now, we are only interested in the Resolution settings, found on the bottom half. They are as follows:

- **Terrain Width:** The total width of the terrain in units.
- **Terrain Length:** The total length of the terrain in units.
- **Terrain Height:** The total possible maximum height of the terrain in units.
- **Heightmap Resolution:** The resolution of the terrain's generated heightmap.
- **Detail Resolution:** The resolution of the terrain's generated detail map. Low numbers here are good for performance, but depending on what you need, you may need to raise it.
- **Control Texture Resolution:** The resolution of the "splat map" used when painting the different terrain textures onto the terrain. (You'll learn more about splat maps later in this chapter.)
- **Base Texture Resolution:** The resolution of the generated texture that is used for the terrain at far distances.

By default, Unity's units equal 1 meter. If you know how big you need your map to be, set it up front. Also, change any of your external applications to match this scale, and you'll have an easier time placing all your assets.

The major decisions you should consider making now are described in the first four settings of the terrain's size and resolution. You'll have time later to change the detail and texture resolutions after you edit the terrain's height, but modifying these settings after you start can cause massive headaches. In particular, if you change any of the resolution features, you will delete all dependent detail information—and that's not fun for anyone. Unity's defaults are a good place to start if you don't have a plan in place, but if you designed your environment first, most of this shouldn't be an issue.

Note

You can have more than one terrain in your scene. In fact, some techniques require you to do so. If you find that you seriously misjudged your terrain's size early on, you may be able to fix the error by using a second terrain.

When using terrain, Unity also gives you some unique movement controls to make editing your game easier. Terrains can get pretty massive, and it can take a while to scroll around or find the one tiny detail you want to tweak. Here are a few:

- With the terrain selected in the Hierarchy view, move your mouse cursor over an area of the terrain in the Scene view you'd like to see and press the F key. The camera will zoom in to that spot.
- If you want to see the entire terrain again, move the mouse off the terrain in the Scene view and press F again. This will zoom out far enough to fit the whole terrain into the Scene view.

Note that you cannot rotate or scale your terrain, and that you can change its dimensions only by using the Set Resolution menu option. The terrain does not act like any other normal GameObject. You can still move the terrain around the world using either the Translate gizmo or by changing its position values in the Inspector, however.

Customizing Terrain

You can edit a terrain in Unity in one of two ways:

- By importing a pre-rendered grayscale image (a heightmap)
- By dynamically painting peaks and valleys onto the terrain's surface using the provided brush tools

Both offer unique advantages and their own associated issues, but you can always switch between the two if you find what you're doing isn't working.

Building Height Using a Heightmap

If you know exactly what you want (and have the tools to make it), using a heightmap can be the fastest way to get the best results. Basically, a *heightmap* is a grayscale image used to represent 3D height changes on a 2D image. Lower elevations are depicted with darker shades of gray going toward black, and higher elevations are shown with lighter shades of gray running toward white. Truly professional-looking heightmaps can be made in external programs such as Terragen or Bryce, but a quick (albeit lower-quality) one can be painted in a 2D graphics editor such as Photoshop or GIMP. Be sure to keep your image sizes square or in powers of two dimensions if you decide to make your own. You can use any program to make your heightmap, as long as it exports to a RAW format. This is the only file format Unity will read in for your maps.

Once you have your heightmap, select your terrain asset in the Hierarchy view, navigate to the Terrain Settings in the Inspector, and click the Import Raw button. If you don't have a heightmap available, you can use any of the ones provided on this book's companion website, in the Chapter 3 > Heightmaps folder. Once you select the file you want to use, a dialog box will display the import choices available for heightmaps:

- **Depth:** Set per your file specifications: either 8-bit or 16-bit. Import using the quality at which you created the file. Use the default for the provided maps.

- **Width:** The width of your heightmap image, which should be grabbed automatically from the image size.

- **Height:** The height of your heightmap image, which should be grabbed automatically from the image size.

- **Byte Order:** Set per your file specifications: Mac or Windows. Use the one that encoded the file (Windows if you're using the files provided on the companion website).

- **Terrain Size:** This links back to the Terrain Set Resolution options and lets you change the size if you find your heightmap image size differs wildly.

In general, a good estimate to use when setting your terrain size to match your heightmap is one square pixel equals 2 meters square. In this case, a 1,000 × 1,000 pixel image maps to a 2,000 × 2,000 unit terrain. These values can be adjusted in your game. If your heightmap is too sparse, it can appear blocky to the player. If your map requires a finer resolution, performance can take a noticeable hit. This type of quality-versus-performance tradeoff is a common balancing act in games. (See Figures 3.3 and 3.4).

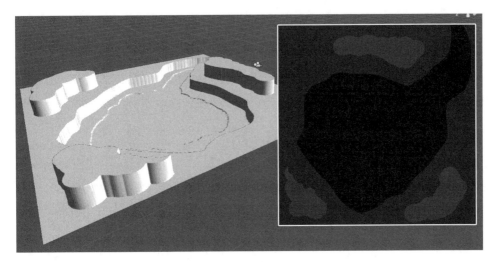

Figure 3.3
A simple terrain and the heightmap used to create it.
Source: Unity Technologies.

Figure 3.4
A more complicated heightmap and its associated terrain.
Source: Unity Technologies.

Painting Height Using Brushes

Creating a heightmap may not be your style or even feasible without the proper tools. That's where the included brush tools come in. To explore them, either create a new terrain or return your current one to its default flat level. To do so, click the Paint Height tool, type a 0 into the Height box, and select the Flatten button to return the terrain to its default starting height. Then, with the terrain selected in the Hierarchy view, examine its information in the Inspector, as shown in Figure 3.5.

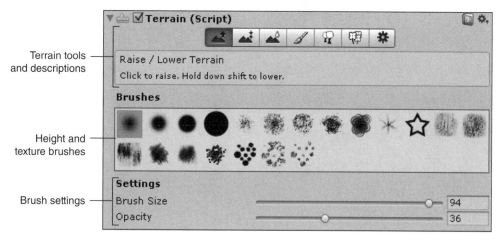

Terrain tools and descriptions

Height and texture brushes

Brush settings

Figure 3.5
The terrain's default Inspector properties.
Source: Unity Technologies.

Tip

You can use the Paint Height tool to set regions of the terrain to any specific height, such as 50 or 100 units. This can be useful if you need to push it down later to create valleys or canyons.

The Terrain component is where the majority of the action happens. Across the top of the component are seven buttons making up the Terrain toolbar, each activating a different submenu for manipulating and editing the terrain. The first three buttons—Raise and Lower Terrain, Paint Height, and Smooth Height—manipulate the general shape of the terrain.

Click the first button in the list to activate the tool to raise and lower the terrain's height. Your cursor will have a blue circle attached to it if you hover over the terrain in the Scene view—this is your selected brush's area of effect. By default, the first brush in the Inspector is selected, but you can change it to any of the other brushes by clicking on them (see Figure 3.6). As in other graphics programs, the brush you select dictates how your painted strokes will look.

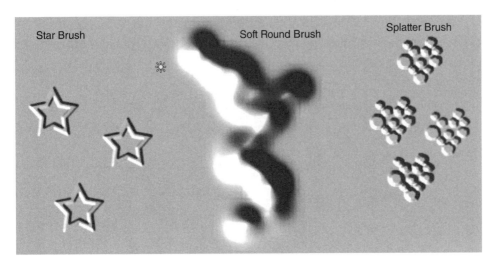

Figure 3.6
Some of the available brushes.
Source: Unity Technologies.

Most brushes come with two available settings:

- **Brush Size:** Brush Size, obviously, dictates how large an area the brush will cover. Small numbers will paint over smaller amounts of terrain, and larger numbers (up to 100) will paint a larger block.

- **Brush Opacity:** Brush Opacity also works the same as in other painting programs. It describes how transparent, or how much height, your brush will paint at once. Low values will move the terrain just a tiny bit, and high numbers (again, up to 100—it's a percentage) will drastically raise or lower the terrain.

Pick one of the brushes and click and drag anywhere on the terrain in the Scene view. The terrain will begin to deform and push up where you painted your stroke. You can change the brush's size and opacity in the Inspector to paint more or less of the terrain in soft, gentle strokes or with harsh, hard lines. Experiment with the different brush offerings and their settings to get a feel for painting on the terrain.

You can also hold down the Shift key while painting to lower the terrain instead of raising it. The terrain will not go below a height of 0, so if you want to create canyons or valleys, you should move your entire terrain's height to a higher level and then lower specific parts down to 0. Your terrain is also limited by the overall height you set in the Set Resolution dialog box, and your brushes will plateau once you reach that height. Using these brushes, you can easily create soft hills, mountain peaks, and streambeds, limited only by the resolution of your terrain (see Figure 3.7).

Figure 3.7
Like any 3D mesh, a terrain's possible deformation is limited only by the resolution available.
Source: Unity Technologies.

While these terrains can be quite natural and beautiful, they're not the most conducive to moving a character across. The second button in the Terrain toolbar will let you paint up to a set height, thereby enabling you to create nice, flat walkways and plateaus for your characters. The Brush Size and Opacity settings work just the same as for the Raise and Lower Height tool, the only difference being the inclusion of a Height slider and a text field. Choose any target height (within the limits of your set maximum height) to paint the terrain and have it plateau at that new height (see Figure 3.8).

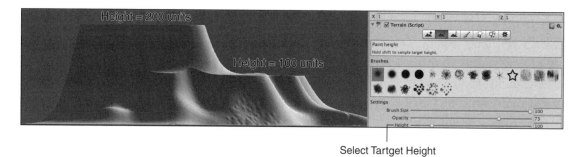

Select Tartget Height

Figure 3.8
By setting the target height to different values, you can create tiered landscapes for your characters to explore.
Source: Unity Technologies.

Holding down the Shift key while painting works a little bit differently when you use this tool. Instead of slowly lowering the terrain based on your opacity settings, it measures the ground and sets the value in the Height box. This is a quick way to find the actual height of an area so you can set other areas to the same height, making it easy to turn any area of your map into a flat walkway. If you want to actually lower a part of the terrain, just set a lower height value and paint normally.

The last tool available to paint the height of terrains is the Smooth Height tool. This works just like the other two tools in that you paint with a chosen brush directly onto the terrain in the Scene view. As you might expect, this brush smoothes out sharp changes in height and makes the terrain look a bit more eroded and natural (see Figure 3.9).

Figure 3.9
Both sides of this mountain range were created with a splatter brush, the left side then being smoothed with a soft round brush.
Source: Unity Technologies.

Of course, you can also mix and match the two approaches. There's nothing saying that once you've decided to import a heightmap, you're stuck only with that. You can always use a heightmap to get the base structures in place and then clean up specific areas using the brushes, or you can paint the terrain using the brushes and then export the generated heightmap to edit in an external program.

When you paint with the brushes on your terrain, you're basically creating your own gray-scale heightmap image within the engine, which is dynamically applied to the terrain as you paint. You can export this 2D image by going to the Terrain Settings tool and choosing Export Raw, which allows you to tweak or edit it on another external package. Unity will export these images only as RAW files, but you can set the resolution and bit depth of the file when you export.

Painting Textures

Once you get the general feel for the terrain's height, it's time to start adding color and detail. Painting color onto the terrain works the same way as painting height: You upload tileable textures to the tool, and you use the same brushes and controls to paint the textures directly onto the terrain in the Scene view. The quickest way to get into terrain painting is to use the textures provided in the Standard Assets package.

Note

This book does not cover how to create your own tileable textures, but there are plenty of free online tutorials that do. Check Appendix D, "Resources and References," for links to these and other helpful tutorials.

Recall that at the beginning of this chapter, when you created the project, you included the Terrain Assets package. This package features several pre-built terrain assets and places them in the Standard Assets folder of your project. Expand the Standard Assets folder in your Project view and open the Terrain Textures folder. The package comes complete with four available textures: two grass variations, a dirt texture, and a decent rocky cliff face texture.

As the textures are painted onto the terrain, Unity is not actually copying the texture details. Instead, it creates what is called a splat map. A splat map tells how much each one of four textures applies to the ground at that location. When Unity creates the texture pages for the terrain, it does so in blocks of four. It's no surprise, then, that the standard textures come in a set of four. If, for example, you have five textures, Unity will still have to create a second splat map for the terrain to fit the fifth texture and will leave three extra slots open. For this reason, you should either try to remake your textures so that you only need four or create three more textures to make use of the available space.

To begin painting textures onto your terrain, make sure the terrain is selected in the Hierarchy view. Then select the Paint Texture button in the Inspector (the one that looks like a paint brush). See Figure 3.10.

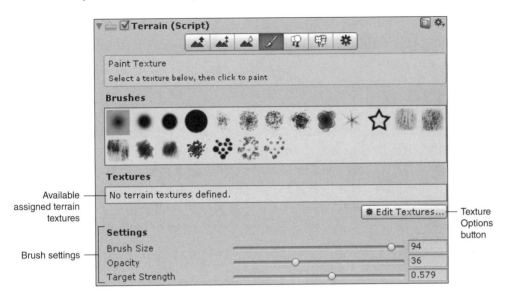

Figure 3.10
The Paint Texture component toolbox.
Source: Unity Technologies.

The main noticeable difference between this mode and the painting height modes is the inclusion of a Textures field and its associated Edit Textures button. Click this button to add, edit, and remove available textures to paint on the terrain. Or, click this button and select Add Texture from the drop-down list to open the Add Terrain Texture dialog box, shown in Figure 3.11.

Figure 3.11
The Add Terrain Texture dialog box.
Source: Unity Technologies.

The first thing you'll need to do is pick a texture to turn into a terrain splat, which you can do by either clicking the box and selecting a texture from the window that appears or dragging a texture over from the Project view into the Texture 2D slot. If you choose the former approach, all the available textures in your Assets folder will be listed. (This underscores the importance of using proper naming conventions.) You may find it easier to just find the file in the Project view and drag it over manually rather than scrolling through the list.

Note

These kinds of dialog boxes are common in Unity. All of them will attempt to give you some sort of helper text explaining what kind of GameObject it expects, like a 2D texture (in this case). Unity won't let you assign a type of asset that won't work with that particular box—for example, you can't assign a model to a texture box.

You can also include a normal map if you have one. *A normal map*, also called a *bump map*, causes highlights to appear at different angles based on any lights in the scene. This may be useful if you are working on a tile or metal floor that has highly reflective bumps or divots. For outdoor terrain, the normal map can be left empty.

You should be a bit savvy about the first texture you upload to the terrain. Unity will tile this one texture for you across the terrain upon upload, so make sure it's something you want to cover the majority of the terrain. Otherwise you may find yourself doing a lot of unnecessary painting. Pick one—Grass (Hill) is a good first choice—and set the tile size for the texture in units. Smaller numbers will make the texture smaller and tile it more times across the terrain, while larger numbers will create a larger splat that tiles less often. Depending on your texture, these numbers could be as small as 4 units or as large as 4,096 units. The default of 15×15 works well for this case. Click Add when you're finished.

Note

If you find you don't like the tile size you picked once you see it on the terrain, either click the Edit Textures button or double-click the texture's swatch in the Inspector to bring up the dialog box again. You can keep changing the tile size until you find something you like.

Now that your terrain is all nice and green, add some variation by adding the three other textures from the Standard Assets > Terrain Assets > Terrain Textures folder using the same method as with the first texture. Click one of the non-grass textures in the Inspector to select it, pick a brush, and start painting in the Scene view. See Figure 3.12.

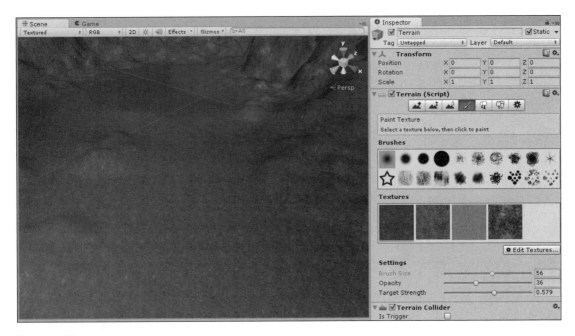

Figure 3.12
The terrain painted with the four available textures.
Source: Unity Technologies.

A good rule of thumb is to start with a low opacity and low target strength and apply the color in thin layers until you get the effect you're after. You can always undo a stroke if you don't like it, but the best terrains feature well-blended and varied textures, which you can only get using thin layers. Also play around with different brush shapes to make painting different shapes easier.

In reality, you're not painting textures, but painting alpha channels as the textures map to the terrain's surface. When you add a new texture to the terrain, Unity basically creates a grayscale texture on the splat map, much like the heightmap. Instead of painting lights and darks to raise the height, you're painting lights and darks to signify where that texture should be placed. This is why the first texture you upload covers the entire terrain at once: Unity makes its default value all white, meaning it covers the entire space. Every other texture defaults to all black (or completely transparent), and then you have to slowly paint in the areas you want to show.

Tip

An interesting technique when painting the heightmap of a terrain is to use an imported texture (like a screen capture of Google Maps) as a guide. Import the texture as a terrain splat and make sure the tile size is the exact size of your terrain. You can then use the color information as a guide for your own hand-painting of the terrain's height and detail information, and the base color is already done for you.

If you find that you don't have the control you'd like with your textures, check the Control Texture Resolution setting under the Terrain Setting tool's Resolution settings. A smaller texture resolution size (such as 512 pixels) will save on memory, but it may not give you the precision you need to paint small details or paths. You can also look at the Base Texture Resolution setting right below it if you feel your textures lose fidelity at far distances. Again, be aware of the possible memory hits that large numbers can mean for your game.

Note

If you're feeling particularly snazzy, you can run your game now and walk around it using a premade first-person camera. Grab the First Person Controller asset from Standard Assets > Prefabs and drop it into your Scene view. Be sure to place it above the terrain. Then click the Play button to start your game. You can use the WASD keys and the spacebar for movement and the mouse to look around.

Placing Trees

Your terrain is probably looking pretty spiffy now that it is all painted, but there is still more you can do to bring it to life—specifically with adding plant life. Unity's Terrain Engine places trees using a special billboard treatment, rendering any trees close-up to the camera in full 3D but transitioning other trees automatically to 2D billboards when they're more than a certain distance away. This enables you to create full, lush scenery without taking the massive memory hit that full 3D trees would produce.

"Painting" Trees

With the terrain still selected in the Hierarchy view, select the Place Trees option from the Terrain toolbar. Much like with textures, you'll need to add some trees to your available library of paintable assets. Terrain trees are special assets (more on this later) and are made a little differently than other assets. The Standard Assets package does include one tree, a palm tree, which you'll use now.

Click the Edit Trees button to open a dialog box with a list of available trees, just like with the Terrain textures. You can find the palm tree under Standard Assets > Terrain Assets > Trees Ambient-Occlusion > Palm. Drag the Palm asset (not the Palm folder) into the Tree field of the dialog box (see Figure 3.13) or select the Palm asset from the drop-down list.

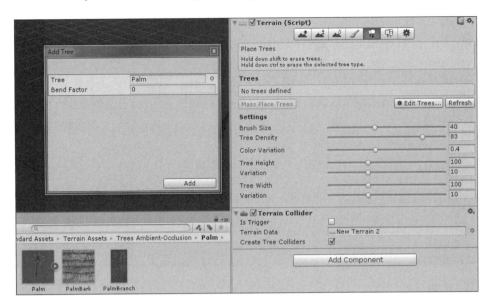

Figure 3.13
Adding a tree GameObject.
Source: Unity Technologies.

This dialog box also offers a Bend Factor value. Besides transitioning trees to billboards, Unity also offers the ability to have your plant life sway and bend in the wind, making it seem more natural. You can set this number to anything you like, but try small numbers first unless you're trying to simulate gale-force winds. (Even a smallish number like 2 will result in large amounts of bending.) Also keep in mind that larger numbers will start to affect your game's performance, as the engine needs to calculate all this swaying and bending.

To place trees, you paint them onto the terrain just like you did with textures, but this time your brush settings are different. Instead of using a selection of different possible brushes, trees use only one round brush that offers seven unique settings:

- **Brush Size:** The brush's radius in units. Larger sizes mean more trees placed at once.

- **Tree Density:** The percentage of each brush stroke that is covered in trees.

- **Color Variation:** The amount of randomness to apply to each tree's color.

- **Tree Height:** Allows adjustment of the asset's base height.

- **Height Variation:** The amount of randomness to apply to each tree's height.

- **Tree Width:** Allows adjustment of the asset's base width.

- **Width Variation:** The amount of randomness to apply to each tree's width.

As you can see from the options, even though there's only one base tree loaded into the engine, each painted tree will be unique, just like in nature. Using these options effectively can really cut back on modeling time if you want a unique-looking landscape. See Figure 3.14. To erase trees, simply hold down the Shift key as you paint.

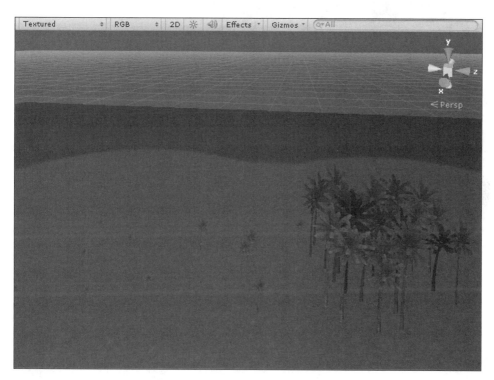

Figure 3.14
Changing a tree's brush settings can result in drastically different trees.
Source: Unity Technologies.

Using the Mass Place Trees Function

Another option available for tree placement is accessible via the Mass Place Trees button. If you know you need a dense forest, this may be the easier route. This feature randomly samples from all the trees you've loaded into your library, so if you only want the engine to use one or two, remove any others you may have added. (See Figure 3.15.) You can also use the Mass Place Trees function to "mass delete" all trees by typing 0 in the Mass Place Trees prompt.

Figure 3.15
100,000 trees, instantly placed. Overkill to some, purely awesome for others.
Source: Unity Technologies.

Making Custom Trees

It's also possible to create your own trees for use in the Terrain Engine, and you only have to follow a few simple steps to do so. In short, to make your own custom trees to use with the Terrain Engine, you must:

1. Place your assets into a folder whose name includes the words "Ambient-Occlusion." The built-in shaders require this name and will not work otherwise. Note that you can nest folders inside this folder if you want to keep your trees separate and organized.

2. Use the Nature/Soft Occlusion Leaves and Nature/Soft Occlusion Bark shaders. Placing the trees in the aforementioned folder will allow these shaders to work.

3. Ensure that your tree mesh is one combined mesh but with two unique materials on it—one material for the leaves and another for the trunk for the two aforementioned shaders. If your tree is not a single mesh, it will not render.

4. Place the pivot point of the tree at the base of the trunk. Otherwise, you could end up with floating trees.

5. Limit the tree model to around 2,000 tris (triangles) or fewer. The sample palm tree only uses 220 tris.

6. Make the tree a prefab if you want to generate collisions for it. (See the upcoming sidebar for more information.)

After you've created your own tree, you may find you need to update it. Unlike other assets, all tree files must be manually updated after you save them. To update it, choose Refresh on the terrain's tree tool. This will update all the trees in the scene to display your changes.

Unity also offers a free package of trees on its website, along with many more trees available in its online store. Although you may not necessarily want to use these in your game, they're helpful for reference when making your own.

Generating Tree Collision

You may want to add collision to your trees, because right now, a character could walk right through them. Adding collision and creating prefabs are covered more fully in later chapters, but the basic steps to add collision are simple:

1. Create a normal instance of your tree by dragging it from the Project view to the Hierarchy view or Scene view. Don't paint it on.

2. Add a capsule collider to the tree. This will break any previous prefab links or data. (A *prefab* is a way to make duplicates of a GameObject, and is covered in the next chapter.) You should use this kind of collider only for trees; the others may not function correctly. Resize this collider to fit the trunk.

3. Make a new prefab using this tree by dragging the GameObject back to the Project view, and use this one to populate your terrain tree library.

4. Ensure that the Create Tree Colliders checkbox is checked (it is by default) on the terrain's Collider component in the Inspector.

Depending on your scene file, however, adding collision may make it too hard to move around and navigate, especially if your trees are close together. With some trees, the capsule collider doesn't fit all that well around the mesh, and you may find that the collision makes your game less fun even if it is more "realistic."

Cluttering It Up with Grasses and Detail Meshes

Trees aren't the only things you can paint onto a terrain. You can also add grasses and detail meshes. The Terrain Engine treats these items differently, drawing and rendering them only when they are near the camera to save on memory and help boost performance.

To paint these objects, click the Paint Details button on the Terrain toolbar—the button that looks like a clump of little flowers. Just as with the other paintable features, you'll need to populate your library of available assets for the engine to use. However, unlike with trees and textures, you can choose to add your asset as either a grass or a detail mesh, each of which offers unique advantages. See Table 3.1 for help in selecting which one to use.

Table 3.1 Basic Differences When Using Trees, Grasses, and Detail Meshes

Variables	Trees	Grasses	Detail Mesh
Wind	Supported	Supported	Not supported
Asset	3D mesh	2D texture	3D mesh
Collision	Supported	Not supported	Not supported
Lighting	Ambient or direct occlusion	Grass only	Vertex or grass
Shadows	Real-time or baked	Not supported	Not supported
Rendering options	3D and 2D billboarding	2D or 2D billboarding*	3D only*

*Viewable only at close distances—objects are not rendered farther away.

Grasses are like trees in that they will bend in the wind, but unlike trees and other detail meshes, they are built only from 2D textures and have no depth. Detail meshes, on the other hand, are displayed as 3D objects, but don't billboard into the distance or bend in the wind like a tree does. These are useful for things like small rocks or other pieces of random clutter you want throughout the world. Both use the same brushes and options to paint.

The Standard Assets package comes with two grass textures ready for use, located here: Standard Assets > Terrain Assets > Terrain Grass. Click the Edit Details button and choose Add Grass Texture to bring up the Add Grass Texture dialog box (see Figure 3.16). Select the Grass asset from the drop-down list or drag the Grass asset onto the Detail Texture field from the Project view.

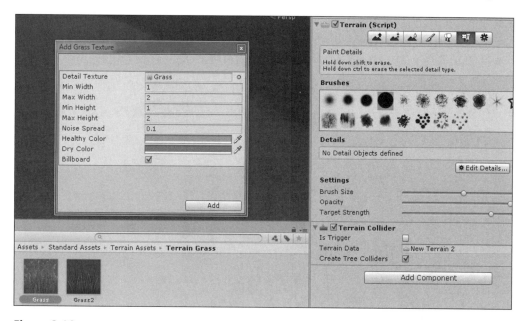

Figure 3.16
The Add Grass Texture dialog box.
Source: Unity Technologies.

The basic options for adding grass are as follows:

- **Detail Texture:** The texture to be used for the grass. The texture file should have an alpha channel to define the individual blades of grass. An *alpha channel* inside an image is much like the red, green, and blue color channels, but instead of controlling color it controls transparency.

- **Min Width:** The minimum width of each individually placed grass texture.

- **Max Width:** The maximum width of each individually placed grass texture.

- **Min Height:** The minimum height of each individually placed grass texture.

- **Max Height:** The maximum height of each individually placed grass texture.

- **Noise Spread:** The size of the clusters of grass.

- **Healthy Color:** This tints the color in the center of the grass clusters.

- **Dry Color:** This tints the color along the outer edges of the grass clusters.

- **Billboard:** Makes the texture always rotate to face the camera.

Instead of placing identical blobs of grass, Unity will randomize several values for each patch. They will vary between the minimums and maximums you set for width and height. They will also have variations in tint based on healthy and dry settings.

Change any of these you like and click Add to finish. Then select a brush and try painting a few strokes in the Scene view. Remember: You can change the brush settings when you paint to vary the look of your grass. You can also click the Play button to see your grasses and trees bend in the wind. See Figure 3.17.

Figure 3.17
Grass and trees reacting to wind on the landscape.
Source: Unity Technologies.

You add a detail mesh the same way, but instead of choosing Add Grass Texture, you pick Add Detail Mesh. These meshes should be created from prefabs, just like the trees, and will show up in the same library as the grasses. See Figure 3.18.

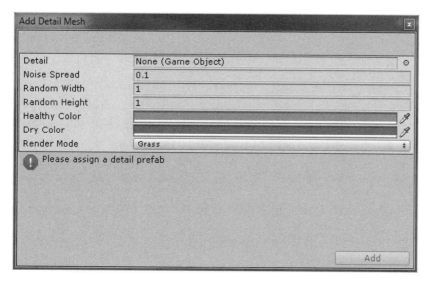

Figure 3.18
Adding a detail mesh is very similar to adding a grass texture.
Source: Unity Technologies.

When adding a detail mesh, you have the following settings available:

- **Detail:** The mesh to be used for the detail painting.

- **Noise Spread:** The size of the generated mesh clusters.

- **Random Width:** The maximum amount of width randomness allowed for each individually placed mesh.

- **Random Height:** The maximum amount of height randomness allowed for each individually placed mesh.

- **Healthy Color:** This tints the color in the center of the mesh clusters.

- **Dry Color:** This tints the color along the outer edges of the mesh clusters.

- **Render Mode:** Select whether this mesh should use the special grass lighting or be vertex lit. For foliage, choose the grass lighting, but for objects like rocks, you must choose vertex lighting for the object to render correctly.

After you add a detail mesh, you paint it onto the terrain exactly as you would with the grass textures.

You can edit grasses and detail meshes after import by clicking the Edit Details button while the terrain asset is selected. You can then change any of the options you selected upon import. As with the trees, if you changed your mesh or texture after placing it on the terrain, you'll need to manually update it by navigating to the Paint Details tool and clicking the Refresh button.

If you find you're having trouble placing grasses or meshes in tight clumps, check the Detail Resolution settings for the Terrain Settings tool. As with the terrain textures, you're not really painting these features onto the terrain; rather, you're painting a generated alpha map that tells the engine how and where to display your assets. If your resolution for this detail texture is too low, you won't have enough resolution to paint fine groupings of objects.

Remember: All these textures and meshes are unlike trees in that they only appear close-up to the camera. They do not billboard into the distance and are only meant to be details, not permanent fixtures of the terrain.

You need not be limited by the words given to each kind of terrain asset: tree, grass, and detail mesh. If you want your grass to be visible in the distance, consider building it as a mesh and adding it as a tree. Want some flags or poles to blow in the wind? Maybe that could be a tree or grass, depending on whether it needs to be 3D. Import your assets for what you want the end result to be, not based on the naming convention alone.

Troubleshooting Steep Terrains

You may have noticed another distinct difference between placing grass and trees: Grasses will tend to nicely follow the shape of the landscape if viewed from head on, but if you try to paint a tree onto a steep cliff, you'll probably end up with a tree partly floating in midair. This is due to the location of the tree's pivot point and how trees are painted onto the terrain. Depending on the size of your trees and how close they'll be to the camera, this may not be an issue, but there are a few steps you can take to make your trees stay firmly rooted to the ground.

■ Try importing your tree into a 3D modeling program and moving the pivot point up a little bit. This will help with the close-up trees, but your 2D billboards may end up floating above the landscape. Depending on your terrain, this could work, and the floating billboards may not be visible.

■ You can individually mold the terrain around the most problematic trees if they are few and far between. This could take too long if you have many trees to individually tweak, however, and can be difficult to get right.

■ If you really need a tree on a slope and don't want to futz around with molding or reimporting, place the trees individually as GameObjects and not as terrain features. These trees won't bend in the wind (unless you add a custom script to make them) or have some of the available features of other terrain items, but you can individually drop and rotate them into place.

■ If you have the memory to spare, try adding an exact copy of your terrain directly below the primary one. To do this, export your terrain as a heightmap, create a new terrain, lower it by about half a meter, and then import the heightmap onto it. This gives you an exact copy. Paint your trees onto this secondary lower terrain, and any floating bits will be hidden under the primary terrain, making it look like your trees are naturally growing from the surface. You do need to be aware of and look for any performance hits using this method.

- The simplest and most memory-friendly method: Avoid placing trees on steep slopes. They probably wouldn't grow there anyway.

Terrain Settings

The terrain has a few other general options you can tweak. You can access these by clicking the final Settings button in the Terrain toolbar. (See Figure 3.19.)

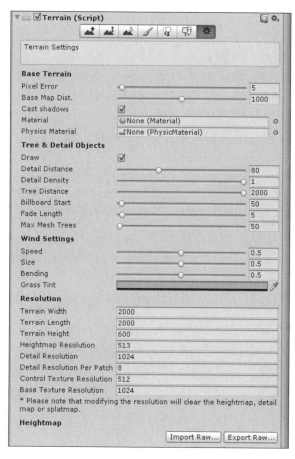

Figure 3.19
The settings for the terrain in the Inspector.

Source: Unity Technologies.

The Base Terrain settings are as follows:

- **Pixel Error:** Dictates how many errors are allowed when drawing the terrain. A higher number will render more quickly, but it won't be as precise.
- **Base Map Dist.:** The distance from the camera before the terrain textures are displayed in low resolution.
- **Cast Shadows:** Makes the terrain cast shadows. The shadows require more processing power but provide eye candy.
- **Material:** Allows a custom shader program for terrains. If you do not specify a value, the default Nature/Terrain/Diffuse shader is applied.
- **Physics Material:** Allows a custom physics system to be applied to the ground.

The Tree and Detail Objects settings are as follows:

- **Draw:** Draws all painted terrain objects. When unchecked, terrain objects are not rendered. This is useful when you need to optimize or tweak a specific section of the terrain and don't want the view cluttered with detail meshes.
- **Detail Distance:** The distance from the camera where detail meshes will stop being displayed.
- **Detail Density:** How much of the details to draw at a distance.
- **Tree Distance:** The distance from the camera where trees will stop being displayed. This includes billboards, too.
- **Billboard Start:** The distance from the camera at which tree meshes will start being displayed as billboards instead of models.
- **Fade Length:** The total distance at which the trees transition from meshes to billboards. Set this high enough so the change isn't too abrupt.
- **Max Mesh Trees:** The maximum number of trees to be displayed as meshes. This will override the fading distances if too many trees are in view.

The Wind settings are as follows:

- **Speed:** The speed of the wind as it blows through the grass. This does not affect trees.
- **Size:** The amount of the grass affected all at once by the wind.

- **Bending:** How much the grass will bend due to the wind. If you want to change the amount of wind bending for the trees, edit their Bend field.
- **Grass Tint:** The overall tint color for all the grasses and detail meshes loaded into the terrain.

The Resolution settings are as follows:

- **Terrain Width:** The total width of the terrain in units.
- **Terrain Length:** The total length of the terrain in units.
- **Terrain Height:** The total possible maximum height of the terrain in units.
- **Heightmap Resolution:** The resolution of the terrain's generated heightmap.
- **Detail Resolution:** The resolution of the terrain's generated detail map. Low numbers here are good for performance, but depending on what you need, you may need to raise it.
- **Control Texture Resolution:** The resolution of the splat map used when painting the different terrain textures onto the terrain.
- **Base Texture Resolution:** The resolution of the generated texture that is used for the terrain at far distances.

For most of these settings, it's helpful to tweak them while previewing the game as it is playing, as they are heavily dependent on motion and camera location. Just remember to record your changes before you stop playing, as they won't be saved while the game is running.

LIGHTING AND SHADOWS

When faced with the three choices on how to light your terrain, you may not be sure exactly where to start. Right now the terrain is lit using vertex lighting provided by one direction light, which is only as good as the terrain's resolution. This lighting is calculated only per vertex, so while it is generally the fastest option to render, it can also look blocky and shaky, depending on how many vertices are actually available.

Objects in Unity can generate shadows, and computing those shadows during runtime can take a lot of processing power. Because objects on the terrain are not very dynamic, you can improve performance by computing the shadows during development and storing them in a lightmap. Unity will mix shadows generated during gameplay with shadows stored in lightmaps. In some scenes, shadows play a very important role, such as revealing enemies running across a rooftop simply by their shadows.

For the terrain, you should consider building a lightmap, which is a texture that bakes in the lighting data provided by your scene. (To *bake* the lighting information means to compute the lighting values when you build the game rather than having them dynamically change during gameplay.) Terrains lit with lightmaps not only look nicer than vertex-lit ones, they also render more quickly than pixel-based lighting. For once, performance and prettiness line up. Creating one is easy:

1. Make sure you have at least one directional light in your scene (which you should have added earlier). You can also add more directional lights and position them if you think you need more lighting and better shadows.

2. Select all the objects you want in the lightmap in the Hierarchy view. Then choose Window > Lightmapping. Mark your lightmap as static (meaning the object will not move or change). Pick a high enough resolution for the generated map and verify that all the lights you want are included in the Lights list. You can edit this list by changing the size of lights, dragging lights into the list to add them, or deleting any lights you don't want.

3. Check if you want to generate shadows and at what resolution they should be made (Shadow Sampling). There are many advanced options you can read about in the Unity online documentation. Click Bake Scene when you're finished.

Now that your lightmap is generated, select the terrain and go back to its settings in the Inspector. Cycle between the three available lighting solutions: Vertex, Lightmap, and Pixel (see Figure 3.20). The vertex lighting is decidedly harsher and darker, whereas the lightmap and pixel lighting solutions are more natural and fluid. The main difference between the latter two can be seen in the foreground slopes—the pixel lighting is a bit special. Up close to the camera, it lights every individual pixel, taking more rendering time but producing a more realistic shadow. As the terrain gets farther away from the camera, it switches to displaying the information from the lightmap. For almost all cases, using the Lightmap setting will work better and more quickly. While the pixel lighting is nice, the increased processing required may not be justifiable for the minimum beauty benefit.

Figure 3.20
The three available terrain lighting solutions.
Source: Unity Technologies.

Shadows are the last piece to look at when lighting your terrain. While the terrain does self-shadow based on the lights, notice that the trees and details cast no shadows on the terrain, causing them to seem almost to float across the top of the landscape. Basically, you have two options to fix this: Either bake the tree shadows into the lightmap using a custom script if you have Unity Pro or hand-paint the shadows. The former probably sounds like the obvious best choice, and while it is quicker, hand-painting does give you finer control and a better end product.

You can hand-paint the shadows either by painting directly onto an exported lightmap or by creating darker terrain textures to paint directly onto the terrain. Creating different terrain textures is as easy as opening a texture in your graphics editor, darkening it a bit, and saving it with a different name. Exporting and painting the lightmap is a bit trickier and more involved, but it does give you even finer control and doesn't affect performance like adding more terrain textures does.

And there you have it: Your lightmap will be applied to your terrain. You can now go back and forth between your graphics program and Unity and tweak your own custom lightmap to your heart's content.

Adding a Skybox and Distance Fog

If you play your game now, your terrain will be looking good and ready to walk on, but there will be one glaring omission in your scene: the sky. Sure, the default blue is okay for prototyping, but it's kind of blah against the lit and painted ground beneath it. Adding a skybox will fix all that right up.

In Unity, a skybox is a special virtual "box" wrapped around your scene. There isn't any real piece of geometry there. It doesn't accept lights or shadows, and it's rendered in the background before anything else in the scene, helping give it the illusion that it's far away.

You can apply skyboxes to your scene in one of two ways: to the entire scene at once using Render settings or to individual cameras, allowing it to change during a scene. The Skybox package comes with nine premade skyboxes you can use. Later, you'll create your own skybox from scratch.

To use a premade skybox, follow these steps:

1. Select Edit > Render Settings. The available options will show up in the Inspector view, not in a dialog box.

2. In the Project view, select the target icon next to Skybox Material, then search for Skybox in the material selector. Alternatively, drag the material into the slot. You can find it under Standard Assets > Skyboxes in the Project view.

3. Your skybox will automatically work when you play the game, but to see it in the Scene view, click the Scene Overlay toggle on the Scene view's Control Bar.

While you're in the Render settings, you may also want to enable fog (click the Fog checkbox to select it) and adjust the Fog Color and Fog Density settings (see Figure 3.21). Right now, your terrain abruptly ends. It doesn't appear to fade off into the distance as it would in real life. Adding fog can help simulate this illusion. Change the fog color to something that matches your sky color and the density to a very low number. You'll definitely want to tweak this while playing the game, as it can be a tricky one to get right. If you haven't yet, add the First Person Controller prefab from the Standard Assets package to your scene in order to walk around.

Figure 3.21
The scene with fog and a skybox in place. This Fog Density setting is set to 0.005.
Source: Unity Technologies.

ADDING WATER TO YOUR TERRAIN

The last terrain-related feature to add to your scene is water. Creating believable and beautiful water shaders is often left to senior graphics programmers, but Unity's Standard Assets comes packaged with Daylight and Nighttime water examples. If you have Unity Pro, your default water will have real-time reflections and refractions. (No such luck, Unity Basic programmers.)

To access the water prefabs in Unity, follow these steps:

1. From the Standard Assets package in the Project view, find the Water folder and expand it.

2. Drag the Daylight Simple Water prefab into either the Scene view or the Hierarchy view to add it to your scene. The Simple Water prefab uses a round mesh. (This can be changed if you like, but it's not necessary for this example.) See Figure 3.22.

Figure 3.22
Even the basic Simple Water prefab turns the drab landscape into an island paradise.
Source: Unity Technologies.

3. Use the Transform tools or the Inspector properties to place the mesh slightly above your lowest terrain level and scale it so it covers the terrain.

It's not perfect, but it's quick enough to throw in to get a point across. You'll also probably want to go back and clean up some of the painted details to make sure you don't have swimming trees. Of course, you can also create your own water from scratch, but the Standard Assets are there if you want them.

You're now an expert on using the Terrain Engine, so it's time to start thinking about importing your own custom assets. In the next chapter, you'll learn to import assets for the *Widget* game and combine them with your new terrain skills to build a simple environment to explore.

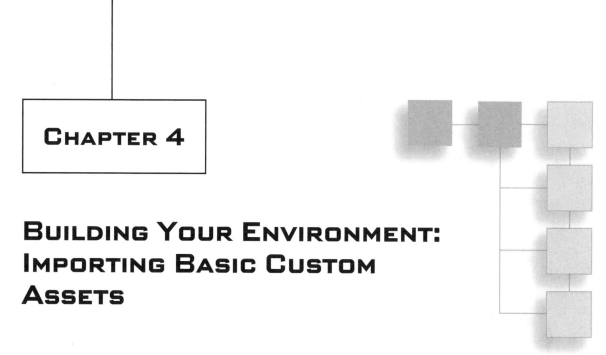

CHAPTER 4

BUILDING YOUR ENVIRONMENT: IMPORTING BASIC CUSTOM ASSETS

Now that you're familiar with using the Terrain Engine, it's time to start looking at creating your own custom environment for your game. The Standard Assets packages have some helpful premade pieces, but to make your game your own, you'll need to import some custom GameObjects.

Starting with this chapter, all examples will use the assets on the companion website and will revolve around creating the game *Widget*. Individual assets referenced in the chapter can be found in each chapter's folder on the companion website, and the compiled final project is contained in the Final Project Files folder. If you get stuck, individual scene files for each chapter are also included in this folder.

DESIGN FIRST, THEN BUILD

Before you jump in and start building your environment, it's helpful to first mock it up either on paper or within the engine using primitive objects. Because designers often use gray or white boxes, this process is often called *grayboxing* or *whiteboxing*. This may seem like a waste of time if you know exactly what it is what you want to do, but getting distances and proportions down first can make working in the engine faster and more fluid.

Drawings of *Widget's* maps and environments can be found on the companion website under Design Documents > Maps and Concept Art. There's no right or wrong way to draw your game's maps, so do what works for you. Some people find it easy to work with blobby shapes and just get down a general feeling for the game's flow, while others like working with graph paper and getting everything "just so" before starting on the computer. Odds are you'll be changing and iterating upon your environments as you work through the game, so nothing's going to be perfect the first time through anyway.

While you're drawing your maps, begin to make notes of the various items you'll need to create. In effect, you need to create your asset list. Creating this list up front will help ensure you don't forget something down the road. This book doesn't cover the basics of how to model or texture your own assets (some suggested sources are listed in Appendix D, "Resources and References"), but everything you need to create the *Widget* game is included on the companion website. You just need to learn how to import them.

Now is also a good time to start arranging your project's Assets folder with sensible sub-folders. You can create your own directory and organization system or you can use the sample one provided with the final game. In general, you may want to consider adding the following folders within your Assets folder:

- Audio
- Characters
- GUI
- Editor
- Particles
- Props
- Scenes
- Scripts
- Skybox
- Terrain

These folders will be referenced throughout the examples to follow, but you can place your imported objects anywhere you like as long as they are within the Assets folder of your project space. The choice is yours.

Importing Textures

To start building the first scene in *Widget*, you'll use an imported texture as a design guide to make sure the terrain is built in the proper place and shape. You could always freehand the map design or sketch something out on a slip of paper, but this way it's sure to fit the dimensions specified on the master map plans.

If you haven't yet, open Unity and start a new scene file. If you need to, set up a new project by choosing File > New Project and saving it to a location that's easy for you to access. Make sure to select the checkboxes to import both the Standard Assets package and the Toon Shader package, as you will need both of these.

Importing custom assets into Unity is extremely easy. If you can save a file, you can import a file. Find the TerrainMap1.jpg file in the Chapter 4 folder on the companion website and drag it into your project's Assets folder on your computer. (If you can't remember where you saved your project, return to the editor, right-click on anything in the Project view and select Show in Explorer. This will open a window in your Assets folder.) After dragging the file into the folder, switch back to Unity. Voilà, instant file import! You can now use TerrainMap1.jpg in your Unity project. Simple, right?

Note

I placed my file in a nested folder hierarchy: Assets > Terrain > Textures. That way, I can keep all the terrain pieces in one easy-to-find area and all the associated textures grouped together as well.

Make a habit to start saving your work directly into Unity's Assets folder. Your file will automatically be imported into your project, and you can always continue to edit it later without having to worry about copying or moving old versions around. This is a major hassle saver, and you should take full advantage of it.

More on Importing

While Unity does perform the bulk of the operation for you, there are a few import settings you should check whenever you import a new file into your project. The Inspector's import settings panel is specific to the type of asset being imported. For example, you will see different options for textures than you will for models.

Select the new texture file in the Project view to bring up its import settings in the Inspector. This brings up the import settings for any custom asset. See Figure 4.1.

Platform overrides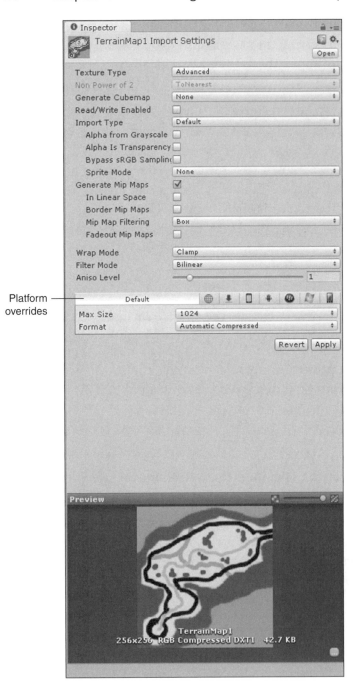

Figure 4.1
The sample terrain map's import settings.
Source: Unity Technologies.

Even though the artwork is automatically imported and configured with values Unity thinks are good, you should still verify them. Selecting the object in the Project view will show the options in the Inspector. These are the settings for images:

- **Texture Type:** Allows you to select default options based on common types of images. The default is a generic texture, but you can also change the image type to a normal map, GUI element, sprite or sprite sheet, cursor, lightmap, and so on. For this example I have set it to Advanced, exposing most major image options.

- **Non Power of 2:** Graphics cards and shader programs can make many optimizations when both dimensions are a power of two (i.e., 32, 64, 128, 256, 512, 1,024, 2,048, etc.). If the texture you're importing has dimensions not represented by a power of two, this option will become available. You can choose Keep Original to have Unity keep your texture its original size, Scale to Nearest to scale to the nearest power of two for each side (for example, a 33 × 247 texture would be scaled to 32 × 256), Scale to Larger to have both sides move to the next larger power value, or Scale to Smaller to do the opposite. In most cases, you'll want to just make your textures a power of two in your graphics program (except for textures you plan to use for GUIs—these can be any size and shouldn't be scaled).

- **Generate Cubemap:** Unity can build a cube map from your texture (more on these later). The texture file must be square for this option to be available.

- **Read/Write Enabled:** Allows scripts to access and modify texture data directly—specifically, functions from the `Texture2D` class. This will create a second copy of the texture for this purpose, so use it wisely and sparingly.

- **Import Type:** The image can be interpreted as a standard texture, as a normal map, or a lightmap. Changing this may enable additional options.

- **Alpha from Grayscale:** Select this checkbox if you want Unity to build an alpha channel from your texture, using its converted grayscale values to render transparency. By default, it's unchecked.

- **Alpha Is Transparency:** If your image has an alpha channel, select this checkbox to use it for transparency. If you leave it unchecked, the alpha channel will not be used for transparency, but shader programs can still use the channel for other purposes.

- **Bypass sRGB Sampling:** Some images may include color calibration information called *sRGB curves*. Adjusting the color for a precise match requires some extra processing and is usually unnecessary. Bypassing the extra work is the default.

- **Sprite Mode:** If you are working on a 2D game or using Unity's 2D rendering tools, you can mark the image as a sprite or a sprite sheet. You can leave this set to "none" for the demo projects in this book.

- **Generate Mip Maps:** Unity generates mip maps of your texture. *Mip maps* are smaller and smaller versions of your texture that are displaced based on where the object is in relation to the camera. When an object is very far away, a tiny version of the texture is displayed (saving some processing power); as the object moves closer, more detailed and larger versions of the texture are displayed. This option is checked by default and should always be used for textures meant for GameObjects.

- **In Linear Space:** When an image contains sRGB color-calibration information, automatically generated mip maps tend to appear slightly darker than the original image. Select this checkbox if you want Unity to attempt to use a linear color space instead of the direct colors.

- **Border Mip Maps:** Clamps the borders of smaller mip maps and stops colors from seeping into edge spaces. This is particularly useful for light cookies. (A *light cookie* is an image used in a light to give it a shape other than the default round shape. A cookie for a window might have drapes or silhouettes, or have a square shape rather than a round one. If colored borders were present, a player might wonder why light was coming through the solid wall. More on these in Chapter 12, "Creating Lighting and Shadows.")

- **Mip Map Filtering:** Specifies which kind of filtering you'd like Unity to use when fading between the different mip levels. Select Box from the list for a simple blurring and smoothing algorithm, or Kaiser if your textures are looking too blurred.

- **Fadeout Mip Maps:** Your mip textures slowly fade to gray as they get smaller. This is useful for detail maps that appear less detailed in the distance. Set the start and end mip level using the two sliders.

- **Wrap Mode:** Determines whether your texture will tile indefinitely or be displayed only once. Choose Repeat to tile or Clamp to have the texture's edges stretch to fill any gaps in sizing.

- **Filter Mode:** Filters how the texture looks when stretched. Choose Point from the drop-down list to allow your texture to look a little blocky when viewed from very close. You can change it to Bilinear to have the texture blur somewhat up close, or to Trilinear to have it also blur between its mip map switches (more on those later as well).

- **Aniso Level:** Sets the level for anisotropic filtering. This is mostly a big word for how well the texture is displayed when viewed from a steep angle. For textures applied to grounds or floors, you'll probably want to bump this up a level or two, but for everything else the default setting is fine. Increased levels of filtering will use some rendering memory on your graphics card, but it can make a huge difference if your ground is looking blurry.

You can modify the final two options, discussed next, on a per-platform basis. If you are making a game that ships on multiple platforms, you may want a different maximum size or a different compression format for each platform. For example, you may want mobile devices to use a smaller version of the texture, or you may want a different compression algorithm when transferred over the Web player. These options are as follows:

- **Max Texture Size:** Available sizes range from 32 to 4,096, with all powers of two represented. This tells Unity at what size it should import your texture, allowing you or an artist to work at any desired resolution.

- **Texture Format:** The compression format or representation used for the texture on import. See Table 4.1 for notes on each format.

Table 4.1 Supported Texture Formats

Format	File Extension	Notes
PSD	.psd	Native Photoshop file. Layers are supported.
TIFF	.tif	Tagged Image File Format. An Adobe format.
JPG	.jpg	Common compression format. Can contain artifacts.
TGA	.tga	Up to 32 bits of precision per pixel.
PNG	.png	Lossless data compression, designed to replace GIFs.
GIF	.gif	Popular Internet format, limited color space.
BMP	.bmp	Can be quite large if uncompressed.
IFF	.iff	Typically used for storing animation frames.
PICT	.pict or .pct	Standard Apple Macintosh format.
DXT or S3T	.dds or .dxt	Compression ratio is constant so graphics cards can use the data directly instead of decoding it into a second buffer.

This may seem like a lot of information at first, but you don't need to deal with most of these selections for the majority of textures you import. Most of the Texture Type presets use only a small number of options. In general, the most important ones to check are the alpha channels, wrap mode, maximum size, and mip map generation. You'll probably use the others on a more case-by-case scenario.

Supported Formats

Unity natively reads a bevy of different file formats and supports most of the more common texture compression formats. Importing your textures at a smaller size is helpful, but most textures are compressed as well to help save on space and memory. A good chunk of a game's available memory can be eaten up by textures alone, so it's important to use the best compression possible to still get the look you want.

If you work with Photoshop files or TIFFs, you can continue to use layers as normal. Unity will flatten the image when it imports it into the project (making it much smaller), but your original file will not be changed, and all your layers will be preserved. This enables you to continue layer edits as often as you want. No more having to export multiple files and flatten images manually now, or worrying about accidently flattening the wrong file! (Refer to Table 4.1.)

In most cases, you'll probably want to work with PSDs, TIFFs, and TGAs for texture work for their superior color quality and layer abilities. There's nothing wrong with the other types of images, but you may find yourself working around artifacts or bad compression when a different file format could have saved you the trouble.

There are many compressed file formats out there. Web pages normally use GIF, JPEG, and PNG compression formats. Those are great at reducing size, but they also require large amounts of memory to decode. Instead, graphics cards use formats like DXT1 and DXT5, which are designed for fast decoding by the hardware.

When it comes to compression, you have a few options. DXT1 is a common compression for textures that just need to act as a diffuse, or just a flat color with no special effects. If your texture has an alpha channel or needs to support a specular map, DXT5 is usually the default selection, but DXT variations 2, 3, and 4 are sometimes used by artists when they want slightly different results in transparency or color details. If you are targeting a specific mobile device, you might override the default and instead target PowerVR or Adreno graphics chips. Some specific texture instances will require you to use a specific format; usually, however, you should stick with Unity's default compression choices.

IMPORTING TEXTURES FOR *WIDGET'S* TERRAIN

Now that you can import textures, you can start building *Widget's* terrain with custom assets. The terrain map is already loaded and ready to go, but you'll need to import the splat map textures for painting and the other custom pieces for things like the skybox. If you look at the Design Documents files on the companion website, you'll see that this terrain map only encompasses the bottom-left of the entire map—the rest of the pieces will be built later. Otherwise, the map could become a bit unwieldy to navigate and take too long to load. No one likes to wait.

To start *Widget's* map:

1. In your new scene, create a directional light and rotate it so that it's pointing straight down (choose GameObject > Create Other > Directional Light). It doesn't matter where it's placed as long as the rotation is to your liking.

2. Expand the Standard Assets folder in the Project view and open the Prefabs folder. Drag the First Person Controller prefab into either your Scene view or your Hierarchy view. You'll use this for testing your terrain for now, until a different character is imported. This controller allows you to walk around using the W, A, S, and D keys, and use the spacebar to jump. If you examine its settings in the Inspector, you can change the Walk Speed and Jump Speed settings to your liking. Delete the default Main Camera object by selecting it in the Hierarchy view and either pressing the Delete key on the keyboard or right-clicking and selecting Delete from the menu. The controller prefab comes with a game camera attached.

3. Create a new terrain (choose GameObject > Create Other > Terrain) and set its resolution to 200 meters long by 200 meters wide (Inspector > Terrain Settings > Set Resolutionvalues). Remember, 1 unit in Unity is equal to 1 meter. Change the terrain's maximum height to 50 meters and the height-map resolution to 1,025. The other resolution settings are fine for now.

4. Rename your terrain to something more meaningful than "New Terrain." (I chose "Terrain–Entry and Villa," since that's what it is.) You can also move your terrain into the project's Terrain folder if you didn't create it there to begin with. You can rearrange any files from within the Project view by clicking and dragging. (Any moving you do should be done here, within Unity. If you move files outside of the editor, sometimes metadata will be lost and links will be broken. It's repairable, but not a good time.)

5. Use the Terrain tools in the Inspector to add Terrainmap1.jpg as a terrain texture splat map. This will automatically apply the map to the terrain, and you can use it to paint more precisely where the height is to go. Change the X and Y tile size to 200 × 200, the size of the terrain's resolution. This will center it squarely on the terrain.

6. Paint the area's height using the map and following pictures as a guide. Feel free to be creative if you want to move some things around. Also see the TerrainMap1 legend shown in Figure 4.2 for tips and hints on how to paint out the map. Start by painting in all the surrounding plateaus to box in the playable space.

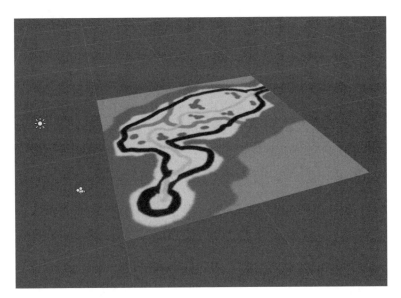

Figure 4.2
The terrain map applied to the terrain.
Source: Unity Technologies.

7. Make the playable space (the light green area) about 2 meters high. That way, you can cut in the path and river and have them at a lower depth.

8. Remember to use all the tools at your disposal. Use different brush shapes to get different effects, paint gentle gradated plateaus using the Paint Height tool, and work up areas in thin layers with a low opacity setting.

As a general guideline, keep these points in mind:

- The green areas are low-lying plateaus covered in trees and vegetation, with a height equal to about 5 meters.

- The light brown areas are higher plateaus, with heights ranging between 10 and 20 meters.

- The heavy black border denotes the playable space—everything within it should be about 2 meters high.

- The light orange line is a path, cut into the terrain at about a depth of 1 meter.

- The light blue line is a river snaking through the map, with its height set to 0. This will make it easier to place the water plane later.

Figures 4.3–4.6 show various views of the heightmap and terrain.

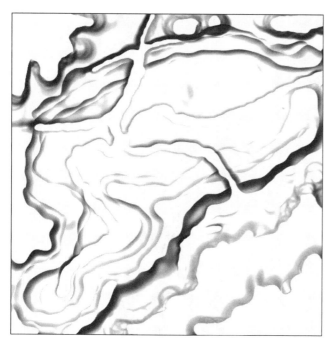

Figure 4.3
An overhead view of the painted heightmap.
Source: Unity Technologies.

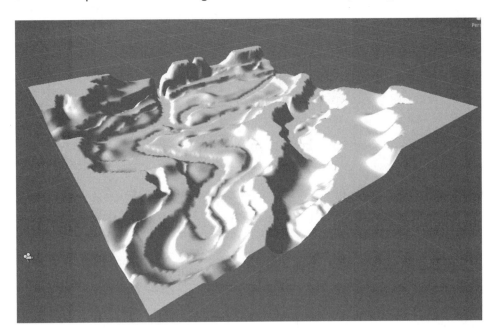

Figure 4.4
A side view of the heightmap, with the texture removed for clarity.
Source: Unity Technologies.

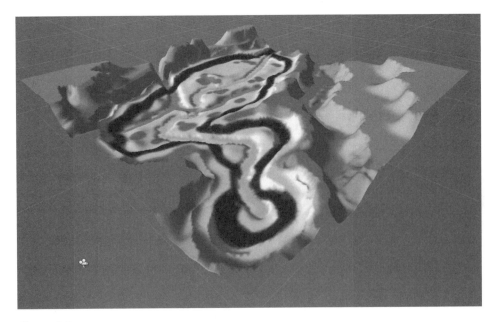

Figure 4.5
The terrain with the texture in place.
Source: Unity Technologies.

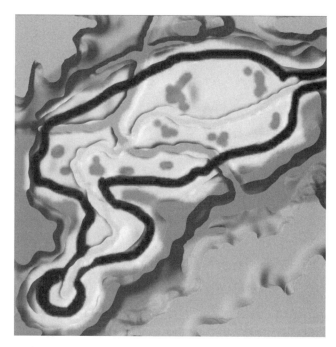

Figure 4.6
An overhead view of the terrain and texture.
Source: Unity Technologies.

Note

> You can also create your lightmap and export it to hand paint if you desire, as described in Chapter 3, "Setting the Stage with Terrain." However, final lighting passes aren't covered until Chapter 12, "Creating Lighting and Shadows."

You now have a pretty respectable custom map. Well done! It's looking a little sad and bland, though, and could really use some real color. The Standard Asset terrain textures are definitely an option, but you can always create your own to match whatever art direction you choose for your game.

The Design Documents files for *Widget* outline the art direction to be cartoon-like and bright, using toon shaders to look more like hand-drawn items. The textures provided in the Standard Assets package are nice, but they don't match the selected style. In the

Chapter 4 folder on the companion website, grab these terrain files and import them into your project:

- Dirt_Dark_DIFF.tif

- Dirt_Light_DIFF.tif

- Grass_Dark_Blotch_DIFF.tif

- Grass_Dark_DIFF.tif

- Grass_Flowers_DIFF.tif

- Grass_Light_DIFF.tif

- Stone_Path_DIFF.tif

- Water_DIFF.tif

Tip

All of these textures end in the suffix _DIFF to denote "diffuse." When you start working with a large number of textures, it's helpful to have a consistent and meaningful naming convention to help you find and sort your files faster.

Import these textures into the Terrain tool and start painting the terrain. If Unity misses a file in your folder or doesn't import something for any reason, you can always force a reimport by right-clicking in the Project view and selecting Import New Asset. Also, you can either continue to use the terrain map texture as a guide or delete it when you start your imports.

1. Import the textures into the Terrain tool with a tiling size of 10 × 10. Set the terrain's Detail Resolution setting to 1,024 and the Control Texture Resolution setting to 512 to match the images.

2. Check each file's individual import settings in the Inspector and verify that they each have DXT1 compression and are no larger than 1,024 in size. Depending on your target computer, you may want to make them all 512 in size or smaller. Artists will sometimes use very large source images because it is easier to scale down than to scale up, but large images can quickly consume available memory. Play with the

aniso levels until you arrive at settings you like. (*Anisotropic scaling* happens when the texture is viewed at a very sharp angle. You'll want to come back to these once you have the textures down on the ground and you can see how they look when stretched out.)

3. Begin painting just like with the height. Get a base color down and then start with low opacities and slowly work in your detail color in layers.

4. Paint the plateaus with the dirt colors, using some grass sparingly along the edges where plant life could grow. Paint some darker browns to define some rocky areas more clearly. Use the different grass textures together to create interesting patterns. All the grasses use the same green detail as a base, allowing them to tile together seamlessly. (See Figure 4.7 and Figure 4.8.)

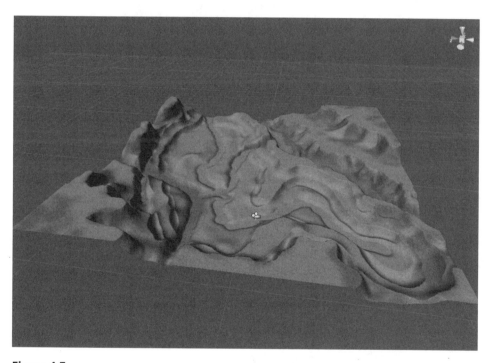

Figure 4.7
Lay down the dirt textures and contour the ridges with the darker dirt texture.
Source: Unity Technologies.

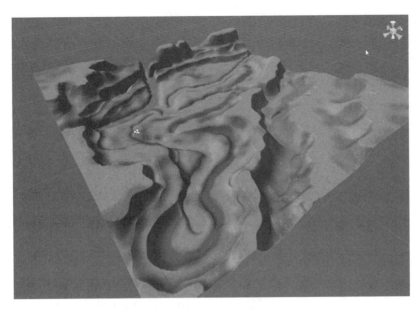

Figure 4.8
Block in the grass textures.
Source: Unity Technologies.

5. You can paint the path using the stone path texture, dirt texture, or a combination of both. (See Figure 4.9.) Also add some dirt along the edges of the stream bank.

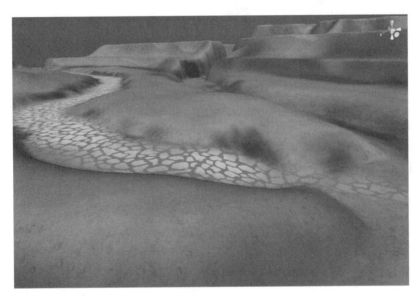

Figure 4.9
Cut in the path and start to detail the small dirt ridges.
Source: Unity Technologies.

6. Paint the bottom of the stream bed with the water texture or the dirt texture. You will add a water plane later to simulate the surface of the water, but the base can be painted in whichever you like.

7. Feel free to take any of these textures into your own graphics editor and customize them. For example, you can change the texture of the tile stones or the color of the flowers. Remember, however, that Unity organizes its terrain textures into blocks of four, so overwrite one, delete one, or add textures in multiples of four to best use the memory space.

8. Save your file often in case of unexpected crashes. Create a new folder in your Project view called Scenes if you haven't already and save your file there. If you need to move your file, do so from only within the Project view. Don't move it outside of Unity.

You can now grab the grass detail texture to give the landscape some life. In the Chapter 4 folder's Terrain Textures folder, import Grass_Terrain_DIFF.tif as a grass detail for the terrain. When importing, make sure it has a DXT5 compression (not DXT1 like the others) to preserve its alpha channel. Paint this item around the terrain. Figure 4.10 and Figure 4.11 show an overhead shot of the finished texture and an in-game render of the painted terrain, respectively.

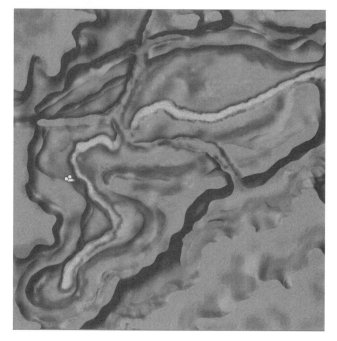

Figure 4.10
An overhead shot of the finished texture.
Source: Unity Technologies.

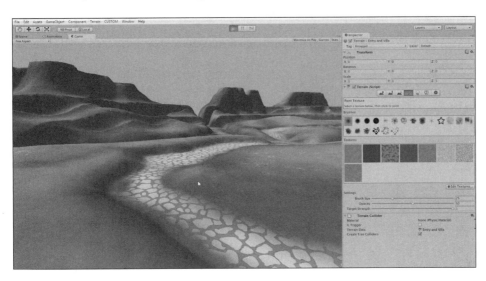

Figure 4.11
An in-game render of the painted terrain.
Source: Unity Technologies.

Play with the wind setting and vary its height, width, and noise patterns until you get something you like. My settings were a minimum height and width of 0.3, a maximum of 1.2, and a noise spread of 0.67. The result of these settings is shown in Figure 4.12.

Figure 4.12
Some grass blowing in the wind.
Source: Unity Technologies.

IMPORTING BASIC MESHES

Importing basic static meshes is no harder than importing textures. Unity can read scene files from Maya, Cinema 4D, 3ds Max, Cheetah3D, and Blender when the files are saved in the Assets folder. Unity also supports popular export formats, like FBX and OBJ, so if your 3D package can export to one of the available formats, you're home free. Here are the supported formats:

- **Maya 8.0 or later (native MA, MB):** Save your Maya file into the Assets folder to have Unity import all nodes, transforms, pivot points, names, meshes (up to two UV sets per), vertex colors, normals, materials, textures, and animations (FK, IK, and all bone-based). Unity will support multiple materials per mesh on imported Maya files.

- **Cinema 4D 8.5 or later (native C4D):** Save your Cinema file into the Assets folder to have Unity import all transforms, pivot points, names, meshes, UV sets, normals, materials, textures (multiple materials per mesh supported), and animations (FK, IK, and all bone-based). Unity will not import point-level animations at this time. You'll have to bake them prior to import.

- **3D Studio Max (native MAX):** Save your MAX file to the Assets folder to have Unity import all transforms, pivot points, names, meshes (up to two UV sets), vertex colors, normals, materials (multiple materials supported), textures, and animations. If you use bone-based animations, you should collapse the motion trajectories before import and export the file as an FBX.

- **Cheetah3D 2.6 or later (native JAS):** Save your Cheetah file to the Assets folder to have Unity import all transforms, pivot points, names, meshes, UVs, normals, materials, textures, and animations.

- **LightWave 8.0 or later (no native file formats—must be exported to an FBX file format):** See the Unity site for FBX exporter plug-ins for LightWave. When converted, Unity will import all transforms, pivot points, names, meshes, UVs, normals, materials (multiple per mesh supported), textures, and animations.

- **Blender 2.45 or later (native .blend):** Save your Blender file into the Assets folder to have Unity import all transforms, pivot points, names, meshes, UVs, and animations. Textures and materials will not be automatically imported and assigned and must be done manually.

- **Modo 501 or later (native LXO):** Unity will import all nodes, transforms, pivot points, names, meshes, normals, UVs, materials, and textures. Unity will support multiple materials per mesh.

- **Other applications:** Unity will natively read in FBX, DAE, 3DS, DXF, and OBJ files, so if your application can save or export to one of these formats, you can import your files without any hassle.

To use the native file formats you must have that program installed on the computer on which you want to run Unity, as the engine runs the 3D application in the background to import your files. If you don't have access to these programs all the time, you can always export your assets into an FBX file format, allowing Unity to read it natively without your application. Visit the Autodesk site (http://autodesk.com/fbx) for available FBX plug-ins and converters. Some 3D applications can also export to Collada files (DAE), so if you're having trouble finding an FBX exporter, try Collada.

The terrain could use some trees and other objects to throw around, so grab the Chapter 4 > Terrain > Meshes folder on the companion website and copy that into your Assets folder. Also copy the remainder of the files located in the Terrain > Textures folder; the meshes will need these to work. Save all of these into your Terrain subfolder in the Assets folder.

Switch back to Unity and allow it to finish importing the files. This could take a few seconds or a few minutes, depending on your computer's speed, but it only happens the first time the file is imported. In the Project view, open the Meshes subfolder in the Terrain folder and find the tree2 file (the file extensions are left off of all assets in the Project view). Clicking on a mesh asset in the Project view brings up its import settings in the Inspector, as shown in Figure 4.13.

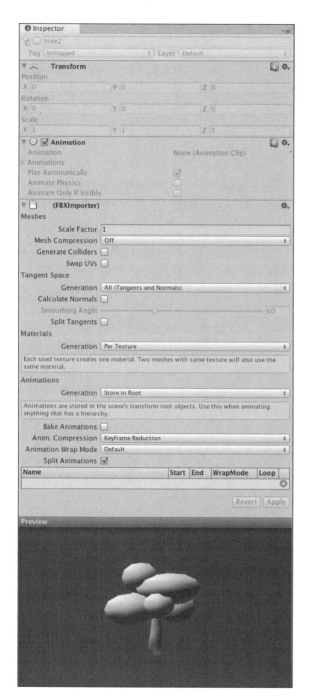

Figure 4.13
The import settings for the tree2 file.

Source: Unity Technologies.

This is similar in nature to the texture importer—all your available options are laid out by function, and a preview of the object is shown at the bottom of the Inspector (you can tumble this around using the mouse). The first field, Animation, is grayed out and unavailable, as this is a static mesh, meaning it has no bones, skinned mesh data, or animation driving it. It just sits there, static—and for a tree that's just fine. Animation, importing, and splitting are covered in Chapter 5, "Creating Characters."

The other settings are as follows:

- **Scale Factor:** If you didn't model your asset using Unity's 1 meter equals 1 unit paradigm, you can use this field to resize the asset upon importation. Set the factor to 1 if the model was created correctly.

- **Mesh Compression:** Select Off, Low, Medium, or High to dictate whether your mesh will be compressed upon import and how much. As with texture compression, this can help save a lot of memory, but you need to be careful to avoid introducing artifacts or other irregularities by setting the compression too high. Test your asset in the game and select the highest compression that still gives you the best look.

- **Generate Colliders:** Select this checkbox to have Unity automatically generate a mesh collider for your object. If the object is to be static, like this one, select this checkbox. This will make your object "solid" in the game world. If your object will move or be animated, a different kind of collider will need to be created, as discussed later.

- **Swap UVs:** Sometimes when you import a mesh, the wrong UV channels get picked up by the shaders. If you notice your asset isn't behaving as it should (with lightmaps in particular), select this checkbox.

- **Tangent Space Generation:** Use these settings to determine which auxiliary parts of the vertex data should be generated during import. Having both normal and tangents allows real-time lighting and bump mapping. Normals alone allow for the lighting but no bump shaders. If you know you don't need either of these, you can set both the normals and tangents to None to save some space and processing.

- **Smoothing Angle:** If you selected the Calculate option, this slider allows you to tell Unity at what point you want the engine to start treating edges as hard edges. If your asset has a normal map applied to it, set this to 180 degrees.

- **Split Tangents:** If you notice that UV seams on your model are showing up in the engine, select this checkbox.

■ **Materials Generation:** Select how you want Unity to handle importing materials, if at all. If you select Off, Unity will not import material data with your mesh or generate a new material for it in the engine. Select Per Texture to have Unity create a new material each time it encounters a new texture file (this is the default). These materials are project wide and can be shared throughout multiple scenes. If you don't want materials shared between scenes, use the Per Material selection. (Materials are covered next in this chapter.)

For the meshes in the Terrain folder, set up all the import settings as follows:

1. Set Mesh Scale Factor to 1 if it is not already.

2. Set Mesh Compression to High and select the checkbox to have Unity generate colliders. None of these assets will be moving around.

3. Change Tangent Space Generation to compute normals and switch Materials Generation to Off. For now, you'll set up the materials manually.

4. Ignore the Animation data (as there is none).

5. Select Apply to finalize any changes you make to the asset and have Unity reimport it, or select Revert to undo any changes.

You can change any of these settings at any time while working on your game. Nothing you select here is set in stone, and any changes you make will propagate to all instances of the asset you've placed in your game. Import the Props folder from the Chapter 4 folder in the same way. Keep these in a separate Props folder, and not in Terrain.

When you import a mesh, Unity will attempt to import all your textures and materials along with it, saving you the trouble of having to re-link them after import. Granted, this isn't always perfect, or you may want to use a preconfigured material you already made in Unity, but it can help speed some imports along. If you want Unity to do this, save your texture files into a folder called Textures, located either at the same level as your mesh in the hierarchy or at any level above it. Unity will look only through these folders to find your textures.

SETTING UP SIMPLE SHADERS AND MATERIALS

Creating materials and assigning shaders to them in Unity is not complicated. It can be done in a few quick clicks. A *shader* is a coded set of instructions describing how to calculate rendering effects on a given object, like lighting. You'll typically run across shaders that either calculate instructions per vertex (called *vertex shaders*) or ones that take up a bit more computational overhead but calculate per pixel (called *pixel shaders*).

You don't apply shaders directly to an object. Rather, you hook them up to individual materials, which are then applied to the mesh. Materials take the shader instructions and link them to a texture file, which is then applied to the asset. Assets can share the same material if they share the same texture file, and many materials and assets can share the same shader. (See Figure 4.14.)

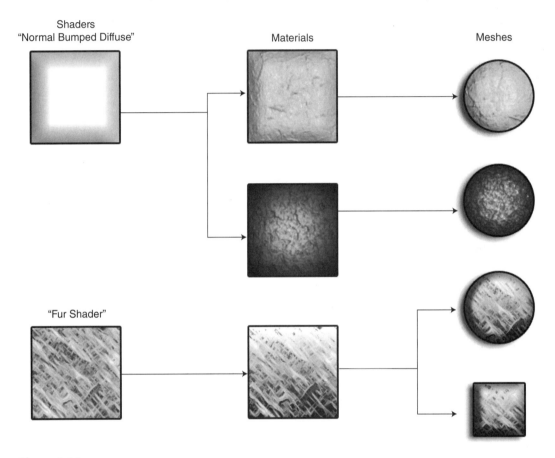

Figure 4.14
A simple diagram showing the relationship between meshes, materials, and shaders.
Source: Unity Technologies.

Without shaders in Unity, your objects would be white, sad, and lifeless, only being colored by the lights around them. Shaders help create the illusion that your objects have depth, are made from a specific kind of real-world material (such as wood, feather, fur, skin, and so on), and drive the artistic direction of your game.

Unity-Provided Shaders

Unity comes with a large library of prebuilt shaders, most of them divided into categories or families: Normal, Transparent, Self-Illuminated, and Reflective, to name a few. There are also special shaders, such as the skybox shader and other unique shaders for displaying particles and text. Some of the more prominently used shaders are shown in Figure 4.15.

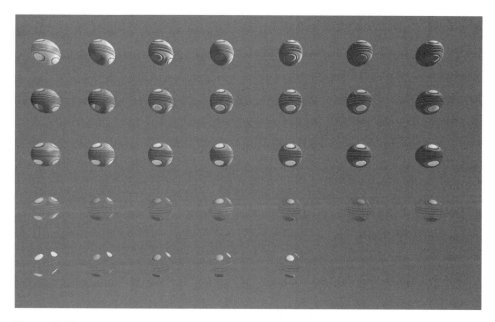

Figure 4.15
Some of the different shaders available for use, all displaying the same textures in their materials for reference.
Source: Unity Technologies.

The scene file used to generate this image is included on the companion website in the Shader Test project folder (choose ShaderTest > Chapter4_shadertest.unity). Browse through the file and tumble around to see how the light affects the different objects. You can see which shader is applied to which object by clicking one of the spheres in the Scene view and viewing its information in the Inspector.

As mentioned, the built in shaders are divided into families. These families are as follows:

- **Normal:** These are the most basic shaders. They're good for opaque objects like wood, cloth, or plastic—things that generally don't have a reflection.

- **Reflective:** As the name suggests, these shaders reflect the surrounding environment onto itself, accomplished through the use of a cube map. These are great for objects like shiny, waxed floors or grease.

- **Self-Illuminated:** These shaders appear to emit their own light and are great choices for objects like lamps or displays. They won't actually emit light onto other objects, just on themselves.

- **Transparent:** For objects that need to be fully or partly transparent, use one of these shaders. Transparent shaders can be used for water, glass, ice, or anything else that is not totally opaque.

- **Transparent Cutout:** These are very similar to the shaders in the Transparent family and are grouped together under the same drop-down menu. Instead of allowing for smooth, gradual shifts from opacity to transparency, the shaders in this family create hard lines between what is drawn and what isn't. This is good for complicated objects such as wire meshes or fences, where you don't want to accidentally bleed into an area that's supposed to be transparent.

The other shaders are used for specific features and effects, like the Nature Soft-Occlusion shaders used for trees. Most of the particle and FX shaders are used only for specific cases—you wouldn't use them for an ordinary mesh. Many other kinds of shaders can be either downloaded from the Unity website or written from scratch.

There's one other kind of shader available for download with Unity: a toon shader. These shaders allow for hand-drawn and cartoony effects, displaying the body of the object in a cel-shaded manner and drawing an outline around the general shape. The Toon Shader package is not automatically installed with every Unity project and must be selected during creation. The *Widget* project will make heavy use of the toon shader, so if you didn't include it at the project's creation, you must add it.

All the families of pixel shaders share similar properties in that they can have a diffuse channel or a specular channel or create the illusion of height with bump and normal maps.

After you determine which family of shaders you need to work with for your item, you need to decide which properties that shader will have. The main properties shared are as follows:

- **Diffuse:** Defines your object's basic color. It can be controlled with a texture or simple color selector. All shaders have some kind of diffuse property.

- **Bump and Parallax Bump:** Shaders with "Bump" or "Parallax" in their name have a property that allows the simulation of height and depth on the object. Modeling every tiny scratch or detail on an object is pricey and a bit silly, so bump maps are used to simulate these small details. Parallax bump shaders are similar but use a different algorithm to calculate the depth of each detail.

- **Specular:** Shaders with specular properties allow the object to have a nice shine or gloss when light hits it, like along the rim of a polished stoneware vase. This is not the same as reflection, which actually reflects objects around it back onto itself using a texture.

Out of the pixel shaders, the normal diffuse shaders are going to be your cheapest to render, followed by shaders with bump maps, and then specular maps, bumped specular, and finally parallax shaders being the most expensive. All the vertex-lit shaders are cheaper than the pixel shaders, but they're a little more limited in use. Of course, these guidelines are relative; every shader is different and has its own unique performance properties.

Shaders in Unity are written in a custom language called ShaderLab, similar in nature to CgFX or HLSL. Although it's not too hard to learn the syntax for the shader language, writing optimized, effective, and beautiful shaders is not trivial. Indeed, a veritable mountain of books has been written on the subject. Detailing how to write a complex shader is beyond the scope of this book, but if you're interested, see Appendix D for good places to start.

Bumps, Spec, Cubes, and Details

Some shaders require more input than others to do their job. Besides providing color to an object, textures are used to describe height, transparency, reflection, details, and many other auxiliary properties. Sometimes a singular texture can be used to provide multiple details at once, but often you'll need to create multiple textures to shade a single object.

Bump Maps

Bump maps are grayscale images that define height or depth on an object. Areas of the texture that are darker seem to recede into the object, and lighter areas on the texture mark spots on the object that should be raised or project out.

An object may be only a simple sphere, but by applying a shader with a bump channel, you can make it look as if the sphere has been sculpted with crevices and raised patches.

In this case, the bump map is just a grayscale version of the diffuse color map, as shown in Figure 4.16.

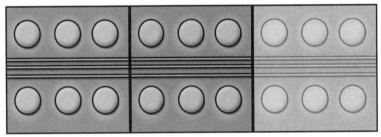

Figure 4.16
The diffuse, bump, and normal textures that lead to the finished Sphere object.
Source: Unity Technologies.

When you import a texture to use as a bump map, select the Generate BumpMap checkbox on the import settings to actually have Unity produce a normal map of your texture. Normal maps are RGB-encoded images, not grayscale ones, that use color data to define the bumps and creases on an object. (They tend to look kind of blue or purple.) Normal maps, depending on their creation method, can often lead to better-looking results than a normal grayscale bump map. When generating a normal map, play with the Bumpiness slider to increase its effectiveness.

Specular and Illumination Maps

Specular maps define which parts of the object are shiny and which parts aren't. Instead of being a separate texture like bump maps, specular information is often stored in the texture's alpha channel as a grayscale image. Parts that are painted white are glossy, and parts that are black are not. Using a map to define individual parts of an object can make your asset more interesting than if you just applied a wholesale specular value to the entire thing. While a person's fingernails and hair may be shiny and glossy, giving her shiny and glossy skin to match would be a little odd. The skin part of the texture can easily be painted out to avoid any gloss highlights.

Illumination maps for self-illuminating shaders work the same way. Instead of having the entire object emit light, you can choose only select parts.

The self-illuminated, bumped, specular shader shown in Figure 4.17 shows it all in one package using only two textures. The base diffuse color (Base RGB) is defined using one texture, and the gloss pattern for the specular highlights is stored in its alpha channel (Gloss A). The bump information for the normal map is a separate texture (Bump RGB), whose own alpha channel houses the illumination data.

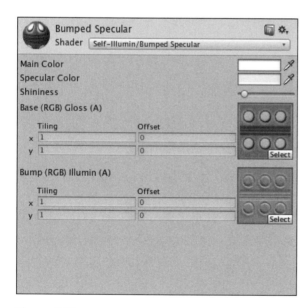

Figure 4.17
Unity clearly marks in the Inspector where you need to store your data.
Source: Unity Technologies.

You can choose a specular color as well (if you don't want the glossy highlight to be stark white), and the overall shininess of the glossy patches can be adjusted with the slider.

Cube Maps

A cube map is another special kind of texture, which in reality is actually made up of six separate textures that map to the faces of a virtual cube. Sound familiar? Skyboxes are in fact a kind of special cube map. Some shaders, like reflective shaders, use cube maps to simulate the world around them. Instead of actually calculating reflections around an object (which is expensive), a cube map basically serves as a snapshot of each cardinal direction around the object, which is then overlaid on top of it. See Figure 4.18.

Figure 4.18
This applied cube map makes it look like the sphere is reflecting its neighbors.
Source: Unity Technologies.

Cube maps fake reflections pretty well. They can be made by hand from six square images, or Unity can generate one from a square image. If you'd like Unity to create a cube map, choose a kind of cube map from the Generate Cubemap drop-down list in the texture's import options. (This option will be grayed out if your image isn't square.) Sphere maps are more common than other selections, but play around with them until you find something you like. The generated cube map is stored underneath the original texture in a hierarchy in the Project view.

Detail Maps

Detail maps are another kind of special texture and are used only by the diffuse detail shader. They act kind of like a reverse mip map in that as you get closer to an object, the special shader begins to take over. Detail textures are used to apply small, fine details to an object, like individual blades of grass on a terrain or bricks on a wall. If the camera is far away from the object, the normal diffuse texture is shown. As the camera gets close, however, the detail texture is slowly overlaid on top of the original, adding interest at a fairly cheap cost.

Detail images are often grayscale and must be completely tileable in all directions or you will see seams. Darker values in the texture will make the diffuse texture darker, and lighter values will make the object lighter. When you import a detail texture, be sure to enable the Fadeout Mip Maps property and set the mip maps levels you want it to function at.

Assigning Shaders and Materials

Linking a material and shader to an object is very simple, following Unity's drag-and-drop principles. Close the Shadertest project (if open) and reopen the *Widget* project. The tree2 object looks like it could use some color, so right-click in Project view and select Create > Material. This will place a new material object in the active folder in the project hierarchy. Just to keep things tidy, create a new folder in the Terrain subfolder and name it Materials. Drag your new material in here and select it to see its properties in the Inspector. See Figure 4.19.

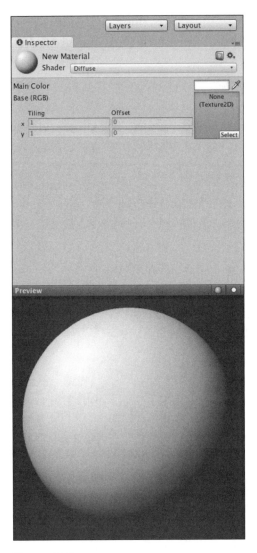

Figure 4.19
The default Material object.
Source: Unity Technologies.

New materials are empty by default and are assigned the basic normal diffuse shader. At this point, you could just pick a color for the material, like a nice green for the leaves, and call it a day, or you can assign a texture to a material—one that fits the UV map of the object. First, in the Inspector, click on the Material component to expand its options. To assign a texture, use the Select button over the dark gray Texture thumbnail or drag and drop one from the Project view to the square where it says "None (Texture 2D)." From your Terrain Texture folder, drag the Tree2_DIFF texture into this space to assign it to the material. The Preview sphere will update to show a green and brown texture wrapping around it, as shown in Figure 4.20.

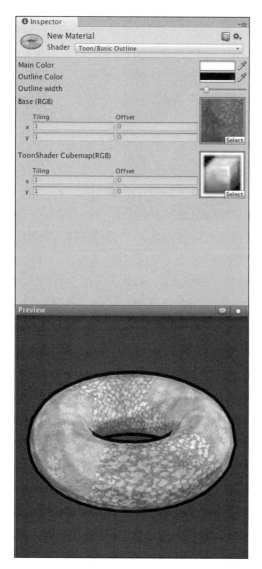

Figure 4.20
The finished toon shader, applied to a torus.
Source: Unity Technologies.

Note

If your sphere disappears and turns into a latticework-looking object, it's not the end of the world. Look at the import settings for the Tree2_DIFF file and make sure its compression setting uses DXT1, not DXT5. These kinds of errors pop up from rogue alpha channels being displayed.

In addition to assigning a texture and color, you can also change the tiling of a texture or its offset values through a material. Leave the default values if your texture has been painted to the UV map of the object; otherwise it won't match. These properties can be useful for creating animated textures on objects, as they can be referenced by scripts to create moving water, fluctuating energy beams, or anything else you can think up.

At the top of the Material Inspector is the Shader drop-down list. Change this to Toon > Basic Outline. This will help give your tree a hand-drawn cartoon look and make it match the terrain better. The material now has some different options available, namely Outline Color, Outline Width, and a toon shader cube map. The default outline values are fine (although you can change them if you want), but you need to get a cube map for the object to display properly.

Luckily, the Toon Shader package comes with a pre-generated cube map. From the Select drop-down list, pick Toony Lighting–Generated Cube map or choose Toon Shading > Sources > toonylighting > generatedCubemap in the Project view and drag that on.

The preview will update with these changes, but the sphere doesn't display the shader all that well due to its shape. At the top-right corner of the Preview window is a small blue sphere—click this to cycle through the basic primitive shapes to see how your shaders behave on different objects.

Now you're ready to apply the material to the asset. To assign new materials to objects, start by dragging the tree2 GameObject from the Project view into the Scene view or Hierarchy view to add it to the game. This creates an instance of the object. Using an instance is slightly different from making a copy. Unity uses a copy of the GameObject called a *prefab* to share information between all the instances. There will be more about instances and prefabs later in this chapter. Notice that the tree2 object has a hierarchy of its own—it's made up of two unique meshes: one for the leaves and one for the trunk. When assets are made up of multiple meshes, each mesh can take a separate material and shader. Right now you're only going to be hand-placing a few trees, so you can keep the toon shader in place.

Click and drag your new material from the Project view onto both of tree2's parts: Leaves and Trunk. Look at your tree in the Scene view to see the new material in effect. Don't forget to name your new material something more meaningful than "New Material." Green Tree or Tree2 are some possibilities. (See Figure 4.21.)

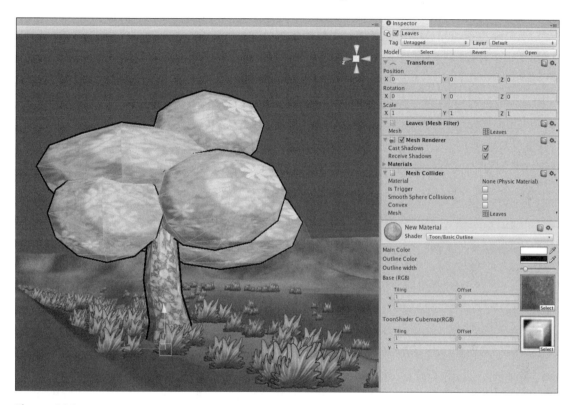

Figure 4.21
The shaded tree and its Inspector properties.
Source: Unity Technologies.

Now the rest of the assets need shaders and materials, too:

1. Make seven new materials and place them in your Terrain Materials folder. Rename them CherryBranches, GreenBranches, LooseRock, Poppy, SunFlower, Greens, and Trunk. These will be the materials for the meshes you imported earlier.

2. All but the CherryBranches and SunFlower materials need to have a toon shader attached to them. For all but these materials, choose Toon > Basic Outline Shader. These two will be a little different.

3. The CherryBranches and SunFlower assets need to use one of the shaders in the Transparency Cutout family, as both of them use alpha channels to define flower parts. For the CherryBranches and SunFlower materials, choose Transparent > Cutout > Diffuse.

4. Now assign the textures and cube maps to these new materials. CherryBranches will receive the Tree1_DIFF file; GreenBranches will receive the Tree2_ DIFF file; the LooseRock Material is assigned the LooseRock_DIFF file; Poppy, Greens, and SunFlowers are assigned the Flowers_DIFF file; and the Trunk material can use either one of the Tree files. All the toon shaders use the same toonylighting cube map.

5. Drag the two rock, two tree, and two flower meshes into the scene (they should be located under Terrain > Meshes if you imported them earlier) and assign the materials to the objects as follows:

   ■ **Flower1:** Flowers receives the SunFlower material, and Leaves_and_Stalk receives the Greens material.

   ■ **Flower2:** Assign the Poppy material.

   ■ **Rock1 and Rock2:** Assign the LooseRock material.

   ■ **Tree1:** Leaves gets the CherryBranches material and Trunk gets the Trunk material.

   ■ **Tree2:** Leaves gets the GreenBranches material and Trunk gets the Trunk material.

You can use the Main Color property of each material to adjust the overall tints of the objects if you think the colors aren't going together so well. The color's alpha channel will determine how much of your tinting shows through. See Figure 4.22 to see the finished version.

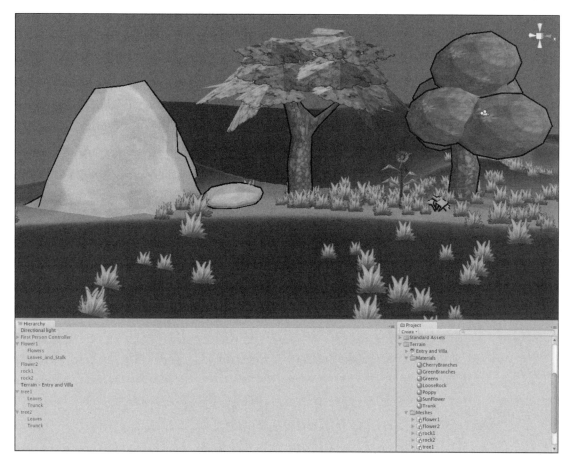

Figure 4.22
The added plant life with materials in place.
Source: Unity Technologies.

Before populating the entire space with these objects, there're a few more things to do. The world looks a little strange without a sky, and the level calls for water.

Making a Custom Skybox Material

The Standard Assets package's skyboxes don't fit the artistic direction for the game, so you need to create a custom one.

Skyboxes are created from six separate textures, each corresponding to one of the six sides of a cube. This virtual cube is rendered around and behind your game scene, giving it the illusion that there's a big ol' sky up there far, far away.

To create a skybox, you'll need to create six seamless, interlocking textures, which can be a bit more complicated than it looks. Or you can find a nice square tiling sky texture and have Unity make one for you. Lucky for you, there's a skybox texture premade for use on the companion website. To use it, follow these steps:

1. Copy the Skybox folder from Chapter 4 on the companion website over to your Assets folder to import the skybox textures.

2. All these textures must have their Wrap mode set to Clamp. If the textures are left at their default Repeat mode, there will be seams.

3. Make a new material in this folder and name it BlueSunnyDay.

4. Skyboxes use one of the special shaders, found under RenderFX. In your new material, select RenderFX > Skybox to create the proper fields.

5. Now assign each of the six sides one of the matching textures. Each has been named to correspond with the correct skybox slot it fits into (left, right, top, and so on). See Figure 4.23 for the result.

Once your material is set up, you need to hook it up to the scene. Because the entire scene will use the same skybox, you can just hook it up to the General properties. Choose Edit > Render Settings to bring up the scene's properties in the Inspector. Drag your new skybox material into the Skybox property or select it from the drop-down list. You can also take this time now to fiddle with the fog, fog color, and ambient light.

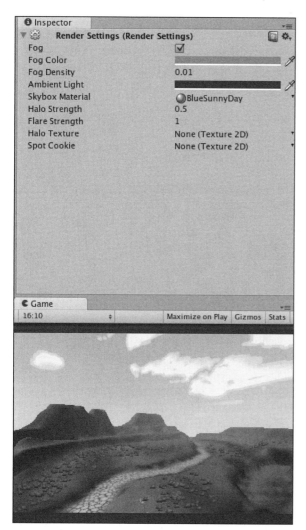

Figure 4.23
Skybox and fog in place, viewable in the game.
Source: Unity Technologies.

Adding Water

The last major addition needed for the map's landscape is water. Right now, the riverbeds are a little dry and don't pose much of a challenge to the player wandering around. In Chapter 3, you just used one of the prefab water objects from the Standard Assets package, so this time you'll make a custom water plane to fit in better with the rest of the game.

To create a custom water plane, follow these steps:

1. Create a new GameObject plane (choose GameObject > Create Other > Plane) and position it at (100,0.2,100) to center it on the map and place it just a hair above the ground. Scale it about 21 times along each axis to make it fit around the entire map.

2. Make a new material, name it Water, and assign it the water shader by selecting FX > Water(simple) from the Shader drop-down list. Put this new material in your Terrain > Materials folder and assign it to the Plane object. (See Figure 4.24.)

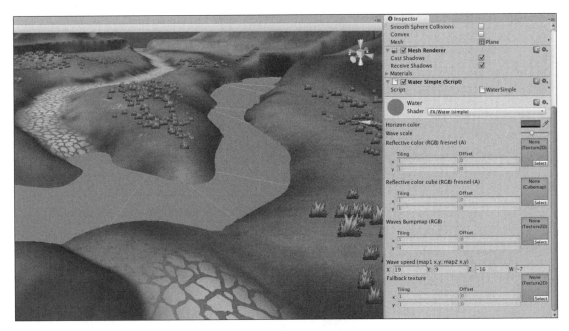

Figure 4.24
The simple water plane in place and its empty Inspector properties.
Source: Unity Technologies.

3. Locate the water script to run the shader. The water material uses a script to animate the different texture fields, giving the water the illusion of movement. Grab the Water(simple) script from the Standard Assets > Water > Sources folder and drag it onto the Plane object. The plane is now covered with a very simple, plain water shader. Spruce up the material by adding some textures.

4. Select the Plane object in the Hierarchy view to view its properties in the Inspector. The wave shader wants four different textures to function: three normal textures and

one cube map. You already have one custom water texture imported: Water_DIFF. Place this texture in both the Waves Bumpmap and Wave Speed texture slots.

5. Select the Water_DIFF texture in the Project view and change its import setting of Generate Cubemap to Spheremap. Click Apply to have Unity reimport this texture and create a cube map from it.

6. Apply this new cube map to your water's Reflective color map. The last file you need can be found in the Chapter 4 folder on the companion website—rivergradient.tif. Import this file into your Terrain Texture folder and add it to the Reflective Color slot. Change the Horizon and Wave sliders until you get an effect you like. Figure 4.25 shows the finished material.

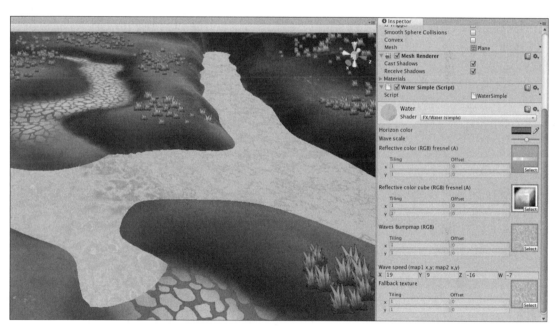

Figure 4.25
The finished water material, all hooked up.
Source: Unity Technologies.

HELPFUL TIPS FOR WORKING WITH ASSETS

Now that you can import textures and meshes, you can begin to populate your map with a wide range of fantastic items. While this is definitely fun to start, the allure can begin to wear off after you've placed your hundredth fence post. Thankfully, there are a few tricks you can employ to make your life easier when working with large arrays of assets.

Prefabs, Prefabs, Prefabs!

Unity has another trick up its sleeve for working with assets more effectively: prefabs. Prefabs are a special kind of GameObject that can only be created from within Unity. Making a normal asset into a prefab creates a template from which all other copies of that prefab can be instanced. If you need to make a change to the prefab—like update a material, edit a mesh, or attach new scripts—all instances of the prefab are updated as well, making it extremely useful.

Making a prefab is pretty simple. In the Project view, right-click and select Create > Prefab. A new Prefab object will be placed into the active folder hierarchy. These new prefabs are empty at first, but they can be easily populated and templated with any object currently in the game. Drag one of the assets currently in the Hierarchy view, like tree2, onto the prefab in the Project view, as shown in Figure 4.26. Rename the new prefab Green Tree or something similar. That's it. Any asset that's currently in the Hierarchy view can be made into a prefab.

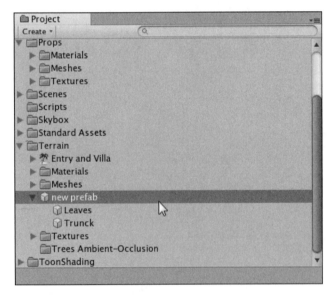

Figure 4.26
A new prefab in the Project view, based off the Tree2 asset.
Source: Unity Technologies.

Now if you want to put more of the green trees around the map, use the prefab Tree2 instead of the base asset. Then if you ever need to change anything, you only have to do it once instead of for each instance of the tree.

Sometimes you may want to change an individual instance of the prefab. These changes are shown in bold in the Inspector. For the most part, you can override any prefab setting and still keep the link back to the parent object, except if you want to add or remove a component or child GameObject. When you override a setting, Unity will ask if you want to propagate the changes to all the other prefabs or just the current one.

Make all the other assets you imported earlier into prefabs, especially if you know you'll be using them more than once. You can always spot a prefab in the Project view by its icon, a little blue box. These are similar to imported assets, but they lack the small file picture attached to those. Make sure you grab these and not the base assets when populating your scene.

Mass-Selecting and Grouping Objects

Scatter 10 or 20 of your new prefab items around. Now if you wanted to move them all 1 meter to the right, you'd have to go around individually moving every single one. Instead of doing this, you can use one of two techniques to group your objects to make selecting and editing easier.

The first way is to create an empty GameObject, place it at (0,0,0), and then make all your objects a child of this GameObject. You can then select the parent object to manipulate all the children at once. (Using empty GameObjects can also be a handy way to clean up your Hierarchy view if it's getting unwieldy.)

The other option is to use Smart Selection groups. To try this, scatter a few of the different trees around and then select them all. Choose Edit > Save Selection > Save Selection 1. Then deselect everything and choose Edit > Load Selection > Load Selection 1. All the items you previously saved are now selected again. This can be useful for saving large sets of like objects that you may want to reference later, like all enemies, all item pickups, or all plant life.

Snapping to the Grid

Depending on the type of game you're making, you may need to snap assets together or align them perfectly with the grid. With the items in question selected, choose Edit > Snap Settings. The Snap Settings dialog box, shown in Figure 4.27, opens. You can now enter the exact measurements for how you want the item to move and whether you want it to snap along all axes or just one in particular.

Figure 4.27
The Snap Settings dialog box.
Source: Unity Technologies.

Reworking the Terrain

As you begin to place items and assets on the map, don't forget to go back and rework the terrain. Often, things will look better if they seem to organically fit into the map and don't look like they were placed right on top without any thought. Using a smaller brush size, slowly work the edges of the terrain up around the edges of trees, fences, houses, or any other feature that would naturally have dirt start to pile up around it.

This doesn't just extend to height, but also to splat painting. Paint in darker areas around assets and put some dirt around well-traveled areas. Darkening the map around the bases of assets can help with shadowing and make it look like the asset fits rather than floats. (Adjusting details can go on for hours and hours. While detail and polish is nice, be careful that you don't neglect other development tasks.)

Now that you've got all the basics down on working with assets, go back to the Props folder you imported at the beginning of the chapter and fix those with materials and prefabs. The Fence asset has two textures for your use: a white variation and a brown variation. Set up two materials so you can use fences in either color.

After you have all these prop pieces and terrain pieces set up with prefabs, place some trees around the borders to keep the player in and hide the world's end. Make some flower beds, line the pathway with fences, or do whatever you want. The final scene file can be found here: Final Projects > Scenes > Chapter4.unity; check it out if you want ideas for how to place things. (Look at Figure 4.28 as well.) You can also check the Design Documentation files for maps and level guides on individual item placement.

Figure 4.28
The landscape, now populated with trees, grasses, textures, and atmospheric effects.
Source: Unity Technologies.

Special trees are also included that can be placed into an Ambient-Occlusion folder if you want to use the Terrain Tree painting feature, prefaced with the term "terrain." Also, don't forget to change the terrain settings from the Toolbar to calculate your lightmap, reconfigure the draw distances, and perfect the wind speed. Name your scene file something like GameStart and save often.

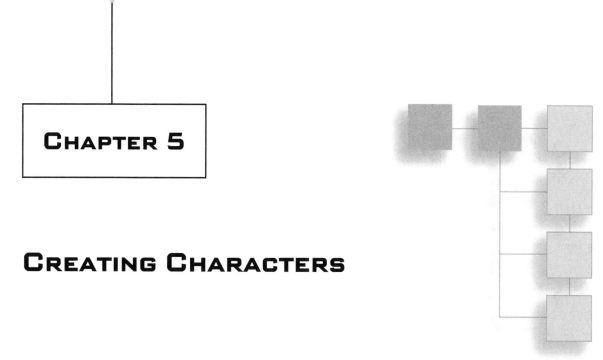

CHAPTER 5

CREATING CHARACTERS

It's all well and good if you have an immaculately designed space for your game to take place in. But most settings need some sort of populace to inhabit them to really come alive. Your players would also probably like to control an actual real character, and not the simple controller thrown in right now.

Player characters, or PCs as they are often called by designers, are simply the avatars that players use to interact with the game. The PC can be handled very differently from game to game, from prewritten characters that develop in accordance to a story to completely player-generated characters that evolve as the player sees fit. Some games don't even have PCs in the traditional sense, and yours doesn't have to, either.

BASIC PC 101

Designing and building unique characters to populate your world will help give your players something on which to focus their interest and with which to empathize. Creating believable characters has been a goal of oral and written literature for thousands of years. With video games, creating a believable character is perhaps even more important, as characters are expected to interact with players at some acceptable level.

In general, the PC will fall into one of three categories:

- First person
- Third person
- Implied/non-existent

Unity will allow all these variations, as the PC is primarily defined by a scripted custom character controller, and not by something predefined and hardcoded in the engine. Right now, the *Widget* scene uses a crude approximation of a first-person PC controller that is lacking a mesh altogether, which is primarily for ease of use when testing the game. The actual game will use a third-person approach common in platformer-type games. To do that, though, you'll need to import some new assets.

Character Capabilities in Unity

Unity offers many powerful features for building animated characters. It includes a comprehensive character animation system called Mecanim. The system is wonderful for animating humans and humanoid characters.

The Mecanim system makes it relatively easy to build and animate humanoids. The system is designed to work with many kinds of models. It can detect heads, bodies, arms, legs—even individual joints of fingers and toes. It isn't just the major bones that you can move. Facial structures, eyeballs and eyelids, and even teeth can be controlled. Joints, muscles, and bones can be grouped together. The parts can all be animated individually or collectively. These avatars can be manipulated as much as your heart desires once you have put together all the pieces.

Unity can combine and blend many animations at once. It can do more than just replay your own animations, however; you can tell it where you want to move your hands or feet and the engine will use inverse kinematics (IK) to figure out the motion. Inverse kinematics uses physics and the knowledge of the character's joints and muscles to compute a good-looking motion that will move all the body parts from their source to their destination.

While the engine provides the functionality, the game developer needs to provide the content. Creating believable and realistic animations for humanoid characters is very time consuming and resource intensive. Professional animators can spend weeks building the animations for a simple interaction. While I would absolutely love to explore the animation system in depth with you, this book just doesn't have room to cover it.

If you are working on a game that has a large group of animators, if you have the skills and want to build articulated models and libraries of animations, or if you have the money to buy fully animated humanoid characters, then the Mecanim system is for you. Animators can create a large collection of animations for large motions and for individual motions, plug them into the game, and the avatars become alive. If you have the resources available to use Mecanim (as most professional studios do), you can achieve amazing results with relatively little work. Because we don't have those kinds of resources, we will need to stick to simpler models and animations in this book.

IMPORTING CHARACTERS AND OTHER NON-STATIC MESHES

Beyond creating just the physical mesh for the character, you'll also need to account for its animation data. Most meshes you'll import will be static (not mobile), but characters will need to move around on their own, react to scripted commands, or be controlled by a player. Generally this means animators will import and link animations created in an outside application.

Introducing Widget

Back in Chapter 3, "Setting the Stage with Terrain," you learned the basics of how to import meshes, but I skipped over the animation properties in the Inspector. We'll return to those now. From the online resources package, drag the contents of the Chapter 5 Widget folder into your project's Assets folder to begin the import process. This is Widget, the star of the game and the character that the player will control. Arrange these files into a folder called Characters to keep everything organized.

Widget has a much more complex hierarchy than any of the previous static meshes. His body is broken into two skinned mesh components, called Body and Wheels (which correspond to the simple meshes Body and Wheels below them); a separate node called root housing his character rig data; and a Take001 animation clip (the one layer of animation his file contains). The animation clip has a separate property displaying the sample rate (how many frames per second the animation was created at) and whether the file has been compressed. The skinned mesh components (the ones with a box and file icon) show the default material that was created for each piece, along with a textured preview of the piece. If you click just the Mesh component (the icon that looks like a mesh box), the particular part will be displayed just showing the wireframe. The number of vertices and triangles that make up the particular mesh (tris) will also be overlaid on the preview.

Note

Unity automatically triangulates all meshes being imported, so this isn't something you must take care of on your own. Model formats allow for many different shapes of polygons, but graphics chips are designed around rendering triangles. The number of vertices and triangles in your game needs to match the capabilities of the hardware. If you are targeting older mobile devices, you might be limited to 20,000 triangles on screen before performance becomes an issue. On a high-end desktop computer, you might reach several million triangles. It is important to understand who will play your game and plan your model complexity accordingly.

Select the root of the Widget hierarchy to bring up all his import properties in the Inspector, shown in Figure 5.1. There are three pages of import settings: Model, Rig, and Animations. The Model page provides settings and options that relate to the mesh. You will probably recognize most of the options from the mesh import in the last chapter.

Figure 5.1
Widget and his import settings.
Source: Unity Technologies.

On the Model page, do the following:

1. Make sure the Scale Factor is set to 1. Some model importers attempt to adjust between scales used on different modeling programs, and the system can be configured with default adjustments based on your modeling programs. Widget should be about 2 meters tall, and you can verify his height by stacking two default cubes next to him. (The default cube is 1 meter tall.)

2. Make sure the Generate Colliders setting is enabled, and allow Unity to generate a material per texture. Apply the settings, and continue to the Rig page.

On the Rig page, do the following:

1. Because we are not using Mecanim to control Widget, change the Animation Type setting to Legacy.

2. Make sure the Generation option is set to Store in Root (New). That's all you need to do on this page.

If you were using a Mecanim-style humanoid, you could change the Animation Type to Humanoid. That change would be followed by mapping model details to the corresponding Mecanim bones and muscles. Unity can guess about most bones and joints, but every one of them must be verified. A humanoid model can easily have over 50 items to match up, so mapping is a task best done by the modeler who created it.

Continue to the Animations page. There, make sure Import Animation is selected, and behold the long list of options. (See Figure 5.2.) Don't worry. Just like the other Inspector pages we'll make quick work of understanding it:

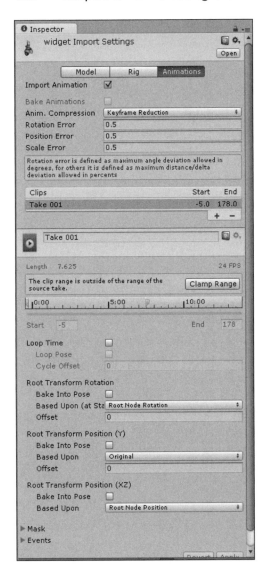

Figure 5.2
The Animations page of Widget's import settings.

Source: Unity Technologies.

■ **Bake Animations:** If you used IK, certain types of blend shapes, or any other forms of non-bone–based or FK animation in the file, the animation data must be baked upon import. Select this checkbox to do so. Widget doesn't need any of his animations baked, so leave this unchecked in this case.

- **Anim. Compression:** Animations can be hefty memory users, and you can set the type of compression you want to apply to the file here. You can select Off to have no compression applied, Keyframe Reduction, or Optimal. The last option will result in a smaller file size but will sometimes introduce artifacts or jittering. Play with different selections and pick the one that looks most like the original file.

- **Rotation Error, Position Error, and Scale Error:** If you chose to compress the animations using the preceding setting, you can fine tune how much error the compressor is allowed to accumulate. Higher numbers mean smaller sizes, but also bigger compression artifacts.

- **Clips:** Collections of animations are stored in clips. A character can have any number of clips associated with it. Each clip can contain many animation segments.

Usually, you'll find animations created for characters stored in one of two ways. Either all the animations will be created in one file and just have buffer keyframes between each unique animation, or each animation will have its own unique file storing only one piece of data, like walk, run, or fire. Widget has all his animations stored within his one file, so you'll use the Split Animations feature to process the different animation sets.

If you want to store the information in unique files (for example, if you had multiple animators working on one model), Unity allows a simple naming mechanic to relink all the files. Name your animation files with the name of the base model file, followed by an @ sign, followed by the name of the animation sequence—for example, widget@walk, widget@run, and widget@fire. The sequence name will be the one you use when you reference particular animations in scripts. Using this naming convention, Unity will link all these animations to the base model file.

Widget has nine animations stored in his FBX file, each spanning a set length of specific keyframes in the animation layer. These are listed in Table 5.1.

Table 5.1 Widget's Animation Data

Name	Frames	WrapMode	Loop Frame
Slow Roll	1–23	Loop	No
Fast Roll	30–53	Loop	No
Taser	60–83	Loop	No

(Continued)

Table 5.1 Widget's Animation Data (*Continued*)

Name	Frames	WrapMode	Loop Frame
Got Hit	90–101	Once	No
Duck	105–128	Once	No
Jump	135–147	Once	No
Fall Down	150–162	Once	No
Idle	170–242	Once	No
Die	250–322	Once	No

In the Clips table, click on the gray plus (+) button to create a new clip. By default, Unity populates the fields with a single Take 001 clip.

Each of the clips has a few options as well. These are visible in Figure 5.2 and are described here:

- **Plus (+) and minus (−) buttons:** Add a new clip to the sequence or delete the selected clip.

- **Name:** This is the given name of the clip and the one you will reference from scripts, so enter something more meaningful than "clip1." Spaces are not allowed in these names, so many developers bunch them together and use capital letters to indicate new words. This is often called "camel case" because the tall letters look like the head and humps of the animal.

- **Start:** The first frame of your animation.

- **End:** The last frame of your animation.

- **Add Loop Frame:** Some animations need an additional frame in order to loop smoothly. Select this checkbox to create a duplicate of the first frame to be played at the end of each loop.

- **Wrap Mode:** How the animation is to loop. The selection, Default, will not loop. Choose Once to play through once or Loop to continuously repeat. Choose Ping Pong to play the clip forward, then play the clip backward, then play the clip forward, repeating endlessly. Choose Clamp Forever to play the clip only once. You'll be required to reset the clip in code before it will play again.

To rename the clip or alter any of the information, simply click the desired cell in the table and retype. Enter all of Widget's animation data as shown in Table 5.1 and click the Apply button to save. The new clips you create are added to Widget's hierarchy in the Project view. (See Figure 5.3.)

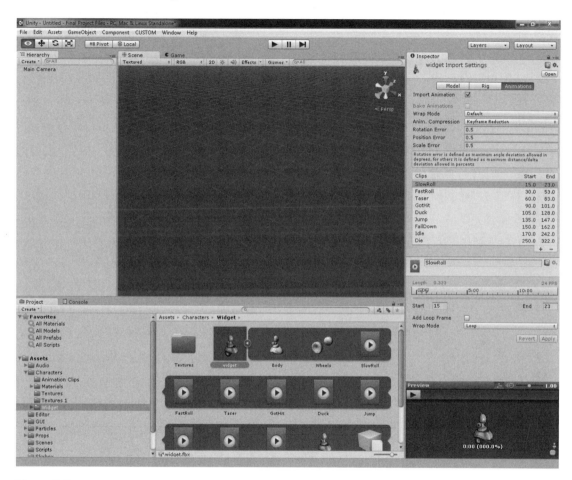

Figure 5.3
Widget's newly created clips.
Source: Unity Technologies.

There are several fold-out panels on the screen that allow animators to fine-tune their animations. They can adjust orientation, position, and mirroring. They can mask out particular items that they don't want animated. You can leave all of these untouched.

The last fold out panel, Events, allows you to trigger events inside your Unity program at a particular frame of your animation. For example, in an animation of the avatar pushing a button, you may use an event to trigger an explosion of particles when the button is fully pressed. In another animation sequence, you might have a rocket launcher that squashes and stretches for a moment, and then on a specific frame it should finally create the rocket.

To test the new animations, add an instance of Widget to the scene and give him a large plane or a terrain to stand on. Select the Widget object in the Hierarchy view to bring up his information in the Inspector. The Animation component describes his basic data and default behavior, as shown in Figure 5.4.

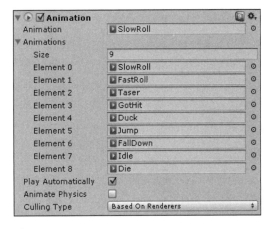

Figure 5.4
Widget's Animation component.
Source: Unity Technologies.

The first Animation field houses Widget's start animation (picked by default from the first clip entered into the sequence), and the Animations array lists all the animations that have been either clipped or linked to the model. The Play Automatically setting will do just that when the game is started (using the selected clip in the Animation field above), and the Animate Physics setting will allow the animation to interact with physics bodies. Changing the culling type lets you control when animation takes place. Selecting Based on Renderers will play the selected model's animations only if it currently is within the view of the active camera or another renderer, saving on memory and processing by not moving things when they are off screen. By default, this and Play Automatically are checked.

Drag one of Widget's animation clips from the Project view into the Animation slot (the top-most slot in Figure 5.4) or select one of his animations from the drop-down list to change his default. Center the view on Widget in the Scene view and click the Play button to view his animation. Remember: you can use the Pause and Step buttons to refine how you view each animation. See Figure 5.5.

Figure 5.5
Widget's Idle animation in action.
Source: Unity Technologies.

Widget is almost ready to be dropped into the game's populated scene file, but he needs a few more tweaks first. First, his materials need to be set up so that he matches the rest of the game world. The default diffuse material applied during import is all right for testing, but he'll need a toon shader to match the rest of the game. Widget should also be made a prefab so that all future updates to him will be easily applied. Many more parts will be added to him through the course of this book (like a character controller and other scripts), and this will be much easier if you work with a prefab from the beginning.

Follow these steps to set up Widget:

1. Assign Widget a material (if you didn't have Unity generate one on import) and give it the Toon > Basic Outline shader. The base RGB file uses the widget_diff texture, and the ToonShader cube map needs the toonylighting-generatedCubemap texture.

2. Change the main color to a darker gray to avoid him being washed out by the lights. (Using the following settings works fairly well: R = 145, G = 145, and B = 145.)

3. Create a Capsule Collider component for Widget's body piece by selecting the Body part in the Hierarchy view and choosing Component > Physics > Capsule Collider (see Figure 5.6). This will allow him to interact with other physics bodies in the world. Change the radius, height, and center of the collider so it fits snuggly around him. Don't try to include the antenna or all the wheels in the collider bounds—just get most of him in.

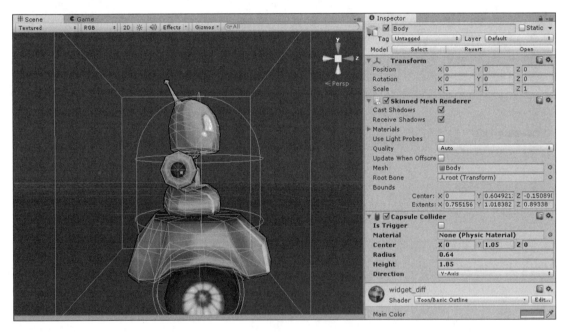

Figure 5.6
Fitting Widget's Capsule Collider component.
Source: Unity Technologies.

4. Create a new Widget prefab and populate it with the current Widget asset.

Your character is now ready to go and can be imported into any scene file in the game (see Figure 5.7). The major thing he lacks now is a controller—that is, some means to move him based upon the player's input. He'll also need an animation state machine, which is a piece of code to drive which animations should be played how and when. In the next chapter, you'll look at the basics of scripting in Unity, followed by creating a simple controller to drive Widget around.

Figure 5.7
Widget overseeing his new environment.
Source: Unity Technologies.

PART III

BRINGING YOUR PROPS TO LIFE WITH INTERACTIVITY

Interactivity is what makes games actually playable. It turns a collection of static artwork and pictures into a living system that responds to your commands. In Unity, most interactivity is achieved through scripting—pieces of instructions that are attached to individual GameObjects that describe how they should behave in a given circumstance. This part explores some of the different ways scripts can be used to enhance your game, from animation control to crafting AI.

141

Chapter 6

Scripting in Unity

If models, textures, and the like give your game environment a physical description and setting, then scripts and code chunks give your game and its contents life. Scripts define the basic interactions, behaviors, and rules of all the pieces in your game. Without them, you'd be hard pressed to call your scene file a game at all.

One of Unity's most powerful aspects is the way it incorporates scripts and their member pieces directly into the editor, allowing for fast, intuitive linking and manipulation of any GameObject in the scene.

This book assumes no prior knowledge of working with a scripting language and covers some basic fundamentals at the end of the chapter—enough to explain the workings of all the scripts needed for the *Widget* game. However, this is no substitution for a more formal approach of learning how to program efficiently and effectively.

One Editor, Three Languages, a Whole Lotta Choice

A brief warning to the new scripting initiates in the room: The first half of this chapter may seem a bit technical in nature, as it details some of the fundamental aspects of working in Unity. Don't be discouraged if you don't understand all of it on the first go—you can always return to it later once you've gotten your feet wet.

In line with the engine's dedication to usability and flexibility, Unity natively supports three scripting languages: C#, Boo (a dialect of Python), and JavaScript, also sometimes referred to as UnityScript. Unity enables programmers to pick their language on a per-script basis, meaning that a single project can contain scripts in all three languages, running in tandem peacefully and quickly. There is no need to choose one particular language at the start of a project and only stick to it; each user on the team can work in a different language based on personal preferences. It's even possible (although not necessarily recommended) for scripts to access functions in other files written in other languages, and a single GameObject can have scripts in all three languages attached to it running at the same time. It's all thumbs up for Unity.

Unity's game logic is based on Mono, an open source .NET platform based around creating cross-platform applications. All three languages have access to the underlying .NET libraries, providing support for common desirable features like file access, networking, and reading XML files. You can find more information on Mono and the .NET framework here: http://mono-project.com/.

To top that off, each language is equally fast at runtime. Yes, equally fast. "How can that be?" scoffs the long-time C# programmer. "Everyone knows JavaScript is an interpreted language and can't possibly be as fast as any compiled language." Well, this is where perhaps officially naming the scripting language "UnityScript" rather than "JavaScript" would have saved on the confusion. Unity's implementation of JavaScript is in fact just-in-time (JIT) compiled to native machine code, thanks to Mono. It runs up to two orders of magnitude faster than any other implementation of JavaScript on the market, giving rise to Unity's claim as to having created the "world's fastest JavaScript." This claim is quite possibly (and happily) completely justified.

So in summary, you can use C#, Boo, or JavaScript, based purely on personal preference. Each language does have its own individual quirks and strengths, perhaps making one better suited to a particular task than another, but as far as Unity is concerned they're all equally valid.

Scripting in C# and Boo: A Few Caveats

Despite the three languages being equally supported by the engine, there are a few non–syntax related issues to look out for if you want to use C# or Boo:

■ To attach a script to a Unity object, it must inherit from MonoBehaviour. Unfortunately neither C# nor Boo behavior scripts automatically inherit from MonoBehaviour unless you created them from directly within the editor. If you created your script file in an outside editor, you must provide the definition yourself. Here's how:

```
//C#
using UnityEngine;
using System.Collections;
public class MyNewBehaviorScript : MonoBehaviour {/*your code here*/}
```

```
#Boo
import UnityEngine
class MyNewBehaviourScript(MonoBehaviour): #your code here
```

- Use the `Awake` and `Start` functions to do any initialization, and do not use the constructor. Unity automatically invokes this; using the constructor elsewhere could create errors.

- The class name you provide in your script must match the file's name because each behavior script file is treated as its own class implementation. So in the previous snippet, "MyNewBehaviourScript" is also the name of the C# and Boo files.

- Only member variables of the class are shown in the Inspector. Properties are not.

PICKING A SCRIPT EDITOR—OR, "DO YOU WANT AUTOCOMPLETION WITH THAT?"

Besides picking which language to use, you'll also need to decide which scripting environment you'll actually do your coding in. Unity comes pre-packaged with a scripting environment right out of the box.

MonoDevelop-Unity is an integrated development environment (IDE). It is much more than a text editor. It is integrated with Unity to view your project, control the project as it is running, pause the program with breakpoints, inspect values of objects in the game, and many other development tasks. The tool is a specialized version of the open-source MonoDevelop system and runs on Windows, Mac, and Linux systems.

Unity has some additional development environments. Before adopting MonoDevelop, the engine relied on different editors. There was the UniSciTE for Windows editor and Unitron for Mac. UniSciTE and Unitron are simple in nature, but they get the job done. Both provide a few options for customizing the workspace and the ability to change the selected language for syntax highlighting, but they lack many features that developers expect in their tools.

Unity can use other programming environments as well:

- **Visual Studio C#:** Unity supports syncing to a Visual Studio C# project. Setting it up is easy: From within Unity, choose Assets > Sync Visual Studio Project. From within Visual Studio, open the newly created SNL file in the root of your Project directory, one level up from the Assets directory. Visual Studio will provide you with much more sophisticated highlighting and autocompletion, and it may give you access to C# features not currently supported by Unity. Debugging from within Visual Studio is tricky and only some features are supported. You can use tools like UnityVS to link more functionality between Unity and Visual Studio. (For more information, see www.microsoft.com/express and UnityVS.com.)

- **Emacs:** This classic editor has been around since the 1970s and many programmers have developed strong ties to it. There have been many branches of Emacs over the decades, and if you are using Unity on Linux chances are good that your programmers already have their favorite versions and settings. To use it, you will need to download and install an Emacs configuration script; the instructions are available online. (For more information, see www.gnu.org/software/emacs.)

- **UnityDevelop:** Modified from the open source FlashDevelop editor, UnityDevelop creates a nicer coding environment for JavaScript users. However, it's for Windows only. Setup is a bit involved; you can find detailed instructions on UnityDevelop's download page. (For more information, see gamejam.ru/unitydevelop/.)

- **TextMate:** This editor for Macs is fairly popular. There are community-supported "bundles" for TextMate that support C#, Boo, JavaScript, and the graphics language ShaderLab. (For more information, see macromates.com.)

- **SubEthaEdit:** This lean text editor, available for Mac users, supports JavaScript and C#. Two Unity-specific modes for the editor are available for download from SubEthaEdit's site. (For more information, see www.codingmonkeys.de/subethaedit/.)

Scripting in JavaScript: A Few Caveats

Not to be left out, Unity's implementation of JavaScript does change some functionality that may seem strange or downright upsetting to longtime "traditional" JavaScript users. Some particularly important ones include the following:

- To initialize a string variable, you need to use Mono's `String` class, not JavaScript's `string` class. Strings also must be designated with double quotation marks, not single ones. Here's an example:

```
var myString : String;
var myOtherString = "Using Double Quotation Marks";
```

- You need to formally declare a variable before using it, and should try to explicitly declare its type whenever possible if not assigning a value straight away. Here's an example:

```
var myName : String;        //myName is a string variable with no assigned value.
var myAge = 35;             //myAge is an int variable containing the value '35'.
myAge = "TreeBranch";       //This will raise an error – myAge is an int.

var myJob;                  //Type is not declared
myJob = "Engineer";         // myJob contains a string type value...
myJob = 7.5;                //...but now it's a float.
```

Unity will dynamically type a variable for you if you don't implicitly set one, but this could lead to undesired effects or errors, as shown here.

- A `switch` statement requires that you insert a `break` for each listed `case`. You cannot declare anonymous functions, and adding semicolons at the end of statements is not optional.

- Each JS file actually implements its own class. While incredibly handy, this does need to be taken into account when organizing your code.

FUNDAMENTALS OF SCRIPTING IN UNITY

Anyone familiar with working in a scripting environment for a game engine will have no trouble picking up Unity's application programming interface (API), but there are some aspects worth mentioning up front. Also, if you're completely new to scripting, make sure you understand the basic concepts presented here; otherwise, the next few chapters may be a little rough.

If you want to try some of the following examples for yourself, choose Assets > Create > JavaScript (either from the top menu or by right-clicking in the Project view) and create a new NewBehaviorScript. Double-click on this script in the Project view to open it for editing.

To run your script, attach it to any GameObject in the Hierarchy view by dragging the script from the Project view onto the object in the Hierarchy view. Click the Play button to start the game and run the script. For simplicity's sake, you can just drag the script onto the default main camera. You can also find all the script examples in this chapter in the Chapter 6 folder, downloadable from the companion website.

If you find that your scripts don't seem to update with changes even if you click the Play button, try clicking on the Options button of the script's component Inspector field and choosing Reset.

Note

Unity is case sensitive, so make sure you follow syntax exactly if you choose to type the examples. `WORD` is not the same thing as `word` or `Word`.

Two Useful Items

There are two items—`print()` functions and comments—that are used everywhere. Get used to seeing them.

The first, `print()`, is a special function that will print anything between the parentheses to the Console view. The last printed line will always be displayed on the status line, but you can open the Console at any time to see all the `print()` statements in order. Inserting `print()` statements makes it easy to see what's going on at any point in your code.

The second, comments, enable you to add notes and explanations inside code. The double slash mark notation, `//`, is a sign for a one-line or inline comment—something in normal speech that you may want to say about your code. Anything on the line after the double slashes isn't compiled or read by the engine. If you need more than one line to make a note, you can use a block comment, denoted by a matched pair of `/*` symbols, as shown:

```
//I'm a one-line comment
/* Anything after the slash-star is a comment.
Including this.
To end a block comment, use : */
```

Variables

Variables are the means by which your script can store data. Think of them as an empty box waiting to be filled. Like boxes (if you extend the analogy a bit further), variables come in different "shapes and sizes" that can fit different kinds of data. Not all data can be stored in every kind of variable, much like how you wouldn't expect to fit a refrigerator inside a shoebox. All variables also have a name, which is a unique identifier to remind you what the data inside is—like writing the contents of a box on its outside face. Simply, variables are comprised of two parts: a symbolic name and a container for data.

After you create a variable in your script (known as *declaring* it), you can assign a value to it—in effect putting something in the box. You can also perform tasks with it, change its value, swap the item in the box with another, or destroy it. Variables allow you to store large quantities of data and then quickly and easily find them again.

To make a new variable, you use a simple statement:

```
var myBox;
```

This line creates a new variable of the name `myBox`, with the keyword `var` declaring that the element `myBox` is a variable. Right now, `myBox` is empty and is waiting to be filled with some type of data.

Buzzword

A *keyword* is any word in a programming language that is reserved to mean something special in that particular language. For example, in Unity, `var` is a keyword that defines the following word as a variable.

Common Variable Types

Unity's JavaScript has many kinds of variables available for use, but you'll run across some kinds more than others. In general, you can break down the available variables into a few categories: numbers, strings, Booleans, arrays, enums, and component-specific. To declare any variable as having a certain type, you can use one of two formulas. The first is as follows:

```
var myVariable : myType; //ex. var myNumber : int;
```

Here's the second:

```
var myVariable = "some assignment value"; //ex. var myNumber = 5;
```

You can also use a combination of the two:

```
var myVariable : myType = "some assignment value";
```

But this is a little redundant and not necessary.

Also note that you cannot use spaces in your variable names, even if it's a multiword phrase like "my variable."

Number Variables

Number variables are available in a couple types, allowing you to pick one that fits your need. Specifically, there are integer number variables and floating-point number variables.

Integer Variables   Integer variable types can store whole numbers, such as 0, 3, or −5. They cannot contain any fractional data or anything beyond a decimal point. If you attempt to assign a number with a fractional component (such as 3.5), everything after the decimal point is discarded. There are several sizes of integer variables; the more common types are shown in Table 6.1.

Table 6.1   Integer Ranges

Type	Size	Range	Notes
int	32-bit	−2,147,483,648 to 2,147,483,647	Ranging between positive and negative 2 billion, this is the most commonly used integer type. Most programmers use int unless they have a specific reason not to.

(Continued)

Table 6.1 Integer Ranges (*Continued*)

Type	Size	Range	Notes
uint	32-bit	0 to 4,294,967,295	These numbers begin at zero and go up to about 4 billion. Programmers frequently use these for sizes and for values that cannot go negative.
byte	8-bit	0 to 255	The byte type is frequently found in graphics colors and in raw data. Colors can have 3 or 4 bytes to represent the red, green, blue, and optional alpha-transparency components.
long	64-bit	−9,223,372,036,854,775,808 to 9,223,372,036,854,775,807	When the range of an int is not enough, the long type provides a range of +/−9 septillion. It is rare for games to need a wider range of numbers than this.

Floating-Point Variables   Floating-point variables can have fractional data, such as 3.5, −20, or 3.14159. Notice that you can in fact assign the value −20 to a float variable, even though it may appear to look like an int. −20 can always be written as −20.0, but the decimal and trailing 0 is unnecessary. Floating-point variables are useful for any calculation that will result in the variable data having non-integer data, such as through division or when multiplying a number by something like a fraction of a second. As shown in Table 6.2, UnityScript supports two types of floating-point variables.

Table 6.2 Floating Point Ranges

Type	Size	Notes
float	32-bit	This type has six significant decimal digits. Anything beyond that is rounded. The exponent can range from 10^{-38} to 10^{38}.
double	64-bit	This type has 16 significant decimal digits. Anything beyond that is rounded. The exponent can range from 10^{-308} to 10^{308}.

You might be used to scientific notation, where numbers are written in the form 1.23456e8, which means there are six significant digits and the value is shifted by an exponent (in this case, 10^8). It gives a decimal value of 123456000. It is important to note that floating-point numbers have only a few significant digits. Anything beyond that value is rounded off. For example, 1.23456e8 is only specified up to six digits. If you tried to store the value 123456123, the extra numbers would round back to 1.23456e8, or 123456000.

Floating-point numbers are used in many math functions and are allowed to have additional special values such as NaN (not a number) and infinity. Because they are stored in binary (base 2) instead of decimal (base 10), many of the numbers do not translate directly into a binary form. Remember that floating-point is an approximation. Avoid directly comparing two floating-point numbers because they gain tiny amounts of error as they get rounded back after every use. Listing 6.1 shows the use of a floating-point variable.

Listing 6.1   Math Example

```
var myFirstInt : int;      //declare the variable as type int
var mySecondInt = 10;

/* print is a special function that prints out anything between the () to the Console. */
print(mySecondInt);

mySecondInt = 7;
myFirstInt = -30;
print(mySecondInt + myFirstInt);

var myFirstFloat = 3.14159;     //declare a variable as type float
print(myFirstFloat);

myFirstFloat = myFirstFloat * 7;
print(myFirstFloat);
```

String Variables

Besides numbers, a variable can also hold data that takes the form of text, giving rise to the ubiquitous and much loved "Hello world" example. Variables of this type, called *strings*, can be a word, a letter, a phrase, or even an entire novel (provided of course you have the memory space to do something like that). Strings allow you to store useful data like overlay text for buttons, players' names, or NPC messages. Listing 6.2 shows a string variable.

Listing 6.2   String Example

```
var myString : String;
var myOtherString = " ";

myString = "Hello,";
myOtherString = "world!";

print(myString + " " + myOtherString);
```

This example takes the two strings and prints them out together, using " " to denote a single empty whitespace (like a single spacebar tap). To assign a text value to a string variable, you must always enclose it in double quotation marks.

Booleans

Booleans are a special kind of variable, and you have run across them before even if the name is unfamiliar. Booleans can only have one of two possible types: `true` or `false`. That's it. Booleans are incredibly useful for when you need to start performing tests on your data, determining if it fulfills some criteria you set. The data either does (`true`) or doesn't (`false`). Yes or no. (See Listing 6.3.)

Listing 6.3   Boolean Example

```
var aTrueVariable : boolean;
var anotherBoolVariable = false;
aTrueVariable = true;

print(anotherBoolVariable);
print(anotherBoolVariable + " doesn't equal " + aTrueVariable);
```

Notice that even though you must set the value of the Boolean variable using a lowercase `true` or `false`, the results will print out capitalized in the Console. Unlike in many other programming languages, `false` does not equate to 0 nor `true` to 1, and you cannot use these to test for equality or assignment.

Arrays and Enums

You should now have a good handle on the basic types of variables you can use. With even this small amount of knowledge, you'd be surprised at how much you can get done. But suppose you want to create some variables that are a bit more interesting.

You may find yourself at some point creating hundreds upon hundreds of integer values, storing your player character's inventory piece by piece. One variable may store how many health potions he has, another how many iron ingots. This, however, can get tediously unwieldy, especially if you have to do something involving the entire inventory at once. Arrays to the rescue!

An *array* is a special kind of object that allows you to store multiple values and objects together in a single variable. Think of it like a numbered list: In slot #1, you have health potions; in slot #2, you have manna potions; in slot #3, you have repair kits; and so on. But all these slots belong to one variable—your item list. All these variables are then stored in one object, the array, making reference and manipulation much easier than if they had been their own unique variables.

Not to make this more confusing than it needs to be, but Unity gives JavaScript users their choice of two different kinds of arrays—ones that can be resized (called JavaScript arrays) and ones that have a fixed size, or number of slots to fill (called built-in arrays).

A built-in array is created with a fixed size (statically sized, so to speak) and is extremely fast to run. Arrays can take the type of any other kind of variable, like `float`, `int`, or `string`, and house only values of that type. To access a value in an array, you specify its slot number using a special `[ ]` notation, as shown in Listing 6.4.

Listing 6.4 Array Example

```
//makes an empty array that could store float values
//an empty array has 0 slots
var myArray: float[];

//makes an empty array that could store string values
var myOtherArray: String[];

//makes an array with 10 slots in it for integer values
//note that to make a non-empty array you use the "new" keyword var
myInventory = new int[10];
var myInventoryLookup = 9;

myInventory[0] = 1;
myInventory[1] = 5;
myInventory[2] = 0;
myInventory[9] = 20;

print(myInventory[0]);    //prints 1
print(myInventory[1]);    //prints 5
print(myInventory[2]);    //prints 0
print(myInventory[7]);    //prints 0
print(myInventory[myInventoryLookup]);        //prints 20
```

There are a few other special bits about arrays:

- Slot numbers don't start counting at 1. Instead, they start at 0. So saying an array has 10 possible slots, or indexes, really means that you can use an index reference number from 0 to 9.

- As shown in the last line of Listing 6.4, you can use another int variable, like myInventory-Lookup, to reference a specific index number. Because myInventoryLookup stores a value of 9, the line of code prints out what value lives in the ninth slot of myInventory.

- Any built-in array you build will have all its default values start at 0, as with myInventory[7]. You didn't explicitly assign a value to it, like with myInventory [1], but it still has a value.

The only thing you must be careful of is not referencing a slot number that doesn't exist in the array, like in this example: myInventory[10]. This hasn't been allocated to the array and will result in an error.

The other kind of array can be resized on the fly, and it's called a JavaScript array. These are very slightly slower to use than the built-ins, but do provide some extra nice functionality. Listing 6.5 shows a JavaScript array in action.

Listing 6.5   Another Array Example

```
var myInventory = new Array();

myInventory.length = 1;
myInventory[0] = 1;

//Oops!     We need to add another item, so increase the size of the array
myInventory.length = 10;
var myInventoryLookup = 9;

myInventory[0] = 1;
myInventory[1] = 5;
myInventory[2] = 0;
myInventory[9] = 20;

print(myInventory[0]);    //prints 1
print(myInventory[1]);    //prints 5
print(myInventory[2]);    //prints 0
print(myInventory[7]);    //prints Null
print(myInventory[myInventoryLookup]);    //prints 20
```

Besides the obvious resizing allowance, there is one more important difference to note here. Observe the result of the print() statement for myInventory[7]. What's going on here? Unlike built-in arrays, which initialize all values to 0, JavaScript arrays initialize all values to null, a fancy way of saying…nothing. It's extremely important to remember that null does not mean 0; it's its own separate thing. If you don't assign a value to a JavaScript array index, it doesn't know what value it should point to, so it points to nothing in memory. The value of 0 is a defined value in programming, and you shouldn't interchange it with "nothing" as we do in colloquial speech. Be very mindful of this or you may find yourself with some errors and bugs down the road.

You can happily convert between the two kinds of arrays if you ever find you need to change your mind!

Note

The JavaScript Array class is only available in JavaScript. The languages C# and Boo have different classes. You'll have to use an ArrayList, Dictionary, or Hashtable class for the same basic functionality.

So in these examples, you could say myInventory[0] holds the number of health potions your character has, whereas myInventory[1] holds the number of fish scales he's picked up. However, there's still one small issue with these: It could be painful or downright impossible to remember what myInventory[0] means a couple of hundred lines of code later. What to do?

Enter the enum. An enum (or enumerated type) is similar to an array, but instead of consisting of a list of index (or slot) numbers and value pairs, an enum contains a list of named identifiers paired with values. So now you really can say in code healthPotions = 1 and not just slot[0] = 1, making it a lot easier to read and understand. The syntax for declaring and using an enum is similar to using arrays. (See Listing 6.6.)

Listing 6.6   Enumeration Example

```
//Here's a list, or enumeration, of all possible inventory items in the game
//Inventory has now been declared as a new variable Type
enum Inventory
{
        HEALTHPOTIONS,
        MANAPOTIONS,
        SWORDS,
        FISHSCALES,
        BESTSHIELDEVER
};
```

```
//To use this enum, you need to make an array Inventory to hold the items
var myInventory: int[] ;
myInventory = new int[5] ;
```

```
//Assignments can now be made using the enum values instead of integers
myInventory[Inventory.HEALTHPOTIONS] = 1;
myInventory[Inventory.MANAPOTIONS] = 5;
myInventory[Inventory.BESTSHIELDEVER] = 1;
print(myInventory[0]);                          //prints 1
print(myInventory[Inventory.MANAPOTIONS]);      //prints 5
print(myInventory[Inventory.FISHSCALES]);       //prints 0
```

It's a bit easier now to see exactly what inventory slot you're updating. You can of course always use numbers (or variables) to reference the same slots, as seen in the first print() statement, because you can think of the enum declaration as actually saying this:

```
HEALTHPOTIONS = 0,
MANAPOTIONS = 1,
SWORDS = 2,
FISHSCALES = 3,
BESTSHIELDEVER = 4
```

You can also use enums to assign the value of a variable, or anywhere a named list just makes more sense. Here's an example:

```
enum GameState
{
        START,
        LOADING,
        PAUSED,
        VICTORY,
        GAMEOVER
};
//Initialize the new GameState Variable. MyGame is now of type GameState var
myGame : GameState;

//Now we can change the state of the game using the named enum. myGame =
GameState.START;
print(myGame);

myGame = GameState.VICTORY;
print(myGame);
```

In this example, you declare myGame to be a variable of the new enum type—GameState—thus allowing it to hold the value of any of your predefined states. This is much easier to read and work with than something like myGame – 0. Do note, however, that you must use the dot notation to reference the enum value. Typing myGame = VICTORY will give you an error.

Component-Specific

Beyond these more normal variable types, you can also declare a variable as having a specific component type—any component that can be found attached to a Unity Game-Object. This basically tells Unity that the variable in question must contain a value (or reference an object) that has this component attached to it. Any object that doesn't have this component can't be assigned to the variable. This is especially important for debugging later on if you start to dynamically assign objects in your world to variables. You'll immediately get an error telling you if the assigned object was missing the requested component type. See Listing 6.7

Listing 6.7   Explicit Type Example

```
//ComponentTest.js
//This creates a variable that must be assigned to
//an object with a Controller attached.
var myController : CharacterController;

//This variable must take a GameObject with a Transform
//component - almost anything could go here
var myGenericObject : Transform;

//This variable looks for an object with an instance of
//a script attached - this one to be precise.
var myTestObject : ComponentTest;
```

Explicitly typing your variables like this, especially when you start to work with Game-Objects and not just script variables, can make reading and working with your code a much more enjoyable experience. Also, it's faster for the engine to run, so it's really a win-win situation.

Options for Declaring Variables

When declaring a variable to use, you have a few more options besides just the plain keyword var, which itself does mean something very specific. In Unity, you have three different kinds of variable keywords to use.

A variable defined only with the keyword var is defined as a member variable of the script class if defined outside of a function (more on that later). However, variables defined in this way have a very special feature associated with them: They can be directly assigned and edited from within the Inspector.

To try this, open a new scene in Unity, create a new JavaScript script file, and create an empty GameObject. Type this small script into your NewBehavior script file and then drag it onto the empty GameObject. (Remember to save it first.)

```
var myCamera : Transform;
```

Yes, it doesn't do anything at the moment. Just wait. Select the GameObject element in the Hierarchy view and look at its components in the Inspector. Under the New Behavior Script (Script) component (yes, this is your script), you'll see the variable listed: My Camera. Setting `myCamera`'s type to Transform tells Unity that `myCamera` can store any kind of data that has a `Transform` component attached to it, which is a very broad type indeed. You can now drag any GameObject you want into the None(Transform) slot (for instance, the Main Camera object) to assign that object to `myCamera`. Try it. `myCamera` can reference and interact with the scene's main camera. Unity will also allow you to choose from the drop-down list attached to the script any available GameObject in the scene that fits this declaration if you don't want to drag and drop.

You should be starting to see the power of this one tiny variable declaration. With it, you can easily find and assign any kind of GameObject in your game to a variable in a script and even update numbers and objects on the fly while playing and debugging the game. Just remember that any changes you make to a variable assignment or value while the game is running won't be saved once you stop.

Go back and look at the sample scripts in the Inspector if you haven't already. Booleans will give you a smart little checkbox to toggle them as true or false, strings will allow you to type a phrase of your choosing, and the `GameState` enum will give you a drop-down list from which to choose items. Almost all types of variables can be exposed to the Inspector in this way. (JavaScript arrays are one exception—they won't work.)

Another option you have is to declare a variable as a private variable, appending the keyword `private` to the front of your variable declaration. Private variables are not visible to the Inspector, nor to any other script at all. They are private and viewable and editable only from the script in which they were declared. This is particularly useful if you have important data that you don't want accidentally overwritten, like a character's maximum health amount or the value of your world's gravity constant.

```
private var mySecretData : Transform;
```

If you replace your previous code line with this one, you will no longer be able to see the variable in the Inspector.

In contrast, you can also create a global variable, in effect making it a super-editable and readable variable. To define a variable as global, append the keyword `static` to the beginning of the declaration. Global variables are shared between all instances of a script in the game world. For example, say you have 10 GameObjects in your scene, each of which has the same enemy team script attached to it. In the script, a global variable is declared:

```
teamColor = someColor
```

The minute you assign one of the enemies a `teamColor`—say, blue—all the other enemy GameObjects will also share that `teamColor`, as they share the global variable.

```
static var enemyTeamColor = "blue";
```

Like private variables, static variables are also not accessible from the Inspector. However, there's nothing stopping you from declaring a normal member variable, setting that variable's value in the Inspector, and then assigning the value of the member variable to the global one. It's a bit silly, but it works.

Note

This isn't quite the same as global variables in other languages you may be familiar with. If you want to access it from another script, you will still need to reference it as if it were a normal member variable:

```
someScript.myGlobalvariable = 42;
```

Operators and Comparisons

Now that you have all these different kinds and types of variables defined, what can you do with them, you may ask? Plenty.

Operators

You've already seen operators at work in the first integer script example: `print (mySecondInt + myFirstInt)`. The plus sign is the operator for addition, just as it is in classroom math. JavaScript has many such operators that allow you to manipulate and map your data from one form or space to another. Listing 6.8 shows some operators in action.

Listing 6.8   Operators Example

```
//Operators you can use in JavaScript
var x = 1.0;

//Addition
print(x+1); //prints 2
//Subtraction
print(x-3); //prints -2
//Multiplication
print(x*5); //prints 5
//Division
print(x/2); //prints 0.5
//Equate or assign to y = 32.0;
print(y);    //prints 32
//Modulus (the remainder after division)
print(x%2); //prints 1
```

The first five operators should be familiar to you, but the last may not be. The modulus operator (%), or mod for short, returns the remainder after division has occurred. So x%2 is just a compact way of saying "give me the remainder of x divided by 2."

As seen in the string example earlier, you can also use the addition operator to join (or concatenate) strings together to form an even longer string:

```
//This....
print("Hello"+ " " + "World!");
//....is the same as this:
print("Hello World!");
```

You may be wondering if it would be possible to concatenate a string and number variable together using the addition operator, since it seems to work on both equally. Yes, with one small warning: While the number (or number variable) is being concatenated with the string, it will also be considered a string itself.

```
print("Hello" + " " + x); //prints "Hello 1"
```

The variable x may be defined as a float, but in the phrase "Hello 1" it is treated as a value of 1.

There are also two other special operators: increment (++) and decrement (--). Sometimes you may find that you just want to quickly increase or decrease the value of a number by 1, and it can get pretty tedious writing "x=x+1" over and over again. An easier way to do this in JavaScript, as well as in many other languages, is to write "x++." This simple phrase tells Unity to take the value of x, increase it by one, and save x with this new number.

```
x=1;
print(x);      //x = 1
x++;
print(x);      //x = 2
x++;
x++;
print(x);      //x = 4
```

On the exact opposite side is the decrement operator, allowing you to systematically decrease the value of your number by one.

```
x=1.5;
print(x);      //x = 1.5
x--;
print(x);      //x = 0.5
x--;
x--;
print(x);      //x = -1.5
```

Notice that the operators work with both floating-point and integer numbers.

Comparisons

Besides adding and subtracting variables, you can also compare them with each other. Many of these comparisons will also be familiar to you from elementary math classes.

The first comparison you can make between two variables is to ask if they are equal in value—does x in fact equal y? Note that the equality comparison operator uses two equal signs, and that the assignment operator only uses one equal sign. In other words, $(x == y)$ is not the same as $(x=y)$. This can be easy to mix up at first, and you don't want to be assigning random values instead of comparing them. See Listing 6.9.

Listing 6.9   Equality Comparison Example

```
var x = 1;
var y = 7;
var z = 1.0;

//is equal to?
print(x == y);        //prints False
print(x == z);        //prints True, even though type doesn't match
//is greater than?
print(x>y);           //prints False
//is less than?
```

```
print(x<y);  //prints True
//is greater than OR equal to?
print(x>=z); //prints True
//is less than OR equal to?
print(x<=y); //prints True
```

These comparisons work with all variable types, not just numbers, allowing you to determine whether two strings are equal, if a random GameObject matches the one you're looking for, or if one array's value is bigger than another one's.

Note

> Be careful when comparing floating-point values. After every operation, the value is rounded back into the floating-point variable's range, and each rounding operation increases the error of the number. For example, if you added a value 100 times in a row, the result may be very slightly different than if you multiplied by 100 and added the result. You might be expecting to see the value 0 but instead see an extremely tiny value, perhaps 5.55112e-17, instead. Always remember floating point is an approximation. The math utility library provides a function `Mathf.Approximately()` to help compare the values.

It is also possible to string and combine comparisons together using logical comparison operators: AND, OR, and NOT. This will allow you to do useful things like query whether an object is, say, both round and blue in one statement, or ask the game engine if your player is not moving. For a statement involving an AND question, you use two ampersands together between the statements: `&&`. For a statement involving an OR question, you use two pipe symbols, also between the different statements: `||`. Finally, to query if something is NOT another thing, you use an exclamation point in front of the conditional question: `!`. See Listing 6.10.

Listing 6.10   Logical Comparison Example

```
var x = 1;
var y = 7;
var z = 1.0;

print( (x == z) && (x < y) );    //prints True
print( (x == 3) || (y == 2) );   //prints False
print( (x == 3) || (y == 7) );   //prints True
print( !(x == z) );              //prints False
print(x != y);                   //prints True
```

The first line asks Unity if x is equal to z AND if x is also less than y. This happens to be a true statement, so the engine prints True. Both statements on either side of the double ampersands (&&) need to be true for the entire statement to return True.

For an OR comparison, only one of the two statements needs to return True, as in the third comparison: *x* is equal to 3 OR *y* is equal to 7. *x* isn't equal to 3, but *y* is equal to 7, so the entire line returns True. If both statements return False, then the entire line will as well.

The NOT comparison is shown in the last two lines. Note that with these, it's very important to correctly place the ! symbol exactly where you mean to create the negative query. One space off can lead to a completely different result. The first comparison is asking Unity what the result is for NOT *x* equal to *z*. Unity needs to ask if *x* is equal to *z* and finds that it is, so Unity returns True. This simplifies the comparison to ! (True) or Not True. Another way of saying something is not true would be to label it false, which is what Unity prints.

The second comparison asks if *x* is not equal to *y*, using the handy unequal operator !=. It is a correct statement that 1 is not equal to 7, so Unity returns True. Out of the two, you'll find that != is a much more common way of phrasing the same question.

It's all well and good to see if some comparison of value is true or false, but wouldn't it be handier if you could also ask that IF this were the case, Unity then do something else afterward? Thankfully, there is.

Conditionals

Conditional statements allow you to execute different actions based on different current criteria. For example, you could play a different background music theme in your game based on the current level. Or you could have your character jump if a certain key were pressed. Anything of the form "if this question is true, then do something" is a conditional.

The if Statement

The simplest form of a conditional is the if statement: "If a given comparison is true, then do something." Any one of the former comparisons (or combinations of) can be used for queries in if statements. See Listing 6.11 for an example.

Listing 6.11   if Example

```
var myGame = "Loading";
if (myGame == "Loading")         // <-If Statement and Comparison
{                                // <-Open body bracket
   print("Game is Loading...");  // <-Code to execute if True
}                                // <-Closing body bracket.
                                 //...Script continues after this...
```

This example defines a variable to store the state of the game: myGame. The if statement that follows asks Unity to check the current value of myGame and see if it is equal to the string "Loading". If this statement returns True, Unity will execute the code in the body of the if statement—the block of code between the curly brackets. if statements execute their body code only if all the comparisons they test return True. If the comparison returns False, no code inside the body will be executed, and your script will continue.

The if-else Statement

The if statement is definitely handy, but what if you wanted to do something else when a condition tested false and not just continue on as if the condition didn't matter? In these cases, you can use an if-else statement: "If a given condition is true, do A. If false, then do B." See Listing 6.12 for an example.

Listing 6.12   if-else Example

```
myGame = "Running";
if (myGame == "Loading")
{
        print("Game is Loading...");
}
else
{
        print("Game has finished Loading");
}
print("Game is now running!");
```

This example again tests for the value of the variable myGame. If myGame is equal to the string "Loading", the first print() statement will be executed. If myGame is equal to anything else, any code in the body of the else statement will be executed instead. As you can see, you can put any number of lines of code inside the body of the statements.

You can also string if and else statements together for more complicated queries (see Listing 6.13).

Listing 6.13   if-else Tree Example

```
if (myGame == "Loading")
{
        print("Game is Loading...");
}
```

```
else if (myGame == "Running")
{
     print("Game is now Running!");
}
else
{
     print("Game is over!");
}
```

Unity will go down the line of if statements until one of them is true or until it gets to the else statement, at which point it will execute that code.

Note

For these kinds of chained conditionals, you need to be mindful of the order in which you place your statements. When more than one conditional is true, only the first one will be run. Having each conditional run a different test can be useful if you want to intentionally filter out conditions, but it can also lead to some tricky bugs if the code meets more than one condition.

The switch Statement

Similar to the if-else statement is the switch statement. This statement performs the same action as the if-else statement, but can be easier to read. See Listing 6.14 for an example.

Listing 6.14   switch Example

```
myGame = "Game Over";
switch (myGame)
{
     case "Loading":
          print("Game is Loading...");
          break;
     case "Running":
          print("Game is now running!");
          break;
     case "Game Over":
          print("Game is over. Thanks for playing!");
          break;
     default:
          print("Game is in an unknown state");
}
```

In the switch statement, you first tell Unity which variable you want to check for in the parentheses—in this case, myGame. Each case statement is then an equality comparison looking to see if myGame is equal to either Loading, Running, or Game Over. Any code between the current case statement and the break statement is executed, just like in the body of the if statement. The break statement is necessary after each case test, as it tells Unity to exit out of the switch statement and no longer look for comparisons. You must have a break statement for each case comparison.

The default keyword is just what it sounds like: Unity will default to this if none of the case statements match. The default keyword should always be placed last in your list and generally serves as an error catch-all. The value of myGame should always match one of the three case statements in the example, but just in case it doesn't, the default is there to keep the game from crashing or otherwise malfunctioning. Unlike the case statements, default doesn't need a break statement, as it's the final step of the switch statement.

The Conditional Operator

One final conditional is the conditional operator, a short and sweet way to write a simple if-else statement. In this form of conditional, you don't have a body to write a set of statements in, so it's particularly useful if you just want to change the value of one specific variable. The conditional operator takes the following form:

```
(comparison test) ? TrueStatement : FalseStatement ;
myGame = " ";          //myGame equals only an empty space character
var x = 1;
var y = 5;

myGame = (x > y)      ? "Loading" : "Running" ;
print(myGame);        //prints "Running"
```

In this example, myGame starts out as an empty string variable, holding only a single white-space character. Suppose you'd like to store a value for its current state based upon a given comparison—in this case, is *x* greater than *y*? If the comparison is true, myGame will be given the value of Loading. If false, it will be assigned the value of Running. This shorthand is nice to use for small assignments like this, but it won't be fitting for every case.

Loops

Loops allow you to perform an action multiple times, either indefinitely or until a certain criterion has been met. There are a few different kinds of loops in JavaScript you could use, but for simplicity's sake you can make do with two basic ones: `for` and `while` loops.

The `for` Loop

`for` loops execute a given body of code while a given condition is true, and you generally know how many times the loop should execute. They take this basic form:

```
for ( startValue; Condition; stepCounter)
{
...code to run every time the loop restarts
}
```

The `for` loop needs some sort of counting value, which keeps track of how many times the loop has executed. At the start of the loop, the counter is compared against some condition. If it's true, the body of the loop executes and the counter is increased by the specified amount. The loop then starts over and again looks at the comparison statement. The loop continues to run until the condition is false.

```
for (i = 0; i < 5; i++)
{
        print("i is now equal to " + i);
}
```

This example asks Unity to print out the value of `i` for as long as it is less than 5. After that, the loop will cease to run. Incrementing step count values is one place where the increment operator gets a lot of use.

Be careful that you don't set up an infinite loop! If there's no way your condition can ever be false, the loop will never end, and your script will be stuck there forever, like this:

```
for (i = 0; i >= 0; i++)
{
        print("i is now equal to " + i);
}
```

(Don't actually run this example, unless you want it to run for a *very* long time.)

`i` will always be either greater than or equal to 0, and the loop will continue to run *ad infinitum*. (Well, not exactly. It will loop more than 2 billion times and eventually overflow the size of an `int`, wrapping around to a negative number.) Be nice to Unity and your computer—don't write infinite loops.

The while Loop

The while loop is similar to the for loop and runs a given piece of code while a specific condition is true.

```
while (some given condition is true)
{
        [...]code to run every time the loop restarts
}
```

Listing 6.15 shows an example.

Listing 6.15   while loop Example

```
var myCounter = 0;
var loopNumber = 1;
while (myCounter <= 20)
{
        print(loopNumber);
        loopNumber++;
        myCounter = myCounter + 2;
}
```

The loop starts looking at the given comparison and executes the body of code as long as it remains true. Because no ending condition is built into the loop definition (like in the for loop), you need to be especially mindful of setting up some way for your loop to finish.

Functions

You've already seen some functions in action even if you're not aware of it. That little print() statement you've been using to show data in the Console? That's a function. When you create a new JavaScript file in Unity, it opens with a default line of code:

```
function Update ()
```

This is also a function. Up until now, you've just been typing code into your script files directly in order, and Unity diligently runs through them line by line. What if you wanted to execute a prewritten block of code only at a specific time, or only when needed? Functions allow this. Anything you don't want Unity to run by default when it starts playing should be placed inside a function.

Functions are simply defined by the keyword `function` and follow this syntax:

```
Function FunctionName ( optional arguments )
{
      [...]some code here
}
```

Unity will not run anything inside a function at startup. To use one, you must call the function from elsewhere in your code, which gives you complete control over when and where it runs. Listing 6.16 shows an example.

Listing 6.16   Function Example

```
//This loop executes at startup
for(var i = 0; i <11; i++)
{
      if(i%2 == 0)
      {
            SayHi();
      }
      else
      {
            SayBye();
      }
}
//These only execute once they're called from within the for loop
function SayHi() {
      print("Hello World!");
}
function SayBye(){
      print("Goodbye Unity!");
}
```

This example defines two functions, `SayHi()` and `SayBye()`. `SayHi()` will print out a greeting phrase when called, and `SayBye()` will print "Goodbye Unity." Neither of these two functions will run when you click Play and will only execute once they're called from within the `for` loop. In the loop, when the counter `i` is even, `SayHi` will be called. When `i` is odd, `SayBye` will be called instead.

Functions can also be defined to have optional arguments (or variables) passed to them when called and return other pieces of data after they've finished running, allowing you to do something more profound than printing out silly messages. An argument is any piece of data you place inside the parentheses of a function—like the bits of code you've been placing inside the `print()` statement parentheses. These are the arguments that give `print()` the data it needs to execute. See Listing 6.17 for an example.

Listing 6.17 Function Argument Example

```
var myGame = " ";

myGame = ChangeGameState(myGame);
print(myGame);        //prints out "Loading"

myGame = ChangeGameState(myGame);
print(myGame);        //prints out "Running"

//Change the name of any string given
function ChangeGameState ( someGame : String ) {
        if (someGame == "Loading")
        {
                return "Running";
        }
        else return "Loading";
}
```

This example defines a ChangeGameState function that takes one argument. When defining arguments, you need to give them some kind of variable nickname, allowing you to work with them in the body of the function. When you run the function, any variable you place in the parentheses will be assigned the value of the argument, so in this case, anywhere you see someGame in the function, it will use the value of myGame, since that was the passed argument.

In this case, the variable someGame is also defined to be of type string. You don't need to explicitly type your arguments, but it makes debugging big functions a lot easier if you do. Any variable that is now passed to ChangeGameState that isn't a string will spit back a detailed error.

ChangeGameState will take in any string variable and compare it to the phrase "Loading". If the string value is equal to "Loading", then it will return a value as well—in this case, "Running". If the comparison is false, then the function returns "Loading" as its value. If you return a value from a function, you must store it in a variable, or else the value is lost. You do this by setting the myGame variable equal to the function call, basically saying: "Change the value of myGame to the one returned by ChangeGameState when it runs."

Return statements can also effectively exit a function prematurely. That is, they can act like a break from a switch statement. You can have them exit with a value, like with "Running", or you can use them singularly to just exit the code without returning a value:

```
function DoNothing() {
        return;
        print("This never runs");
}
DoNothing();  //function exits before the print statement is reached.
```

Unity will attempt to give you a warning if ever it finds code in a function, like the previous example, that will never, ever run.

Variable Scope

An important concept to understand at this point is variable scope. Up until now, you've been declaring all your variables as member variables outside of all functions. But what happens if you declare a variable from within the body of a function, like so?

```
var myNumber = 0;
SetNumber();
print (myNewNumber);

//Function to change the value of the number?
function SetNumber(){
      var myNewNumber = 10;
      myNewNumber = myNumber;
}
```

In this example, you define a function `SetNumber ()`, in which a new variable `myNewNumber` is declared. `SetNumber()` then attempts to take this new variable and give it the value of the old variable, `myNumber`. After calling the function, a `print()` statement is made, asking for the value of `myNewNumber`. What do you expect to happen—for `myNewNumber` to get the value of `myNumber` and print out 0?

Well…no. It isn't that simple.

Any variables defined inside a function are local to that function. They exist only inside that function and while the function is currently being run. A local variable only comes into being when its enclosing body of code begins to run. The minute the `SetNumber()` function finishes executing and exits, `myNewNumber` ceases to exist, and the `print()` statement can no longer find the variable called `myNewNumber`. This code will result in an error.

Any variables defined outside the body of a function or other closed body (like inside an `if` statement) can be referenced anywhere else in the script—like with the case of `myNumber`. A variable's scope is defined by its closest container. `myNumber` is a member of the ScopeTest.js object and can be accessed anywhere within the file. `myNewNumber` is only defined inside the function body of `SetNumber()` and can only be accessed in that one tiny space in the file.

Naming Conventions

Before moving on to some actual scripting for the *Widget* game, it's good to be aware of some of Unity's naming conventions. You are free to name your variables and functions anything you like, but you and anyone else you work with will have an easier time of it if there's some sort of systematic approach to it. Keep these points in mind:

- **Most variables:** Variable names in Unity follow a mixed case convention of using a lowercase first letter with capitalized words, and do not use dashes or underscores between separate words. One example is `deltaTime`.

- **Keywords:** Keywords are always lowercase, including the inherited Unity keyword variables like `audio` or `transform.position`.

- **Enums:** Enumerated types generally are all capitalized and often use underscores between words, such as `CRITICAL_HIT`.

- **Functions:** Functions defined in Unity's API always follow the convention CamelCase, making it easy to identify them from other variables.

- **Classes:** As with functions, Unity class names also follow the naming convention CamelCase.

Remember that while this chapter gives you the basics you need to understand and use the scripts presented for the game, it is no substitute for a more formal approach to learning to program. Learning the syntax for a language is one thing, but learning how to build beautiful, maintainable code is a whole 'nother story! Now it's time to actually start giving some functionality to little Widget and his world.

CHAPTER 7

WRITING THE CHARACTER AND STATE CONTROLLER SCRIPTS

To get the Widget character up and running, he needs both a character controller and a state controller script. The character controller defines exactly how he moves and behaves while parsing the input from the player to direct him. The state controller holds all his necessary vitals and information, such as his current health and energy points and which functions can directly affect these stats. The state controller could also define more broad aspects of the character, such as whether he is controllable, dead, or alive.

To get started, load your last save from Chapter 5, "Creating Characters," with the newly imported Widget character. All the scripts for this chapter are included on the companion website; you can import them into the scene by putting them in the Assets folder. Alternatively, you can build your own as you go along.

SETTING IT UP AND LAYING IT OUT

Before jumping in and scripting, you need some idea of what it is you're setting out to do. You know at the moment that the Widget character needs some sort of controller script, but what exactly does that mean? How is Widget going to be controlled? Is it going to be first-person or third-person perspective? How should the camera follow him? The list of questions can go on and on, and they all need answers before you can effectively write his controller.

Although you won't always have the luxury of knowing all the answers up front or working with a finished, immutable design, it still helps to develop some kind of plan of action before sitting down to code. Writing code without any clear plan of attack and organization will quickly lead to code-management hell, and it's not a fun place to be. A simple game like *Widget* will require only a couple hundred lines of code, which is tiny compared to the hundreds of thousands of lines a commercial title may use, so it's a good, small place to start practicing.

To get started, lay out a plan for what you'll need in Widget's controller. The Design Documents on the website have a basic rundown of Widget's needs and are a good place to start for gathering information. If you haven't checked them out yet, now could be a good time to do so.

As described in the game's details, Widget's controller will need to handle these basic functions in some way:

- The player should be able to use the W, A, S, and D keys to control the character's movement. The character should rotate with the D and A keys and move forward and backward with the W and S keys.

- Widget needs to be able to jump, "boost roll" (roll faster with energy consumption), and duck down. Ducking down should make his physics collider smaller.

- The controller should have editable variables for the character's movement and rotate speeds and some variable to keep track of whether he's controllable or not (such as if he died during his adventure—the player shouldn't be able to control him during the respawn).

- The script should also make sure that he's on the ground when accepting move input so he doesn't end up accidentally floating or flying. This robot is definitely earthbound!

- Some kind of camera hookup to follow Widget smoothly.

With even this simple plan in mind, you can begin putting together the first scripts to get Widget rolling.

A Simple Third-Person Controller

To make Widget move, you're going to need to take the previous list and turn that into usable code. To get started, create a new JavaScript file in the Scripts directory of your Assets folder and name it Widget Controller. You'll be doing all your work for the controller in here. Load your final scene file from Chapter 5 and ensure that Widget is imported in the scene as a prefab. Create an instance of the Widget prefab in the game world if needed and position him somewhere in a nice open spot.

First you should do a little bit of cleanup on the scene to get it ready for Widget's big debut. Follow these steps to clean up the scene:

1. Unparent the main camera from the first-person controller and make sure you don't parent it to something else by accident. Just leave it as its own free GameObject in the Hierarchy view. Remove the Mouse Look script component from the main camera.

2. Delete the first-person controller. This was added only as a convenience to view the scene while you were building the environment, and it won't be needed any longer.

3. Select the Widget prefab in the Project view and choose Component > Physics > Character Collider. Agree to and click Replace if a dialog box appears, asking you if you're sure you want to do this.

4. Resize the new collider so that it fits around the character. A base setting of Height = 2, Radius = 0.7, and Center Y = 1 works fairly well.

The old capsule collider would work fine if Widget needed to interact only with other physics bodies in the environment, but it doesn't always perform as expected if used on a moving, controlled character. The character controller, on the other hand, gives you the abilities and responsiveness you want for player-controlled movement. Unfortunately, character controller colliders do not react with rigid bodies or other physics objects by default, but it's always possible to add custom code to allow them to do so.

Most of the settings for the character collider are self-explanatory, like Height, Radius, and Center. Some of the others could use some description:

- **Slope Limit:** The character cannot climb slopes greater than the specified number. The controller won't be able to climb up vertical walls due to its shape, so that's not a concern by default. The default value of 90 usually works for most cases.

- **Step Offset:** This limits how tall a step or stair can be; the character won't climb anything taller than the specified value. For a normal 2 meter humanoid-size character, a value smaller than 0.4 works nicely.

- **Skin Width:** This can be a finicky value. Basically, two different colliders (like your character and the ground) can overlap each other a little bit, up to the depth of the specified skin width. A larger value will reduce movement jitters, but it can make it look like your character is walking into the ground. A small number may look nicer but could cause your character to get stuck on tiny little bits of geometry. A good rule of thumb to try is to make the initial value 10% of your collider's radius and then fine-tune it from there.

■ **Min Move Distance:** The minimum distance the character must cover if he is to actually move. If the attempted movement value is below this number, the character won't move. For most cases, the default of 0 will be fine.

Widget is now ready to start moving.

Controller Variables

It's best to begin by defining the variables you know you'll need in the script file and assigning some base values. Open Widget Controller in your editor of choice, delete any helper text that Unity added at creation (like the Update function call), and add the following to the first couple of empty lines:

```
var roll Speed = 6.0;
var fastRollSpeed = 2.0;
var jumpSpeed = 8.0;
var gravity = 20.0;
var rotateSpeed = 4.0;
var duckSpeed = 0.5;
```

These are all defined as member variables and can be edited from within the Inspector. These variables will control how quickly Widget moves during any one of his actions and can be easily changed during play-testing so that they're just right. You need the gravity variable to apply to Widget in every frame to keep him on the ground. A value of 20 gives a relatively good approximation of Earth-like gravity, but it can be changed to anything you find suitable for your game. The other variables directly control how quickly he rolls, moves, and pivots around the world.

You'll also need a few private variables to keep track of Widget's current direction of movement, whether he's on the ground or not, and his current height if ducking. Although you could get away with making all these variables normal member ones, you don't want to accidentally edit something like the direction Widget is moving. Only the player through his controls should be able to do that.

```
private var moveDirection = Vector3.zero;
private var grounded : boolean = false;
private var moveHorz = 0.0;
private var normalHeight = 2.0;
private var duckHeight = 1.0;
private var rotateDirection = Vector3.zero;
```

The rotate and move directions are defined as 3D vectors, allowing movement to be calculated in all three planes simultaneously if need be. Writing Vector3.zero is a quick way of saying that the X, Y, and Z values all equal zero: (0,0,0). The moveHorz variable determines which direction the player is turning, and the grounded Boolean stores whether Widget is currently on the ground.

Widget will need one last variable to control whether he's actually currently controllable by the player:

```
var isControllable : boolean = true;
```

If, for example, Widget is dead, the player shouldn't be able to still input commands and move him around.

Now that you have your variables defined, you'll need to start making the loop to read in the player's input every frame and direct his movements.

Unity's MonoBehaviour Class

Whenever you create a new JavaScript script in Unity, it automatically derives itself from the MonoBehaviour class, giving the script access to all its built-in functions and inherited members, like special variables. MonoBehaviour controls most of the functions that involve collision detections, mouse events, camera events, component fetching and comparing, and functions that are called every frame or at fixed timestamps. This is exactly what you need to implement the game's behavior.

Tip

The MonoBehaviour class is discussed more fully in Appendix B, "Common Classes," and on Unity's online documentation. Being familiar with this class and all its offerings will prove a worthwhile investment in time.

There are five MonoBehaviour functions that control when code is executed in the game, whether it be once per frame or only at startup. Placing custom code inside these functions will enable you to do things like move a box a little per frame or initialize a player's inventory only when the game starts up. Unity will run these time- and frame-related functions automatically—you don't need to call them somewhere else yourself to use them.

- **Update:** Code placed inside this function is called once every frame. You've probably noticed that Unity places an empty Update function in every script file you create.

- **LateUpdate:** Like the Update function, LateUpdate is also called every frame, but only right after Update finishes.

- **FixedUpdate:** FixedUpdate is called every physics time-step and is not the same as and should not be confused with Update. FixedUpdate should be used for objects dealing with rigid bodies or anything requiring physics calculations and a set, dependable calculation speed (like player movement).

- **Awake:** Code placed in the Awake function is called when the script is loaded at runtime. This can be a good place for some initializations.

- **Start:** Start is called after Awake and before the very first Update function is called. Start is another handy place to put any initializations, caches, or checks you want to make only once.

You should also at this point cache your new character controller component for use later in the script. The script will act directly on the character controller component you've placed on Widget to move him, so it makes good sense to cache the link to the component. Otherwise, you have to find the link to the component every frame again and again, which is a silly waste of computing power.

```
var controller : CharacterController ;
controller = GetComponent(CharacterController);
```

The GetComponent() function call is also inherited from the MonoBehaviour class and can be used in all your JavaScript files. It enables you to look for any component currently part of the GameObject to which your script is attached and save a reference to it for later. Now when you move the controller every frame, you don't need to look up the link to the component every frame as well—a good time saver and scripting practice to remember. If you know you're going to need a component or variable frequently, cache a reference to it outside of any update functions.

FixedUpdate: **Make Widget Move**

Your character controller is set and ready, as are the needed variables and references. Widget is just moments away from being completely player controllable.

The simple third-person controller script will follow the basic logic outlined here:

- If the character is controllable, allow movement input from the player.

- If the character is on the ground, allow normal ground movement input from the player.

- Get the player's input and transform it so that it's applicable to the world-space coordinates.

- Apply any special player controls to the movement, like jumping, ducking, or boosted speed.

- Factor in the world's gravity so that Widget can fall and jump naturally.

- With all the movement possibilities now taken into account, actually move the character and make note of whether his new position keeps him on the ground.

Laying out your thoughts like this before you start coding can help you spot any flaws in your logic or conditions you didn't think of, without wasting any implementation time or effort. Writing pseudo code (even small and loose examples like this) is a good practice to get into when dealing with new systems or large projects.

First, you know that because you'll be moving a GameObject based on input and calculations, you should place your code in the FixedUpdate function call, not just the default Update. The first block of code to go in, according to the outline you created, is to determine whether Widget is controllable by the player:

```
function FixedUpdate() {
    if(!isControllable)
        Input.ResetInputAxes();
    else{}
}
```

This tests for controllability every fixed update frame. If the character is not controllable (recognize the ! operator?), reset any controls the player may have input and continue. (The Input class is discussed later in this chapter.) The else block will contain all the code for when your character is controllable.

Moving down the outline, you now need to test for whether the character is grounded. Inside the else statement, add the following:

```
if (grounded) { }
```

Simple. If grounded is true, Widget is on the ground, and the code will continue.

Moving forward, now that you've established that the character is grounded for this frame, you need to collect the player's input and translate that into a direction in the world. Inside this grounded if statement's brackets, add this block of code:

```
moveDirection = new Vector3(Input.GetAxis
    ("Horizontal"), 0, Input.GetAxis("Vertical"));
moveDirection = transform.TransformDirection(moveDirection);
moveDirection *= rollSpeed;
```

Tip

In the previous code, moveDirection makes use of the compound assignment operator, *=. If you're new to scripting, this may seem a little enigmatic, but it's pretty straightforward. Basically, this is shorthand for writing moveDirection = moveDirection * rollSpeed. You're multiplying the original variable by a new value and then saving this new result over the original variable. Other commonly used compound assignment operators include +=, -=, and /=.

All right, now things are getting a little more complicated. The moveDirection variable gets populated with a new vector of the player's input, although only along the X and Z planes of movement. So leave the Y part of the vector at 0 since that'll be controlled by jumping or gravity. The moveDirection vector is then transformed using the TransformDirection function, which takes a given direction and transforms its coordinates from local to world space—just what you need to translate the player's controls into movement. The vector's length isn't affected by this transformation. You then take the modified moveDirection vector and multiply it by the rollSpeed variable, giving it a base speed to go with its direction.

This works to give the base direction you want Widget to face and roll, but what if you want the controller to pivot and turn based on the input as well? Right now the mesh would just translate around the screen, always facing one direction—not very believable for a working robot. Time to factor in some rotation values. Continuing where you left off, add the following:

```
moveHorz = Input.GetAxis("Horizontal");
if (moveHorz > 0)        //Right turn
        rotateDirection = new Vector3(0, 1, 0);
else if (moveHorz < 0)        //Left turn
        rotateDirection = new Vector3(0, -1, 0);
else                //not turning
        rotateDirection = new Vector3 (0, 0, 0);
```

You'll find the rotation of the character based on the player's Horizontal input, for example, the left and right arrows on the keyboard. The horizontal (and vertical for that matter) input axis is mapped from positive to negative, with any positive value mapping to the right and any negative value mapping to the left (for the vertical axis, positive and negative values map up and down, respectively). To find Widget's movement rotation, you just query to see which direction key the player is currently pressing. If no horizontal axis key is pressed, then the character must be moving forward or backward only along the vertical axis.

Now that Widget's base movement is decided, you need to get the player's input for special commands. Below the text for the rotation, add these lines:

```
if (Input.GetButton ("Jump")) {
     moveDirection.y = jumpSpeed;
}
if(Input.GetButton("Boost")){
     moveDirection *= fastRollSpeed;
}
if(Input.GetButton("Duck")){
     controller.height = duckHeight;
     controller.center.y = controller.height/2 + .25;
     moveDirection *= duckSpeed;
}
```

These three if statements look for specific button presses from the user, which you define using the key phrases Jump, Boost, and Duck (the keys themselves will be set up shortly). If the player presses the Jump key, you make the character move upward by his jumpSpeed variable value. If boosted, Widget's speed is multiplied again to make it even faster. Finally, if the player ducks, Widget's speed is reduced, and his controller is made tinier so it's harder to hit. controller is the reference to Widget's character controller that you set earlier, allowing you access to its Height and Center variables. You can access any of the component's variables and settings.

Since you're changing the height and placement of the character controller on a duck move, you should also make sure you're resetting the default values at some point. Otherwise, Widget will duck forever! Return to the moveDirection *= rollSpeed line and add this directly after:

```
controller.height = normalHeight;
controller.center.y = controller.height/2;
```

This will make sure the character controller is back to the normal default values at the start of every movement frame.

You're almost done with the outline, the only tasks remaining being the gravity and actual controller movement. Outside the grounded if statement (but still inside the else statement for the controllable query), add the following:

```
moveDirection.y -= gravity * Time.deltaTime;
```

This will ensure Widget remains on the ground or will fall down toward the ground if he ever jumps up. Just like on Earth, you want gravity to constantly act as a downward force.

This line also introduces another important class for scripting in Unity: time. The Time class gives you access to some nice read-only data, like how long the game has been running or how much time has passed since the level was loaded. The value deltaTime is another piece of read-only data, detailing how much time in seconds it took the last frame to complete. By multiplying the gravity constant by how much time it takes for the frames to complete, you are effectively calculating how much gravity should affect your characters per second.

Tip

Anytime you want to do something per second, multiply it by Time.deltaTime.

Finally, all you have left to do is to move the controller. The character controller class comes with its own predefined Move function, which you can use to do most of the work for you. Under the last line, add the following:

```
var flags = controller.Move(moveDirection * Time.deltaTime);
controller.transform.Rotate(rotateDirection * Time.deltaTime, rotateSpeed);
grounded = ((flags & CollisionFlags.CollidedBelow) != 0 );
```

Move takes any direction vector and moves the attached GameObject by that amount. Multiplying it by Time.deltaTime ensures that you get a nice, even movement at all times. The Move function also does something else: It has a return value that marks any colliders it came into contact with during its move, so you can store that in the variable flags. These CollisionFlags will store whether the controller collided above, below, along the sides of, or with nothing during its movement.

The Rotate function is another predefined function to which all character controllers have access. It uses a rotation vector and speed variable to rotate the controller along its center axis. Multiplying the rotation vector by Time.deltaTime ensures a nice, even pivot.

After rotating the controller, test to see if the character's new position keeps it grounded for the next frame of movement. A handy check to see if the character collided with anything below it will work for this. If the Move function returns any CollisionFlags from below the controller, grounded is set to True, and the character can be controlled in the following frame. The & is a logical operator that acts like the word AND. So grounded is set to True only if both flags AND CollisionFlags.CollidedBelow are not equal to zero.

Now that you have something workable, you'll want to attach it to Widget and see it in action. However, there's just one small problem: Widget is currently a prefab. If you try to attach the script to the instance of Widget in the Hierarchy view by the normal dragging and dropping method, you'll lose the link to the prefab. To attach the script, you need to select the Widget prefab in the Project view and add the script manually by choosing Component > Scripts and selecting it from the list.

Right now this isn't so bad, but what if your game has hundreds or thousands of scripts? Finding it this way could be tedious. Luckily, Unity has an answer to this in the form of a special command line:

```
@script AddComponentMenu("SomeFolder/SomeScriptName")
```

By adding this line to your scripts (outside of any function), you can have Unity index it in the Component menu in the subfolder of your choice. For the controller script, add this line to the bottom:

```
@script AddComponentMenu("Player/Widget'sController")
```

Now you can easily find the script by choosing Component > Player > Widget's Controller and clicking there. Attach the controller script to the prefab and save.

Note

The complete files are available on the accompanying website. The completed Widget_Controller.js file is located in the Chapter 7 folder for easy attachment.

If you can't wait and want to take Widget out for a test drive now, comment out the Boost and Duck if statements using block comments (you'll hook up these keywords next). Make sure that the camera is focused on Widget and then click the Play button. You should now be able to drive Widget around using either the arrow keys or the W, A, S, and D keys for basic movement. Victory, your first controller class! Just remember to delete the comment blocks later if you did this. But what about those special buttons, like Boost and Duck, which were defined earlier?

Setting Up Unity's Input Manager

Setting up custom control schemes in Unity requires only a few simple button clicks and is easily accomplished from within the editor. Unity supports input from keyboards, mice, gamepads, and joysticks. You can mix and match any number of these input devices for a single game, giving your players the choice to use their preferred control method. Every new project has 15 input axes defined by default, encompassing both standard keyboard and mouse controls. An *axis* is any defined movement or button press. Examples of axes include Jump, Run, Strafe, and Left Mouse Click.

To view or edit Unity's Input Manager, choose Edit > Project Settings > Input. The Input Manager will be displayed in the Inspector, as shown in Figure 7.1.

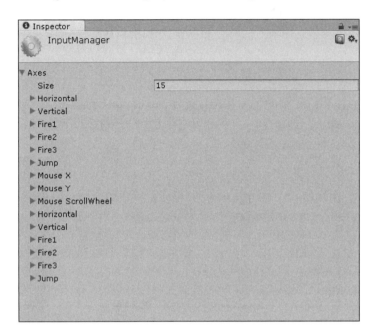

Figure 7.1
Unity's default input axes.
Source: Unity Technologies.

Each axis defines one type of control command, such as horizontal movement, jumping, or an attack called Fire1. Each of these axes has settings that describe how the control works. You can set up the control axes in advance, and players can also customize these controls later through a provided configuration dialog box in the game. You may notice that some axes appear to be listed twice—for example, horizontal and vertical. It's possible in the Input Manager to define completely different control schemes that share a name, allowing two separate control devices to share the same role for the player. One could define keyboard presses, for example, and another could define joystick controls. Unity will handle the input choice for you, enabling you to reference only one value in your scripts. Horizontal movement would in the end be the same to Unity, whether it came from a keyboard press or a gamepad control stick.

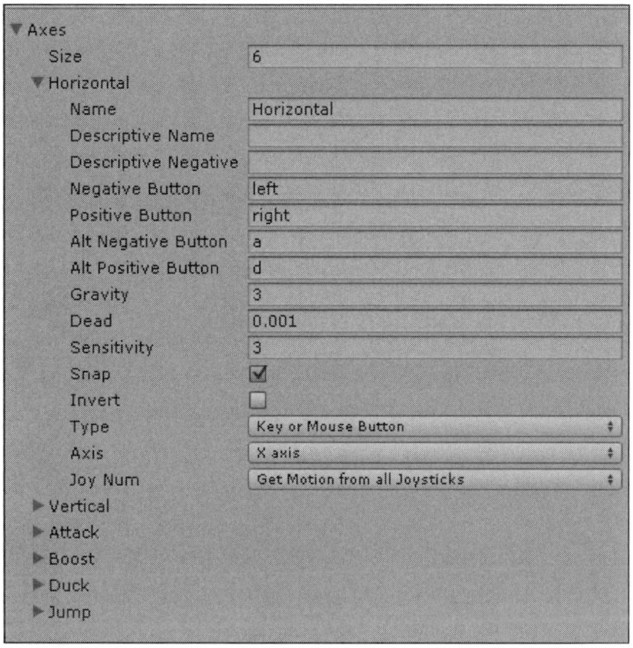

Figure 7.2
Input axes needed by Widget.
Source: Unity Technologies.

To see and edit the settings, click on the arrow next to the axis's name. (See Figure 7.2.) The settings are as follows:

- **Name:** This is the axis's name and reference for scripting. As written in the character controller class script, you use names to access the controls directly, like Input.GetButton ("Jump"). Any control can be accessed in this way by using its given name.

- **Descriptive Name:** The name displayed for the positive control value in the configuration dialog box in the game's standalone, finished build. By default, this is blank, but you can enter a descriptive name if you like.

- **Descriptive Negative Name:** The name displayed for the negative control value in the configuration dialog box in the game's standalone build. So, for example, if your game used the arrow keys for control, the descriptive name for the right arrow could be "Right Turn," and the negative descriptive name for the left arrow could be "Left Turn." This can make it easier for players to know which control they're overwriting.

- **Negative Button:** The button the player presses to move the axis in the negative direction. For something like horizontal movement, this corresponds to the left direction.

- **Positive Button:** The button the player presses to move the axis in the positive direction. Again, for horizontal movement, this would correspond to the right direction.

- **Alt Negative Button:** An alternative button that the players can use. Assigning values to both normal buttons and alternative buttons enables you to define two separate control schemes under one label in one go, like allowing the players to use, for example, either the arrow keys or the W, A, S, and D keys for movement.

- **Alt Positive Button:** An alternative button that the players can use.

- **Gravity:** The speed in units per second that the axis will return to neutral or zero if the player stops providing input. A larger number will return faster.

- **Dead:** For use with analog controls. Any values within this range from the analog controller will map to neutral and not provide any input.

- **Sensitivity:** For use with digital controls. The speed in units per second that the axis will move toward the given value, positive or negative. Some digital controllers require a very high value here, such as 1,000, to respond quickly and smoothly.

- **Snap:** If selected, this ensures the axis value is neutral if you press both the positive and negative control button at once. For example, if you enable this option and the player presses both the left and right arrows together, the controller will keep moving forward in a straight line, not wobbling between the two directions.

- **Invert:** Quickly swaps the positive and negative controls.

- **Type:** The type of input device to which the axis corresponds. You can select Key or Mouse Button, Mouse Movement, or Joystick Axis. Make sure the correct selection is made here for the controls defined.

- **Axis:** Indicates the axis of the input device that directs this control schema (such as a gamepad control stick). Choices include X axis, Y axis, and options for six additional axes, available only on some kinds of gamepads and joysticks.

- **Joy Num:** If multiple joysticks are connected to the machine, determines which one will control this given axis. You can choose to get motion from all joysticks or assign a specific joystick, from 1 to 4.

You don't need to use these default axes and can overwrite or delete them as you see fit. You can change the number of possible control axes by typing a new number in the Size field.

Unity provides you with a few default axes to describe the most common, basic controls. The Horizontal and Vertical axes are premapped to the W, A, S, and D keys and the arrow keys. Fire1, Fire2, and Fire3 are respectively mapped to Ctrl, Alt, and Command. Mouse X and Mouse Y read in the delta of the mouse movement.

For Widget, you'll only need a few basic controls to begin with:

- Change the Size field to 6 to remove the unneeded axes. Widget's controls are fairly simple, and the default options aren't needed.

- Leave the Horizontal and Vertical axes as they are. These two axes are already mapped to use both the W, A, S, and D keys and the arrow keys.

- Expand the Fire1 selection and rename it Attack. You can also enter a new value in the Descriptive Name field if you want. The Attack button only needs a positive button assignment—you care only if players are pressing it, not what direction it is. You can keep the default left Ctrl and mouse 0 assignments or enter new ones.

- Rename the Fire2 axis to Boost and the Fire3 axis to Duck. Make Boost use the left Shift key and Duck use Caps Lock. You can keep the alternate mouse button assignments if you want.

- Leave the Jump axis as is.

And there you have it. Now if you play your game again, you can use the Duck, Boost, and Jump buttons to control Widget.

A Redux of the *Input* Class

The Widget example used `Input.GetAxis` and `Input.GetButton` to read in the player's commands. The `Input` class has a few other useful functions with which you'll want to be familiar, especially if you plan to use other control devices like joysticks or mice.

- `GetAxis`: Returns the value of the specified axis, such as Horizontal or Vertical. These are mapped from −1 to 1, with neutral sitting at 0.

- `GetButton`: Returns `True` if the specified named button is pressed. You need to use this function to reference joystick and gamepad buttons. This can also work on keyboard keys.

- `GetKey`: Returns `True` if the specified key is pressed. This will not return joystick button commands.

- `GetMouseButton`: As suggested, returns `True` if the specified mouse button is pressed.

- `ResetInputAxes`: This doesn't take a named axis like the other functions. Instead, you use this function to reset all input and return it to neutral or 0, overriding any input from the players.

The Input class also has a few useful variables, giving you access to some important read-only data. Two of the more commonly used ones are listed here:

■ **anyKey:** Access this variable by typing Input.anyKey. Its value will be set to True if the player presses any key, button, or mouse button. "Press any key to continue" never looked so easy!

■ **mousePosition:** Stores the current position of the mouse on the screen as a vector. For reference, the bottom-left corner of the screen maps to the coordinate (0,0).

Naming Conventions for the Axes

You can use any key or button to map controls, and Unity's naming scheme is pretty straightforward and easy to remember. No need for lookup tables or pesky ASCII codes! Here's how it works:

■ **Main keyboard keys:** Simply type the full English name of the key as it appears, such as a, w, 3, enter, page up, or f1. For keys that appear more than once on the keyboard (such as Ctrl and Alt), you need to specify which one you mean—for example, left ctrl or right shift. Note that the key names are lowercase, Unity rejects an uppercase key name, immediately blanking out the box.

■ **Arrow keys:** Just type the direction of the arrow, such as right, left, up, and down.

■ **Keypad keys:** To reference the keys on the keypad, enclose the key in brackets, like so: [1], [3], [+], or [=]. (The keypad is the small attached number pad located on the right side of full-sized keyboards.)

■ **Mouse:** Mouse buttons all use the moniker "mouse" followed by a number, like so: mouse 0, mouse 1, and so on.

■ **Joysticks:** Joysticks follow the same convention as mice: joystick button 0, joystick button 1, and so on. If you want to reference a specific joystick—not just any one attached to the computer—simply add a reference to the joystick number: joystick 0 button 1, joystick 2 button 1, and so on.

Sample Xbox-Style Controller Setup

Using the available named axes and buttons, it's possible to set up a USB-powered game controller to work with Unity. Just make sure first that your controller is set up correctly with your computer, calibrated, and turned on before starting Unity.

The basic settings are as follows:

■ **Left Control Stick:** Horizontal movement maps to the X axis and vertical movement to the Y axis.

- **Right Control Stick:** Horizontal movement maps to the fifth axis and vertical movement to the fourth axis.

- **Left D-Pad:** Horizontal movement maps to the sixth axis and vertical movement to the seventh.

- **Shoulder Triggers:** These map to the third axis. Left maps to −1 and right to 1.

- **Shoulder Buttons:** The right shoulder button maps to joystick button 5, and the left to joystick button 4.

- **Back or Select Button:** Maps to joystick button 6.

- **Start Button:** Maps to joystick button 7.

- **A Button (Bottom):** Maps to joystick button 0.

- **B Button (Right):** Maps to joystick button 1.

- **X Button (Left):** Maps to joystick button 2.

- **Y Button (Top):** Maps to joystick button 3.

Any controller in this style should map similarly, but you may need to fiddle with an axis name or two. Just remember that when using joysticks or gamepads, you need to use the proper Input function call to read in the controls.

Hooking Up the Camera

Now that Widget is fully functional and controllable, you need some way to keep the camera always locked on him. Otherwise, it will be really easy for the player to roll outside the camera's field of view. To do that, you'll make a smooth follow script to control the camera's movement and rotation. There are some free available camera scripts in the Standard Assets > Camera Scripts folder, and you can always use those if you want.

For the custom camera here, you'll want it to do a few basic things:

- Follow Widget from a set, specified distance at all times.

- Put a slight delay in the follow speed so that the camera's movement isn't jerky or jittery. You want it to smoothly change course and update its position as the player moves around.

- Always update its current rotation angle so that it's looking at Widget. Otherwise, a jump action may send him flying out of view.

Create a new JavaScript file in the Scripts directory and name it Widget_Camera. Delete the default Update function in the new file.

To start off, you know you'll need a few basic variables to define the following distance and the speed at which the camera catches up to Widget. You'll also need to create a variable to hold the reference to the Widget GameObject. Otherwise, the camera won't know what to look at. At the beginning of the file, add the following:

```
var target : Transform;
//The distance for X and Z for the camera to stay from the target
var distance = 5.0;
//The distance in Y for the camera to stay from the target
var height = 4.0;

//Speed controls for the camera--how fast it catches up to the moving object
var heightDamping = 2.0;
var rotationDamping = 3.0;
var distanceDampingX = 1;
var distanceDampingZ = 1;
```

The previous damping variables define how much delay your camera uses before following Widget. These can be rather finicky to get right (and you may want to change some of them as you go along), but luckily you can change them on the fly in the Inspector.

On the next line, add the following:

```
function LateUpdate () {
        //Check to make sure a target has been assigned in Inspector
        if (!target)
                return;
}
```

This code uses the LateUpdate function instead of Update for one specific reason: Widget's controller is based in the FixedUpdate loop, and you want to make sure that the player has finished inputting commands and that the controller has finished moving. If the camera script were to run before Widget had finished moving, it wouldn't necessarily know where to look or go.

The if statement is a safety check. If for whatever reason you forget to assign a target for the camera to follow and look at, or if something happens to Widget during the game, the camera script will stop working gracefully instead of crashing and generating errors. These kinds of statements help your game stay stable in case of unforeseen errors or bugs.

After the `if` statement, you need to grab references for the target's current position and the camera's current position. This will enable you to compute the distance and angle between the two. Add the following code:

```
//Calculate the current rotation angles, positions,
//and where you want the camera to end up
RotationAngle = target.eulerAngles.y;
wantedHeight = target.position.y + height;
wantedDistanceZ = target.position.z - distance;
wantedDistanceX = target.position.x - distance;

currentRotationAngle = transform.eulerAngles.y;
currentHeight = transform.position.y;
currentDistanceZ = transform.position.z;
currentDistanceX = transform.position.x;
```

The `wanted` variables record the target's current angle and position and then factor in the desired distance and height specified earlier. The `current` variables grab the camera's data with the shorthand transform reference. Because the script will be attached as a component to the camera, the `transform` keyword references the camera's position and rotation automatically.

Now that you know where the camera is and where it's pointing, as well as where the target is located, you can start to update the camera and move it if necessary, continuing in the `LateUpdate()` function:

```
//Damp the rotation around the Y axis
currentRotationAngle = Mathf.LerpAngle
        (currentRotationAngle, wantedRotationAngle, rotationDamping * Time.deltaTime);
```

Let's start with fixing the camera's rotation. `Mathf` is Unity's built-in math library. It contains a list of common math functions and constants, like the value of pi, trigonometry functions, exponentials, and rounding. It also has a few interpolation functions, one being `LerpAngle`. `LerpAngle` takes three arguments—a beginning value, end value, and time step—and interpolates the starting value toward the end one. This is exactly what you want the camera to do. By multiplying `Time.deltaTime` by the `rotationDamping` variable, you can change and vary the speed at which it interpolates.

After interpolating the rotation, you need to do the same for the distance of the camera to the target in all three axes. Continue the function by adding the following code:

```
//Damp the distance
currentHeight = Mathf.Lerp (currentHeight, wantedHeight, heightDamping * Time.deltaTime);
currentDistanceZ = Mathf.Lerp(currentDistanceZ,
     wantedDistanceZ, distanceDampingZ * Time.deltaTime);
currentDistanceX = Mathf.Lerp(currentDistanceX, wantedDistanceX,
     DistanceDampingX * Time.deltaTime);
```

Now that you have these new positions and rotation angles, it's only a few more steps to assign these back to the camera's current position. You'll also add a line to index the script in the Component menu:

```
//Convert the angle into a rotation
currentRotation = Quaternion.Euler (0, currentRotationAngle, 0);
//Set the new position of the camera
transform.position -= currentRotation * Vector3.forward * distance ;
transform.position.x = currentDistanceX;
transform.position.z = currentDistanceZ;
transform.position.y = currentHeight;
}
@script AddComponentMenu("Player/Smooth Follow Camera")
```

Attach this script to the Main Camera object and drag the instance of Widget onto the target variable or select it from the drop-down list. Even without looking at the functionality implemented, you can get a good sense of how the camera's looking. Play with the distance and damping variables until you arrive at a feeling you like. Getting the camera to feel right can be a lengthy, tedious process, but it's well worth it, and your players will thank you.

Now you'll build the function to make the camera look at Widget at all times. Outside of and below the LateUpdate() function, add the following line:

```
function LookAtMe(){        }
```

As suggested, this function will make the camera look at a specified target. To do this, you'll need to add two more variables. At the top of the file, by the other variable declarations, add this:

```
//The camera controls for looking at the target
var camSpeed = 2.0;
var smoothed = true;
```

This will enable you to control how quickly the camera rotates and whether you want the look at functionality to be smooth. (This is just a personal preference.) Inside the LookAtMe function brackets, add the following:

```
if(smoothed)
{
    //Find the new rotation value based upon the target and camera's
    //current position. Then interpolate smoothly between the two
    //using the specified speed setting.
    var camRotation = Quaternion.LookRotation(target.position -
transform.position);
    transform.rotation = Quaternion.Slerp(transform.rotation, camRotation,
Time.deltaTime * camSpeed);
}
//This default will flatly move with the targeted object
else{
    transform.LookAt(target);
}
```

If smoothed is set to True in the Inspector, the camera will use a smooth interpolation to rotate to look at Widget. If not, it will use the default LookAt() function, which is a part of all transform components. Back in the LateUpdate function, add a call to LookAtMe() as the last action to perform:

```
//Make sure the camera is always looking at the target
LookAtMe();
```

Quaternions

The LookAtMe() function uses functionality from the quaternion library. A *quaternion* is a four-dimensional vector (x,y,z,w) used extensively for the calculation of rotations in three dimensions. Unity uses quaternions to represent all its internal rotation values, as they don't have problems with gimbal lock and can be easily interpolated between. Gimbal lock occurs in some notation systems when you rotate an axis to be very close to another axis. For example, telling someone at the North Pole to walk east is an example of gimbal lock. On the pole, there is no east or west; every direction becomes south.

Instead of using the more intuitive values of yaw, pitch, and roll, quaternions extend the complex number system. They're defined with an imaginary number component—$i2 = j2 = k2 = ijk = -1$. As such, they may not be innately intuitive to every individual, and the thought of working extensively with them can be offputting if you're completely unfamiliar with them.

Thankfully, you don't need to edit the direct components of quaternions (and you shouldn't, unless you really know what you're doing). Instead, you can use the included class functions and identities. The two functions in the camera example are two of the most commonly used—LookRotation creates a rotation along the forward direction and Slerp spherically interpolates one value to another.

There are a few other things you could add to the camera at this point (like collision detection so it doesn't run through geometry), but for basic functionality it gets the point across. Try Widget with his completed camera script in action.

Assembling the Status Controller

Now that Widget is mobile, he needs to be able to store his states and vitals so that they can be updated when he encounters things like items and enemies. He'll need the following:

- Variables to keep track of his health, such as energy, max health, and max energy, as well as any other variables to determine how much energy is used to boost roll.

- At some point, he'll need audio variables for being hit and dying.

- Functions to add health and energy and to apply damage and remove health.

- Some kind of death function to handle an unfortunate early end and his respawning back into the game.

You'll add the audio cues later, but you currently have the skills and knowledge to start putting together the basics of his state controller. To start, create a new JavaScript file in the Scripts directory and name it Widget_Status. You can also delete the Update function created here because this script won't need to do anything frame to frame. As with his controller, he'll need some basic variables to store his pertinent data:

```
//Vitals---------------------------------------------------
var health: float = 10.0;
var maxHealth: float = 10.0;
var energy: float = 10.0;
var maxEnergy: float = 10.0;
var energyUsageForTransform: float = 3.0;
var WidgetBoostUsage :float = 5.0;
```

Widget has two main stats: health and energy. Besides defining the starting values for each of these, you need to record the maximum amount for each stat so they can be easily reset in case of death. You also need to define some base usage amounts for energy, specifically when he transforms, and boost rolls. All these values can be updated or changed during play via the Inspector.

The script will also need to access data in the Widget_Controller.js script—specifically, to some of the variables stored within. To do that, you'll cache a link to that component to allow easy reference:

```
//Cache the controller-------------------------------------
var playerController: Widget_Controller;
playerController = GetComponent(Widget_Controller) ;
```

Because this script will also be attached to the Widget object, the GetComponent function is the easiest way to create the link. With Widget's base stats now in place, all you need according to the outline is a few functions to help change and manage these variables.

The first function to create is an AddHealth function, something you can use later to give extra health points to Widget. To do this, all you need to do is take a given number of health points and add it to his current health. You should then check to make sure the new amount isn't more than his maximum health, and if it is, reset his health to the allowed maximum.

```
function AddHealth(boost: float) {
        //Add health and set to min of (current health + boost) or health max
        health += boost;
        if(health >= maxHealth) {
                health = maxHealth;
        }
        print("added health: " + health);
}
```

Pretty straightforward. Now you can call this function any time to add any number of health points to Widget. Widget will also need a similar function, but for energy:

```
function AddEnergy(boost: float) {
        //Add energy and set to min of (current en + boost) or en max
        energy += boost;
        if(energy >= maxEnergy) {
                energy = maxEnergy;
        }
        print("added energy: " + energy);
}
```

With the two positive functions out of the way, Widget will also need some sort of function to subtract points from his health in case he is damaged by something out in the world. Make a new function called ApplyDamage and have it take a single float argument:

```
function ApplyDamage(damage: float){          }
```

This is also pretty straightforward. You simply subtract the given damage amount from Widget's current health. If this dips his health below zero, you need to call some sort of function that (sadly) kills Widget and removes him from the scene. Add the following to the ApplyDamage function:

```
health -= damage;
//Check health and call Die() if need to
if(health <= 0) {
        health = 0; //Keep it from ever displaying negative
        Die();
}
```

Now let's make this `Die()` function. The design for the Widget game allows him to be respawned at passed waypoints if ever killed, so you need to be able to remove him from the game and then place him back at a given location. You won't learn about the respawn or waypoint scripts until Chapter 9, "Using Triggers and Creating Environment Interactions," but you can get the rest of it written now. Create a new function called `Die()`:

```
function Die(){
    print("dead!");
    HideCharacter();
    yield WaitForSeconds(1);
    ShowCharacter();
    health = maxHealth;
}
```

This function uses two more helper functions, `HideCharacter` and `ShowCharacter`, both of which will take care of removing Widget from the scene and then having him reappear later. The middle statement, however, is the most important part to take away—the `yield` keyword.

Co-routines

As you've seen a bit of now, when writing code for games, you often want things to occur in a set sequence: Event A must occur and finish before the start of event B, and then only after those two events are finished can event C begin. For example, you can't update the camera controls until the character finishes moving for the frame. Using the `yield` keyword tells Unity to stop executing the current function, wait a frame, and then continue where it left off on the subsequent frame.

Chaining together a collection of `yield` statements in this manner allows you to write *co-routines*, or special functions that can basically start up and pause without losing their place and then continue where they last stopped with a certain command.

The `yield` statement will also stack with a few other instructions—specifically, `WaitForSeconds`, `WaitForFixedUpdate`, and any named co-routine. For example, in the `Die()` function, `yield` is paired with `WaitForSeonds (1)`, telling Unity to stop the execution of the `Die()` function, wait one second, and then continue where it left off. Without this `yield` statement, the function would continue without pausing, which wouldn't give the player any time to recollect himself after dying. Note that `yield` statements cannot be used in any of the various `Update` function calls.

Note

If you're using C#, you need to use MonoBehaviour's StartCoroutine to begin any co-routine. For example, if you had a co-routine named MyCoroutine, you would need to invoke it using the following:

```
yield return StartCoroutine( MyCoroutine() );
```

The HideCharacter and ShowCharacter helper functions are also pretty straightforward. The first needs to hide the Widget object and take away the player's input controls, and the second needs to restore the controls and object to view. Add the following to the script:

```
function HideCharacter(){
     GameObject.Find("Body").GetComponent(SkinnedMeshRenderer).enabled = false;
     GameObject.Find("Wheels").GetComponent(SkinnedMeshRenderer).enabled = false;
     playerController.isControllable = false;
}
function ShowCharacter(){
     GameObject.Find("Body").GetComponent(SkinnedMeshRenderer).enabled = true;
     GameObject.Find("Wheels").GetComponent(SkinnedMeshRenderer).enabled = true;
     playerController.isControllable = true;
}
```

Here is where you need to reference the controller. In the controller script you wrote, the isControllable variable defines whether Widget currently accepts input from the player. To take that control away, you just need to set it to False. The GetComponent (SkinnedMeshRenderer) statement finds Widget's renderer and turns it off, thereby making him invisible. He's still on the screen, but the player won't be able to see or interact with him. In Chapter 9, you'll add more functionality to the Die() function and make Widget reappear at a different spot rather than just staying in his current location when he returns to the scene.

Add the indexing line to the bottom of the script and attach the state controller to Widget:

```
@script AddComponentMenu("Player/Widget'sStateManager")
```

Updating the Character Controller

Now that Widget has stats defined and working, you can update his controller script. Currently, Widget can boost roll without using any energy, but this isn't in line with the design. Changing this is a simple rewrite of the Input.GetButton("Boost") conditional.

Open the Widget_Controller script and create a link to Widget's status manager. Underneath the cache to the `CharacterController`, add the following:

```
var WidgetStatus : Widget_Status;
WidgetStatus = GetComponent(Widget_Status);
```

This will allow easy access to how much energy Widget currently has. Now to rewrite the boost conditional:

```
//Apply any boosted Speed
if(Input.GetButton("Boost")){
    if(WidgetStatus){
        if(WidgetStatus.energy > 0){
            moveDirection *= fastRollSpeed;
            WidgetStatus.energy -= WidgetStatus.WidgetBoostUsage *Time.deltaTime;
        }
    }
}
```

First you make a safety check to make sure that there is a status controller script attached to Widget. (You don't want to try to access the energy stat if the Widget_Status script doesn't exist.) Then, after a simple check to make sure that Widget has energy, you subtract from Widget's current energy amount the amount of energy it takes to boost roll every second. Now when Widget rolls quickly, he will continually consume energy until he has none left. If Widget has no energy, the player cannot boost roll.

You'll find that, despite any best-laid plans, you'll be working constantly between scripts, updating one after you make a significant change in another. This is completely normal, but it does highlight the importance of clean writing and good naming conventions. If, a few months down the road, you can't figure out what you wrote, you can't really expect anyone else to be able to, either.

In Chapter 8, "Hooking Up the Animations," you'll start to hook up Widget's animation state machine. It's all wonderful news that he can be controlled and can move, but it won't look right until he starts to use his animations in conjunction with the movement.

COMPLETED SCRIPTS

These can be found on the website, but are included here for reference. The Widget_Controller.js script appears in Listing 7.1.

Listing 7.1   Widget_Controller.js

```
//Widget_Controller: Handles Widget's movement and player input

//Widget's movement variables------------------------------
//These can be changed in the Inspector
var rollSpeed = 6.0;
var fastRollSpeed = 2.0;
var jumpSpeed = 8.0;
var gravity = 20.0;
var rotateSpeed = 4.0;
var duckSpeed = .5;

//Private, helper variables------------------------------
private var moveDirection = Vector3.zero;
private var grounded : boolean = false;
private var moveHorz = 0.0;
private var normalHeight = 2.0;
private var duckHeight = 1.0;
private var rotateDirection = Vector3.zero;

private var isDucking : boolean = false;
private var isBoosting : boolean = false;

var isControllable : boolean = true;

//Cache controller so we only have to find it once----
var controller : CharacterController ;
controller = GetComponent(CharacterController);
var widgetStatus : Widget_Status;
widgetStatus = GetComponent(Widget_Status);

//Move the controller during the fixed frame updates---
function FixedUpdate() {

    //Check to make sure the character is controllable and not dead
    if(!isControllable)
        Input.ResetInputAxes();

    else{
        if (grounded) {
            //Since we're touching something solid,
            //such as the ground, allow movement
            //Calculate movement directly from input axes
            moveDirection = new Vector3(Input.GetAxis("Horizontal"), 0,
Input.GetAxis("Vertical"));
            moveDirection = transform.TransformDirection(moveDirection);
            moveDirection *= rollSpeed;
```

```
//Find rotation based upon axes if need to turn
moveHorz = Input.GetAxis("Horizontal");
if (moveHorz > 0) //Right turn
      rotateDirection = new Vector3(0, 1, 0);
else if (moveHorz < 0) //Left turn
      rotateDirection = new Vector3(0, -1, 0);
else //Not turning
      rotateDirection = new Vector3 (0, 0, 0);

//Jump controls
if (Input.GetButton ("Jump")) {
      moveDirection.y = jumpSpeed;
}

//Apply any boosted speed
if(Input.GetButton("Boost")){
      if(widgetStatus){
            if(widgetStatus.energy > 0)
            {
                  moveDirection *= fastRollSpeed;
                  widgetStatus.energy -=
widgetStatus.widgetBoostUsage *Time.deltaTime;
                  isBoosting = true;
            }
      }
}

//Duck the controller
if(Input.GetButton("Duck")){
      controller.height = duckHeight;
      controller.center.y = controller.height/2 + .25;
      moveDirection *= duckSpeed;
      isDucking = true;
}

if(Input.GetButtonUp("Duck")){
      //Reset height and center after ducks
      controller.height = normalHeight;
      controller.center.y = controller.height/2;
      isDucking = false;
}

if(Input.GetButtonUp("Boost")){
      isBoosting = false;
}

}
```

```
                //Apply gravity to end jump, enable falling, and make sure he's touching
                //the ground
                moveDirection.y -= gravity * Time.deltaTime;

                //Move and rotate the controller
                var flags = controller.Move(moveDirection * Time.deltaTime);
                controller.transform.Rotate(rotateDirection * Time.deltaTime, rotateSpeed);
                grounded = ((flags & CollisionFlags.CollidedBelow) != 0 );
                }

        }
//-----------------------------------------------------
function IsMoving(){

        return moveDirection.magnitude > 0.5;
}

function IsDucking(){

        return isDucking;
}

function IsBoosting(){

        return isBoosting;
}

function IsGrounded(){

        return grounded;
}


//Make the script easy to find
@script AddComponentMenu("Player/Widget'sController")
```

The Widget_Status.js script appears in Listing 7.2.

Listing 7.2   Widget_Status.js

```
//Widget_Status: Handles Widget's state machine.
//Keep track of health, energy and all the chunky stuff

//Vitals------------------------------------------------
var health: float = 10.0;
var maxHealth: float= 10.0;
var energy: float = 10.0;
var maxEnergy: float = 10.0;
var energyUsageForTransform: float = 3.0;
var widgetBoostUsage :float = 5.0;
```

```
//Sound effects----------------------------------------
var hitSound: AudioClip;
var deathSound: AudioClip;


//Cache controllers------------------------------------
var playerController: Widget_Controller;
playerController = GetComponent(Widget_Controller) ;
var controller : CharacterController;
controller = GetComponent(CharacterController);



//Helper controller functions--------------------------
function ApplyDamage(damage: float){
        health -= damage;
        //Play hit sound if it exists
        if(hitSound)
        {
                audio.clip = hitSound;
                audio.Play();
        }
        //Check health and call Die() if need to
        if(health <= 0){
                health = 0; //For GUI
                Die();
        }

}

function AddHealth(boost: float){
        //Add health and set to min of (current health + boost) or health max
        health += boost;
        if(health >= maxHealth){
                health = maxHealth;
        }
        print("added health: " + health);
}

function AddEnergy(boost: float){
        //Add energy and set to min of (current en + boost) or en max
        energy += boost;
        if(energy >= maxEnergy){
                energy = maxEnergy;
        }
        print("added energy: " + energy);
}
```

```
function Die(){
       //Play death sound if it exists
       if(deathSound)
       {
              audio.clip = deathSound;
              audio.Play();
       }
       print("dead!");
       playerController.isControllable = false;

       animationState = GetComponent(Widget_Animation);
       animationState.PlayDie();
       yield WaitForSeconds(animation["Die"].length -0.2);
       HideCharacter();

       yield WaitForSeconds(1);

       //Restart player at last respawn checkpoint and give max life
       if(CheckPoint.isActivePt){
              controller.transform.position = CheckPoint.isActivePt.transform.position;
              controller.transform.position.y += 0.5; //So not to get stuck in the
platform itself
       }
       ShowCharacter();
       health = maxHealth;
}
function HideCharacter(){
       GameObject.Find("Body").GetComponent(SkinnedMeshRenderer).enabled = false;
       GameObject.Find("Wheels").GetComponent(SkinnedMeshRenderer).enabled = false;
       playerController.isControllable = false;

}
function ShowCharacter(){
       GameObject.Find("Body").GetComponent(SkinnedMeshRenderer).enabled = true;
       GameObject.Find("Wheels").GetComponent(SkinnedMeshRenderer).enabled = true;
       playerController.isControllable = true;

}
@script AddComponentMenu("Player/Widget'sStateManager")
```

The Widget_Camera.js script appears in Listing 7.3.

Listing 7.3 Widget_Camera.js

```
//Widget_Camera.js: A script to control the camera and make it smoothly follow widget.
//The object we want to follow and look at
var target : Transform;

//The distance for X and Z for the camera to stay from the target
var distance = 10.0;
//The distance in Y for the camera to stay from the target
var height = 5.0;

//Speed controls for the camera--how fast it catches up to the moving object
var heightDamping = 2.0;
var rotationDamping = 3.0;
var distanceDampingX = 0.5;
var distanceDampingZ = 0.2;

//The camera controls for looking at the target
var camSpeed = 2.0;
var smoothed = true;


function LateUpdate () {
        //Check to make sure a target has been assigned in Inspector
        if (!target)
                return;

        //Calculate the current rotation angles, positions, and where we want the
        //camera to end up
        wantedRotationAngle = target.eulerAngles.y;
        wantedHeight = target.position.y + height;
        wantedDistanceZ = target.position.z - distance;
        wantedDistanceX = target.position.x - distance;

        currentRotationAngle = transform.eulerAngles.y;
        currentHeight = transform.position.y;
        currentDistanceZ = transform.position.z;
        currentDistanceX = transform.position.x;


        //Damp the rotation around the Y axis
        currentRotationAngle = Mathf.LerpAngle (currentRotationAngle,
wantedRotationAngle, rotationDamping * Time.deltaTime);

        //Damp the distance
        currentHeight = Mathf.Lerp (currentHeight, wantedHeight,
heightDamping * Time.deltaTime);
```

```
        currentDistanceZ = Mathf.Lerp(currentDistanceZ, wantedDistanceZ,
distanceDampingZ * Time.deltaTime);
        currentDistanceX = Mathf.Lerp(currentDistanceX, wantedDistanceX,
distanceDampingX * Time.deltaTime);

    //Convert the angle into a rotation
    currentRotation = Quaternion.Euler (0, currentRotationAngle, 0);

    //Set the new position of the camera
    transform.position -= currentRotation * Vector3.forward * distance;
    transform.position.x = currentDistanceX;
    transform.position.z = currentDistanceZ;
    transform.position.y = currentHeight;

    //Make sure the camera is always looking at the target
    LookAtMe();
}


function LookAtMe(){
        //Check whether we want the camera to be smoothed or not--can be changed
        //in the Inspector
        if(smoothed)
         {
            //Find the new rotation value based upon
            //the target and camera's current position;
            //then interpolate smoothly between the two
            //using the specified speed setting
            var camRotation = Quaternion.LookRotation(target.position -
transform.position);
            transform.rotation = Quaternion.Slerp(transform.rotation,
camRotation, Time.deltaTime * camSpeed);
         }
        //This default will flatly move with the targeted object
        else{
            transform.LookAt(target);
         }
    }
@script AddComponentMenu("Player/Smooth Follow Camera")
```

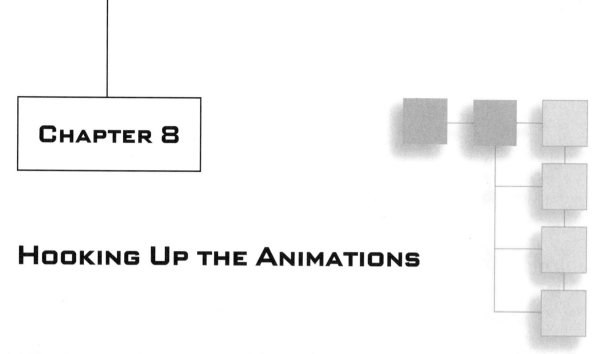

Chapter 8

Hooking Up the Animations

Animations are an important part of the visual structure of a game. They help breathe life and character into an otherwise static collection of objects. They can also help provide important bits of information for the player: Am I running or walking? Jumping or falling? Did that enemy actually just hit me or did I dodge? Without clear and constant visual feedback, playing a game can be much harder and more frustrating than ever intended. Animations can help with this.

Animation in Unity

You can handle animations in Unity in a few ways:

- You can create them in a third-party editor and import them.
- You can procedurally generate them using scripts.
- You can create them directly from within Unity in the Animation view.

Each of these methods has its own pros and cons, with some befitting a certain task more than others. A complex, multipart character can be animated from within the Animation view, but the character artist may find he's more at home with a separate editor like Maya. A health or ammo pickup can be animated in an outside package, but some simple animation effects can be created more efficiently with a simple script. On the other hand, if you don't have access to a different animation editor, you can do everything you need from within Unity itself. Analyze the task at hand and try to pick the best method for it. Work smarter, not faster.

ANIMATION API

Unity's Animation API is extremely powerful and comprehensive. Unity also includes the integrated Animation editor. Often, when one thinks of animation, one has visions of multiboned, carefully weighted character antics. However, animation extends far beyond that. In Unity, it's possible to animate materials, light intensities, audio cues, procedurally created objects, and even variables inside your custom scripts. Some of this is easily handled through the Animation view, whereas other tasks can be quickly and deftly scripted using the API.

The Mecanim Animation System

Unity is always growing and improving. With release 4, Unity introduced a powerful new animation system called Mecanim, which allows developers to build sophisticated animations for characters. The system has been mentioned a few times already in this book.

The Mecanim system enables animators and programmers to collaborate by first jointly building a flowchart describing the groups of animations and placing arrows to describe all the transitions that are permitted. Once the flowchart is created, programmers can write the code even when animations are missing, and animators can add animation clips before programmers hook them up.

With that power comes a bit of complexity. The process of setting up bones, muscles, blending trees, animation layers, and all the other pieces takes time and skill. If you are working in a professional environment, you will probably be working with Mecanim-powered animations. Unfortunately, the system is extensive and beyond the scope of this book.

Instead, the book will focus on the generic animation system, which Unity renamed the Legacy animation system. The Legacy system does not provide as many new bells and whistles, but it has been the workhorse since Unity's initial release.

From a development perspective, there is relatively little difference between the two systems. Mecanim provides additional features and options for animators and modelers, but the tasks for everyone else in the development process remain the same. The game script still animates the characters, and Unity still plays, mixes, blends, and fades animations. And that brings us to our first stop on the Legacy animation system tour: the Animation class.

The Animation Class

The Animation class handles all the functionality to play, mix, blend, and fade animation clips. It can also change a few import settings, like whether an animation is to play automatically or what an individual clip's WrapMode is set to. With just a few simple function calls, you can set up a working, dynamic system.

The class derives from the Behaviour class, so it contains some of the functions and variables you're getting used to seeing, like GetComponent and Transform. The unique members of the class are relatively small in number and are easy enough to become familiar with.

One of the most critical aspects of the API to grasp is the concept of animation layers. In Unity, all the available animation clips on a given GameObject are assigned a layer—0 by default. Depending on the layer number, a clip will be given a higher priority when the blending weights are assigned. Animations in lower layers can then be easily overwritten by one in a higher layer that needs to take precedence.

For example, you might have a general walking animation and a waving animation that affects only one arm. The animation with the highest number is given the most importance when the calculations take place, so you will want the full-body walking animation to have a higher number than the waving animation.

It doesn't matter what layer numbers you use, only that they are larger or smaller than the others. Because the default is 0, you can have animations that are lower than default priority use negative numbers.

To set up a layer, initialize the clip when your animation script starts as follows.

```
animation["myClipName1"].layer = -1;
animation["myClipName2"].layer = 10;
```

Keeping your clips on different layers allows more than just priority differences. It also allows Unity to crossfade and blend the weights to create more beautiful animations. Continuing the previous example, if a player would attempt to attack while also running, the system could blend the two animation clips together and create a running attack animation on the fly, since the two exist on different layers.

Additive animation mixing also allows for the same, but in a much more controlled and sophisticated manner. Using an additive mixing state instead of a blending mixing state would allow for more complex custom animations, like procedural facial animations or animation clips influenced by player input. A character's default run cycle could have a dynamic lean applied to it based on whether the player was pushing the analog stick left or right. This kind of planned mixing can help to save on animation time and resources.

To set up a clip to use additive blending, simply reset its default blend mode when you initialize the clip:

```
myAnimationClip.blendmode = AnimationBlendMode.Additive;
```

Important Member Variables

A few member variables enable you to change the import settings of any clip, as well as query if any animation is currently playing. They are as follows:

■ wrapMode: While a clip's wrap mode may be set up during import, you can change it during your script's initialization. You can also easily loop through all the given animation clips on a GameObject (sometimes abbreviated as GO) and set their wrap mode at once, which is especially handy if your character has hundreds of possible animations.

■ isPlaying: This will return True if any animations are currently playing on the GameObject.

■ clip: An easy way to reference the default animation clip of the GameObject. Usually this will be the first clip in the animation list (Element 0) unless a different one was specified in the import settings.

Often-Used Functions

The Animation class functions give you the abilities to play, stop, blend, and fade clips at a moment's notice. To do so, you use the following functions:

■ Play: A simple and fast way to play the named clip animation. This will not apply any blends or mixing.

■ IsPlaying: Not to be confused with the variable isPlaying (note the capitalization difference). This function takes a single string argument, the name of any animation clip, and returns True if that particular clip is playing.

■ Blend: This blends a named clip toward a target weight over a given amount of time, mixing with any other weighted animations on the same layer.

■ CrossFade: Similar to Blend, this function fades in an animation over a given amount of time, but will fade out and stop any other animations on the same layer.

■ SyncLayer: Call this during initialization to sync all the playback speeds of any animation clips in the specified layer. Useful for when you have multiple kinds of runs or walks in the same layer.

■ CrossFadeQueued, PlayQueued: Crossfades or plays the named clip after any other previous animations have finished playing. This is particularly useful for setting up scripted sequences and cut scenes.

There are a few other variables and functions available in the class, but these are the most commonly used and referenced.

SETTING UP THE PC'S ANIMATIONS

For the Widget character, you imported a selection of different animations back in Chapter 5, "Creating Characters." Nine clips were split up, named, and stored in the root of Widget's base mesh. Now it's time to actually hook these up to the character movement and player's input.

Defining the Problem

Much like with the other systems, it helps to first define what it is exactly you want to do. Now you not only need to figure out how you want the system to run, but also what order the clips need to be in. You will also need a class that coordinates the state of the animations, which we will call an animation state manager.

- The system will need to hook up to the controller class to get access to the player's input and determine what Widget is currently doing.
- The script will need to account for the player when she isn't doing anything and play an idle-fidget animation after a set amount of time.
- The controller class will need to be updated with a few helper functions to allow the animation state manager access to the pertinent information.
- Widget's animation clips will need to be set up in an appropriate layer order, with idle being the lowest and the death clip taking top priority.

With that together, it's time to give Widget some animations.

Updating the Controller

First, you should update the controller with the few basic needs of the animation state manager. Open the Widget_Controller file and add these member variables to the top of the file:

```
private var isDucking : boolean = false;
private var isBoosting : boolean = false;
```

These will help tell the animation state manager what Widget is currently doing. In the `Input.GetButton(@Boost@)` conditional, add this line beneath the energy management statements:

```
isBoosting = true;
```

Do the same for the `Duck` conditional. Add the following beneath the update to the `moveDirection` speed:

```
isDucking = true;
```

Now you need to add two new small conditional statements. Right below the `Input.GetButton(@Duck@)` statement body, add these two new conditionals:

```
if(Input.GetButtonUp("Duck")){
      controller.height = normalHeight; //Reset for after ducks
      controller.center.y = controller.height/2;      //Re-center for after ducks
isDucking = false;
}
if(Input.GetButtonUp("Boost")){
      isBoosting = false;
}
```

These will help you control when the animation will stop playing, as the `GetButtonUp` event will be triggered whenever the player lets go of one of the keys.

Finally, the controller needs these quick helper functions to return the private data so other scripts can access it. Add these to the bottom of the file, outside of the `Update` function:

```
function IsMoving(){
      return moveDirection.magnitude > 0.5;
}
function IsDucking(){
      return isDucking;
}
function IsBoosting(){
      return isBoosting;
}
function IsGrounded(){
      return grounded;
}
```

Now the Animation Manager will be able to tell if the player is currently pressing any special buttons or if Widget is in the air or grounded. Using functions like this is an easy way to get read-only access to a private variable from another script. A complete version of the controller script is available on the accompanying website in the Chapter 8 folder.

Creating the Animation State Manager

Now for the animation state manager itself. Create a new JavaScript file in the Scripts directory and name it Widget_Animation. You can keep the `Update` function that's provided, as that's where all the animation calls will be made.

You'll need very few variables for this one, as the majority of the information will be driven from the controller script itself. In fact, the only ones you need are the ones to manage the idle time wait and the variable link to the player controller. At the top of the file outside of the Update function, add the following:

```
private var nextPlayIdle = 0.0;
var waitTime = 8.0;
var playerController: Widget_Controller;
playerController = GetComponent(Widget_Controller) ;
```

The value in nextPlayIdle will be updated based on the system time, but you can also change the amount of buffer time between idle animation calls from the Inspector with the waitTime variable.

Next up is to initialize all the clips into their respective layers and make any necessary updates to their individual wrap modes. Make a new Start function:

```
function Start(){
        //Set up layers - high numbers receive priority when blending
animation["Idle"].layer = 0;
        //We want to make sure that the rolls are synced together
animation["SlowRoll"].layer = 1;
        animation["FastRoll"].layer = 1;
        animation["Duck"].layer = 1;
        animation.SyncLayer(1);
        animation["Taser"].layer = 3;
        animation["Jump"].layer = 5;
        //These should take priority over all others
        animation["FallDown"].layer = 7;
        animation["GotHit"].layer = 8;
        animation["Die"].layer = 10;
        animation["Duck"].wrapMode = WrapMode.Loop;
        animation["Jump"].wrapMode = WrapMode.ClampForever;
        animation["FallDown"].wrapMode = WrapMode.ClampForever;

        //Make sure nothing is playing by accident,
        //then start with a default idle.
        animation.Stop();
        animation.Play("Idle");
}
```

This may look a little long and complicated, but it's all pretty straightforward. Remember the clips you imported back in Chapter 5? The clip names need to be entered here exactly as they were in the animation importer, or Unity won't be able to find them. The idle clip is set at the bottom of the layer stack on layer 0, followed by the various movement animations, and then by the unique one-off animations at the highest layers. Changing the Duck wrap mode to loop will make it look like the character is actively ducking while the button is pressed. The Clamp Forever wrap modes will help the jump and fall-down animation clips last for however long they need to, based purely on input.

Now that the clips are organized correctly for proper blending and weighting, it's time to start hooking them up. First is the basic walk—or in this case, roll cycle—for Widget. In the Update function, make the conditional statement to control Widget's roll:

```
if(playerController.IsGrounded()){
      animation.Blend("FallDown", 0, 0.2);
      animation.Blend("Jump", 0, 0.2);
      //If boosting
      if (playerController.IsBoosting()){
            animation.CrossFade("FastRoll", 0.5);
            nextPlayIdle = Time.time + waitTime;
      }
      else if(playerController.IsDucking()){
            animation.CrossFade("Duck", 0.2);
            nextPlayIdle = Time.time + waitTime;
      }
      //Fade in normal roll
      else if (playerController.IsMoving()){
            animation.CrossFade("SlowRoll", 0.5);
            nextPlayIdle = Time.time + waitTime;
      }
      //Fade out roll and fast roll else
      {
            animation.Blend("FastRoll", 0.0, 0.3);
            animation.Blend("SlowRoll", 0.0, 0.3);
            animation.Blend("Duck", 0.0, 0.3);
            if(Time.time > nextPlayIdle){
                  nextPlayIdle= Time.time + waitTime;
                  PlayIdle();
            }
      }
}
```

First, you check to make sure Widget is in fact on the ground by querying the controller with the new helper function. If so, you quickly blend out any falling or jumping animations that might be lingering. Otherwise, there could be some degenerate cases where Widget has landed but the falling animation hasn't stopped playing. Blend takes three arguments: the animation clip in question, the weight you want it to receive, and the time you want the blending to take. Because you want the clips not to provide any visual information, you should set the weight to 0.

The next few conditionals determine if the player is boosting, ducking, moving normally, or not moving at all. The new piece of information is the inclusion of the nextPlayIdle variable. After each test of movement, the nextPlayIdle time is updated with the result of the current time plus the buffer wait time. During the else statement, the current time will be tested against this nextPlayIdle time. If Widget hasn't moved at all for the past couple of seconds, nextPlayIdle will not be updated, and eventually the idle animation will play when the current system Time.time surpasses the amount of buffer wait time. This keeps the idle from continuously playing if the player stops moving.

Next you need to play the animations for when Widget is jumping or falling down. After the preceding block of code, add the following:

```
else{
    if(Input.GetButtonDown("Jump")){
        animation.CrossFade("Jump");
    }
    if(!playerController.IsGrounded()){
        animation.CrossFade("FallDown", 0.5);
    }
}
```

First the script checked to see if the player is currently pressing the jump key. If the player is not grounded for any reason, the jump animation will fade to the falling down animation after a period of 0.5 seconds. CrossFade can take one, two, or three arguments, depending on how much control you want. The first—the animation clip name—you must specify, but then you can choose to provide the time in seconds you want the cross-fade to occur as well as if you want all other clips to stop playing immediately. Usually, this isn't the case.

Finally, you need to just make a safety check to make sure the player isn't pressing any keys. If the player is doing something onscreen, the idle animation shouldn't ever play. Add this code underneath the else statement:

```
//Safety test for idle
if(Input.anyKey){
    nextPlayIdle = Time.time + waitTime;
}
```

The only other thing missing from the Animation Manager is the `PlayIdle` function and the other small functions to call the unique, context-specific animations. Add the following outside of the `Update` function:

```
function PlayTaser(){
     animation.CrossFade("Taser", 0.2);
}
function PlayIdle(){
     animation.CrossFade("Idle", 0.2);
}
function GetHit(){
     animation.CrossFade("GotHit", 0.2);
}
function PlayDie(){
     animation.CrossFade("Die", 0.2);
}
@script AddComponentMenu("Player/Widget'AnimationManager")
```

These other functions, with the exception of `PlayIdle`, will be used and called once you get combat up and running. The current settings will do for playing any of the clips in a pinch.

Update the controller script on Widget and add this script to the prefab. Now when you play the game, Widget's imported custom animations will play along with the proper input. Go give him a test spin. (The completed script is also available on the companion website in the Chapter 8 folder.)

CREATING ANIMATIONS INSIDE UNITY

Writing a custom class to handle all your animation needs isn't the only option available to you. You can also add new animation clips from within Unity's integrated Animation editor. If you've animated in a different 3D package, the basic concepts and controls won't be drastically unfamiliar to you. If you're new to animation in general, don't worry. The concepts themselves aren't particularly hard to grasp; it's just a lot of new terminology.

The integrated Animation editor is particularly useful for a few tasks, such as adding new animation clips to objects or components created from within Unity, setting up in-game rendered cut scenes, and adding events that you want to occur at an exact point of time in a given animation.

Some Basic Concepts

Animations in Unity are controlled by keys, which in turn define animation curves. A *key* basically stores a snapshot of a given object's state at a specific time. For example, suppose a GameObject is located at point (0,0,0) at time 0 and then moves to point (1,1,1) at time 5.

Each of these two position states would be stored with a key. A curve can then be defined, connecting the two (or more) keys, interpolating a full path of motion for the given object. The smoother the curve, the smoother the resulting animation.

Each part or component of an object can hold its own keys and curves for any given animation clip. For example, in Widget's SlowRoll animation, his wheel child objects are made to turn with some key data. But in the Idle animation, they're not. Any part of a GameObject can be edited in this manner, whether it's a physical piece of geometry, a color value, a texture offset, or even an audio cue.

All these keys and curves can be edited directly within Unity's Animation view.

Animation View

To start working with the editor, choose Window > Animation or press Ctrl+6 to bring up the Animation view, shown in Figure 8.1. Select an object in the Hierarchy view to view its animation data in the Animation view. By selecting Widget, you can view his imported clips, with the Idle clip being shown here.

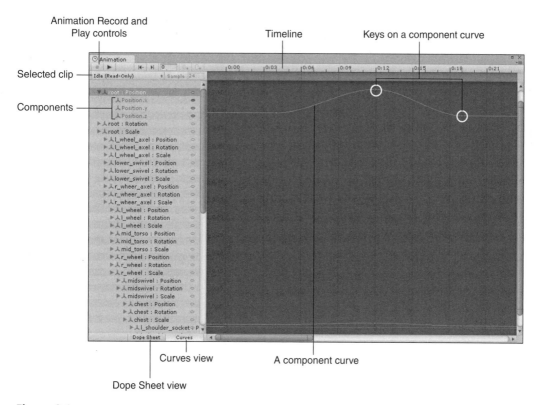

Figure 8.1
The Animation view.
Source: Unity Technologies.

You can select a different clip for the current object from the drop-down list. You can also create a new animation clip through this view. Any clips created from within Unity can then be edited directly through this view. Right now, all of the Widget character's clips are read only, as they were made and imported from another package.

Without equivocation, it's a complicated screen with a lot going on. The best way though to figure it out is to dive right in. It's far easier to use than it looks. To facilitate this, you'll make a simple new idle animation clip for Widget to play while he's not doing anything.

Setting Up a New Animation Clip

Make a new scene for testing and give it some name, like AnimationTest. Because you'll need to have a good view of your test subject, it'll be a lot easier to just work in a flat, new environment.

Creating the Custom Animation

To create your custom animation, follow these steps:

1. Drop in an instance of the current Widget prefab and zoom in on him so he takes up most of the Scene view.

2. Open the Animation view and position it so you can still see Widget in the Scene view. Select Widget in the Hierarchy view to populate the Animation view with his data.

3. Expand Widget's root component and keep expanding until you reach his head. Widget is made up of a hierarchy of smaller component pieces, and you'll need access to these to animate them individually. Your view should now look something like Figure 8.2.

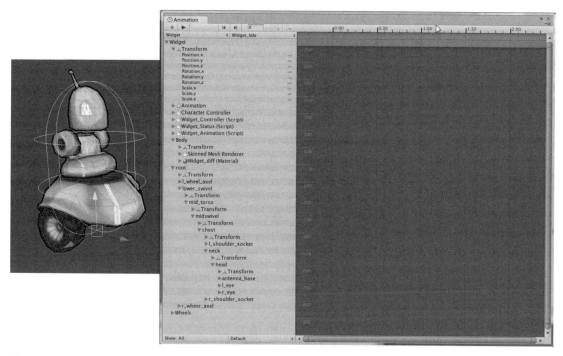

Figure 8.2
Expanding all of Widget's component parts.
Source: Unity Technologies.

4. To make a new animation clip, open the drop-down list in the Animation view that currently says Idle (Read-Only) and select the Create New Clip option. Unity will prompt you to name the clip and save it somewhere in the Project folder. Save it to the Characters directory and name it something like Widget_Idle.

5. Now you're ready to animate. Click the Record button (the one with a red circle) to allow the Animation editor to start recording changes. A red line will appear in the Animation view, signifying your current space in the clip's timeline. By default, it will start at 0:00. (All times displayed here are in seconds and frames.) The play buttons at the top of the editor will turn red to indicate you're recording.

6. At time 0:00, set a key to save Widget's default stationary stance. Expand the Transform component underneath Widget's lower_swivel node, select the Rotation.z component, and click the Add Keyframe button, as shown in Figure 8.3. This will save all of Widget's base information. To add keys, you can select all the Position and Rotation components, right-click on the small dash mark to the right of their names, and select Add Key.

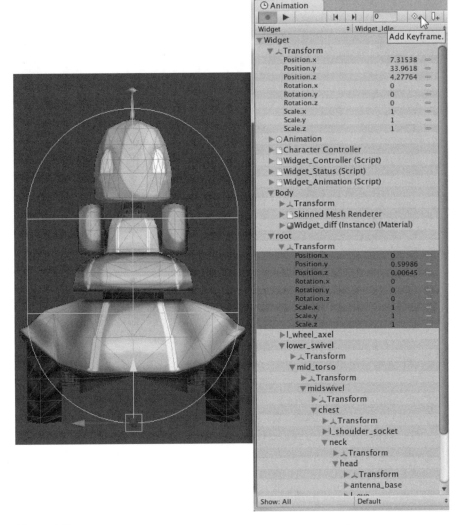

Figure 8.3
Adding a key to Widget's new animation clip.
Source: Unity Technologies.

7. Now to add some movement. Click and drag on the red line in the timeline to move it to a new frame position—roughly 2 seconds. You can also type an exact frame number in the small box to the left of the Add Keyframe button if you prefer. By default, each second has 60 frames, so 2 seconds would be 120 frames.

8. Expand the Transform component below the lower_swivel node. (You can now see why good naming conventions are always a plus! Trying to do this with poor names

would be all but impossible.) Also expand the root node of the Widget instance in the Hierarchy view to gain access to the lower_swivel object. Switch to the rotate gizmo and rotate Widget's lower_swivel object in the Scene view slightly around the Z axis. The Animation view will update to display your changes. Unity will automatically add a keyframe for you at the current time. Figure 8.4 shows the current workspace.

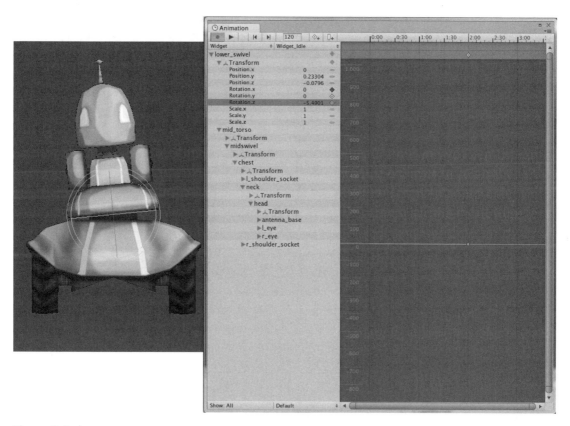

Figure 8.4
Adding a key to Widget's new animation clip.
Source: Unity Technologies.

9. Move the red line forward in time to around 4 seconds (240 frames). Then rotate Widget's lower_swivel node back the opposite direction, as shown in Figure 8.5. If you zoom in, you can see a nice curve forming. Now if you scrub the red line back and forth you can see Widget slowly bobbing. You can also click the small Play button next to the Record button to have Unity play all the keyed frames in time.

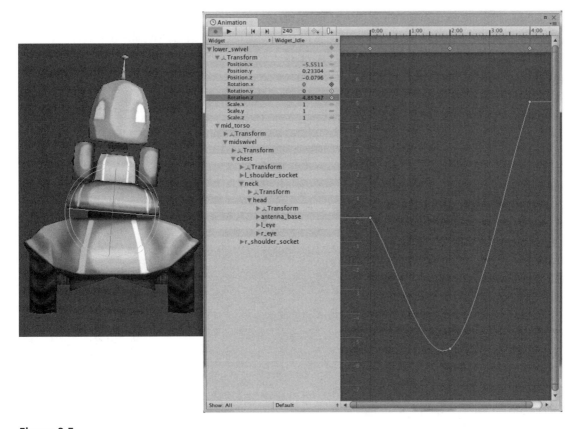

Figure 8.5
Widget's three new keyframes and interpolated curves.
Source: Unity Technologies.

Granted, this isn't the most masterful animation in the world, but it's all your own! Continue to add new keys in this manner and animate an interesting-looking animation for Widget's idle. Don't forget that you can access all his other nodes, too. Make him look around, bob his antenna up and down, or whatever—it's up to you. A finished Widget_ Idle animation clip is provided in the Chapter 8 contents on the accompanying website.

If you make a mistake, don't worry. You can delete a key by selecting it on the curve and pressing the Delete key. You can also right-click and select the Delete Key option from the menu that appears. The right-click menu will also give you access to more advanced options like tangent editing. In a nutshell, tangents will change the shape of the curve around a key. The default Auto selection will attempt to keep all your curves smooth and nice, but you can either edit the tangents freely or select one of the premade options. Play around with it and see how it affects Widget's animation.

When you're finished, click the Record button to stop all recording. Now all that's needed are a few quick final steps, and your new animation will be in the game.

Hooking It Up

First, you need to explicitly hook up the new clip to Widget. Otherwise, the script will never be able to find it. Follow these steps to hook up the new clip:

1. In the Project view, select the Widget prefab and expand its Animation component in the Inspector. Expand the Animations array and change the size to 10. Under the last element, select the new animation clip from the drop-down list. Your prefab should now look like Figure 8.6

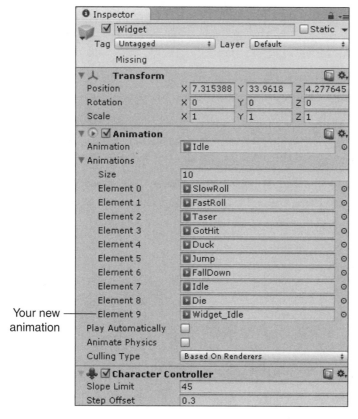

Figure 8.6
The new animation clip loaded into the prefab.
Source: Unity Technologies.

2. Because you've already done the bulk of the work on the Animation Manager, getting this new clip to play will be pretty painless. Open the Widget_Animation script to start working.

3. Create a new layer for the Widget_Idle clip at layer number −1. This will give it the lowest priority of the current clips.
```
animation["Widget_Idle"].layer = -1;
```

4. Then update its WrapMode and set it to PingPong. This will keep it running smoothly from 0:00 to 4:00 then back to 0:00.
```
animation["Widget_Idle"].wrapMode = WrapMode.PingPong;
```

5. In the Update function, add an else statement to tie into the PlayIdle if statement, as shown here:
```
if(Time.time > nextPlayIdle){
        nextPlayIdle= Time.time + waitTime;
        PlayIdle();
}
else
        animation.CrossFade("Widget_Idle", 0.2);
```

This will fade in the new idle animation while the player sits around doing nothing.

6. Try the new animation clip by playing the current scene and sit back to watch. Using the Animation editor, you can create small clips like this or complex, multi-character cut scenes.

Adding Animation Events

The Animation editor enables you to add one more useful function: synchronized events to the animation clips. For complex animations that need to correlate with other actions happening onscreen, this is an extremely handy ability to have right at your fingertips.

For example, say you have a four-legged character with a complex walk cycle animation clip attached to it. You recently found a nice sound effect that you want to play each time the character puts his foot down. To do this manually, you'd have to figure out exactly when each foot hits the ground and try to time the sound to match. But what happens if your frame rate varies or slows down for a second? Your effect could be completely mismatched, and it won't look or sound very good.

Using an Animation event ties an event directly to the clip's frame so it's always in sync. For this example, you can simply open up the Animation view, find on the graph where the foot hits the ground, and add your event call to your sound effect. Then, regardless of how fast or slow the animation plays, your sound effect will always be in time.

Unity's Animation events can call any function that takes one or no arguments and works similar to MonoBehaviour's SendMessage. The function argument can be of type float or string or an object reference. Any functions currently attached to the same GameObject as the animation clip that fit this definition can be called.

To illustrate, try adding a sample event to one of Widget's clips:

1. Open the Animation view and select Widget in the Hierarchy view. Select the new Widget_Idle clip from the drop-down list and move the red line to time 2:00.

2. Click the Add Event button (the one that looks like a small pointed line next to the Add Keyframe button) or right-click the red line and select Add Event from the menu that appears. (When right-clicking the red line, you must do so in the medium gray bar underneath the timeline.) This opens a dialog box from which you can select your function, as shown in Figure 8.7.

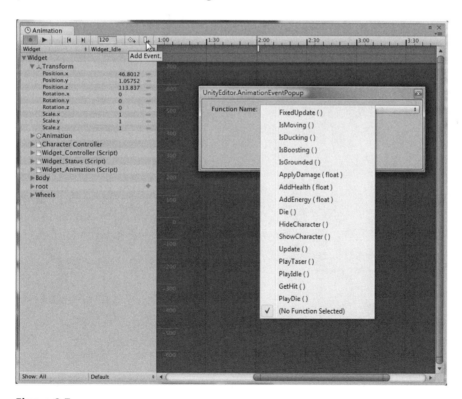

Figure 8.7
Widget's available functions to call from the event.
Source: Unity Technologies.

3. For now, select the `AddHealth( float )` function. Then type some number into the Parameters box, such as 10. Close the dialog box; then check to see that the Animation event works by playing the scene. Whenever the event is triggered, 10 health points are added to Widget, as indicated by the small print statement in the Console.

If you ever want to edit the event, you can click the event marker and drag it around the timeline. You can also select it and delete it, much in the same way as the keys. You can also change the event's function and parameter by clicking on the marker. Feel free to delete the event after you're satisfied it works and are comfortable with the workflow.

Widget is now fully controllable and animated. The world is his to explore! Next you need to give him something to actually do out there in the wild world with the introduction of triggers and enemies.

COMPLETED SCRIPTS

These can also be found on the accompanying website in the Chapter 8 folder but are included here for reference. Widget_Controller.js Update appears in Listing 8.1.

Listing 8.1   Widget_Controller.js Update

```
//Widget_Controller: Handles Widget's movement and player input

//Widget's movement variables-------------------------
//These can be changed in the Inspector
var rollSpeed = 6.0;
var fastRollSpeed = 2.0;
var jumpSpeed = 8.0;
var gravity = 20.0;
var rotateSpeed = 4.0;
var duckSpeed = .5;

//Private, helper variables--------------------------
private var moveDirection = Vector3.zero;
private var grounded : boolean = false;
private var moveHorz = 0.0;
private var normalHeight = 2.0;
private var duckHeight = 1.0;
private var rotateDirection = Vector3.zero;

private var isDucking : boolean = false;
private var isBoosting : boolean = false;

var isControllable : boolean = true;

//Cache controller so we only have to find it once-----
var controller : CharacterController ;
```

```
controller = GetComponent(CharacterController);
var widgetStatus : Widget_Status;
widgetStatus = GetComponent(Widget_Status);

//Move the controller during the fixed frame updates---
function FixedUpdate() {

        //Check to make sure the character is controllable and not dead
        if(!isControllable)
                Input.ResetInputAxes();

        else{
                if (grounded) {
                        //Since we're touching something solid, like the ground, allow movement
                        //Calculate movement directly from input axes
                        moveDirection = new Vector3(Input.GetAxis("Horizontal"),
0, Input.GetAxis("Vertical"));
                        moveDirection = transform.TransformDirection(moveDirection);
                        moveDirection *= rollSpeed;

                        //Find rotation based upon axes if need to turn
                        moveHorz = Input.GetAxis("Horizontal");
                        if (moveHorz > 0) //Right turn
                                rotateDirection = new Vector3(0, 1, 0);
                        else if (moveHorz < 0) //Left turn
                                rotateDirection = new Vector3(0, -1, 0);
                        else //Not turning
                                rotateDirection = new Vector3 (0, 0, 0);

                        //Jump controls
                        if (Input.GetButton ("Jump")) {
                                moveDirection.y = jumpSpeed;
                        }

                        //Apply any boosted speed
                        if(Input.GetButton("Boost")){
                                if(widgetStatus){
                                        if(widgetStatus.energy > 0)
                                        {
                                                moveDirection *= fastRollSpeed;
                                                widgetStatus.energy -=
widgetStatus.widgetBoostUsage *Time.deltaTime;
                                                isBoosting = true;
                                        }
                                }
                        }
```

```
                    //Duck the controller
                    if(Input.GetButton("Duck")){
                         controller.height = duckHeight;
                         controller.center.y = controller.height/2 + .25;
                         moveDirection *= duckSpeed;
                         isDucking = true;
                    }

                    if(Input.GetButtonUp("Duck")){
                         controller.height = normalHeight; //reset for after ducks
                         controller.center.y = controller.height/2;  //Re-center for
                         //after ducks
                         isDucking = false;
                    }

                    if(Input.GetButtonUp("Boost")){
                         isBoosting = false;
                    }

              }

         //Apply gravity to end Jump, enable falling, and make sure he's touching
         //the ground
         moveDirection.y -= gravity * Time.deltaTime;

         //Move and rotate the controller
         var flags = controller.Move(moveDirection * Time.deltaTime);
         controller.transform.Rotate(rotateDirection * Time.deltaTime, rotateSpeed);
         grounded = ((flags & CollisionFlags.CollidedBelow) != 0 );
              }
         }
//-----------------------------------------------------


function IsMoving(){

      return moveDirection.magnitude > 0.5;
}
function IsDucking(){

      return isDucking;
}
function IsBoosting(){

      return isBoosting;
}
```

```
function IsGrounded(){

      return grounded;

}
```

```
//Make the script easy to find
@script AddComponentMenu("Player/Widget'sController")
```

Widget_Animation.js appears in Listing 8.2.

Listing 8.2   Widget_Animation.js

```
//Widget_Animation: Animation Manager for Widget
//Controls layers, blends, and play cues for all imported animations

private var nextPlayIdle = 0.0;
var waitTime = 10.0;

var playerController: Widget_Controller;
playerController = GetComponent(Widget_Controller) ;

//Initialize and set up all imported animations with proper layers
function Start(){

//Set up layers--high numbers receive priority when blending
      animation["Widget_Idle"].layer = -1;
      animation["Idle"].layer = 0;

      //We want to make sure that the rolls are synced together
      animation["SlowRoll"].layer = 1;
      animation["FastRoll"].layer = 1;
      animation["Duck"].layer = 1;
      animation.SyncLayer(1);

      animation["Taser"].layer = 3;
      animation["Jump"].layer = 5;

      //These should take priority over all others
      animation["FallDown"].layer = 7;
      animation["GotHit"].layer = 8;
      animation["Die"].layer = 10;

      animation["Widget_Idle"].wrapMode = WrapMode.PingPong;
      animation["Duck"].wrapMode = WrapMode.Loop;
      animation["Jump"].wrapMode = WrapMode.ClampForever;
      animation["FallDown"].wrapMode = WrapMode.ClampForever;
```

```
        //Make sure nothing is playing by accident, then start with a default idle.
        animation.Stop();
        animation.Play("Idle");

}

//Check for which animation to play--------------------
function Update(){

        //On the ground animations
        if(playerController.IsGrounded()){

                animation.Blend("FallDown", 0, 0.2);
                animation.Blend("Jump", 0, 0.2);

                //If boosting
                if (playerController.IsBoosting())
                {
                        animation.CrossFade("FastRoll", 0.5);
                        nextPlayIdle = Time.time + waitTime;
                }

                else if(playerController.IsDucking()){

                        animation.CrossFade("Duck", 0.2);
                        nextPlayIdle = Time.time + waitTime;

                }
                //Fade in normal roll
                else if (playerController.IsMoving())
                {
                        animation.CrossFade("SlowRoll", 0.5);
                        nextPlayIdle = Time.time + waitTime;

                }
                //Fade out walk and run
                else
                {
                        animation.Blend("FastRoll", 0.0, 0.3);
                        animation.Blend("SlowRoll", 0.0, 0.3);
                        animation.Blend("Duck", 0.0, 0.3);
                        if(Time.time > nextPlayIdle){
                                nextPlayIdle= Time.time + waitTime;
                                PlayIdle();
                        }
                        else
                                animation.CrossFade("Widget_Idle", 0.2);

                }

        }
```

```
        //In air animations
        else{
                if(Input.GetButtonDown("Jump")){
                        animation.CrossFade("Jump");
                }
                if(!playerController.IsGrounded()){
                        animation.CrossFade("FallDown", 0.5);
                }
        }
        //Test for idle
        if(Input.anyKey){
                nextPlayIdle = Time.time + waitTime;
        }
}
//Other functions-----------------------------------
function PlayTaser(){
        animation.CrossFade("Taser", 0.2);
}
function PlayIdle(){
        animation.CrossFade("Idle", 0.2);
}
function GetHit(){
        animation.CrossFade("GotHit", 0.2);
}
function PlayDie(){
        animation.CrossFade("Die", 0.2);
}
@script AddComponentMenu("Player/Widget'AnimationManager")
```

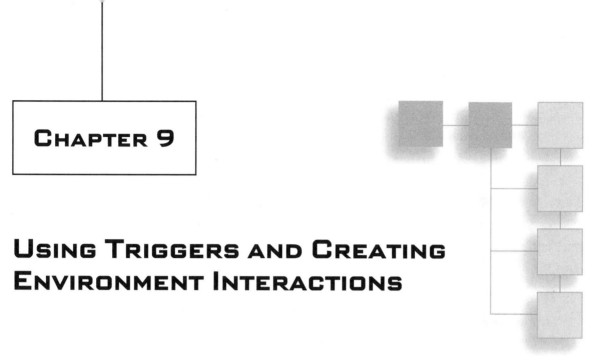

CHAPTER 9

USING TRIGGERS AND CREATING ENVIRONMENT INTERACTIONS

Triggers and other forms of environment interactions form an important part of environment and game design. They help create moving doors as well as pickup items, puzzles, traps, and all sorts of pieces not directly controlled by enemy artificial intelligence (AI). Setting up a trigger in Unity is as simple as setting up a collision mesh.

Triggers allow for an infinite number of possible events for your players to experience and explore. Your gameplay doesn't have to revolve around enemies and combative interactions; indeed, many successful games are solely based on unique and interesting environment puzzles and interactions. Learning to effectively use and manage triggers will open a whole new host of game design possibilities for you.

TRIGGERS AND COLLISION

In games, a *trigger* is basically anything that can be activated or tripped, which in turn sends some sort of message or starts an event. Triggers are generally invisible areas or volumes that enclose a given space, activating when the player either enters the space or performs a specific action while in the area (like pressing a button). Many activities that involve the player—such as opening a door or chest, starting an elevator lift, and picking up a dropped item—work because of triggers and their volumes.

All game engines define triggers and trigger volumes differently. In Unity, triggers are tied directly to GameObjects—you can't have one without the other. The GameObject's collision component (a box, sphere, mesh, and so on) is set to act as a trigger instead of a physics volume in the Inspector, thereby defining the space in which the player can interact. Whenever the player then collides with this GameObject's collision volume, the trigger can be activated via scripts. The GameObject itself can be invisible (that is, have no mesh renderer) and define a loose area, or it can depict a tangible object the player can see, like a door. Each has its own uses, and you have to set up your own triggers case by case. There isn't really any generality to draw from.

Setting Up a Basic Trigger Object

You've already had a bit of experience setting up collision components for GameObjects, and setting up a trigger volume isn't any more difficult. For your first trigger object, you'll set up a simple pickup item with which the Widget character can interact.

Follow these steps to create a simple pickup item:

1. Import the Pickup_Gear object and the Generic_Pickups texture from the Chapter 9 > Props folder into your game. (You can download the chapter material from the companion website.) If necessary, review Chapter 4, "Building Your Environment: Importing Basic Custom Assets," on importing assets. Ensure that the mesh is scaled correctly in the FBX Importer. Set it up with a new material called generic_pickups and give it a lighted outline toon shader.

2. Create a prefab of the object and name it Pickup_Gear. Drop this item somewhere near the Widget character in your latest scene file and ensure that the scale of the item is something big enough for you to comfortably work with. Your scene should look something like Figure 9.1.

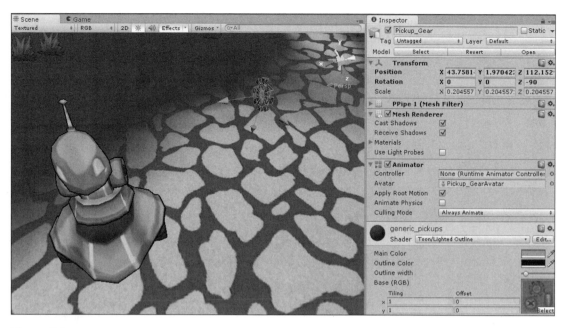

Figure 9.1
The newly imported and instanced gear prefab.
Source: Unity Technologies.

3. Give the gear a new sphere collider by highlighting the object and choosing Add Component > Physics > Sphere Collider. Change the Radius setting to something around 0.5 and make sure the sphere is centered at 0 for all three axes.

4. Above the Radius setting in the Sphere Collider component, select the Is Trigger checkbox. Voilà, instant trigger! The sphere collider will now act as a trigger volume instead of a physics one. If you try to run Widget into the gear now, he'll roll right through it. All physics collisions from the component are removed when you select the Is Trigger checkbox. You can always add a second physics component if you want the object in question to still have basic collision and serve as a trigger. Figure 9.2 shows the finished gear.

Figure 9.2
The gear trigger, with Widget demonstrating the lack of physics collision.
Source: Unity Technologies.

With the base item now finished, you need to indicate exactly what it is this pickup is going to do. In the game, Widget will be able to pick up gears and screws dropped by fallen enemy robots. When a certain number have been collected, he can spend them on new upgrades. This gear will form the basis of one of these pickups. For now, you'll work on making it act as a proper pickup item, and you'll learn about having an enemy drop it in Chapter 10, "Building Adversaries and AI."

Basically, you want Widget to be able to roll over one of these items on the ground and, in effect, pick it up, adding it to his in-game inventory (which you'll set up in a bit). The pickup item will then need to disappear after it's been dutifully catalogued in the inventory. To do this, you'll need to create a script to handle all the pickup functionality.

Make a new JavaScript script and name it PickupItems. Place it in the Scripts directory. This script will be a generic one to run all possible pickup items in the game, not just the gear. Because they all have the basic same functionality, it doesn't really matter to the system what the attached GameObject looks like. Also, feel free to delete the Update function—you'll use a new MonoBehaviour function this time around.

Start off by defining the few variables you'll need:

```
var itemType;
var itemAmount = 1;
private var pickedUp = false;
```

Because the script will be attached to all types of items in due time, you need to keep track of what type of item the particular one in question is, as well as how many there are. You could, for example, have a single GameObject be worth 10 gears and another one be worth only five. The private variable will track whether the item is currently picked up by the player in case of any buggy cases whereby the trigger tries to fire off more than once.

Now for the new behavior. Add the next line:

```
function OnTriggerEnter(collider: Collider){        }
```

This is another one of those special Unity functions that you don't have to ever call yourself. It's handled by the engine automatically whenever an object enters the trigger's defined volume area, hence the OnTriggerEnter and collider arguments. OnTriggerEnter will activate every time a collidable GameObject enters the trigger's defined collision volume, so you'll need to check to make sure it's Widget doing the picking up and not something else. For some games, this may be a desirable trait; for this one, not so much.

Add the following to the body of this function:

```
var playerStatus : Widget_Status = collider.GetComponent(Widget_Status);
if(playerStatus == null) return;
```

This code will test to see if the GameObject colliding with the trigger in question has the Widget_Status script attached to it. Because Widget is the only one who ever will have this component, you know it's safe to continue. If the GameObject doesn't have the Widget_Status script attached to it, the function will return, and the pickup will stay where it is.

Next, you need to add the safety check to make sure the trigger hasn't been called twice by accident and then add the item to Widget's inventory.

```
if(pickedUp) return;
//Everything's good, so put it in Widget's Inventory
/* Add Inventory Code Here! */
pickedUp = true;
```

Well, Widget's inventory doesn't exist quite yet, so you'll just make a placeholder reminder to come back to it later. Now the only thing remaining is to remove the pickup, as it's completed its task of rewarding Widget with a cool new item. This is an easy one-line solution:

```
Destroy(gameObject);
```

`Destroy` is a handy function that all GameObjects possess. It tells Unity to remove the instance of the passed GameObject from the scene. The keyword `gameObject` here automatically refers to the GameObject to which the script is attached. With that, your pickup will work! However, you should add one more safety mechanism just in case something goes wrong when the pickup is added to the scene. It would be incredibly frustrating to the player to have a ton of pickups spawn from a defeated enemy, only to be unusable. Outside the `OnTriggerEnter` function, add the following:

```
function Reset (){
        if (collider == null){
                gameObject.AddComponent(SphereCollider);
        }
        collider.isTrigger = true;
}
@script AddComponentMenu("Inventory/PickupItems")
```

This will ensure that the trigger always has some form of set trigger volume. The last line, of course, is the handy shortcut to allow easy attachment of scripts to prefabs. With that being said, attach this script to the gear prefab and try rolling Widget over it in the game. The gear disappears!

Gizmos for Sanity

For something singular like this, it's pretty easy to maneuver the player character over the indicated space and trigger the event in question. However, with more complicated or invisible trigger volumes, it can be incredibly difficult or tiresome to try to get the volume placed just so and the gameplay feeling just right. You could always switch between the Scene and Game views, selecting any finicky triggers one by one to see where their bounding areas lie. As you might think, however, this is also highly tiresome.

Thankfully, Unity gives you a better way: gizmos. Not only the term for the UI elements you use to move and rotate objects in the scene, *gizmo* is also the name for any small visual element you can place on the screen, usually for debugging or placement aids. Gizmos are created and drawn from their own class (aptly named the `Gizmo` class) and can be either basic wireframe pictures or custom icons and textures. Some main highlights of the Gizmo class follow:

- **Color:** A class variable that sets the color of the next drawn gizmo. You can either use one of the available color enums (like Color.Red) or specify an RGB value.

- **DrawWireSphere:** A function that draws a wireframe sphere with a given center location and radius.

- **DrawIcon:** A specified icon is drawn at the given location. If you want to use a custom icon, you need to place the icon file either in the Assets/Gizmos folder or the Unity/ Contents/Resources folder for the engine to be able to find it.

- **DrawGUITexture:** Similar to DrawIcon, you can draw a specified texture spanning the given set of coordinates. As well as for debugging, this particular function can be quite useful for drawing GUI backgrounds that you want to display all the time—for example, a player HUD.

You can place your gizmo in the OnDrawGizmos() or the OnDrawGizmosSelected function call, depending on what you're after. The former will render all the gizmos every frame, while the latter will only render a selected GameObject's gizmos. To set up a sample gizmo to view the radius of the gear pickup, add this block of code to the pickup's file:

```
function OnDrawGizmos(){
    Gizmos.color = Color.yellow; Gizmos.DrawWireSphere ( transform.position,
GetComponent(SphereCollider).radius);
}
```

This will draw a yellow wireframe sphere around the gear with the trigger volume's current radius. If you're having trouble viewing a particular item's boundaries, you can always add a similar piece of code to it.

Inventory Management

With the pickup finished and working, you need to create an inventory manager to allow Widget to actually store his newfound prize. You'll need some sort of object or array in which to store the available items and to keep track of what Widget has actually collected, variables to keep track of what each of these items does, and some helper functions to manage the addition and removal of items.

Make a new JavaScript file in the Scripts directory. Name it Widget_Inventory, and delete the Update function from it. To facilitate the creation of an easy-to-read inventory, you'll make a new `enum` type called `InventoryItem`. This will house all the available items in the game and can be easily expanded in the future. Add the following to the top of the file:

```
enum InventoryItem{
        DEBUG_ITEM,
        SCREW,
        NUT,
        BOSS_TRAY,
        BOSS_PLOWBLADE,
        BOSS_WINDBLADE,
        ENERGYPACK,
        REPAIRKIT,
        COUNT_NUM_ITEMS
}
```

`DEBUG` and `COUNT` aren't actually used in the game. As you might expect, `DEBUG` is used purely as a placeholder item (in case you need to try anything and don't want to mess with real items), and `COUNT` stores the number of the rest of the items in the list (it is always placed last in the list). Any new inventory values should be placed between `DEBUG` and `COUNT` so that `DEBUG` is always first (in slot 0) and `COUNT` is always last. You'll use the value of `COUNT` to create the inventory array.

Next, create the inventory and a link back to the player's state manager. Also add the variables describing the usage of two of the more common items:

```
var widgetInventory: int[] ;
var playerStatus: Widget_Status;
playerStatus = GetComponent(Widget_Status);
private var repairKitHealAmt = 5.0;
private var energyPackHealAmt = 5.0;
```

The array is of type `int`, because you'll just be storing the number of each kind of item Widget has available. You also need to define the amount of health and energy Widget can regain after using the two healing items: the repair kits and energy packs.

With the basic setup out of the way, you need to initialize Widget's inventory so it'll be ready to go at the start of the game.

```
function Start(){
        widgetInventory = new int[InventoryItem.COUNT_NUM_ITEMS];
        for (var item in widgetInventory){
                widgetInventory[item] = 0;
        }
```

```
//Give Widget some starting items
widgetInventory[InventoryItem.ENERGYPACK] = 1;
widgetInventory[InventoryItem.REPAIRKIT] = 2;
}
```

This is pretty straightforward. You initialize the inventory to be the same size as the number of available items and then iterate through each available item, setting them all to 0. This kind of `for` loop is an efficient and easy way to iterate through an array of this type. Using this method, you need not hard-code the exact size of the array using a real number like 5 or 7. Because of the `COUNT_NUM_ITEMS` variable, the inventory will always be initialized to the proper size, even if you add more items later.

The enum comes into play here and makes it easy to see and update Widget's inventory whenever you need to. No need to remember that energy packs are stored in array index 6—just use the enum's name to reference the item directly.

The only thing remaining now is to provide a few helper functions to give Widget the ability to add and remove items from his inventory:

```
function GetItem(item: InventoryItem, amount: int){
    widgetInventory[item] += amount;
}
function UseItem(item: InventoryItem, amount: int){
    if(widgetInventory[item] <= 0)
        return;
    widgetInventory[item] -= amount;
    switch(item){
    case InventoryItem.ENERGYPACK:
        playerStatus.AddEnergy(energyPackHealAmt);
        break;
    case InventoryItem.REPAIRKIT:
        playerStatus.AddHealth(repairKitHealAmt);
        break;
    }
}
```

The `GetItem` function is for the pickup items. An item of type `InventoryItem` is passed to the function, along with how many of it are picked up at once, and the proper amount is added to the inventory. The `UseItem` does just the opposite, checking to make sure Widget actually has the item in question in the first place. It then makes a call to the player's state manager if the item used was a healing one, updating Widget's energy or health in the process.

You'll add two more helper functions that will come in handy later when you need to start checking how many of an item Widget currently has:

```
function CompareItemCount(compItem: InventoryItem, compNumber: int){
    return widgetInventory[compItem] >= compNumber;
}
function GetItemCount(compItem: InventoryItem){
    return widgetInventory[compItem];
}
@script AddComponentMenu("Inventory/Widget's Inventory")
```

Attach this new script to the Widget prefab.

With Widget's inventory now created (albeit still invisible to the player), you just need to update the PickupItems script to actually add the new item to Widget's inventory. Open PickupItems.js for editing and make the following changes:

1. Change the `var itemType` declaration at the top of the file to `var item- Type : InventoryItem`. This will enable you to quickly pick a correct item type for each pickup from within the Inspector.

2. Add these couple of lines to the `OnTriggerEnter` function, after the `if (pickedUp) return` statement:

   ```
   var widgetInventory      = collider.GetComponent(Widget_Inventory);
   widgetInventory.GetItem(itemType, itemAmount);
   ```

   This will call the new helper function and add the pickup to Widget's inventory before it gets destroyed.

3. Update the gear pickup's PickupItems component and change the Item Type field to NUT. This will save the pickup into the correct inventory slot.

Save and try running the game again. If you have Widget selected in the Inspector and the Inventory script component expanded, you can watch the inventory update as Widget rolls over and collects the item. Any new pickup item can now be created with an instance of the PickupItems script, and Widget will dutifully add all the newly collected finds to his inventory array.

Setting Up Other Kinds of Triggers

Triggers can provide players with boundaries in the world and repercussions for their gameplay decisions. Being a robot, Widget has a natural fear and distrust of water, which will quickly short circuit all his wiring if he were ever to come in contact with it. A trigger placed on the water plane in the game level could easily handle the effects if such an unfortunate event were to occur. Triggers could then be used to craft checkpoints and spawn locations were Widget ever to need their use.

Death Triggers

Creating the death trigger is incredibly simple, as you already have most of the work done for you! The water plane already exists in the environment, and you've already written functions to apply damage to Widget and kill him if necessary (both in the Widget_Status.js file). Because you've been writing the code to be as generic and reusable as possible, creating these kind of one-off effects isn't too hard or time consuming.

To create a death trigger, follow these steps:

1. With the plane selected, add a box collider to the water plane. To do so, use the Component Physics Box Collider. If your plane already has a mesh collider attached, you will see a confirmation dialog box asking you to add or replace the collider. Select Add. Then select the Is Trigger checkbox on the component in the Inspector.

2. Resize the collider so that Size.y = 0.05.

3. Create a new JavaScript file in the Scripts directory and name it DamageTrigger. Delete the Update function and add these few lines:

```
var damage: float = 20.0;
var playerStatus : Widget_Status;
function OnTriggerEnter(){
       playerStatus = GameObject.FindWithTag("Player").GetComponent(Widget_Status);
       playerStatus.ApplyDamage(damage);
}
@script AddComponentMenu("Environment Props/DamageTrigger")
```

4. Attach this script to the water plane.

5. In the Inspector, ensure that Widget's tag value is set to Player. This field is located right beneath Widget's object name and right above the first Transform component. Using tags like "Player" can be an effective and fast way to find a specific object in the world.

That's it—short and sweet. The amount of damage can be changed in the Inspector, and this simple script can be attached to any kind of object to make it subtract health from Widget. Try rolling Widget into the water and watch his sad fate unfold.

Checkpoints: The Anti-Death Trigger

That's really no way for players to end their journeys and they should have the opportunity to restart from some earlier point in their adventures. This can easily be achieved through the use of another trigger object. In the game, Widget can activate a string of checkpoints to track his journey. If he dies, he can spawn at the last activated one. These checkpoints will also serve as the mechanism to enter the store, where Widget can sell screws and gears to buy repair kits and energy packs.

1. Start off by importing the new StationRobotRelay.fbx file from the Chapter 9 folder, found on the accompanying website. Import his texture (of the same name) and drop both of them in the Props folder. Create a prefab of this new object and name it Checkpoint. Make sure the Scale Factor setting is set to 1.

2. Drop one of these new checkpoint prefabs into the scene somewhere near Widget. Your scene should now look something like Figure 9.3.

Figure 9.3
The physical checkpoint added.
Source: Unity Technologies.

3. Give the checkpoint prefab a mesh collider (choose Component > Physics > Mesh Collider) and select the robot_station mesh from the drop-down list in the Mesh field.

4. Add a second capsule collider (click the Add Button on the pop-up dialog box that appears) and set this one to be a trigger. Set the Radius setting to 3, the Height setting to 2, and the Center.y setting to 2. This will place an invisible trigger volume around most of the checkpoint.

Now that the physical trigger object is set up, you need to plan how you want the checkpoints to work. Keep these points in mind:

- You'll need some sort of variable to keep track of which checkpoint is the last one selected by the player. While you only have one checkpoint right now, you want the ability to have multiple checkpoints spread out throughout a larger level.

- The checkpoint's trigger will need to be able to play some sort of effect when it becomes active or inactive, to give the player some visual feedback.

- The checkpoint should restore the player's health and energy to full whenever he enters the trigger area.

- The player's Die() function will need to be updated with the pertinent checkpoint information so Widget will know where to respawn.

All right, that doesn't sound too bad. To do this, you'll use static var for the first time. This will let you keep track of which checkpoint is the current one across any and all checkpoints in the level, since it's global.

Create a new JavaScript file and name it CheckPoint, placing it in the Scripts directory. Again, feel free to delete the Update function, as you won't need it. First, you should declare the variables you'll need:

```
static var isActivePt : CheckPoint;
var firstPt : CheckPoint;
var playerStatus : Widget_Status;
playerStatus = GameObject.FindWithTag("Player").GetComponent(Widget_Status);
```

The first two variables are defined as type CheckPoint, as you'll be attaching this script to only that kind of prefab object. The first variable will keep track of which checkpoint is the last selected, and the second will be used only for startup initialization. You'll also need the link to the player's state manager to update his health and energy.

Next, initialize the first checkpoint in the level on startup. You want something to be active immediately, or the player's death will be permanent.

```
function Start(){
     //Initialize first point
     isActivePt = firstPt;

     if(isActivePt == this){
          BeActive();
     }
}
```

You're using a new keyword here: this. It's a handy way to refer to the GameObject in question. Whenever Widget rolls over a checkpoint, it will reference its particular instance of the script, which will use this checkpoint as the new active point. BeActive() is a helper function you'll define to add in the visual feedback for the player.

Now you need to set up the actual trigger functionality:

```
function OnTriggerEnter(){
     //First turn off the old respawn point if this is a newly encountered one
     if(isActivePt != this){
          isActivePt.BeInactive();
          //Then set the new one isActivePt = this;
          BeActive();
     }
     playerStatus.AddHealth(playerStatus.maxHealth);
     playerStatus.AddEnergy(playerStatus.maxEnergy);
}
```

Again, you'll make use of the this keyword functionality. If the currently activated checkpoint isn't "this one," make it so. You'll also need to set the old active one inactive. Lastly, the player's stats are restored to maximum. The two helper functions will be defined now but not fleshed out until later in Chapter 13, "Using Particle Systems." Add the following to the bottom of the script:

```
function BeActive(){
     //Stuff here. . .
}
function BeInactive(){
     //Stuff here. . .
}
@script AddComponentMenu("Environment Props/CheckPt")
```

Hook this script up to the checkpoint prefab. You need to set up the first checkpoint variable now or the script won't function. Select the CheckPoint object in the Hierarchy view and drag it onto the First Pt field of the CheckPoint component in the Inspector. Later, you can make whatever checkpoint you want the first point, but for now this will work.

All that's left is to update Widget's status to handle the new checkpoint functionality. Now is also a perfect time to hook up his death animation, as you finally have a reason to use it. Open the Widget_Status.js file and update his `Die()` function to read as follows:

```
function Die(){
      print("dead!");
      playerController.isControllable = false;
      animationState = GetComponent(Widget_Animation);
      animationState.PlayDie();
      yield WaitForSeconds(animation["Die"].length -0.2);
      HideCharacter();
      yield WaitForSeconds(1);
      //Restart player at last respawn checkpoint and give max life
      if(CheckPoint.isActivePt){
            controller.transform.position = CheckPoint.isActivePt.transform.position;
            controller.transform.position.y += 0.5;
            //So not to get stuck in the platform itself
      }
      ShowCharacter();
      health = maxHealth;
}
```

First, this makes doubly sure that the player loses control of Widget the minute his health drops to 0. Next, you find the animation manager and call the `PlayDie()` function to set that clip running. You then ask the `Die()` function to yield as it plays—it wouldn't do any good to keep going with the respawn and not see any of the death animation. Widget is hidden briefly (as the script yields yet again) and is then respawned at the last available checkpoint. After Widget's position is moved to that of the checkpoint, he's made visible and controllable again and has his health reset to maximum.

Try the new chain of events by driving Widget into the water plane's death trigger and watch as he's happily brought back to life. See Figure 9.4.

Figure 9.4
Widget will be in need of that checkpoint now.
Source: Unity Technologies.

This chapter provided a good introduction to using triggers and chaining their effects together to create more complex gameplay experiences. With this knowledge alone, you can create many kinds of fun and meaningful interactions for your players. Play around with combining triggers and co-routines to create new kinds of interaction, such as scripted sequences, removable blockades, moving death traps, and floating health potions.

The only major piece of interaction you still need to create is the enemies—the other robots roaming the world who aren't too keen to share it with Widget. Chapter 10 covers basic AI, spawning, and combat.

COMPLETED SCRIPTS

The newly completed and updated scripts are available on the companion website. PickupItems.js appears in Listing 9.1.

Listing 9.1   PickupItems.js

```
//PickupItems: handles any items lying around the world that Widget can pick up
var itemType : InventoryItem;
var itemAmount = 1;
private var pickedUp = false;
//When Widget finds an item on the field--------------
```

```
function OnTriggerEnter(collider: Collider){
      //Make sure that this is a player hitting the item and not an enemy
      var playerStatus : Widget_Status = collider.GetComponent(Widget_Status);
      if(playerStatus == null) return;

      //Stop it from being picked up twice by accident
      if(pickedUp) return;

      //If everything's good, put it in Widget's inventory
      var widgetInventory = collider.GetComponent(Widget_Inventory);
      widgetInventory.GetItem(itemType, itemAmount);
      pickedUp = true;

      //Get rid of it now that it's in the inventory
      Destroy(gameObject);
}
// Make sure the pickup is set up properly with a collider
function Reset (){
      if (collider == null){
            gameObject.AddComponent(SphereCollider);
      }
      collider.isTrigger = true;
}
@script AddComponentMenu("Inventory/PickupItems")
```

Widget_Inventory.js appears in Listing 9.2.

Listing 9.2   Widget_Inventory.js

```
//Widget_Inventory: All of Widget's collected items are updated here
//Also handles functions for item use and inventory management
//All the items in the game available for the character to find
enum InventoryItem{
      DEBUG_ITEM,
      SCREW,
      NUT,
      BOSS_TRAY,
      BOSS_PLOWBLADE,
      BOSS_WINDBLADE,
      ENERGYPACK,
      REPAIRKIT,
      COUNT_NUM_ITEMS
}
//We'll use a statically sized BuiltIn array rather than a
//JavaScript array here.
var widgetInventory: int[];
```

```
var playerStatus: Widget_Status;
playerStatus = GetComponent(Widget_Status);

//Item Properties-------------------------------------
private var repairKitHealAmt = 5.0;
private var energyPackHealAmt = 5.0;

//Initialize Widget's starting Inventory--------------
function Start(){
      widgetInventory = new int[InventoryItem.COUNT_NUM_ITEMS];
      for (var item in widgetInventory){
            widgetInventory[item] = 0;
      }
      //Give Widget some starting items
      widgetInventory[InventoryItem.ENERGYPACK] = 1;
      widgetInventory[InventoryItem.REPAIRKIT] = 2;
}
//Inventory Management Functions----------------------
function GetItem(item: InventoryItem, amount: int){
      widgetInventory[item] += amount;
}
function UseItem(item: InventoryItem, amount: int){
      if(widgetInventory[item] <= 0) return;
      widgetInventory[item] -= amount;
      switch(item){
            case InventoryItem.ENERGYPACK:
                  playerStatus.AddEnergy(energyPackHealAmt);
                  break;
            case InventoryItem.REPAIRKIT:
                  playerStatus.AddHealth(repairKitHealAmt);
                  break;
      }
}
function CompareItemCount(compItem: InventoryItem, compNumber: int){
      return widgetInventory[compItem] >= compNumber;
}
function GetItemCount(compItem: InventoryItem){
      return widgetInventory[compItem];
}
@script AddComponentMenu("Inventory/Widget's Inventory")
```

DamageTrigger.js appears in Listing 9.3.

Listing 9.3   DamageTrigger.js

```
//DamageTrigger.js: A simple, variable damage trigger that can be
//applied to any kind of object.
//Change the damage amount in the Inspector.
var damage: float = 20.0;
var playerStatus : Widget_Status;
function OnTriggerEnter(){
     print("ow!");
     playerStatus = GameObject.FindWithTag("Player").
          GetComponent(Widget_Status);
     playerStatus.ApplyDamage(damage);
}
@script AddComponentMenu("Environment Props/DamageTrigger")
```

CheckPoint.js appears in Listing 9.4.

Listing 9.4   CheckPoint.js

```
//Checkpoint.js: checkpoints in the level--active for the
//last selected one and first for the initial one at startup
//the static declaration makes the isActivePt variable global
//across all instances of this script in the game.

static var isActivePt : CheckPoint;
var firstPt : CheckPoint;
var playerStatus : Widget_Status;
playerStatus = GameObject.FindWithTag("Player").GetComponent(Widget_Status);
function Start(){
     //Initialize first point
     isActivePt = firstPt;
     if(isActivePt == this){
          BeActive();
     }
}
//When the player encounters a point, this is called when the collision occurs
function OnTriggerEnter(){
     //First turn off the old respawn point if this is a newly encountered one
     if(isActivePt != this){
          isActivePt.BeInactive();
          //Then set the new one
          isActivePt = this;
          BeActive();
     }
```

```
        playerStatus.AddHealth(playerStatus.maxHealth);
        playerStatus.AddEnergy(playerStatus.maxEnergy);
        print("Player stepped on me");
}
//Calls all the FX and audio to make the triggered point "activate" visually
function BeActive(){
        //Stuff here. . .
}
//Calls all the FX and audio to make any old triggered point
//"inactivate" visually
function BeInactive(){
        //Stuff here. . .
}
@script AddComponentMenu("Environment Props/CheckPt")
```

Widget_Status.js appears in Listing 9.5.

Listing 9.5   Widget_Status.js

```
//Widget_Status: Handles Widget's state machine.
//Keep track of health, energy, and all the chunky stuff

//Vitals------------------------------------------------
var health: float = 10.0;
var maxHealth: float= 10.0;
var energy: float = 10.0;
var maxEnergy: float = 10.0;
var energyUsageForTransform: float = 3.0;
var widgetBoostUsage :float = 5.0;

//Cache controllers-----------------------------------
var playerController: Widget_Controller;
playerController = GetComponent(Widget_Controller) ;
var controller : CharacterController;
controller = GetComponent(CharacterController);

//Helper controller functions-------------------------
function ApplyDamage(damage: float){
        health -= damage;
        //Check health and call Die if need to
        if(health <= 0){
                health = 0; //For GUI
                Die();
        }
}
```

```
function AddHealth(boost: float){
      //Add health and set to min of (current health+boost) or health max
      health += boost;
      if(health >= maxHealth){
            health = maxHealth;
      }
      print("added health: " + health);
}
function AddEnergy(boost: float){
      //Add energy and set to min of (current energy + boost)
      //or energy maximum
      energy += boost;
      if(energy >= maxEnergy){
            energy = maxEnergy;
      }
      print("added energy: " + energy);
}
function Die(){
      print("dead!");
      playerController.isControllable = false;
      animationState = GetComponent(Widget_Animation);
      animationState.PlayDie();
      yield WaitForSeconds(animation["Die"].length -0.2);
      HideCharacter();
      yield WaitForSeconds(1);
      //Restart player at last respawn checkpoint and give max life
      if(CheckPoint.isActivePt){
            controller.transform.position = CheckPoint.isActivePt.transform.position;
            controller.transform.position.y += 0.5;
            //So not to get stuck in the platform itself
      }
      ShowCharacter();
      health = maxHealth;
}
function HideCharacter(){
      GameObject.Find("Body").GetComponent(SkinnedMeshRenderer).enabled = false;
      GameObject.Find("Wheels").GetComponent(SkinnedMeshRenderer).enabled = false;
      playerController.isControllable = false;
}
```

```
function ShowCharacter(){
     GameObject.Find("Body").GetComponent(SkinnedMeshRenderer).enabled = true;
     GameObject.Find("Wheels").GetComponent(SkinnedMeshRenderer).enabled = true;
     playerController.isControllable = true;
}
@script AddComponentMenu("Player/Widget'sStateManageer")
```

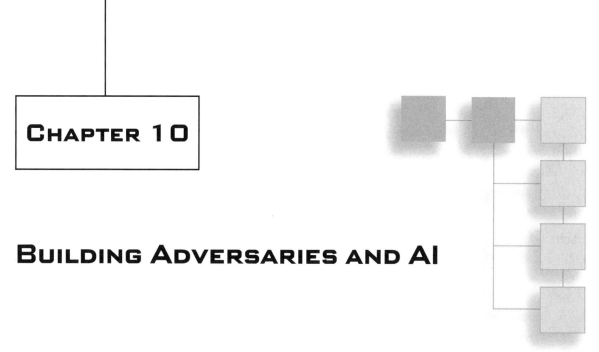

CHAPTER 10

BUILDING ADVERSARIES AND AI

Widget's travels would be a lot more interesting if he faced a band of rival robots, seeking to impede his progress through the level. Through the scripting of artificial intelligence (AI), props and lifeless characters can be given commands, routines, and goals, making them appear to be alive, thinking, and functioning.

Like many other aspects of game development, writing good AI routines is an art form unto itself and is a specialized field of study. Although it's pretty easy to give an enemy a list of commands to perform, it's much harder to make the player believe that the enemy is actively thinking and behaving in a manner that's just out to get him.

That said, it's still possible to write good, fun AI behaviors, even as a beginning game scripter. After you're finished with some basics, you can further your knowledge by checking out Appendix D, "Resources and References," for recommendations on further reading.

ARTIFICIAL INTELLIGENCE: DEFINITELY ARTIFICIAL, NOT MUCH INTELLIGENCE

Although games and game programmers refer to the realm of computer-driven adversaries as AI, the name is really at heart a misnomer, and it's important to recognize that from the very start. Modeling intelligence, or true "thinking" behaviors, in a computer is incredibly difficult and perhaps not completely possible. Instead, programmers create and script behaviors that dictate how the computer will interact with and react to stimuli around it.

Many different conditions and stimuli can play into a single AI's script, and the numerous behaviors are often prioritized to make it seem as if the computer is actually thinking about how it will respond to its given situation. An amount of randomness can be added into the mix as well to make it seem less computer like. But in the end, AI does not think; it only reacts. An AI's effectiveness, then, is only as good as its behaviors and conditions and how adept the programmer was at predicting what kinds of situations it would find itself in. When AI programmers say they're "teaching" the AI new tricks and abilities, they're really giving it new conditions and situations to respond to.

Players want different things at different times. In the early stages, players want an AI that teaches them how to play the game. In the middle stages, players want an AI that presents a good, entertaining challenge. And in the final stages, players want an AI that presents a strong challenge. Players don't mind losing occasionally, but when an AI has perfect aim or is allowed to cheat in obvious ways, the player may become frustrated or angry with your game.

One key to writing a good AI is to understand your game's mechanics from the inside out. Test and play your game often to see where possible exploits may lie, and look to see what paths or options players tend to pick most often. If you're not the best at playing your game, your AI probably won't be, either.

AIs come in many different shapes, sizes, and flavors—no game necessarily approaches them the same way. Some games may need complex creations, which need to be able to take the role of missing human players. Others may only need to follow a set of nodes around a map and patrol a set path, firing a weapon every couple of seconds. The complexity of your scripts and defined behaviors depends on the nature of your game. Don't try to force something more complex if it doesn't fit; on the other hand, don't oversimplify a problem so that players become bored with their opposition.

Some Simple AI Guidelines

Many tips and skills are learned as you go, but there are a few general pointers you should think about on your first foray into AI scripting:

- There is no one-size-fits-all AI script—no "easy" button, so to speak. Because each AI script is created to respond to given criteria and circumstances, each one needs to be individually made. Don't get sidetracked looking for an easy answer. Although there are tools to make generating AIs faster and easier, there is no "AI" button.

- You need to think about creating meaningful experiences for your players and not just worry about making some numerical quota of encounters. What can a particular AI provide for the character that another couldn't? Will the player take away something important?

- Pure randomness does not always lead to good things. Some randomness may be added to behaviors or numbers to make them seem more realistic to a player, as things in life rarely happen exactly the same every time. However, most players expect and want a particular distribution of randomness, usually something like a Gaussian or Poisson distribution. (Both of these are bell-shaped curves in statistics that allow for smooth variations within a range.) These kinds of distributions fit nature more readily than pure randomness does. Notice when you employ randomness in your code, and check to make sure you shouldn't be using a distribution of some kind instead. Players learn by recognizing patterns and repetition, and pure randomness is antithetical to this.

- The AI needs to provide an appropriate challenge level for the players, not play the best game it can. A computer can out-react a player in any given circumstance every time, and you should take care when planning exactly how good the AI actually is. Players want to feel like they have a chance of beating any AI in your game. Impossible AIs are not fun AIs, and your players will pick this up readily enough. Don't forget that AIs are there to be a fun challenge for the player, not an impossible hurdle. Constant iteration and testing are a must.

- Your goal should be to define a good AI system that makes your players feel clever and awesome about themselves. Don't baby your players by giving them only easy AI adversaries to defeat. Your AIs should ramp up and become more difficult as players gain more skills and experience in your game. If all the enemies in your game share the same AI patterns, players will quickly pick this up and then stop having fun with your game.

- Sometimes it's easier to make your AI better by giving it unfair advantages—more health, faster reflexes, better skills or attacks—rather than actually teaching it to behave in a "smarter" manner. Players almost always pick up on this and think of it as cheating—the game plays by different rules than they do. If used in moderation, this can be a good challenge for your players, but if the AI is constantly playing with a different rule set, your players will get frustrated.

With that in mind, you can begin to craft an effective AI. Your goal shouldn't be to make a system that always beats the players, but rather to craft a meaningful and fun experience that ramps up with your players.

A Simple Workflow

Starting off writing your first AI can be a bit daunting, but like with any problem, if you break it into smaller chunks, it'll be easier to approach and solve. Here are a few points to consider:

- Think critically think about what exactly it is you want your AI to do. Be as specific as possible. "Attack the player" isn't much of a behavior. What does it mean to attack? How will it know to attack? How should it attempt to attack? Will it need to move to the player or see him first? Try to think of all the steps and required conditions that make up your desired behavior.

- Implement your basic outline. If you were detailed enough, your plans from the previous bullet point will form the basic structure of your code. Flowcharts and other diagrams can help ensure all the paths are covered.

- Before trying to add more complex behavior or conditions, test your AI. Then test it some more. Trying to spot edge cases and unforeseen circumstances that your AI might find itself in isn't always easy or obvious, and testing is the only way to figure them out. Testing methods will depend on the system. It might mean navigating complex mazes of moving objects, filling an enclosed area with hundreds of AI avatars, or pitting AI against AI in thousands of automated competitions. Test early and often.

- After ensuring that your AI is performing as expected, sit back and question whether it is *fun*. While your AI functions may be designed or even behave realistically, it doesn't matter if the end result isn't fun for the players. Get some outside opinions, test some more, and teach away.

- If you need to implement more than one kind of AI script in your game (such as multiple enemies), make sure they are both different from each other and also recognizable by the players. Remember: Game design is heavily rooted in patterns, and you want your players to be able to learn your rules, not be continually dumbfounded at every turn.

SETTING UP A SIMPLE ENEMY

Widget's first enemy encounter will be a simple robot bunny, native to the hills where Widget roams. The AI for this enemy will be fairly straightforward and allow the player to get used to the controls without any real danger of dying. You don't want to scare players away from the game with presenting a challenge they can't handle from the offset.

Before you get to scripting, you need to get the assets set up in Unity and ready to go. Open your saved project and create a new scene. It will be easier to set up and test the enemy in his own simple environment rather than trying to do it all in the main game scene. With the content from the companion website ready, follow these steps:

1. Create a new scene in the project and place a basic plane GameObject into the world. Resize it so it provides ample space to run around on.

2. Import the contents of the Chapter 10 > Characters folder and place the pieces in their matching folders inside the project. Ensure that you keep the root directory the same so that the links to the prefab are not lost.

3. Change the Scale factor of the E_Bunny object to 1 if it isn't already. (E_Bunny is located under Materials > Meshes.)

4. Create a new prefab for the bunny character and populate it with this E_Bunny object.

5. Set up the provided material with the toon shader and assign the provided texture to it. Use the same steps as for setting up the Widget character.

6. Add an Animation component to the bunny prefab (Component > Miscellaneous > Animation) and change the Size setting of the animation's array in the Inspector to 3. The bunny enemy happens to have three animations she can play, based on what she is up to. Find the provided animation sequences in the Animation Clips folder and populate the elements with these clips. After attaching them to the character, you can play them back in the Animation view.

7. Because the bunny will need to interact with and move around the world, she'll also need a character controller. Add the component from the Component > Physics menu. Then change the height and radius of the collider to 0.65 and the center to (0,0.52,0). Your enemy bunny should look like the one in Figure 10.1.

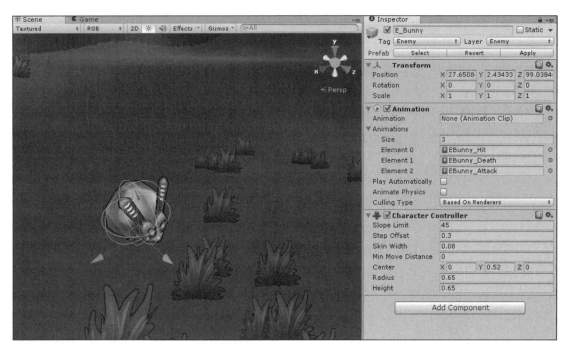

Figure 10.1
The preliminary "electronic bunny of doom."
Source: Unity Technologies.

The AI Controller

Now that your new enemy character is hooked up and ready to go, you'll need to define how you want her to behave. Simply put, you want the bunny to wander freely until she spots a player and then turn to hunt him down.

This doesn't lend itself very well to implementation. A more structured approach can yield better results. Often, breaking the behavior into a series of individual steps makes it easier to design, easier to code, and easier to test:

1. Slowly and randomly wander a small area.

2. If the character is within some set area bounds, face and head toward him.

3. If you collide with the character, attack. Then pause briefly to allow for a counterattack.

4. Move toward the character again if it is still within bounds and you can see him.

5. If not, try to find him.

6. If the character moves out of bounds, return to wandering.

7. If defeated, drop some random small items and disappear.

From this list, it will be much easier to implement the bunny's behaviors. Many of the conditions and criteria for her behaviors are already defined and laid out in a logical order. Much like the Widget character, the bunny will also need a controller class script to dictate how she will behave and move around and a state script to handle her health and state functions. Because you don't need to check for the player's input or actions, playing the proper animations for the bunny is a much more straightforward process and can be handled in the same script as the controller.

Make a new JavaScript file in the Scripts directory, name it EBunny_AIController, and delete the provided Update() function. As with Widget's controller, you'll need to start off with some variables to define how quickly the character can move:

```
var walkSpeed = 3.0;
var rotateSpeed = 30.0;
var attackSpeed = 8.0;
var attackRotateSpeed = 80.0;
```

The bunny will use one base walk and rotate speed for when she's wandering around aimlessly, and a faster, more pointed one for when she actually spots the player. Setting these kinds of variables as public will make iteration and testing time much quicker.

Next, you'll need some variables to define how the bunny aimlessly wanders around, as per condition 1, and set the distance for when the bunny can see the player, as per condition 2.

```
var directionTraveltime = 2.0;
var idleTime = 1.5;
var attackDistance = 15.0;
```

The first variable defines how often the bunny will change directions as she wanders.

Finally, you'll need to set up a few last variables for the bunny's attacks:

```
var damage = 1;
var viewAngle = 20.0;
var attackRadius = 2.5;
var attackTurnTime = 1.0;
var attackPosition = new Vector3 (0, 1, 0);
```

These variables define exactly where the attack is generated with respect to the bunny's position, how much of an area the bunny can hit with one attack, and how long it takes the bunny to complete each attack. You'll also set her base damage output here, to make it easy to change later.

The bunny will also need a few `private` variables to handle the switches between attacking, pausing, and changing direction:

```
private var isAttacking = false;
private var lastAttackTime = 0.0;
private var nextPauseTime = 0.0;
private var distanceToPlayer;
private var timeToNewDirection = 0.0;
```

You also need to define a target for the bunny to chase after and cache a reference to the bunny's controller:

```
var target : Transform;
//Cache the controller
private var characterController : CharacterController;
characterController = GetComponent(CharacterController);
```

With this in place, you're ready to start working on the script. Unlike the Widget controller, which needs to constantly look for and execute player commands every frame, the bunny doesn't really need this kind of overhead. Instead, this character will be performing a simple action repeatedly (wandering around) until certain criteria are met (finding the player, at which point the bunny attacks). These two actions, idling and attacking, encompass all of the bunny's behaviors and will simply switch between each. Rather than checking to see if the player is within reach of the bunny every frame, you can instead use the power of co-routines to have the bunny switch from one state to the other!

This simplifies the code quite a bit. Now you can set up everything in the `Start()` function and have the two main co-routines, `Idle()` and `Attack()`, handle everything.

Create a `Start()` function and begin to initialize the bunny's basics:

```
function Start ()
{
if (!target)
target = GameObject.FindWithTag("Player").transform;
}
```

Because you didn't specify a target earlier in the variable definition, you need to set one now. You also need to initialize and set up the animation information, much like for Widget. Within the Start() function and below the target setup, add the following:

```
animation.wrapMode = WrapMode.Loop;
animation["EBunny_Death"].wrapMode = WrapMode.Once;
animation["EBunny_Attack"].layer = 1;
animation["EBunny_Hit"].layer = 3;
animation["EBunny_Death"].layer = 5;
```

Because the bunny's animations weren't embedded in the FBX file, you need to make sure the wrap modes are correctly set up for all the available clips and then ensure that they reside in the proper layers for blending. The bunny's first and default behavior is Idle()—wandering aimlessly around the world. Create a new Idle() function in the EBunny_AIController file:

```
function Idle (){
    while (true) {
    }
}
```

Rather than call the Idle() function every frame with something like Update(), set it up to run a while loop an infinite number of times until some condition is met. This will make it easier to bounce to the second routine, Attack().

Inside the while loop, create the if statement that controls how often the bunny should change direction:

```
if(Time.time > timeToNewDirection)
{
    yield WaitForSeconds(idleTime);
    if(Random.value > 0.5) {
        transform.Rotate(Vector3(0,5,0), rotateSpeed);
    } else {
        transform.Rotate(Vector3(0,-5,0),rotateSpeed);
    }
    timeToNewDirection = Time.time + directionTraveltime;
}
```

First you check to see if the allotted amount of time wandering in one direction has been reached and, if it has, to look for a new direction to move. The bunny also takes this time to wait for a few idle seconds, giving the illusion she's "thinking" about where to go next.

After the bunny's direction has been set, she needs to start moving forward along that path. Still within the `while` loop and below the `if` statement, add the following:

```
var walkForward = transform.TransformDirection(Vector3.forward);
characterController.SimpleMove(walkForward * walkSpeed);
```

These two simple lines grab the bunny's current facing direction, forward, and cause her to move along that vector at her default walk speed.

If you tried to run this function as it stands now, the bunny would continue to wander for the entire game. You need to create the condition that pops the bunny's controller out of idle and allows her to continue into the attack. Right below the walk code, add the following:

```
distanceToPlayer = transform.position - target.position;
if (distanceToPlayer.magnitude < attackDistance)
        return;
yield;
```

Every loop iteration, the bunny checks to see how far away she is from the specified target. If this distance is smaller than her attack radius, the `Idle()` function returns and stops executing, allowing the bunny to move into her attack.

Create a new function named `Attack()` and add it below the `Idle()` function in the file.

```
function Attack (){
}
```

Because the `Attack` function will start only when the player is in range, you only need to check to see whether the bunny can "see" the player. If she can see the player, she should move toward him and attack. If she can't see the player, she should search until she can.

Set the bunny's `Attack` state to `True` and begin playing her animation. Within the `Attack()` function, add the following:

```
isAttacking = true;
animation.Play("EBunny_Attack");
```

Now set up the bunny for the attack by turning her toward the player and moving toward him:

```
var angle = 0.0;
var time       = 0.0;
var direction : Vector3;
while (angle > viewAngle || time < attackTurnTime){
}
```

You'll need to figure out what angle the bunny is actually facing in relation to the player to reset the variable angle. To do so, create a new function at the bottom of the file and name it FacePlayer(). Because you'll also use this function to rotate the bunny, give it two arguments: one for the player's current position and how fast you want the bunny to rotate while attacking.

```
function FacePlayer(targetLocation : Vector3, rotateSpeed : float) : float{
}
```

First, you need to figure out the relative angle between the player and the bunny. Using simple trigonometry, you can find the corresponding angle. Add the following within the FacePlayer() function:

```
var relativeLocation = transform.InverseTransformPoint(targetLocation);
var angle = Mathf.Atan2 (relativeLocation.x, relativeLocation.z) * Mathf.Rad2Deg;
```

Now knowing where the player is, you can turn the bunny to face toward him, clamping the speed down by the passed-in speed argument. Allowing the bunny to turn on a dime without clamping would not only be jarring to watch but also difficult to respond to.

```
var maxRotation = rotateSpeed * Time.deltaTime;
var clampedAngle = Mathf.Clamp(angle, -maxRotation, maxRotation);
transform.Rotate(0, clampedAngle, 0);
```

Now that the bunny is being rotated toward the player correctly, all you need to do is return her current angle for the Attack function to use later. Add the following code to the very bottom of the FacePlayer() function:

```
return angle;
```

With the helper function completed, you can return to working on the bunny's attack. Back within the while loop, set up the Attack() function:

```
time += Time.deltaTime;
angle = Mathf.Abs(FacePlayer(target.position, attackRotateSpeed));
move = Mathf.Clamp01((90 - angle) / 90);
animation["EBunny_Attack"].weight = animation["EBunny_Attack"].speed = move;
direction = transform.TransformDirection(Vector3.forward * attackSpeed * move);
characterController.SimpleMove(direction);
yield;
```

Depending on the bunny's angle, you adjust the attack animation's speed and blend weight and then begin to move the bunny toward the player at the increased attack speed. You need to also insert a yield statement because you'll be running this as a co-routine.

With the bunny moving toward the player, you need to ensure that you can in fact still see the target. After all, there's nothing to prevent the player from moving out of the way when he notices the bunny making a beeline straight for him. Create a new `while` loop beneath the one you just finished:

```
var lostSight = false;
while (!lostSight){
}
```

First, you need to make sure that the player is still within the bunny's eyesight range. Add the following within the `while` loop:

```
angle = FacePlayer(target.position, attackRotateSpeed);
if (Mathf.Abs(angle) > viewAngle) {
        lostSight = true;
}
if (lostSight) {
        break;
}
```

If your player's current relative angle is greater than the bunny's field of vision, the bunny will lose sight of the player. If this is the case, the bunny should bounce out of this loop and begin looking again. If the bunny hasn't in fact lost sight of the player, you need to check to see if she is within attack range. If the player is in fact so unlucky, the bunny will attack:

```
var location = transform.TransformPoint(attackPosition) - target.position;
if(Time.time > lastAttackTime + 1.0 && location.magnitude < attackRadius){
        //Deal damage
        target.SendMessage("ApplyDamage", damage);
        lastAttackTime = Time.time;
}
```

The `SendMessage` function calls the specified method—in this case, `ApplyDamage`—on the target object every time it is found. If multiple scripts have a function called `ApplyDamage()`, each one would be called in turn using `damage` as its argument. This can be a useful way to trigger multiple scripts on one GameObject—just ensure they share the same function declaration.

You'll also check to make sure the bunny can actually attack again. You want to give the player a second or so between each of the bunny's attacks, allowing him time to move out of the way. Otherwise, the bunny will bite the player every frame he's within range, which can quickly kill the player in a not-so-fun manner. Conversely, if the player *isn't* within the attack range, you need to break out of the loop and begin looking again. Within this while loop after the earlier statements, add the following:

```
if(location.magnitude > attackRadius){
    break;
}
//Check to make sure our current direction didn't
//collide us with something
if (characterController.velocity.magnitude < attackSpeed * 0.3){
    break;
}
yield;
```

Now is also a good time to make sure the bunny's sprint toward the player didn't cause her to collide with something she can't jump over, like a big rock.

One last thing to do to the Attack() function is to reset the bunny's Attack state to false, which would happen if the bunny lost sight and had to start looking again. Outside the while loop and at the very bottom of the Attack() function, reset her state:

```
isAttacking = false;
```

For ease of use, finish the script with the menu command at the bottom:

```
@script AddComponentMenu("Enemies/Bunny'sAIController")
```

Attach this finished controller script to the Bunny prefab. You can now run the test scene by dropping a Bunny prefab object and Widget onto the plane and watching as the bunny hunts Widget down, as shown in Figure 10.2. The bunny isn't quite finished yet, however. She still needs a state manager.

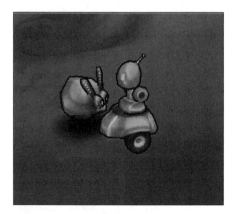

Figure 10.2
Widget meets an untimely end at the paws of the evil bunny.
Source: Unity Technologies.

A Simple State Manager for a Simple Bunny

Unlike Widget, the bunny doesn't have many things to keep track of—pretty much only her health. Create a new JavaScript file in the Scripts directory and name it EBunny_Status. Delete the Update function and give the bunny two simple variables:

```
var health: float = 10.0;
private var dead = false;
```

That's all she'll need for the moment. Like Widget, she'll need a function to handle any damage dealt to her and another to deal with her if she dies. Create a new function named ApplyDamage(). Note that you give it the same name as Widget's for a reason. If you were to have any environment-type damage, like from the water, you can send the ApplyDamage() message to any robotic target that steps foot into the trap, regardless of whether it's the player or an NPC. Add the following to the file:

```
function ApplyDamage(damage: float){
        if (health <= 0){
                return;
        }
        health -= damage;
        animation.Play("EBunny_Hit");
        if(!dead && health <= 0){
                health = 0;
                dead = true;
                Die();
        }
}
```

Whenever the bunny gets hit, she plays the proper animation. If the bunny's damage takes her health below 0, she dies. Now create her death handler:

```
function Die (){
        animation.Stop();
        animation.Play("EBunny_Death");
        Destroy(gameObject.GetComponent(EBunny_AIController));
        yield WaitForSeconds(animation["EBunny_Death"].length - 0.5);
        Destroy(gameObject);
}
@script AddComponentMenu("Enemies/Bunny'sStateManager")
```

First you stop all attack and hit animations; then you'll begin playing the death one. Then you'll remove the bunny's AI controller, preventing her from continuing any behaviors, wait the length of the death scene, and then finish the destroying process by removing her entire asset from the scene. Pretty straightforward. Attach the script to the Bunny prefab.

HOOKING UP WIDGET'S ATTACKS

Now that the enemy can move and attack, you need to make Widget able to defeat it in battle. Widget doesn't currently stand a chance, even against this tiny robot bunny, without some attack moves of his own. Widget starts life with a simple laser type attack, called taser. With it, he can blast any enemy within range, a sphere extending around him for two units on all sides.

Create a new script in the Scripts directory named Widget_AttackController and then add some simple attack-handling variables to the top:

```
var attackHitTime = 0.2;
var attackTime = 0.5;
var attackPosition = new Vector3 (0, 1, 0);
var attackRadius = 2.0;
var damage = 1.0;
```

These describe the basic details of how long it takes Widget to attack, how often he can attack, and where on his body the attack originates. He'll only need a few private variables to finish this off:

```
private var busy = false;
private var ourLocation;
private var enemies : GameObject[];
```

While the first two are self-explanatory, the enemy's array will hold the information for all objects within his attack range that can be declared as an enemy. Widget's attack is known as an area of effect, and you need to make sure that any and all enemies caught within its range take damage.

Because you'll be taking input from the player, you also need to cache Widget's controller to make sure any move is valid:

```
var controller : Widget_Controller;
controller = GetComponent(Widget_Controller);
```

Just like with Widget's base controller, you first need to determine if the player pressed the Attack button. Recall in Chapter 7, "Writing the Character and State Controller

Scripts," that you set up Widget's Attack input button, so calling it now is pretty easy. Within the provided `Update()` function, add the following:

```
if(!busy && Input.GetButtonDown ("Attack") && controller.IsGrounded() &&
!controller.IsMoving()){
     DidAttack();
     busy = true;
}
```

You allow the player to attack again only if Widget isn't busy—that is, if he's not currently attacking. The player must wait until Widget is finished with his current attack before attacking again. This loop calls the `DidAttack()` function, which you need to write now. Create a new function named `DidAttack()` and add it to the bottom of the file:

```
function DidAttack (){
}
```

First, you need to provide feedback to the player by starting the taser animation, letting the player know that his or her attack went through successfully. Inside this function, add the following:

```
animation.CrossFadeQueued("Taser", 0.1, QueueMode.PlayNow);
yield WaitForSeconds(attackHitTime);
```

Now you need to determine which enemies, if any, are within the attack radius. Unity came with a predefined `Player` tag, but you'll need to make a new tag for all the enemy robots to use.

Select the E_Bunny prefab in the Project view and navigate to its Tag field in the Inspector. This is right up at the top, underneath its name. Select Add Tag from the drop-down menu. This takes you to the Tags & Layers Manager, shown in Figure 10.3.

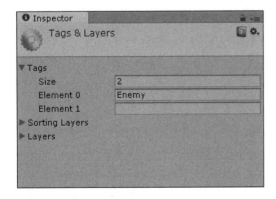

Figure 10.3
The Tags & Layers Manager.
Source: Unity Technologies.

Here you can define any number of tags you want to assign to GameObjects in your scene. To do so, change the Tags Size field to any number greater than 0 to populate the array with new elements. Double-click an element to rename it with the tag of your choice—for example, Enemy. Create a new Enemy tag and reselect the E_Bunny prefab from the Project view. Assign this new tag to the prefab.

With your enemy now tagged appropriately, you can easily search for it. Back in Widget's attack controller script, continue working in the DidAttack() function where you left off.

Add the following to the function:

```
ourLocation = transform.TransformPoint(attackPosition);
enemies = GameObject.FindGameObjectsWithTag("Enemy");
for (var enemy : GameObject in enemies){
    var enemyStatus = enemy.GetComponent(EBunny_Status);
    if (enemyStatus == null){
        continue;
    }
    if (Vector3.Distance(enemy.transform.position, ourLocation) < attackRadius){
        enemyStatus.ApplyDamage(damage);
    }
}
```

After populating the enemy's array with all the tagged objects in the scene, you search through them item by item to see if any one of the enemies is a bunny. If it is, you check to make sure that it is within range of the attack and then deal it the appropriate amount of damage.

The only thing remaining is to wait for the attack to finish and reset Widget's status to not busy, allowing the player to attack again when ready. Finish off the DidAttack() function with the following:

```
yield WaitForSeconds(attackTime - attackHitTime);
busy = false;
```

Add the component string to the bottom of the file and attach this script to Widget's prefab:

```
@script AddComponentMenu("Player/Widget's Attack Controller")
```

Test your hard work in the test scene and battle the nefarious rabbit.

REWARDING THE PLAYER FOR A JOB WELL DONE

You have only one thing left to do: Give the player a reward for his or her victory over the enemy! Recall in Chapter 9, "Using Triggers and Creating Environment Interactions," that you wrote a script to allow Widget to pick up items and place them in his inventory. Now you need to make enemies spawn and release items into the level upon their defeat, giving Widget a tangible reward to roll over and collect.

Reopen the EBunny_Status script file and add some new variables to the top:

```
var numHeldItemsMin = 1;
var numHeldItemsMax = 3;
var pickup1: GameObject;
var pickup2: GameObject;
```

Each bunny enemy can hold a range of items and can hold up to two items at once. These items will be set via the Inspector later.

Go to the Die() function and begin working before the last Destroy(GameObject) line. You basically want the bunny to fall over and finish her death animation, drop the pickups, and then finish disappearing.

At this location in the script, add the following:

```
var itemLocation = gameObject.transform.position;
yield WaitForSeconds(0.5);
var rewardItems = Random.Range(numHeldItemsMin, numHeldItemsMax);
for (var i = 0; i < rewardItems; i++){
        var randomItemLocation = itemLocation;
        randomItemLocation.x += Random.Range(-2, 2);
        randomItemLocation.y += 1; //Keep it off the ground
        randomItemLocation.z += Random.Range(-2, 2);
        if (Random.value > 0.5){
                Instantiate(pickup1, randomItemLocation, pickup1.transform.rotation);
        } else {
                Instantiate(pickup2, randomItemLocation, pickup2.transform.rotation);
}
```

First you should save the location of the bunny—you'll use this to assign the drop location of the new items. Then, after figuring out how many items you want to give the player, you figure out what each one will be—whether pickup1 or pickup2. Each of these items is then created near the bunny's final resting place. Save the script.

You already have one pickup ready from Chapter 9, the simple gear prefab. Here, you'll add another pickup to give Widget some variety:

1. From the Chapter 10 folder on the accompanying website, import the contents of the Props folder. Assign the Pickup_Screw.fbx object the same material and texture as the gear object.

2. Create a prefab for the screw using the same settings and information as the gear. (Refer to Chapter 9 if needed.)

Armed with two distinct pickups, fill in the variables in the EBunny_Status script component on the Bunny prefab with the Gear and Screw prefabs. Your Inspector view for the Bunny prefab should now look like Figure 10.4. Test your new script and collect your rewards!

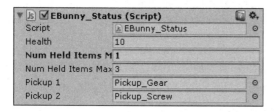

Figure 10.4
The pickups are ready to go.
Source: Unity Technologies.

SPAWNING AND OPTIMIZATION

You can add one more bit of functionality to the bunny enemy while also cutting back on some memory space for better game optimization. Right now, after your player kills the bunny, she drops her rewards and disappears. However, with the addition of a spawn point, you can have new bunnies appear and give Widget more adversaries to face. Using this point, you can at the same time remove these same enemies if Widget drops out of their radar, saving on unneeded space. There's no need to populate the scene full of enemies and objects if Widget can't even see them, so having enemies spawn only when needed can really help cut back on unneeded calls.

Create a new JavaScript file in the Scripts directory and name it Enemy_RespawnPoint. Give it some starting variables to function:

```
var spawnRange = 40.0;
var enemy: GameObject;
```

```
private var target : Transform;
private var currentEnemy : GameObject;
private var outsideRange = true;
private var distanceToPlayer;
```

You can now set the exact range of the particular spawn point and set which enemy you want to appear from within the Inspector. You also need to save information on your currently generated enemy, currentEnemy, to allow the point to spawn only one at a time. Otherwise, each frame that Widget is caught within the radius, a new enemy will appear.

Initialize the script with a simple Start() function, creating a link to the player:

```
function Start (){
        target = GameObject.FindWithTag("Player").transform;
}
```

Now within the provided Update() function, begin checking if the player has crossed the threshold of the spawn's radius of effect:

```
function Update (){
        distanceToPlayer = transform.position - target.position;
        if (distanceToPlayer.magnitude < spawnRange){
        }
}
```

If the player is in fact within the spawn point's range, you'll create a new enemy if one already doesn't exist. Add the following to the body of the if statement:

```
if (!currentEnemy){
        currentEnemy = Instantiate(enemy, transform.position, transform.rotation);
}
//The player is now inside the respawn's range
outsideRange = false;
```

As long as the player remains inside the spawn point's range, it will keep one enemy alive to patrol the area.

Create an else case within the Update() function to handle when the player does actually begin to move outside the spawn point's area:

```
else{
        if (currentEnemy) Destroy(currentEnemy);
}
outsideRange = true;
```

If an instantiated enemy does exist, remove it and reset the state of the spawn point to not create any others. Create the obligatory menu reference at the bottom of the file to find the script easily later on:

```
@script AddComponentMenu("Enemies/Respawn Point")
```

Now you just need to hook it up. Back in the test file, create a new empty GameObject by choosing Game Object > Create Empty. Rename this object Spawn Point and put it somewhere on the plane. Attach the Enemy_Respawn script to the point and assign the Enemy variable using the E_Bunny prefab. Test your scene and play with the spawn range until you get something you like. Try placing more than one spawn point around the level so you can see how the effect of multiple enemies can change the difficulty.

You can now use your new enemy and enemy spawner in any of your scene files, giving Widget some new gameplay options.

In the next few chapters, you'll hook the remaining important bits for gameplay—namely the user interface (UI) and some particle effects—thus making the player's interactions with props and enemies in the world more fun.

COMPLETED SCRIPTS

The newly completed scripts are also available on the accompanying website in the Chapter 10 folder. EBunny_AIController.js appears in Listing 10.1.

Listing 10.1   EBunny_AIController.js

```
//EBunny_AIController: Handles the electronic bunny's AI and animations
//Because we don't need to be checking for the player's input or
//actions, playing the proper animations is much more
//straightforward and can be handled in the same script.
//-------------------------------------------------------
var walkSpeed = 3.0;
var rotateSpeed = 30.0;
var attackSpeed = 8.0;
var attackRotateSpeed = 80.0;

var directionTraveltime = 2.0;
var idleTime = 1.5;
var attackDistance = 15.0;

var damage = 1;
var attackRadius = 2.5;
var viewAngle = 20.0;
```

```
var attackTurnTime = 1.0;
var attackPosition = new Vector3 (0, 1, 0);

//-----------------------------------------------------
private var isAttacking = false;
private var lastAttackTime = 0.0;
private var nextPauseTime = 0.0;
private var distanceToPlayer;
private var timeToNewDirection = 0.0;
var target : Transform;

//Cache the controller
private var characterController : CharacterController;
characterController = GetComponent(CharacterController);

//-----------------------------------------------------
function Start (){
      if (!target)
            target = GameObject.FindWithTag("Player").transform;

      //Set up animations----------------------------
      animation.wrapMode = WrapMode.Loop;
      animation["EBunny_Death"].wrapMode = WrapMode.Once;
      animation["EBunny_Attack"].layer = 1;
      animation["EBunny_Hit"].layer = 3;
      animation["EBunny_Death"].layer = 5;
      yield WaitForSeconds(idleTime);
      while (true){
            //Idle around and wait for the player
            yield Idle();
            //Player has been located, prepare for the attack
            yield Attack();
      }
}
function Idle (){
      //Walk around and pause in random directions
      while (true){
            //Find a new direction to move
            if(Time.time > timeToNewDirection){
                  yield WaitForSeconds(idleTime);
                  var RandomDirection = Random.value;
                  if(Random.value > 0.5)
                        transform.Rotate(Vector3(0,5,0), rotateSpeed);
```

```
                  else
                        transform.Rotate(Vector3(0,-5,0),rotateSpeed);
                  timeToNewDirection = Time.time + directionTraveltime;
            }

            var walkForward = transform.TransformDirection(Vector3.forward);
            characterController.SimpleMove(walkForward * walkSpeed);
            distanceToPlayer = transform.position - target.position;

            //We found the player! Stop wasting time and go after him
            if (distanceToPlayer.magnitude < attackDistance)
                  return;
            yield;
      }
}
function Attack (){
      isAttacking = true;
      animation.Play("EBunny_Attack");
      //We need to turn to face the player now that
      //the bunny is in range
      var angle = 0.0;
      var time = 0.0;
      var direction : Vector3;
      while (angle > viewAngle || time < attackTurnTime){
            time += Time.deltaTime;
            angle = Mathf.Abs(FacePlayer(target.position, attackRotateSpeed));
            move = Mathf.Clamp01((90 - angle) / 90);
            //Depending on the angle, start moving
            animation["EBunny_Attack"].weight =
animation["EBunny_Attack"].speed = move;
            direction = transform.TransformDirection(Vector3.forward *
 attackSpeed * move);
            characterController.SimpleMove(direction);
            yield;
      }
      //Attack if bunny can see player
      var lostSight = false;
      while (!lostSight){
            angle = FacePlayer(target.position, attackRotateSpeed);
            //Check to ensure that the target is within the bunny's eyesight
            if (Mathf.Abs(angle) > viewAngle)
                  lostSight = true;
```

```
            //If bunny loses sight of the player, she jumps out of here
            if (lostSight)
                break;
            //Check to see if bunny is close enough to the
            //player to bite him.
            var location = transform.TransformPoint(attackPosition) - target.position;
            if(Time.time > lastAttackTime + 1.0 && location.magnitude < attackRadius){
                //Deal damage
                target.SendMessage("ApplyDamage", damage);
                lastAttackTime = Time.time;
            }
            if(location.magnitude > attackRadius)
                break;
            //Check to make sure our current dir didn't
            //collide us with something
            if (characterController.velocity.magnitude < attackSpeed * 0.3)
                break;
            //Yield for one frame
            yield;
        }
        isAttacking = false;
}
function FacePlayer(targetLocation : Vector3, rotateSpeed : float) : float{
        //Find the relative place in the world where the player is located
        var relativeLocation = transform.InverseTransformPoint(targetLocation);
        var angle = Mathf.Atan2 (relativeLocation.x, relativeLocation.z) * Mathf.Rad2Deg;
        //Clamp it with the max rotation speed so bunny doesn't move too fast
        var maxRotation = rotateSpeed * Time.deltaTime;
        var clampedAngle = Mathf.Clamp(angle, -maxRotation, maxRotation);
        //Rotate
        transform.Rotate(0, clampedAngle, 0);
        //Return the current angle
        return angle;
}
@script AddComponentMenu("Enemies/Bunny'sAIController")
```

EBunny_Status.js appears in Listing 10.2.

Listing 10.2   EBunny_Status.js

```
//EBunny_Status: Controls the state information of the enemy bunny

//--------------------------------------------------
var health: float = 10.0;
private var dead = false;
```

```
//Pickup items held----------------------------------
var numHeldItemsMin = 1;
var numHeldItemsMax = 3;
var pickup1: GameObject;
var pickup2: GameObject;

//State functions----------------------------------
function ApplyDamage(damage: float){
      if (health <= 0)
            return;
      health -= damage;
      animation.Play("EBunny_Hit");
      //Check health and call Die if need to
      if(!dead && health <= 0){
            health = 0; //for GUI
            dead = true;
            Die();
      }
}
 function Die (){
      animation.Stop();
      animation.Play("EBunny_Death");
      Destroy(gameObject.GetComponent(EBunny_AIController));
      yield WaitForSeconds(animation["EBunny_Death"].length - 0.5);

      //Cache location of dead body for pickups
      var itemLocation = gameObject.transform.position;
      //Drop a random number of reward pickups for the player
      yield WaitForSeconds(0.5);
      var rewardItems = Random.Range(numHeldItemsMin, numHeldItemsMax);
      for (var i = 0; i < rewardItems; i++){
            var randomItemLocation = itemLocation;
            randomItemLocation.x += Random.Range(-2, 2);
            randomItemLocation.y += 1; // Keep it off the ground
            randomItemLocation.z += Random.Range(-2, 2);
            if (Random.value > 0.5)
                  Instantiate(pickup1, randomItemLocation,
pickup1.transform.rotation);
            else
                  Instantiate(pickup2, randomItemLocation,
pickup2.transform.rotation);
      }
```

```
        //Remove killed enemy from the scene
        Destroy(gameObject);
}
function IsDead() : boolean{
        return dead;
}
@script AddComponentMenu("Enemies/Bunny'sStateManager")
```

Widget_AttackController.js appears in Listing 10.3.

Listing 10.3 Widget_AttackController.js

```
//Widget_AttackController: Handles the player's attack
//input and deals damage to the targeted enemy

//------------------------------------------------------
var attackHitTime = 0.2;
var attackTime = 0.5;
var attackPosition = new Vector3 (0, 1, 0);
var attackRadius = 2.0;
var damage= 1.0;

//------------------------------------------------------
private var busy = false;
private var ourLocation;
private var enemies : GameObject[] ;
var controller : Widget_Controller;
controller = GetComponent(Widget_Controller);

//Allow the player to attack if he is not busy
//and the Attack button was pressed
function Update (){
        if(!busy && Input.GetButtonDown ("Attack") && controller.IsGrounded()
&& !controller.IsMoving()){
            DidAttack();
            busy = true;
        }
}
function DidAttack (){
        //Play the animation regardless of whether we hit something or not
        animation.CrossFadeQueued("Taser", 0.1, QueueMode.PlayNow);
        yield WaitForSeconds(attackHitTime);
        ourLocation = transform.TransformPoint(attackPosition);
        enemies = GameObject.FindGameObjectsWithTag("Enemy");
```

```
        //See if any enemies are within range of the attack
        //This will hit all in range
        for (var enemy : GameObject in enemies){
                var enemyStatus = enemy.GetComponent(EBunny_Status);
                if (enemyStatus == null){
                        continue;
                }
                if (Vector3.Distance(enemy.transform.position, ourLocation)
< attackRadius){
                        enemyStatus.ApplyDamage(damage);
                }
        }
        yield WaitForSeconds(attackTime - attackHitTime);
        busy = false;
}

@script AddComponentMenu("Player/Widget's Attack Controller")
```

Enemy_RespawnPoint.js appears in Listing 10.4.

Listing 10.4   Enemy_RespawnPoint.js

```
//Enemy_RespawnPoint: Attach to a game object in the scene to serve
//as a respawn point for enemies. When the player walks into the
//specified area, a new enemy will respawn.

//-------------------------------------------------------
var spawnRange = 40.0;
var enemy: GameObject;
private var target : Transform;
private var currentEnemy : GameObject;
private var outsideRange = true;
private var distanceToPlayer;

//-------------------------------------------------------
function Start (){
      target = GameObject.FindWithTag("Player").transform;
}
function Update (){
      distanceToPlayer = transform.position - target.position;
      // check to see if player encounters the respawn point.
      if (distanceToPlayer.magnitude < spawnRange){
              if (!currentEnemy){
                      currentEnemy = Instantiate(enemy, transform.position,
transform.rotation);
              }
```

```
                //The player is now inside the respawn's range
                outsideRange = false;
        }
        //Player is moving out of range, so get rid of the
        //unnecessary enemy now
        else
        {
                if (currentEnemy)
                        Destroy(currentEnemy);
        }
        outsideRange = true;
}

@script AddComponentMenu("Enemies/Respawn Point")
```

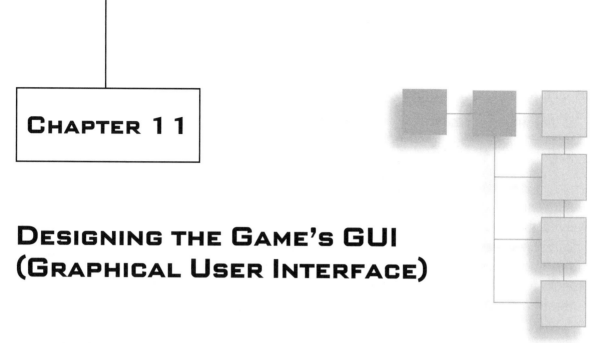

CHAPTER 11

DESIGNING THE GAME'S GUI (GRAPHICAL USER INTERFACE)

A graphical user interface (GUI) can be one of the most time-consuming and most-iterated systems in your game. Although it may look like a simple collection of images and text arranged prettily on the screen, good, usable, attractive, efficient, and friendly GUIs aren't just stumbled upon after one quick sketch or two. Not only does the GUI need to provide players with all the bits of pertinent information they need at any time, it also needs to fit within the game's artistic vision, not clutter up the screen, and be easy enough for anyone to use without instruction.

GUIs are the gateway to your game. A difficult, hard-to-use GUI will stop players in their tracks and make some stop playing altogether. It doesn't matter how great the gameplay is—if the GUI sucks, the game sucks. A well-designed GUI will often fade away into the background because the player doesn't need to pay any attention to the interface, just the game itself. A good GUI is an open pathway leading to your gameplay, not a stumbling block the player has to master first.

BASIC INTERFACE THEORY

One of the first things to understand before you start designing your own GUI is how people interact with computers. Sure, you've used hundreds if not thousands of different computer interfaces, but knowing how to use one doesn't necessarily give you the right information on how to start designing one.

Steps of Interaction

Human-computer interaction can be broken into three basic steps:

1. Forming a goal

2. Executing an action

3. Evaluating the action

Before users click anything in an interface, they first determine what they want to achieve. Maybe they want to open a menu or use an item. After deciding what they want to accomplish, they then have to abstract that goal into something the system can understand and provide. Perhaps the user sees a button on the screen that's labeled "Main Menu," providing her with the necessary information to deduce that perhaps clicking this button can help her achieve her goal. Once an intention of using the system is formed, the user executes her action—in this case, clicking the menu button.

Now she needs to evaluate her action and determine if she has reached her goal. This is where timely and descriptive feedback is vitally necessary. The user doesn't know, nor *can* she know, how the underlying menu system works or is written. The only way she can glean any information is from the system updating itself and providing her with some sort of feedback for her action. With the button click, this could be a new menu screen opening or a tooltip describing what she did. Without feedback, the user wouldn't ever know if the button she clicked did anything, if the button was perhaps disabled because of some random state, or the button was activated too quickly for her to notice. Feedback is what helps teach the users how to understand your GUI—and through it, your game.

Designing for Your Users

With this in mind, your first thoughts when you start laying out an interface should be, "What do users need to do?" or "What do users think they need to do?" As the designer, you have a pretty good handle on all the different functions and mechanics that the user could run across, but you need to be able to take a step back and think from a user's perspective. Consider these main rules:

- **Don't throw all the information at your users at once.** Rather, think of what they would want to know or need to know.

- **Be consistent.** Users learn by doing, and you want to help that process along as much as possible. Pick a style for buttons, labels, and anything else with which users will interact and stick with it. Nothing is more frustrating than seeing a style used for an interactive button on one screen and then finding it used again on another as a static label. Users recognize available functionality as much from visual art cues as from text.

- **Use the standards and paradigms your users are familiar with.** There's no need to reinvent the wheel for some basic principles. For example, most Windows users are comfortable seeing the Minimize, Maximize, and Close buttons for their applications on the top-right corner of the window. Sure, you could move those buttons wherever you wanted, but you'd only end up confusing and irritating your users for no real gain. If there's a standard interface option that your user base will be aware of, make sure you're not willfully ignoring it.

- **Make feedback quick and meaningful.** Feedback that is too late is just as bad as no feedback at all. GUIs need to be responsive, optimized, and descriptive. Users learn from the causality chain of "perform action, get response." If the response is late coming, users might not always pair it correctly with their previous action.

- **Be clear about the current state of the system.** If the game is paused, make sure there's a pause screen up that obscures the rest of the field of play so there's no way to miss it. If the user's character is dead, make sure that it's obvious visually. Don't just disable the controls.

- **Be mindful of your users' movements.** It may look nice to ring the screen with lots of different buttons, but be aware of what that means for the users. Especially for faster-paced games, users want to make quick mouse or controller movements; they don't want to have to scroll all the way across the screen and back again to perform a simple action. If there are multiple buttons or controls that users can interact with in a short span of time, try to group them closer together so your screen is easier to navigate.

- **Above all, test early and test often.** A successful GUI is developed with the game from the very beginning. Trying to slap a GUI onto a mostly finished game will lead to a poor GUI that lacks deep integration with the systems and isn't part of the cohesive whole. Grab a friend who's unfamiliar with your game and watch him try to play without helping him along. If he can figure out your interface by himself, you're doing something right. If he needs to ask for help or clarification about anything, make a note and address those issues as you develop. Professional developers have their GUIs studied by designers, producers, art directors, full-time test teams, and normal folk brought in from the street for usability testing. An interface that seems intuitive to you may be confusing to someone else.

UNITY'S GUI SYSTEM

Unlike other event-driven GUI systems you may already be familiar with, Unity's GUI system is based on an immediate mode model. Instead of driving the interface with a series of messages like OnMouseHover or OnClick combined with art objects placed on a screen, a single interface element is drawn and declared in one step:

```
function OnGUI(){
    if( GUI.Button( Rect( 10, 10, 320, 80), "Quit Game")) ){
        Application.Quit();
    }
}
```

The function OnGUI() works similarly to the Update() function. It is called at least twice every game frame: once to draw the GUI elements on the screen and then at least one more time to process any user input. In this example, a new button is drawn at the screen position (10,10) with a width of 320 pixels and a height of 80. The words "Quit Game" are displayed on the button. When the button is clicked, the GUI.Button() function returns True, fulfilling the condition of the if statement, which then closes the current game.

Note

Any GUI element you want drawn to the screen *must* be called within the OnGUI() function to appear correctly. Calling it outside the function will probably result in the element being drawn somewhere unexpected or with an incorrect scale.

Caution

The OnGUI() function is called at least twice every *frame*. This is different from being called every *update*. Recall that your game update rate and the graphics frame rate are independent. This allows you to have visually smooth GUI elements that respond quickly to input, but it can become a performance concern. If you want to do advanced processing instead of simple controls like buttons and sliders, consider creating scripted game objects that are attached relative to the camera.

All of Unity's GUI controls follow this basic idea of evaluating the return Boolean of any given GUI interaction. The controls themselves are another basic pattern: control type (screen position, control content). The type declares what kind of control you want, like a button, slider, box, and so on; the screen position specifies in pixels where the control is to be displayed; and the content handles the actual visual display of the control.

Unity provides a range of prebuilt basic controls, but you can define your own custom controls using this simple process. You can follow along with the overview of the basic controls by navigating to the Chapter 11 folder of the accompanying material and opening the Chapter11_Test scene in the GUI Test folder.

Buttons

The first kind of control most people think of when asked about interfaces is the simple button. When users click the button, the button returns True, and some piece of code is executed.

```
if( GUI.Button(Rect(10, 10, 100, 40), "I'm a Button" )){
    print("You clicked the button.");
}
```

Regardless of how long the button is held down, the action executes only once, when the user finally releases the button. Besides simple text phrases, buttons can also take images and other complex content forms as arguments, allowing you to create skinned buttons with tooltips and other advanced functionality. Custom buttons like this are covered later in this chapter.

The Rect() function defines a rectangular space that the button uses for its display, following this pattern: (left X corner, left Y corner, total width, total height). This sample button is defined at the space (10,10) and is 100 pixels wide by 40 pixels tall. The Rect() function is used for all kinds of GUI controls.

A button can also be formatted as a RepeatButton(), which will continuously fire as long as the user holds it down. Declaring and using a RepeatButton() is done exactly like a normal button:

```
if( GUI.RepeatButton(Rect(10, 60, 200, 40), "I'm a Repeat Button" )) {
    number = Time.deltaTime + number;
    print("You clicked the button for " + number + " seconds.");
}
```

These kinds of buttons are useful for power-ups or anything else that the users need to time.

Sliders

Sliders are another popular form of basic control, and Unity provides you with a basic horizontal and vertical option. The current position of the slider knob is returned from the function as a float, allowing users to click and drag it to a new location.

```
slidervalue = GUI.HorizontalSlider( Rect(10, 110, 200, 40),
slidervalue, 0.0, 100.0);
```

```
slidervalue = GUI.VerticalSlider ( Rect(240, 60, 200, 60),
slidervalue, 0.0, 100.0);
print("Slider value: " + slidervalue);
```

By setting the current value of the slider as the return value, the slider becomes interactive. If you didn't save the return value of either slider function, the user wouldn't be able to drag the slider around, making it more of a display than an interaction object.

Labels and Boxes

Besides these basic interactive controls, Unity also defines a set of basic labels and boxes, making it easy to group and manage your different GUI fields. Labels are your most basic form of display, allowing you to show a line of text or a simple texture anywhere on the screen. Labels have no form of interaction and do not catch mouse clicks.

```
GUI.Label( Rect(10, 150, 200, 40), "I'm a simple label.");
```

To display a label with an image instead of text, simply replace the second argument with a link to a texture instead of providing a string.

A box is similar in nature to a label, but is used when you want to provide a bit more visual information for the players. The box is drawn with a default texture background and the string is applied, much like the label.

```
GUI.Box( Rect(10, 200, 200, 40), "I'm a simple box.");
```

Boxes can also display textures, but are still static and shouldn't be confused with buttons. You can also stack boxes beneath buttons to make a defined button group, complete with a title label.

Text Entry

Sometimes you may want to capture user text input, like storing a custom name for a character. If the text to be entered is relatively short, you can use a one-line text field for the job. If you think users will need a bit of space to type (say, for a journal entry), use a text area instead.

```
shortText = GUI.TextField( Rect(10, 250, 200, 40), shortText);
longText = GUI.TextArea( Rect(10, 300, 200, 100), longText);
```

Text fields allow only one line of text, whereas text areas allow the users to enter newline carriage returns. Both types of text fields support copy and paste functionality. Much like the sliders, you need to return and save the string if you want the control to be interactive.

You can also specify a maximum string length for both kinds of text entries by adding an optional third integer argument to the text function:

```
shortText = GUI.TextField( Rect(10, 400, 200, 40), shortText, 40);
```

Unity will stop the users from entering any new text once the character length has been reached.

Toggle

While looking like a radio button, the Unity toggle functions like a Boolean checkbox: click once to set it to true, and click again to set to false. The current status of the toggle is returned from the function and should be captured to make the control function.

```
toggleState = GUI.Toggle( Rect(10, 400, 200, 40), toggleState, "I'm a Toggle/Checkbox");
```

Clicking on either the box or phrase will activate the toggle.

Toolbars and Selection Grids

Toolbars and selection grids are Unity's answer to radio buttons. These compound controls allow users to choose between one of many states but only keep one active at any given time. A toolbar encapsulates a single row of options, whereas a selection grid allows you to create a matrix of options. A toolbar control is created with an array of either string or image variables, with each index of the array corresponding to a new button on the toolbar. The control's function returns the index of the selected button, which must be captured and stored for use.

```
var toolBarState = 0;
var toolBarLabels : String [] = ["Button 1", "Button 2", "Button 3"];
toolBarState = GUI.Toolbar( Rect(10, 450, 300, 40) toolBarState, toolBarLabels);
```

Selection grids are defined almost exactly the same way, except you also need to specify how many columns you want the controls to span. In this example, only one column is used, in effect creating a vertical toolbar.

```
var selectionState = 1;
var selectionLabels : String[] = ["Button 1", "Button 2", "Button 3", "Button 4", "Button 5"];
selectionState = GUI.SelectionGrid( Rect( Screen.width - 150, 10, 100, 300),
selectionState, selectionLabels, 1);
```

Note

While being able to switch between states is a great thing, you'll also probably want to know when a user actually clicks one of these kinds of buttons or changes anything else on the GUI. Rather than checking manually every frame, you can make a simple call to the GUI.changed() function. GUI.changed() will return True anytime the user clicks a button, selects a box, enters text, or changes anything else on the interface.

Windows

The last basic control Unity provides is a bit more complex: a draggable window. These controls float above the other GUI controls and can be clicked to acquire focus. Besides being drawn themselves, windows also need to take a separate function as an argument, declaring what other kinds of controls and goodies should be displayed inside them. An empty window wouldn't be all that interesting.

```
var windowPosition = Rect(Screen.width - 100, Screen.height - 100, 200, 200);
function OnGUI(){
      windowPosition = GUI.Window(0, windowPosition, MyWindowFunction, "My Window");
}
function MyWindowFunction(windowID : int){
      if( GUI.Button(Rect(10, 30, 180, 40), "I'm a Window Button" )){
            print("You clicked the Window button");
      }
      if( GUI.Button(Rect(10, 90, 180, 40), "I'm also a Window Button" )){
            print("You clicked the other Window button");
      }
      GUI.DragWindow (Rect (0,0,1000,1000));
}
```

Each window you create must be given a unique integer ID number—in this case, 0. An initial position is then specified, followed by the function detailing the contents of the window. Like other controls, a window can take a string label or an image to define its look.

The helper function MyWindowFunction() defines the basic behavior of the window. In it are two simple buttons and an additional GUI element called GUI.DragWindow(). Including the GUI.DragWindow() function in your windows makes them draggable. (If you don't want this functionality, don't include it.) The GUI.DragWindow() function only needs a rectangle to define the space within the window that the user can click to drag. You may only want to make a title bar draggable, or perhaps you don't mind if the user can grab the entire window. If the rectangle you specify is larger than the window itself, it crops itself automatically to the size of the window.

All these control examples are displayed in Figure 11.1 for your reference. With these basic controls under your belt, you're ready to create your own custom GUI system.

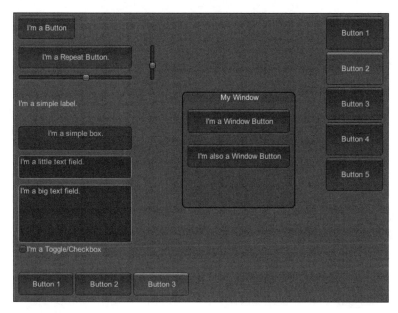

Figure 11.1
The basic Unity controls.
Source: Unity Technologies.

Tip

If you want your GUI elements to show up in the editor without having to click Play, add this command to the button of any of your scripts:

```
@script ExecuteInEditMode()
```

Now the Game view will update live as you edit your GUI, without you having to stop and play your scene every time you change something.

A Custom Skin for *Widget*

Unity's default controls come with a simple blue template, but this won't necessarily work with every game you make. Although you can customize each individual button or toggle as you come across it in your code, this can quickly get tedious and create lots of extra work. Fortunately, Unity provides you with the option of using GUIStyles and GUISkins to help push your workflow along at a speedy pace.

Applying a GUIStyle overrides the appearance of any default control and contains options like displayed texture image, text color, font, or even what highlights to use on a rollover. Defining a single style once and then applying it to multiple controls can save you hours of work. A GUIStyle applies to one type of control at a time, like a button or slider.

GUISkins take customization one step further. A *skin* is a collection of all the basic, default GUIStyles defined in Unity. Your game can handle more than one GUISkin at once (if you wanted to allow the users to pick their interface wrapper, for example), and you can even add your own custom styles to a GUISkin template. To illustrate, you'll make a new master GUISkin for *Widget*.

Creating the GUISkin

Open your main *Widget* project's latest scene and save it as a new Chapter 11 scene. In the Project view, right-click and select Create > GUI Skin. Place this new skin in a folder labeled GUI, making it easier to find later. Your new skin will look like Figure 11.2 upon inspection. Rename it something more meaningful, like Widget_Skin.

Figure 11.2
A default GUISkin.
Source: Unity Technologies.

As you can see, the GUISkin lists all the major GUI controls, and then some. Each control listing is its own GUIStyle definition. If you expand any one of the controls, like Button, you can edit and create new default values for all the button's properties, like its hover image, border, font, or normal view. Any value you don't change in the skin reverts to Unity's default.

The Settings tab at the bottom of the list allows you to set some of the basic functionality for text manipulation—whether double-clicking selects a word, the cursor color, and cursor flash speed, to name a few.

The last point of interest is the Custom Styles entry near the bottom. If you expand this section, you can enter a new size for the element, allowing you to create new control styles at will. If, for example, you create a new compound control for your game, you can define a default style for it here.

Defining Custom Styles

Creating a custom style is simple and follows the same steps as assigning a texture to a new material. To start, import all the GUI pieces in the Chapter 11 > GUI folder on the website and place these assets into the GUI folder in your project. In it you'll find a collection of buttons, window panels, and backdrops that match the *Widget* art style.

You can now start off by creating a simple, default button for the game:

1. Expand the Button selection on the GUISkin object you just created. Once inside the Button style, expand the Normal, Hover, and Active definitions for the button.

2. Drag (or select from the drop-down list) the ShortButton_Up image found in the GUI > Buttons folder into the Normal Background field. This will set all buttons to display this image.

3. Populate the Hover and Active Background fields with the ShortButton_Hover texture. This texture will make it look like the button glows when users click or hover the mouse over it. Set all the text colors for the buttons to a black or dark color by clicking the colored bar.

4. Farther down the list, change the Alignment setting to Middle Center, as you want any text to center along the entire length of the button. Your GUIStyle for the button should now look like Figure 11.3.

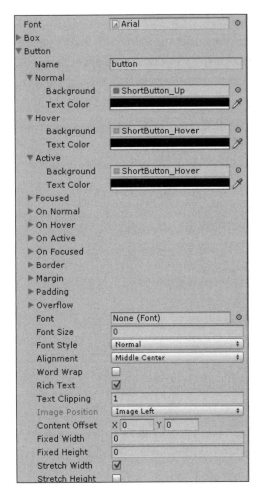

Figure 11.3
The completed GUIStyle.

Source: Unity Technologies.

Using these simple steps, you can replace and customize any and all of the remaining GUIStyles in the skin.

Importing New Fonts

In addition to importing new textures to use as backdrops for controls, you can also import your own custom fonts. The default font may work well for your project (usually this is something like Courier or Arial), but odds are you're going to want to develop or use a font that reflects your game's visual theme.

Unity can import and read any TrueType font. Although you may have hundreds of fonts already installed on your computer, Unity will not read these fonts automatically—a new font must be manually imported. Thousands of free fonts are also available for download on the Internet, and you may find something fitting there. Whichever the case, be sure you have the legal right and license to use a font before displaying it in your game.

The *Widget* game makes use of a custom, freeware font, available for download from Marco Rullkötter's site, Designer in Action (www.designerinaction.de/fonts/detail.php?id=206). This is a condensed, futuristic font and goes well with the visual atmosphere of *Widget*. To access the font, follow these steps:

1. Download the font from the aforementioned link or copy the included font from the companion website, in the root of the Chapter 11 folder (078MKMC_.ttf). Or, if you want to use a font already on your computer, locate it on your hard drive.

2. Drag the font onto the Project view to import it. Alternatively, you can copy and paste it directly into the Project folder. Once it's imported, click it to display the properties in the Inspector, as shown in Figure 11.4.

Figure 11.4
Unity's Font Import settings.
Source: Unity Technologies.

3. Here you can change the font size, character coding, and how much anti-aliasing (if any) you want to apply to the font. Click Apply to save any changes. For now, change the font size to 24.

4. Now you can apply this new font to the button style you just customized. Reopen the GUISkin in the Inspector and change the button's font from Courier to the newly imported one.

If you want to change the font size of your text later, you'll need to go back in and change the master font file in the Inspector. However, this updates all cases of the font in the game, which may not be what you want. The easiest way to handle multiple font sizes is to create copies of any given font you want in the project, giving each a different default size. You can then easily assign the different font sizes to different GUIStyles, giving you more options. Try this by importing a second copy of the font (give it a different name, like 078MKMC_small) and changing its font size to 16. Assign this new font to the master font style in the GUISkin.

Note

You may notice multiple "Font Size" labels in Unity. The size located in the font's import settings should be your default font size. In the preceding examples, the font size is 16 or 24. Inside the skin properties when you pick the imported font, set Font Size to 0 to inherit the default value.

SETTING UP THE HUD

Now that you know how to create basic controls and define their styles in a skin, you're ready to start making the custom heads-up display (HUD) for the game. Looking at the game design, you know you'll need to keep track of a few basic pieces of information for the player and display them when relevant. Primarily, you'll need to show the following:

■ Widget's current health and energy status

■ The current health and energy of any enemy Widget encounters

■ How many energy packs Widget has left

■ How many health packs Widget has left

■ How many screws and nuts Widget has collected on his journey (effectively the world's "cash" commodity)

You'll need to define custom controls for all these pieces of information, as Unity's basic control options don't quite provide you with everything you'll need. The item displays will need to handle a combined picture of the object and text display of how many Widget has in his inventory, and the character displays will need to show both stats in real time plus a picture of the character in question. The inventory buttons can also handle click functionality, allowing the players to quickly use them directly from the main screen.

To start, you'll make the custom inventory button for the item displays. Create a new JavaScript file in the Scripts directory and name it GUI_CustomControls. All the new controls will be stored in this directory, making them easier to reference in the future.

Delete the Update() function and create a new function as follows:

```
function InvoHudButton(screenPos: Rect, numAvailable : int, itemImage:
Texture, itemtooltip: String ) : Boolean {
}
```

This new button, `InvoHudButton()`, takes many of the same kinds of arguments as the normal Unity button but adds a few more for the advanced functionality. You also need to make sure that this function returns a Boolean value (as it is still a button), or else the user wouldn't be able to interact with it. First, you'll make the simple button part using a new GUI concept, called `GUIContent()`.

GUIContent()

`GUIContent()` arguments can be used by most of Unity's basic controls and allow you to pass labels, images, and tooltips as one package to any control. The `InvoHudButton()` will use `GUIContent()` to handle the button's image and tooltip.

Inside the `InvoHudButton()` function, add the following:

```
if( GUI.Button(screenPos, GUIContent(itemImage, itemtooltip), "HUD Button") ){
    return true;
}
```

The first little bit should look familiar. First you call the normal `GUI.Button()` function (placed inside the `if` conditional to allow interactivity) and give it a `Rect()` screen position. The `GUIContent()` argument then feeds in a display image and tooltip to the button. The last argument, `"HUD Button"`, may look like a normal button label, but it isn't—don't get this confused. If you want to pass a label, you need to include it in the `GUIContent()` package. This last piece of information defines what GUIStyle the button should use. Any control can use an optional last argument to define a custom style. For now, finish the button and then go back and define the new HUD button style.

After this conditional, add a new label to display how many units you have of this current item:

```
GUI.Label( Rect(screenPos.xMax - 20, screenPos.yMax - 25, 20, 20 ),
numAvailable.ToString() );
```

This `Rect()` aligns the label to the bottom right of the whole button, using the larger master `Rect()` as a reference.

Lastly, you need to define the space where your tooltips will appear:

```
GUI.Label( Rect( 20, Screen.height - 130, 500, 100), GUI.tooltip);
```

All the `InvoHudButton()` tooltips are now displayed in this one area of the screen.

Having finished the code definition, you need to define the visual style of your new button. Open the Widget_Skin GUISkin object in the Inspector and navigate to Custom

Styles. Increase the size of the object to 1 and name the newly created element HUD Button. This will now allow the script to reference this style.

Change the Normal Background field to ItemButtonBackUp and the Hover and Active Background fields to ItemButtonBackDown, both found in the GUI > Buttons folder. Set the font to the small version of the imported custom font and change the Alignment setting to Middle Center. Change the font colors to white and uncheck Stretch Width. Your new style should now look like Figure 11.5.

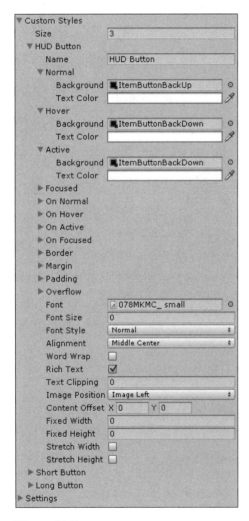

Figure 11.5
The finished custom style.

Now that your custom button's defined, you need to hook it up to the actual game. Follow these steps to do so:

1. Create a new JavaScript file in the Scripts directory and name it GUI_ HUD. Delete the Update() function.

2. Create a new variable at the top of the script named customSkin. This will enable you to tell Unity to use your newly defined GUISkin and not the default one. Also create image variables to hold the special item textures you'll display on the buttons.

```
var customSkin: GUISkin;
var screwImage : Texture2D;
var gearImage : Texture2D;
var repairkitImage : Texture2D;
var energykitImage : Texture2D;
```

3. Create a new Awake() function so you can cache some of Widget's data up front. The InvoHudButton needs information stored in Widget's inventory manager, so you'll need to link to it at startup:

```
private var customControls : GUI_CustomControls;
private var playerInvo : Widget_Inventory;
function Awake(){
        customControls = FindObjectOfType(GUI_CustomControls);
        playerInvo = FindObjectOfType(Widget_Inventory);
}
```

4. With this set up, create the initial OnGUI() function and set the GUISkin:

```
function OnGUI(){
        if(customSkin)
        GUI.skin = customSkin;
}
```

If a GUISkin is defined in the Inspector for the script to use, all of its defined styles will replace those in the game. Pretty straightforward.

5. Next, you just need to write calls to the new custom button. In the OnGUI() function, add the following:

```
//Inventory buttons------------------------
if(customControls.InvoHudButton(Rect(10, Screen.height - 100, 93, 95),
playerInvo.GetItemCount(InventoryItem.ENERGYPACK), energykitImage, "Click to use an
Energy Pack.")){
        playerInvo.UseItem(InventoryItem.ENERGYPACK, 1);
}
```

```
if(customControls.InvoHudButton(Rect(110, Screen.height - 100, 93, 95),
playerInvo.GetItemCount(InventoryItem.REPAIRKIT), repairkitImage, "Click to
use a Repair Kit.")){
        playerInvo.UseItem(InventoryItem.REPAIRKIT, 1);
}
//Non-usable inventory buttons------------------------
customControls.InvoHudButton(Rect(Screen.width - 210, Screen.height - 100, 93, 95),
playerInvo.GetItemCount(InventoryItem.SCREW), screwImage, "Number of screws you've
collected.");
customControls.InvoHudButton(Rect(Screen.width - 110, Screen.height - 100, 93, 95),
playerInvo.GetItemCount (InventoryItem.NUT), gearImage, "Number of gears you've
collected.");
```

This may look a little complicated, but just refer to your `InvoHudButton()` definition. First you define a rectangular space for the button to occupy and then pass it the number of items the player has in her inventory using the `GetItemCount()` function. The overlay image of the item is then passed, followed by the tooltip. For the `EnergyPack` and `RepairKit` items, these are housed within an `if` conditional so the player can click them to use—the appropriate use function is called in each case. (Remember writing those a few chapters ago?) The `SCREW` and `NUT` displays don't need to respond, so they are simply displayed outside of any `if` statement.

To see your new buttons in action, attach the GUI_Hud and GUI_CustomControls scripts to the Main Camera object. Populate the Inspector variables for the two scripts as follows:

- **Custom Skin:** Widget_Skin(GUISkin)
- **Screw Image:** Item_Overlay_1
- **Gear Image:** Item_Overlay_2
- **RepairKit Image:** Item_Overlay_4
- **EnergyPack Image:** Item_Overlay_3

The Item_Overlay images can be found in the GUI > Buttons folder. Once you're set up, click Play to see your new HUD in action, as shown in Figure 11.6. Try clicking on the RepairKit or EnergyPack button to see the number update live.

Figure 11.6
The new custom buttons in action.
Source: Unity Technologies.

Note

If you ever have problems clicking on the buttons, go to Edit > Project Settings > Input and verify that mouse clicks aren't being used for any of the axes actions.

Character Displays

Now that the inventory buttons are functioning, you need to add the character displays for Widget and whatever enemy he may be facing. Widget's display will need to always be in view so the player can keep tabs on his current health and energy stats. The enemy's status display, however, needs to be adjustable based on whatever Widget is facing. It should appear only when Widget is close enough to notice the enemy and update accordingly with any enemy's specific information. You'll begin with Widget's display, since it's a little more straightforward.

Widget's Character Display

Open the GUI_CustomControls script again, as you'll be adding a new custom control to it. Create a new function called LeftStatusMeter(), as follows:

```
function LeftStatusMeter(charImage : Texture, health :
float, energy : float, bBarImage : Texture, hBarImage : Texture, eBarImage : Texture){
}
```

First, the control gets a portrait of Widget, followed by his current health and energy stats. Next, three more images are loaded: two to handle the current health and energy display and a third one to provide a nice frame. As you have so many pieces to organize, it's best to use a GUI group to help.

In the function, begin a new group as follows:

```
GUI.BeginGroup( Rect(0,0, 330, 125) );
```

GUI groups are basically large rectangular containers that can hold other kinds of GUI controls, making it easier to move them together *en masse*. Groups can also nest inside each other, allowing you to create table-like structures of controls. The rectangle defined in the group describes where everything inside the group will be shown on the screen.

Next, you need to create the back framing images of the control. Unity draws the controls onscreen as it comes to them in the code. Images that should be drawn first (and therefore placed in the back) should be listed first.

```
GUI.Label( Rect(40, 10, 272, 90), bBarImage );
```

This line creates a simple label control using a texture. The rectangle defining this label does not use world coordinates. Instead, this rectangle is defined relative to that of the group.

With the frame in place, you can add the health and energy bars, each of which uses its own nested group:

```
GUI.BeginGroup( Rect(40, 10, 218 * (health/10.0) +35, 90) );
GUI.Label( Rect(0, 0, 272, 90), hBarImage );
GUI.EndGroup();
GUI.BeginGroup( Rect( 40, 10, 218 * (energy/10.0) +10, 90) );
GUI.Label( Rect(0, 0, 272, 90), eBarImage );
GUI.EndGroup();
```

The rectangle for each subgroup is defined based on Widget's current health and energy, in effect creating a moving status bar. The rectangle will clip and update every frame based on his current vital stats. Full stats will display the bar's full length, whereas decreasing health or energy will shorten the bar.

Lastly, you just need to add another texture displaying Widget's face, notifying the player that these stats belong to Widget and not someone else. You can also end the master group for the control:

```
GUI.Label( Rect(0, 0, 330, 125), charImage );
GUI.EndGroup();
```

Switching back to the GUI_HUD script, it's now time to implement it into the scene. Add some more variables to the file to help define the new images and information you'll need:

```
var lbarImage: Texture2D;
var lhbar : Texture2D;
var lebar : Texture2D;
var widgetImage : Texture2D;
private var playerInfo : Widget_Status;
```

Also add a new line to the Awake() function to cache Widget's status manager:

```
playerInfo = FindObjectOfType(Widget_Status);
```

Now in the OnGUI() function, you can call the new custom display:

```
customControls.LeftStatusMeter(widgetImage, playerInfo.health, playerInfo.energy,
lbarImage, lhbar, lebar);
```

The control grabs Widget's current health and energy from the state manager and populates the control with the proper textures. In the Inspector, assign the textures to GUI_HUD as follows:

- **Lbar Image:** LeftCornerBarsBack
- **Lhbar:** LeftCornerHealthBar
- **Lebar:** LeftCornerEnergyBar
- **WidgetImage:** WidgetCornerCircle

You can find these images in the GUI > Panels folder. Play your game to see Widget's stats in action. Try using his boost power to see the energy decrease, or add your new enemy from Chapter 10, "Building Adversaries and AI," and allow her to bite Widget a few times to test the health decrease. Using the item buttons will now fill Widget's health or energy back up, too! See Figure 11.7.

Figure 11.7
It may soon be time for an energy pack!
Source: Unity Technologies.

The Enemy's Display Panel

The enemy's display panel follows much of the same format as Widget's but will require a little more setup as it needs to be dynamically shown. First, you need to update your enemy's state manager to house all the information the display panel will need. Currently, the E_Bunny from Chapter 10 has a health stat, but you'll need to add an energy stat and image variable.

Open the EBunny_Status script and add these two variables to the top:

```
var energy: float = 10.0;
var charImage : Texture2D;
```

Populate the charImage variable with the Enemy_Overlay_1 texture, found in the GUI > Panels folder. From now on, each enemy that Widget faces should have a health, energy, and character image variable to take advantage of the new display.

You'll also need to add a new accessor function to the enemy's status class, allowing you to grab and reference its image for later:

```
function GetCharImage(): Texture2D{
    return charImage;
}
```

Next you need to update Widget's attack controller to add some functionality for finding the closest enemy to him. The enemy display will pop up only for the closest enemy, and then only if that enemy is within a certain range.

Open the Widget_AttackController script and add a new function and variables:

```
private var enemies : GameObject[] ;
function GetClosestEnemy() : GameObject {
}
```

This will allow you to store a list of all current enemies in the scene. In the GetClosestEnemy() function, define the enemy list and a few other helper variables:

```
enemies = GameObject.FindGameObjectsWithTag("Enemy");
var distanceToEnemy = Mathf.Infinity;
var wantedEnemy;
```

The Enemy variable is now populated with a list of all the objects in the scene tagged with Enemy. If you haven't yet, populate the scene with at least one E_Bunny and ensure that it's tagged with Enemy.

Now you can loop through this list of enemies and find which one is the closest to Widget. Starting like you did with a default distance equal to infinity (or in reality, a really, really big number) will make it easy to compare and find the closest one. Add the following to the function:

```
for (var enemy : GameObject in enemies){
    newDistanceToEnemy = Vector3.Distance(enemy.transform.position,
transform.position);
    if (newDistanceToEnemy < distanceToEnemy){
        distanceToEnemy = newDistanceToEnemy;
        wantedEnemy = enemy;
    }
}
return wantedEnemy;
```

After looping through all the enemies, you return the closest one. Save and close this file and return to the GUI_CustomControls script.

Writing the custom display control for the enemy panel is basically the same as writing the one for Widget, only the direction is reversed. The enemy's panel will be displayed in the top-right corner across from Widget's, taking into account that the bars should move toward the right side of the screen, mirroring Widget's.

Create the new control function:

```
function RightStatusMeter(charImage : Texture, health : float, energy : float,
bBarImage : Texture, hBarImage : Texture, eBarImage :
Texture, bCircleImage :Texture){
     GUI.BeginGroup( Rect(Screen.width - 330,0, 330, 125) );
}
```

Next, create the bar groups for the enemy's health and energy:

```
GUI.Label( Rect(40, 10, 272, 90), bBarImage );
GUI.BeginGroup( Rect(40 + (218-218*(health/10.0)),10, 218*(health/10.0), 90) );
GUI.Label( Rect(0, 0, 272, 90), hBarImage );
GUI.EndGroup();
GUI.BeginGroup( Rect( 40 + (218-218*(energy/10.0)), 10, 218*(energy/10.0), 90) );
GUI.Label( Rect(0, 0, 272, 90), eBarImage );
GUI.EndGroup();
```

All you have left to do is to add a blank circle frame and then an overlay for whichever enemy Widget is currently facing:

```
GUI.Label( Rect(208, 0, 330, 125), bCircleImage );
GUI.Label( Rect(208, 0, 330, 125), charImage );
GUI.EndGroup();
```

Calling this new control in the GUI_HUD script will require a little bit of extra work. You want the display to appear only when there is an enemy in the scene and only when it's close enough to Widget to be an immediate threat. Add some variables to the GUI_HUD script to help out with this:

```
var rbarImage: Texture2D;
var rhbar :Texture2D;
var rebar : Texture2D;
var enemyImage : Texture2D;
var circBackImage : Texture2D;
private var playerAttack : Widget_AttackController;
private var closestEnemyStatus ;
```

```
private var player;
var closestEnemy;
var enemyDistance;
```

Then set up the necessary links in the `Awake()` function:

```
playerAttack = FindObjectOfType(Widget_AttackController);
player = GameObject.FindWithTag("Player");
```

Now, in the `OnGUI()` function, you need to determine whether the display should be shown, and if so, what to populate it with:

```
closestEnemy = playerAttack.GetClosestEnemy();
if (closestEnemy != null){
      enemyDistance = Vector3.Distance (closestEnemy.transform.position,
player.transform.position);
      if(enemyDistance < 20.0){
            closestEnemyStatus = closestEnemy.GetComponent(EBunny_Status);
            enemyImage = closestEnemyStatus.GetCharImage();
            customControls.RightStatusMeter(enemyImage, closestEnemyStatus.health,
closestEnemyStatus.energy, rbarImage, rhbar, rebar, circBackImage);
      }
}
```

First you find the closest enemy to the player. If such an enemy exists, the distance is then computed. If the enemy is deemed to be close enough (under 20 meters in this case), the enemy's status is grabbed and the new custom control is populated with its information.

In the Inspector, set up the new HUD variables as follows:

- **Rbar Image:** RightCornerBarsBack
- **Rhbar:** RightCornerHealthBar
- **Rebar:** RightCornerEnergyBar
- **Circ Back Image:** RightCornerCircle

You can find all these images in the GUI > Panels folder. Leave the Enemy Image field blank because it's populated on the fly when you need it. Try your new enemy display and take down that bunny. See Figure 11.8.

Figure 11.8
The battle of the bots has begun.
Source: Unity Technologies.

Resolution

Although you have been docking all your UI images to the sides of the screen, allowing them to be sized somewhat dynamically, early on in your development you should decide what your game's resolution will be. Some games (especially browser-based ones) allow for one specified resolution, whereas others allow players to pick one of many options.

Widget will officially support only the standalone app's default size of 1,024 × 768, and all the control images have been authored to that exact size. If you want to support different screen resolutions, you should either ensure that your UI is small enough to fit on the lowest resolution or create multiple UI art packs.

The latter option is more time consuming, but it does create a more professional package in the end. Thankfully, with Unity's GUISkins, it's also not that hard to implement. Basically, you need to create a new GUISkin for each supported resolution, populating the styles with the correct version of each control's image. Then, upon startup, when the players select their resolution preference, you simply load the GUISkin variable with the correct option.

Now would also be a good time to change your game's test resolution to the supported 1,024 × 768 setting (found on the Game tab in the top-left corner) to best view the UI images at their proper resolution.

A Sample Pop-Up Screen

The HUD is coming along nicely now, but what if you wanted to add some dynamic pop-ups to the scene based on what the player was doing? You can try this by adding a store-front functionality to the CheckPoint prefab object you've already made. While standing on the checkpoint platform, Widget can receive a notification that he can begin shopping at the robot's latest, greatest, and classiest boutique if he so wishes. By clicking a button that appears, the player can open and close the store at will.

First you need to make a new script to handle the actual store display. Make a new Java-Script file in the Scripts directory and name it GUI_WaypointStore. Add some basic variables to handle the GUI images and player information:

```
var storeBG : Texture2D;
var customSkin: GUISkin;
private var playerInventory : Widget_Inventory;
private var openStore = false;
```

You'll need to link to the player's inventory and also keep track of whether the storefront is currently open or closed. Delete the Update() function and add a new Awake() function, linking the inventory to the script:

```
function Awake(){
    playerInventory = FindObjectOfType(Widget_Inventory);
    if (!playerInventory){
        Debug.Log("No link to player's inventory.");
    }
}
```

Now you just need to determine when to display the store window. Create a new OnGUI() function and link the custom skin to it:

```
function OnGUI(){
    if(customSkin)
    GUI.skin = customSkin;
}
```

Inside the `OnGUI()` function, add an `if` statement that displays the store images only if `openStore` is true:

```
if(openStore)
{
     GUI.Box(Rect(0,0,Screen.width, Screen.height), " ");
     GUI.Label(Rect(Screen.width/2 - storeBG.width/2, Screen.height/2-
storeBG.height/2, storeBG.width, storeBG.height ), storeBG);
      if(GUI.Button(Rect(Screen.width/2 -126, Screen.height - 100, 252,
113), "Close      Store")){
          StoreFrontToggle();
     }
}
```

The label handles the actual store display and the button appears to toggle the store on and off. The box creates a dark backdrop across the entire screen, dimming the rest of the game while the player is in the store.

All that's left to do is to create the `StoreFrontToggle()` helper function and add an accessor function for the status of the store:

```
function StoreFrontToggle(){
     if(openStore == false)
          openStore = true;
     else
          openStore = false;
}
function GetStoreStatus(){
     return openStore;
}
```

Open the GUISkin in the Inspector so you can set up the default box. Open the box style and assign the DarkenScreen image to the Normal Background field, found in the GUI > Backdrops folder. This small, tileable image places a light gray overlay across the entire field of the box control. Ensure also that the DarkenScreen image was imported with DXT5 compression to preserve the alpha channel. Otherwise the image will appear black and opaque.

Assign the storeBG variable from the GUI_WaypointStore script the Inventory Screen_bg file (found in the GUI > Panels folder). Populate the Custom Skin variable with the Widget_Skin (GUISkin) object. Attach this script to the CheckPoint prefab.

The last step to get the store operational is to create the WaypointBehavior script. Create a new JavaScript file and name it WaypointBehavior. This will handle the actual GUI implementation of the robot checkpoints. This could be incorporated into the original Check-Point script, but I prefer to keep it separate in case one of the two systems needs a drastic change.

Delete the provided Update() function and add this to the file:

```
var customSkin: GUISkin;
private var isTriggered = false;
```

Next you need to set up two simple triggers to determine whether Widget is the one who has entered the waypoint, not some random enemy. Add these two new functions to the script:

```
function OnTriggerEnter(collider: Collider){
    //Make sure that this is a player hitting the platform and not an enemy
    var playerStatus : Widget_Status = collider.GetComponent(Widget_Status);
    if(playerStatus == null)
        return;
    isTriggered = true;
}
function OnTriggerExit(collider: Collider){
    //Make sure that this is a player leaving the platform and not an enemy
    var playerStatus : Widget_Status = collider.GetComponent(Widget_Status);
    if(playerStatus == null)
        return;
    isTriggered = false;
}
```

Now you only need to hook up the GUI bits to make the store operational. Continuing in the script, add to the bottom a new function:

```
function OnGUI(){
    if(customSkin)
        GUI.skin = customSkin;
}
```

Because you've already got a variable in place tracking whether the player is triggering the waypoint, hooking up the store button trigger is easy. Add the following to the OnGUI() function:

```
if(isTriggered){
    var store = this.GetComponent(GUI_WaypointStore);
```

```
        //Display open button only if store is currently closed
        if( !store.GetStoreStatus() ){
                if(GUI.Button(Rect(Screen.width/2 -126, Screen.height - 100,
252, 113), "Open Store")){
                        store.StoreFrontToggle();
                }
        }
}
```

If the player is currently standing on the checkpoint and the store isn't already open, an Open Store button will appear on the screen, allowing the player to bring up the pop-up at will. Save the script and attach it to your CheckPoint prefab, populating the CustomSkin variable with your *Widget* GUISkin. Figure 11.9 shows the empty storefront in all its glory.

Figure 11.9
Open for business.
Source: Unity Technologies.

From here, you can populate the storefront with any kind of button or list you want. Perhaps a nice window or two would make it easy to use the same basic functionality while easily switching stock between different stores.

ADDING FULL-SCREEN MENUS

One other kind of UI option is a full-screen menu, useful for such things as pause screens and main menus. Although these can be created inline in the current scene, some full-screen menus function better as their own unique scene files. To try this out, you'll make a main menu screen for the *Widget* game and allow the player to click a button to start.

Save your current scene and create a new empty one, naming it Chapter11_MainMenu. The only object you need in here is the Main Camera; delete anything else. With the camera selected, change the background color in the Inspector to black. The default blue is a little much for the main menu. Now if you preview your scene, you're met with a nice blank canvas, perfect for putting main interface elements on.

Create a new JavaScript file in the Scripts folder and name it GUI_MainMenu. Delete the Update() function, as normal. For the main menu, you'll need to link to your custom skin and then provide a link to a title and background image. Create some new variables at the top of the file:

```
var customSkin: GUISkin;
var mainMenuBG : Texture2D;
var mainTitle : Texture2D;
```

You should also create one more variable, a Boolean, to track whether the game is currently loading. Otherwise, the player may think the game is just hanging if he clicks on the Load Game button and nothing happens.

```
private var isLoading : boolean;
```

In a new OnGUI() function, make a link to the custom skin:

```
function OnGUI(){
     if(customSkin)
     GUI.skin = customSkin;
}
```

Now create another dark box to hide the screen (just in case) and a label to display the splash image and title.

```
GUI.Box(Rect( 0, 0, Screen.width, Screen.height), " ");
GUI.Label(Rect( 0, 30, Screen.width, Screen.height), mainMenuBG);
GUI.Label(Rect(Screen.width - 500, 50, mainTitle.width, mainTitle.height), mainTitle);
```

All that's left to add is the two buttons: one to load the game and one to quit the application. Because these buttons are going to be a whole lot bigger, you'll also need to define a new button style in the custom skin.

Follow these steps to create a new button style:

1. In the Widget_Skin object, create a new custom style by increasing the size count, and name it Long Button.

2. Expand the Normal, Hover, and Active fields, setting Normal Background to the LongButton_Up file and the Hover and Active Background fields to LongButton_Hover. Both of these textures can be found in the GUI > Buttons folder.

3. Change the Alignment to Middle Center and place the larger of your two font files in the Font field.

Back in the GUI_MainMenu file, create the two buttons in the OnGUI() function:

```
if(GUI.Button( Rect(Screen.width - 380, Screen.height - 280, 320, 80),
"Start Game", "Long Button")){
     isLoading = true;
     Application.LoadLevel("Chapter_11");
}
if(GUI.Button( Rect(Screen.width - 380, Screen.height - 180, 320, 80),
"Quit Game", "Long Button")){
     Application.Quit();
}
```

The Application class is a special class used to access and control runtime data, like whether to quit the game or load a specific scene. It will be covered in greater detail in Chapter 16, "Creating the Final Build"; for now, you'll use these two simple functions.

The last thing you should add to the menu is a small text pop-up letting players know the game is loading. In the OnGUI() function, add the following:

```
if (isLoading){
     GUI.Label( Rect(Screen.width/2 - 50, Screen.height - 40, 100, 50), "Now Loading");
}
```

When the player clicks the Loading button, this conditional will begin to fire, and a Now Loading tag will be displayed at the bottom of the screen. To make it easier for testing, add the customary script tags at the bottom of the file:

```
@script ExecuteInEditMode()
@script AddComponentMenu("GUI/MainMenu")
```

Note

Beyond starting up the Loading string, these buttons will not function as expected yet. They will give an assert in the Debug Console. Before you can load different levels in the application, they need to be set up in the build settings. This is covered in full in Chapter 16.

To see your main menu in action, attach it to the Main Camera already populating the scene and set up the texture variables as follows:

- **Main Menu BG:** MainMenu_SplashScreen

- **Main Title:** WidgetTitle

These two new textures can be found in the GUI > Panels and GUI > Backdrops folders. The finished main menu with the loading tag active is displayed in Figure 11.10.

Figure 11.10
Now loading, or will be shortly.
Source: Unity Technologies.

You're now ready to make custom interfaces of your own. By combining small and simple controls, it's possible to create complex UI pieces capable of displaying any kind of information you want.

In its current state, *Widget* is mostly playable from a systems point of view and is only lacking in expanded content and polish. Moving forward, you'll look at how to add those last little bits of extra shine such as lighting, particle effects, and sound.

COMPLETED SCRIPTS

The newly completed and updated scripts are also available on the companion website in the Chapter 11 folder. GUI_CustomControls.js appears in Listing 11.1.

Listing 11.1   GUI_CustomControls.js

```
//GUI_CustomControls: Contains the custom compound control
//classes for use elsewhere in the GUI_CustomControls

//Item HUD Button--------------------------------------
//Displays the button, correct overlay item picture, and the
//number of the item currently in Widget's Invo.
function InvoHudButton(screenPos: Rect, numAvailable : int, itemImage: Texture,
itemtooltip: String ) : Boolean {
    if( GUI.Button(screenPos, GUIContent(itemImage, itemtooltip), "HUD Button") )
        return true;
    GUI.Label( Rect(screenPos.xMax - 20, screenPos.yMax - 25, 20, 20 ),
numAvailable.ToString() );

    //Display area for tooltips
    GUI.Label( Rect( 20, Screen.height - 130, 500, 100), GUI.tooltip);
}
//Left hand health------------------------------------
function LeftStatusMeter(charImage : Texture, health : float, energy : float,
bBarImage : Texture, hBarImage : Texture, eBarImage : Texture){
    GUI.BeginGroup( Rect(0,0, 330, 125) );

    //Place back bars
    GUI.Label( Rect(40, 10, 272, 90), bBarImage );

    //Place front bars
    GUI.BeginGroup( Rect(40, 10, 218 * (health/10.0) +35, 90) );
    GUI.Label( Rect(0, 0, 272, 90), hBarImage );
    GUI.EndGroup();
    GUI.BeginGroup( Rect( 40, 10, 218 * (energy/10.0) +10, 90) );
```

```
        GUI.Label( Rect(0, 0, 272, 90), eBarImage );
        GUI.EndGroup();

        //Place head circle
        GUI.Label( Rect(0, 0, 330, 125), charImage );
        GUI.EndGroup();
}

//Right hand health---------------------------------
function RightStatusMeter(charImage : Texture, health : float, energy : float, bBarImage :
Texture, hBarImage : Texture, eBarImage : Texture, bCircleImage :Texture){
        GUI.BeginGroup( Rect(Screen.width - 330,0, 330, 125) );

        //Place back bars
        GUI.Label( Rect(40, 10, 272, 90), bBarImage );

        //Place front bars
        GUI.BeginGroup( Rect(40 + (218-218*(health/10.0)), 10, 218*(health/10.0), 90) );
GUI.Label( Rect(0, 0, 272, 90), hBarImage );
        GUI.EndGroup();
        GUI.BeginGroup( Rect( 40 + (218-218*(energy/10.0)), 10, 218*(energy/10.0), 90) );
        GUI.Label( Rect(0, 0, 272, 90), eBarImage );
        GUI.EndGroup();

        //Place back circle
        GUI.Label( Rect(208, 0, 330, 125), bCircleImage );

        //Place head circle
        GUI.Label( Rect(208, 0, 330, 125), charImage );
        GUI.EndGroup();
}
@script AddComponentMenu("GUI/CustomControls")
```

GUI_HUD.js appears in Listing 11.2.

Listing 11.2   GUI_HUD.js

```
//GUI_HUD: Displays the pertinent information for Widget,
//his items, and any current enemy

//Set up textures--------------------------------
//For larger games, this should be done programmatically
var customSkin: GUISkin;
var screwImage : Texture2D;
var gearImage : Texture2D;
var repairkitImage : Texture2D;
var energykitImage : Texture2D;
```

```
//Left vital tex
var lbarImage: Texture2D;
var lhbar :Texture2D;
var lebar : Texture2D;
var widgetImage : Texture2D;

//Right vital tex
var rbarImage: Texture2D;
var rhbar :Texture2D;
var rebar : Texture2D;
var enemyImage : Texture2D;
var circBackImage : Texture2D;

//-----------------------------------------------------
private var customControls : GUI_CustomControls;
private var playerInfo : Widget_Status;
private var playerInvo : Widget_Inventory;
private var playerAttack : Widget_AttackController;
private var closestEnemyStatus ;
private var player;
var closestEnemy;
var enemyDistance;

//Initialize player info-----------------------------
function Awake(){
     playerInfo = FindObjectOfType(Widget_Status);
     customControls = FindObjectOfType(GUI_CustomControls);
     playerInvo = FindObjectOfType(Widget_Inventory);
     playerAttack = FindObjectOfType(Widget_AttackController);
     player = GameObject.FindWithTag("Player");
}

//Display--------------------------------------------
function OnGUI(){
     if(customSkin)
          GUI.skin = customSkin;

     //Widget's vitals
     customControls.LeftStatusMeter(widgetImage, playerInfo.health,
playerInfo.energy, lbarImage, lhbar, lebar);

     //Inventory buttons----------------------------
     if(customControls.InvoHudButton(Rect(10, Screen.height - 100, 93, 95),
playerInvo.GetItemCount (InventoryItem.ENERGYPACK), energykitImage, "Click
to use an Energy Pack.")){
          playerInvo.UseItem(InventoryItem.ENERGYPACK, 1);
     }
```

```
        if(customControls.InvoHudButton(Rect(110, Screen.height - 100, 93, 95),
playerInvo.GetItemCount (InventoryItem.REPAIRKIT), repairkitImage, "Click to
use a Repair Kit.")){
                playerInvo.UseItem(InventoryItem.REPAIRKIT, 1);
        }

        //Non-usable inventory buttons------------------
        customControls.InvoHudButton(Rect(Screen.width - 210, Screen.height - 100, 93, 95),
playerInvo.GetItemCount(InventoryItem.SCREW), screwImage, "Number of screws you've
collected.");
        customControls.InvoHudButton(Rect(Screen.width - 110, Screen.height - 100,
93, 95), playerInvo. GetItemCount(InventoryItem.NUT), gearImage, "Number of gears
you've collected.");

        //Enemy vitals
        closestEnemy = playerAttack.GetClosestEnemy();
        if (closestEnemy != null){
                enemyDistance = Vector3.Distance(closestEnemy. transform.position,
player.transform.position);
                if(enemyDistance < 20.0){
                        closestEnemyStatus = closestEnemy.GetComponent(EBunny_Status);
                        enemyImage = closestEnemyStatus.GetCharImage();
                        customControls.RightStatusMeter(enemyImage,
closestEnemyStatus.health, closestEnemyStatus.energy, rbarImage, rhbar, rebar,
circBackImage);
                }
        }
}
@script ExecuteInEditMode()
@script AddComponentMenu("GUI/HUD")
```

Widget_Attack_Controller.js appears in Listing 11.3.

Listing 11.3   Widget_Attack_Controller.js

```
//Widget_AttackController: Handles the player's attack input
//and deals damage to the targeted enemy

//----------------------------------------------------
var attackHitTime = 0.2;
var attackTime = 0.5;
var attackPosition = new Vector3 (0, 1, 0);
var attackRadius = 2.0;
var damage= 1.0;
```

```
//----------------------------------------------------------
private var busy = false;
private var ourLocation;
private var enemies : GameObject[] ;
var controller : Widget_Controller;
controller = GetComponent(Widget_Controller);

//Allow the player to attack if he is not busy and the
//Attack button was pressed
function Update (){
      if(!busy && Input.GetButtonDown ("Attack") && controller.IsGrounded()
&& !controller.IsMoving()){
            DidAttack();
            busy = true;
      }
}
function DidAttack (){
      //Play the animation regardless of whether we hit something or not
      animation.CrossFadeQueued("Taser", 0.1, QueueMode.PlayNow);
      yield WaitForSeconds(attackHitTime);

      ourLocation = transform.TransformPoint(attackPosition);
      enemies = GameObject.FindGameObjectsWithTag("Enemy");

      //See if any enemies are within range of the attack
      //This will hit all in range
      for (var enemy : GameObject in enemies){
            var enemyStatus = enemy.GetComponent(EBunny_Status);
            if (enemyStatus == null){
                  continue;
            }
            if (Vector3.Distance(enemy.transform.position, ourLocation) <
attackRadius){
                  enemyStatus.ApplyDamage(damage);
            }
      }
      yield WaitForSeconds(attackTime - attackHitTime);
      busy = false;
}
function GetClosestEnemy() : GameObject{
      enemies = GameObject.FindGameObjectsWithTag("Enemy");
      var distanceToEnemy = Mathf.Infinity;
      var wantedEnemy;
```

```
        for (var enemy : GameObject in enemies){
                newDistanceToEnemy = Vector3.Distance(enemy.transform. position,
transform.position);
                if (newDistanceToEnemy < distanceToEnemy){
                        distanceToEnemy = newDistanceToEnemy;
                        wantedEnemy = enemy;
                }
        }
        return wantedEnemy;
}
@script AddComponentMenu("Player/Widget's Attack Controller")
```

EBunny_Status.js appears in Listing 11.4.

Listing 11.4   EBunny_Status.js

```
//EBunny_Status:        Controls the state information of the enemy bunny

//----------------------------------------------------
var health: float = 10.0;
var energy: float = 10.0;
private var dead = false;
var charImage : Texture2D;

//PickupItems held-------------------------------------
var numHeldItemsMin = 1;
var numHeldItemsMax = 3;
var pickup1: GameObject;
var pickup2: GameObject;

//State functions--------------------------------------
function ApplyDamage(damage: float){
        if (health <= 0)
                return;
        health -= damage;
        animation.Play("EBunny_Hit");

        //Check health and call Die if need to
        if(!dead && health <= 0){
                health = 0; //For GUI
                dead = true;
                Die();
        }
}
```

```
function Die (){
      animation.Stop();
      animation.Play("EBunny_Death");
      Destroy(gameObject.GetComponent(EBunny_AIController));
      yield WaitForSeconds(animation["EBunny_Death"].length - 0.5);

      //Cache location of dead body for pickups
      var itemLocation = gameObject.transform.position;

      //Drop a random number of reward pickups for the player
      yield WaitForSeconds(0.5);
      var rewardItems = Random.Range(numHeldItemsMin, numHeldItemsMax) + 1;
      for (var i = 0; i < rewardItems; i++){
            var randomItemLocation = itemLocation;
            randomItemLocation.x += Random.Range(-2, 2);
            randomItemLocation.y += 1; //Keep it off the ground
            randomItemLocation.z += Random.Range(-2, 2);

            if (Random.value > 0.5)
                  Instantiate(pickup1, randomItemLocation,
pickup1.transform.rotation);
            else
                  Instantiate(pickup2, randomItemLocation,
pickup2.transform.rotation);
      }

      //Remove killed enemy from the scene
      Destroy(gameObject);
}
function IsDead() : boolean{
      return dead;
}
function GetCharImage(): Texture2D{
      return charImage;
}
@script AddComponentMenu("Enemies/Bunny'sStateManager")
```

GUI_WaypointStore.js appears in Listing 11.5.

Listing 11.5   GUI_WaypointStore.js

```
//GUI_WaypointStore: Handles the interface for the store transactions
//Shows the available items for purchase, allows the player
//to sell his own inventory and buy transforms
```

```
var storeBG : Texture2D;
var customSkin: GUISkin;
private var playerInventory : Widget_Inventory;
private var openStore = false;
//----------------------------------------------------
function Awake(){
     playerInventory = FindObjectOfType(Widget_Inventory);
     if (!playerInventory)
          Debug.Log("No link to player's inventory.");
}

//Enable and disable script as needed-----------------
function OnGUI(){
     if(customSkin)
          GUI.skin = customSkin;

     if(openStore){
          GUI.Box(Rect(0,0,Screen.width, Screen.height), " ");
          GUI.Label(Rect(Screen.width/2 - storeBG.width/2, Screen.height/2-
storeBG.height/2, storeBG.width, storeBG.height ), storeBG);
          if(GUI.Button(Rect(Screen.width/2 -126, Screen.height - 100,
252, 113),    "Close Store")){
               StoreFrontToggle();
          }
     }
}
function StoreFrontToggle(){
     if(openStore == false)
          openStore = true;
     else
          openStore = false;
}
function GetStoreStatus(){
     return openStore;
}
@script AddComponentMenu("GUI/Store")
```

WaypointBehavior.js appears in Listing 11.6.

Listing 11.6   WaypointBehavior.js

```
//WaypointBehavior: Handles the scripts on all the waypoints
//Gives the player the option of
//opening the store or not.
```

```
var customSkin: GUISkin;
private var isTriggered = false;

function OnTriggerEnter(collider: Collider){
        //Make sure that this is a player hitting the platform and not an enemy
        var playerStatus : Widget_Status = collider.GetComponent(Widget_Status);
        if(playerStatus == null)
                return;
        isTriggered = true;
        playerStatus.energy = playerStatus.maxEnergy;
        playerStatus.health = playerStatus.maxHealth;
}
function OnTriggerExit(collider: Collider){
        //Make sure that this is a player leaving the platform and not an enemy
        var playerStatus : Widget_Status = collider.GetComponent(Widget_Status);
        if(playerStatus == null)
                return;
        isTriggered = false;
}
function OnGUI(){
        if(customSkin)
                GUI.skin = customSkin;
        if(isTriggered){
                var store = this.GetComponent(GUI_WaypointStore);
                //Only display open button if store is currently closed
                if( !store.GetStoreStatus() ){
                        if(GUI.Button(Rect(Screen.width/2 -126,  Screen.height - 100, 252,
113), "Open Store")){
                                store.StoreFrontToggle();
                        }
                }
        }
}
@script AddComponentMenu("GUI/WaypointGUI")
```

GUI_MainMenu.js appears in Listing 11.7.

Listing 11.7   GUI_MainMenu.js

```
//GUI_MainMenu: Adds the backdrop and main navigation buttons to the scene.
//This scene will be the first thing the app loads and
//will allow the player to pick a level to load or quit.

var customSkin: GUISkin;
var mainMenuBG : Texture2D;
var mainTitle : Texture2D;
private var isLoading : boolean;
```

```
//Main menu-----------------------------------------------
function OnGUI(){
     if(customSkin)
          GUI.skin = customSkin;

     //BG images
     GUI.Box(Rect( 0, 0, Screen.width, Screen.height), " "); GUI.Label(Rect( 0, 30,
Screen.width, Screen.height), mainMenuBG);

     //Title and buttons
     GUI.Label(Rect(Screen.width - 500, 50, mainTitle.width, mainTitle.height),
mainTitle);
     if(GUI.Button(Rect(Screen.width - 380, Screen.height - 280,
320, 80), "Start Game", "Long Button")){
          isLoading = true;
          Application.LoadLevel("Chapter_11");
     }
     if(GUI.Button( Rect(Screen.width - 380, Screen.height - 180, 320, 80), "Quit Game",
"Long Button")){
          Application.Quit();
     }

     //If game is currently loading, display a notification to the user
     if (isLoading){
          GUI.Label( Rect(Screen.width/2 - 50, Screen.height - 40, 100, 50),
"Now Loading");
     }
}
@script ExecuteInEditMode()
@script AddComponentMenu("GUI/MainMenu")
```

PART IV

POLISH AND THE FINISHING TOUCHES

All that remains now is for you to add some artistic and audio refinements to your game. Although your game is technically playable at this stage, some important feedback systems and ambience are still missing. Chapter 12, "Creating Lighting and Shadows," and Chapter 13, "Using Particle Systems," will help provide some extra feedback for the player's attacks and movements by employing particle systems. Chapter 14, "Adding Audio and Music," will take a look at boosting the world's atmosphere with the addition of environment lights and sound effects.

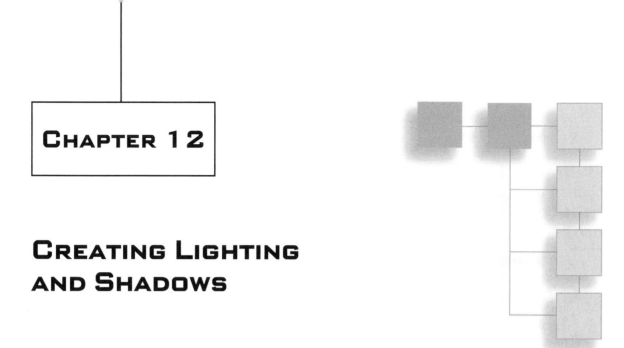

CHAPTER 12

CREATING LIGHTING AND SHADOWS

Although it's easy to add some quick working lighting to any given scene, lights are one of the most important parts to get right when trying to set a mood. A small change in the temperature of a light can make a scene seem inviting and open or dark and sinister. Lights can also be used in a more gameplay-oriented manner. Lights and shadows can be used to guide a player down particular paths, illuminate an important object, or draw attention to an often-overlooked detail. Lights can make your textures look dull and flat or bring out all the little details in your world and make it come to life.

TYPES OF LIGHTS

Unity comes packaged with three kinds of lights, each simulating a common source of light in the real world:

- **Directional:** Directional lights function similarly to the sun. They simulate a large, distant light source that points in one direction. Everything in the scene is illuminated from this light in the same manner, and any shadows cast would follow the same path. A combination of directional lights can quickly illuminate an entire scene, but they can also blow some details out or light some areas that you want to remain hidden.

- **Point:** Point lights function like a common light bulb. They emit light from a central point outward in a sphere. The light can either taper off naturally or be made to stop on a hard line. The size of the sphere of influence can change, and only the objects within the point light's radius will be affected by the light.

■ **Spot:** Spotlights function in a game exactly as they do in real life. With a spotlight, light is emitted from a defined point outward in one direction, taking the shape of a cone. The light also can taper off naturally, and the angle of the spot's cone can be changed.

Although this may not seem like a great number of possibilities to play with, once you begin to mix different kinds of lights (and their shadow effects) together, just about any lighting effect is possible. Figure 12.1 demonstrates some of the possibilities available with just these simple lights.

Point light

Spotlight

Directional light

Default light

Figure 12.1
Different base lighting effects.
Source: Unity Technologies.

To add a light to a scene, from the main menu, choose GameObject > Create Other and select the desired light from the list. Open Unity and add any light to a scene. Click it to view its properties in the Inspector.

Light Properties

Light properties dictate the size, intensity, color (or temperature), and angle of a light. Properties can also change any cast shadows or add special effects like halos or lens flares. All lights have the same basic list of properties, as shown in Figure 12.2.

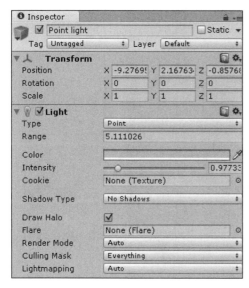

Figure 12.2
Light properties.
Source: Unity Technologies.

- **Type:** This property changes what kind of light is being emitted. You can select from the drop-down list the different lights available. Doing so will not overwrite any other properties you have set, so it can be a quick way to test different options if you're unsure of what kind of light to use.

- **Range:** For point lights and spotlights, this dictates how far away the light is emitted from the central point. This has no effect on the directional light.

- **Spot Angle:** For the spotlight only, this changes the activated angle of the emitted light. A smaller number will create a clean, pointed cone of light, while a larger one will illuminate a larger area.

- **Color:** Changes the color of the emitted light. This can be extremely useful for setting a particular mood or achieving a special effect.

- **Intensity:** Determines how "bright" the light is.

- **Cookie:** Cookies are textures assigned to lights to create the illusion of more complex lighting rigs or to apply special effects. (More on these later in the chapter.) Directional and spotlights use a 2D texture, whereas point lights need a cube map.

- **Shadow Type:** Dynamic shadows are available only in Unity Pro. If you have access to dynamic shadows, the lighting will be updated as the object moves. Hard shadows are rendered with a crisp edge. Soft shadows are rendered with a tapered edge, and require more computing power to draw.

- **Strength:** How dark the shadow is. Numbers closer to 0 will cast a more transparent and light shadow, whereas numbers closer to 1 will be very dark and opaque.

- **Resolution:** The detail level of the shadow cast. High will have smoother, more accurate lines, whereas the lowest option may look more blobby but will render more quickly.

- **Bias:** When using shadow mapping, you can adjust the bias of the shadow map. If the bias is too low, values might be sampled too distantly, causing spots of shadow on objects. If the bias is too high shadows may not appear crisply on the edges of objects, making the object appear to fly.

- **Draw Halo:** Selecting this checkbox will render a hazy halo effect equal to the light's range. This can be useful for mood or effect lighting.

- **Flare:** Assigns a lens flare effect to the light. Choose the desired flare type from the drop-down list—some are included with the Standard Assets package.

- **Render Mode:** Choose how the light will render on any objects it illuminates. The Important setting will force the rendering of the light on a per-pixel basis. The Not Important setting will render the light on a faster vertex-based routine. The Auto setting will automatically switch between the two settings based on performance and other nearby light settings.

- **Culling Mask:** Used for optimization and effects. With this setting, you can choose which layers the light can affect. You can create new layers in the Layers drop-down list and then select them from there.

- **Lightmapping:** Determines the kind of lighting to apply. BakedOnly will only use lights that were applied when building a lightmap. RealtimeOnly will ignore baked lighting and always compute the light directly. Auto allows both types of lighting to appear based on the distance to the shadow and other properties.

Drop a few random objects into your scene and play around with some of the basic settings on your test light to get a feel for how the properties affect the light.

Note

Placement in the world is vital to the proper functioning of spotlights and point lights. The directional light, because of its nature, can be placed anywhere and still emit the same kind of light. All that matters for the directional light is its current rotation, unless you're attaching a flare to it, in which case the light's position is used for the flare.

Basics of Lighting

Creating a light rig for a game is very similar to the processes used by movie and stage lighting technicians. In all three cases, you are trying to simulate natural or mood lighting conditions in an artificial setting. Most scenes, even simple ones, are lit with a combination of lights working in tandem, which together help to mimic the quality of natural lights and bounce effects seen in the real world.

A Simple Three-Point Lighting Rig

Many basic scenes start with a three-point lighting rig. These are especially useful when the scene's camera is fixed and you have complete control over how the user will view the scene. As suggested by the name, the rig uses three basic lights for the composition. (Any default lighting should be removed prior to setting up the first light or it could throw off the entire final result.) These lights are as follows:

- **Key light:** The key light is the scene's main light and should be added first. This light mimics the strongest light source available in the scene, whether that's the sun, a large overhead lamp, or a giant bonfire. Spotlights and directional lights work well as key lights. Make sure you like the effects of your key light before placing additional lights in the scene.

- **Fill light:** The fill light (or lights, in some cases) helps create the illusion of light bouncing around the scene and helps to fill in and soften some of the darker shadows cast by the key light. Secondary light sources, like candles or small lamps, should be implemented as fill lights. Point lights make excellent fill lights, but you can use low-intensity directional lights and spotlights to great effect. Keep the intensity low for all fill lights at first and build up to create the effect you want.

- **Back light:** Back (or rim) lights help define important objects and pop them out from the scenery. Placed directly behind the subject and opposite the camera, they create a nice, bright outline around the given subject.

Try setting up a sample scene in Unity using a three-point rig. Experiment with moving the relative positions of the lights, like moving the key light higher or lower relative to the subject than the fill light. Light rigs like this can either lie independently in a scene or be attached to moving objects, like a character. A sample diagram of a three-point rig is shown in Figure 12.3.

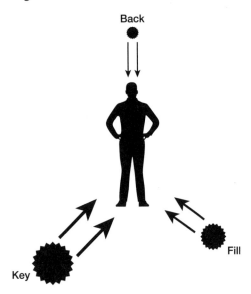

Figure 12.3
An overhead schematic of a three-point rig.

Remember, this is just a simple lighting rig example and isn't a one-catch-all solution for every scene you may create. Start with a practical look at which objects in your scene would be casting light, determine the mood you want to achieve, and work from there.

Lighting for Different Functions

Besides the obvious purpose of lighting a scene so players know where they are going, lighting can serve multiple purposes simultaneously in any given level. When placing a light in a scene, try to identify what purpose (or purposes) it's currently serving.

On the most basic level, lights are used for simple illumination. If your level isn't lit, the players won't be able to see where they are going or what they are doing. Providing enough light for the players to adequately judge their surroundings should be one of the first parts tackled when lighting a new scene.

Lights can also be used as gameplay devices to help direct or attract players to a particular point or object. Players tend to follow lit paths rather than explore only dark corners, and placing a subtle string of lights around your level can help guide the players without resorting to more obvious means. Lights can also be used to illuminate levels, triggers, or other important objects that the players should focus on. A dim light in the distance can help players discover treasures placed off the beaten path.

Mood is one of the biggest visual factors that lights can influence. One scene can have multiple different moods associated with it, based solely on lighting alone. A wash of red tinted lights can make a scene seem more sinister or dangerous, whereas blues and greens are more calming and tranquil. Also, play with the contrast of strong lights and dark shadows when trying to make more intense scenes.

For an outdoor scene, lights play an important role in determining the time of day. While this sounds painfully obvious, the color of the light is almost more important than the intensity when setting the scene. Blue lights are effective for simulating moonlight and night skies, oranges and reds are used for dawn and dusk, and very pale green lights are perfect for noon-day skies.

Lights can also be controlled via scripts and can be shut on or off or have their properties changed on the fly. The possibilities for achieving the look you want are just about endless.

Lighting the World

Currently, the *Widget* scene has only one directional light in it, placed in Chapter 4, "Building Your Environment: Importing Basic Custom Assets." This light works well as a base key light for the scene, but it can use a few tweaks.

The scene could also use some more ambient and mood lighting. Let's do that now:

1. Open your latest scene in Unity and save a new copy of it, naming it Chapter 12. Click your directional light in the Hierarchy view to bring up its properties in the Inspector.

2. The light probably hasn't been changed from any of its default values, so begin by setting its color to a pale green. (R=253, G=255, B=218 works well.) The effect on the terrain is subtle, but it helps.

3. Import the Props folder from Chapter 12 on the website and place the objects and textures into their respective folders. Make sure the Scale Factor settings on the meshes are at 1 and assign basic outline toon shaders to the materials. This package includes a cottage, some wooden structures, and two light props. Make prefabs of the new objects (by dragging them to the Project view) if you plan to reuse or change any aspects of them in the future.

4. Find a nice open spot in your scene and drop the cottage there. Place a few fences and lights and span the river with the included bridge piece. A sample placement is shown in Figure 12.4.

Figure 12.4
A pastoral setting. Pretty, but it lacks lighting.
Source: Unity Technologies.

5. Now that you've got some light-emitting props down, you can set up some mood lighting. Find one of your lamps and create a new point light around it. (Choose GameObject > Create Other > Point Light.) Set this lamp up with an appealing light color and intensity.

6. Duplicate this light and leave it sitting on top of the first one. This second light will serve as a halo for the lamp, so select the Draw Halo checkbox and turn the intensity down until you like the effect. Also play with the range and color. You can apply this double light/halo light effect to other lamps in the scene if you want.

7. Find the checkpoint object you placed previously in the scene and add some lights to it as well. You want to draw the player's attention to the checkpoint, and lights are an easy way to do this. Figure 12.5 and Figure 12.6 show the finished cottage and checkpoint robot.

Figure 12.5
The lit cottage and fencing.
Source: Unity Technologies.

Figure 12.6
Lights and halos adorning the checkpoint robot.
Source: Unity Technologies.

8. Continue adding lights around the scene as you see fit. Try adding some subtle light cues along the path to direct the player along it.

Tip

If you notice strange lines or clipping from lights on the ground, this usually means your terrain resolution is too low.

CREATING SHADOWS

Light and shadows can be visually stunning. Several dynamic shadowing features are available in Unity Pro but are disabled in the free version of Unity. Even without the Pro version, you can still add the effects of shadows on your terrain and objects. Primarily, you can use a combination of terrain painting, lightmaps, and projectors to give the effect of objects casting shadows.

Lightmaps

Chapter 3, "Setting the Stage with Terrain," briefly mentioned lightmaps and how they can be useful for painting shadows on terrain. Now you'll actually create the illusion of cast shadows on the terrain by painting up a custom lightmap.

To create a shadow with a lightmap, follow these steps:

1. Grab the LightmapExport.cs file from the Chapter 12 > Scripts folder on the companion website if you didn't import this in Chapter 3.

2. In your own project Assets folder, create an Editor folder and drop the copied script file into it. This Editor folder is special in that it allows custom scripts to be run directly from within the editor. Failure to place the script in the properly named folder will result in it not working.

3. A new menu option will appear between Terrain and Window: CUSTOM. If you look in here, the custom script called Duplicate Texture is now available. This is exactly what you need to export your lightmap for edits.

4. In the Project view, find your terrain asset (probably called New Terrain unless you changed it earlier). Expand its hierarchy to see its Lightmap texture. Select this texture and then run the Duplicate Texture option from the menu.

5. Your new texture file LightmapDuplicate will be placed in the root of your Assets folder. It may not show up in the Project view until you manually refresh (press Ctrl+R to do so).

Now take this file into your graphics editor of choice and paint onto it. Make your adjustments on new layers to save yourself headaches later. GIMP is a free graphics editor (read more about GIMP in Appendix D, "Resources and References") if you need to install one.

To determine where to place your edits, take a screenshot of your current level from a top-down view and import it into your graphics editor. You can then apply this as a layer or mask and know exactly where to edit. Figure 12.7 shows an example of this.

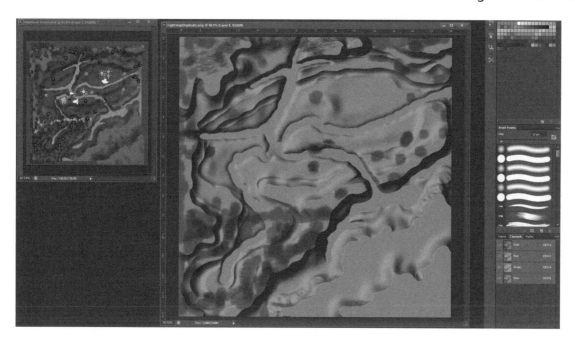

Figure 12.7
Aligning layers in Photoshop to paint shadows.
Source: Unity Technologies.

After painting, you just need to assign your new lightmap to the terrain:

1. Click your new Lightmap file in the Project view to bring up its properties. In the Inspector, change its Texture Format setting to RGB 24-bit. Your lightmap will not work if you forget to do this.

2. Click your base terrain asset in the Project view (not the Hierarchy view).

3. Its Inspector view will show only one option: Lightmap. Drag your new Lightmap texture file onto this slot (or select it from the drop-down list) to apply it.

Take a spin around your level and verify that the shadows you painted look the way you want them to. If you saved your edits on separate layers in your Lightmap file, you can continuously tweak and edit even as you add new content to your scene.

Projector-Made Shadows

Another method for applying shadows is to use projectors. A Unity projector acts just like one in real life—it projects a material or image onto a surface. This can be used to project pictures and patterns onto objects in the scene (like bullet holes or footprints) or, when used with a dark material, to project blobby shadows underneath characters and objects.

To create a simple projector object, make an empty GameObject and then add a Project component by selecting Component > Rendering > Projector. A sample projector is shown in Figure 12.8.

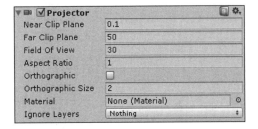

Figure 12.8
A sample projector object.
Source: Unity Technologies.

Many of a projector's properties are similar to those of a camera or light source:

- **Near Clip Plane:** Any object that is closer than the distance specified will not be projected upon.

- **Far Clip Plane:** Any object that is farther away than the distance specified will not be projected upon.

- **Field of View:** The degrees of the projector's field of view. If the projector is orthographic, this value is not used.

- **Aspect Ratio:** The aspect ratio of the projector. You can change this to project quadrilateral shapes besides squares.

- **Orthographic:** Select this checkbox if you want to disable perspective for the projector.

- **Orthographic Size:** If the projector is orthographic, this dictates how big an area it covers.

- **Material:** The material and texture to be projected onto any object the projector encounters.

- **Ignore Layers:** Select layers in the drop-down list to disable the projector's effects. This is useful to disable a character so his own projector doesn't place him in shadow.

The Standard Assets package comes with a blob-shadow projector premade, so all you need to do is hook it up:

1. Find the blob-shadow projector in the Standard Assets folder by choosing Standard Assets > Blob-Shadow > blob shadow projector.

2. Make an instance of this prefab in the scene and then parent it to a Widget object. Allow this to break the link to the parent Widget prefab.

3. Maneuver the projector so that it points down directly over Widget. A position of (0,5,0) and a rotation of (90,0,0) work well. Widget should now be cast in darkness, as shown in Figure 12.9.

Figure 12.9
The early shadow projector.
Source: Unity Technologies.

4. Now you need to set up a new layer so the projector can ignore the Widget mesh while still projecting the blobby shadow onto the ground. From the Layers drop-down list in the top-right corner, select Edit Layers.

5. Click the empty space to the right of User Layer 8 (the first editable layer) when the mouse cursor changes to the text editing cursor. Enter a new name for this layer, such as Player.

6. Select the Widget prefab and change the Layer option (directly under the name in the Inspector) to Player. Also change this field on the Widget model in the scene. Select Apply to All Children when prompted.

7. Return to the blob shadow projector. In the Ignore Layers property field, select the new Player layer from the drop-down list. Voilà! Widget is now casting a shadow! Update the links to the Widget prefab with this new shadow version, shown in Figure 12.10.

Figure 12.10
Widget's final shadow.
Source: Unity Technologies.

Add more projectors to the enemies or to any other object you want in the scene. You can also place projectors over all the trees to simulate dappled foliage rather than painting individual lightmaps.

You can also use projectors to create the effect of moving clouds when tied to an appropriate script. The material can be slowly animated, making it look like rolling clouds are crossing the landscape. Even without dynamically cast shadows, many kinds of shadow effects are possible by combining clever projector usage and texture painting.

OTHER LIGHT EFFECTS

There are a few last effects you can add to your lights to add a final layer of polish to your game. These should be used sparingly and only when appropriate so they don't appear cheesy or overused to your players.

Lens Flares

Unity supports the classic lens flare and comes prepackaged with a few flare options. Flares are built from a Flare component and a specially laid texture, which can be attached to any GameObject in the scene—not just lights. The flare works by reading the texture file, splitting it into a set number of component images, and then stringing these images out in a line. The line is calculated by comparing the position of the Flare object to the center of the screen.

To make a basic Lens Flare effect, create an empty GameObject in the scene and then attach the Lens Flare component by selecting Component > Rendering > Lens Flare. Rename your GameObject to something like Lens Flare and view its properties in the Inspector. They are as follows:

- **Flare:** Select the kind of flare effect you want from the drop-down list. Standard Assets comes prepackaged with a Sun, 50mm Zoom camera, and Small Flare effect. Try each of these to see the different effects.
- **Color:** This tints the flare's texture.
- **Brightness:** Change the overall brightness of the flare effect.
- **Directional:** Select this checkbox to make the flare appear far away in the distance. It will attach itself to the positive end of the Z axis.

If you decide to attach your flare to a GameObject and not through a light component, be careful where you place the object. Flares should always be tied to a light source in some way. Players will easily become distracted by misplaced flare effects.

Cookies

Cookies are another form of lighting effect, useful for creating the illusion of light being obstructed in some way. Cookies are like gobos in stage lighting—you basically place a black and white texture mask over the light, which acts to obstruct the light according to its pattern. Fully white areas will allow the light to pass through unobstructed, and fully black areas will not emit any light at all. Cookies can be used to create illusions ranging from light passing through barred windows to sun dappling between tree leaves.

Unity comes with two cookies in the Standard Assets packages, but it's simple to create and import your own:

1. To start, find a black and white image or make one in the graphics editor of your choice. Make sure the edges of the image are all black; otherwise, it'll look like light is "leaking" out the sides of the image. A sample cookie image is included with the Chapter 12 contents as well.

2. Import the image into the Assets folder and set the wrap mode to Clamp.

3. Select Build Alpha from Grayscale and Border Mipmaps from the import settings list.

4. Change the Texture Format setting to Alpha 8 and click Apply to save all your import changes.

5. Create a new spotlight (choose GameObject > Create Other > Spot Light) and position it so you can see the cone of light easily in the scene.

6. Duplicate this light and move it so that the two lights sit side by side. With one light selected, assign the new cookie texture to the Cookie property in the light's Inspector view. Figure 12.11 shows the simple spot and the spot with the cookie applied.

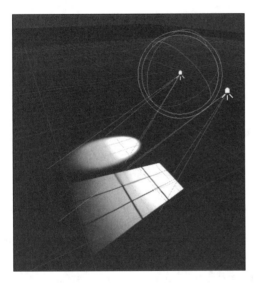

Figure 12.11
A window-esque cookie's effect on a spotlight.
Source: Unity Technologies.

You can apply 2D texture cookies to directional lights and spotlights, and point lights can take a cube map texture as a cookie as well. A simple and quickly authored black-and-white image can lend the illusion that you have complicated geometry in your scene, saving both time and rendering power.

Lights are a fast and relatively cheap way to add depth, personality, and interest to your scenes. A few mood and interest lights can be all that differentiates a fun and interesting game from a boring and lifeless level.

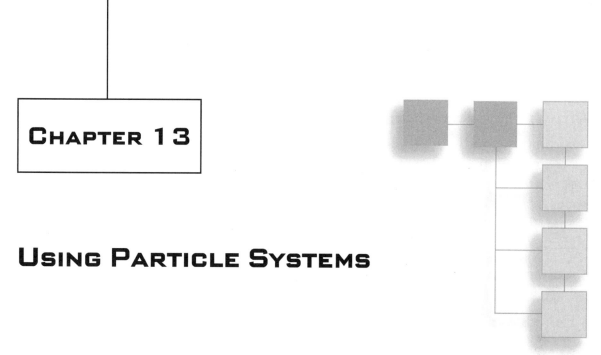

CHAPTER 13

USING PARTICLE SYSTEMS

Particles are another way you can add life and polish to your game levels. Particles can provide feedback to players based on their actions, can be a useful method to grab the player's attention, or can simply help illustrate a pretty area of the scene with special effects. You can hook up and control particle systems like any other object in Unity, and you can easily start and stop them from within scripts. Although they are computationally expensive when overused, particles can add a pleasing amount of movement and interest to an otherwise static scene.

Unity's particle system engine, called Shuriken, is quite powerful and can be fun to play with. You might want to set some time limits when adjusting particles because it is easy to get caught up in the fun.

PARTICLES: FROM SMOKE TO STARDUST

In 3D graphics and games, particles are a way to render certain kinds of effects and materials that aren't simple or efficient to model in a traditional way—for example, smoke, stars, sparks, fire, and dust clouds. Particles are generally represented by 2D planes known as *billboards* or *sprites*, which are discharged from an object called an *emitter*. The combination of rendered particles and emitter is what makes up a basic particle system.

To render a complex object like a flickering torch or a plume of smoke, you first attach an emitter to the object in question. The emitter can be a basic shape, like a sphere, or use a detailed mesh to create special effects. The sprites are discharged along the surface of the emitter (usually at the vertices) at a set rate and velocity and are layered on top of each other to create the illusion of substance. Animations and forces are also applied to the sprites to achieve different effects.

Sometimes, the textures used by sprites are tiled with different images, allowing for even more complex effects with minimal work. Figure 13.1 shows a sample explosion effect that was created using only a single-texture sprite. Depending on the forces and animations applied, the same particle emitter can take on wildly different effects, as illustrated in Figure 13.2. Getting the exact effect you want can sometimes be a lengthy process of trial and error, but the end result is worth it.

Figure 13.1
A simple particle system.
Source: Unity Technologies.

Figure 13.2
The same particles as in Figure 13.1, but with different forces.
Source: Unity Technologies.

SETTING UP A SIMPLE SYSTEM

Creating a new particle system is as easy as making a new GameObject. Open a new scene in Unity and navigate to GameObject > Create Other > Particle System. This places a new, ready-to-go particle system in the scene. If you select it in the Hierarchy view and focus on it in the scene, it will begin animating with the default selections. Figure 13.3 shows the basic particle system in action.

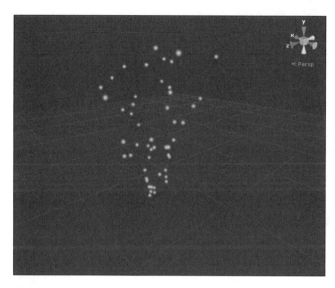

Figure 13.3
A default particle system.
Source: Unity Technologies.

The default system uses a cone particle emitter and comes prepopulated with a particle animator and renderer. To customize the system to fit your needs, from dust cloud to bonfire, you just need to tweak the particle system modules.

Particle Systems

Unity's particle emitters are built out of a collection of modules. Figure 13.4 illustrates the various properties used to discharge the default particle sprites.

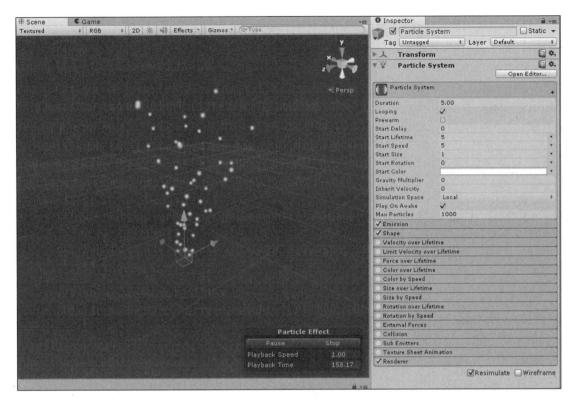

Figure 13.4
The Particle System component.
Source: Unity Technologies.

The emitter randomizes the particles rendered, changing the size, visible duration, and velocity of each sprite based on the set properties in the component. To make it easier to see the details of particle systems, you can click Open Editor in the Inspector. That opens a window with the same particle system details, but with a large window for editing curves and details (see Figure 13.5).

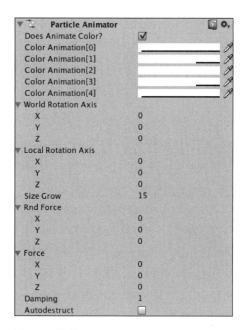

Figure 13.5
The Particle Effect editor.

Source: Unity Technologies.

The first cluster module specifies the overall details of the particle system:

- **Duration:** The number of seconds to run the particle system. If the system is marked as looping, this is the time of a single loop.

- **Looping:** When checked, the particle system will loop until stopped by script.

- **Prewarm:** When a particle system starts running, you might want to make it look like it has been running for a while. This will simulate a full loop of the system when the scene is loaded so all the particles will be in motion. This is useful if you have a water fountain and want it to look like it has been running for a while, or if you have a fire and want a pillar of smoke rising from it as you enter.

- **Start Delay:** The opposite of Prewarm. It tells the particle system to wait x number of seconds before starting.

- **Start Lifetime:** How long an individual particle should last after being emitted.

- **Start Speed:** How fast an individual particle should travel when emitted.

- **Start Size, Rotation, and Color:** Other values to use when the particle is first emitted.

- **Gravity Multiplier:** Set to 1 if you want your particles to follow the same gravity values as the physics engine. Values between 0 and 1 cause the particles to float down more slowly.

- **Max Particles:** Keep the number reasonable. Too many particles can harm performance.

Each of the built-in modules has its own set of details. Rather than going in depth on each X, Y, and Z component, I'll cover the modules generally:

- **Emission:** Allows you to generate new particles. You can generate new particles based on a time, with bursts happening periodically. Or you can generate new particles when old particles leave the system. Turn the module off if you only want to keep the initial particles.

- **Shape:** Specify where particles will be generated. By default, they will be generated in a cone fountain. Generating them on a sphere or hemisphere can produce nice bubble effects. Generating particles from a mesh requires more processing, but can be satisfying if you want your particles to match a model. For example, if you are detonating an object, you want particles to appear from the shape of the model, not from a sphere. You can also indicate if you want particles to be generated everywhere inside the shape or only from a specific region.

- **Velocity over Lifetime:** Effectively acts as gravity or as a drift. You can make the wind flow relative to the particle system or relative to the world.

- **Limit Velocity over Lifetime:** Keep particles from going too fast if they are accelerating for gravity or other reasons.

- **Force over Lifetime:** Lets you change the speed over time. This is useful if you are following your own gravity rules or if you want to treat your wind as a steady force.

- **Color over Time:** Many types of particles change color over time. Smoke may fade out to transparency, sparks may fade from a hot bluish-white through reds and oranges, and eventually fade to a transparent gray.

- **Color by Speed:** Perhaps your particles change color based on how far they are from the emitter. This will give a more spherical effect than Color over Time.

- **Size over Lifetime:** Allows particles to grow and shrink over time. You can build a curve that lets your particle start at a medium size, grow large, and then shrink to obscurity.

- **Size by Speed:** Faster particles can be bigger or smaller than slower particles.

- **Rotation over Lifetime:** Control the angular velocity of particles, making them turn as a constant or as curves.

- **Rotation by Speed:** Allow speed to determine the velocity, again as curves or constants.

- **External Forces:** If you use the physics system's wind zones, this allows the particles to be affected by wind and other forces.

- **Collision:** Some particles should react to the world. They can collide with built-in planes or, if you have processing power available, they can collide and interact with other physics objects. Beware of performance issues.

- **Sub Emitters:** Like an aerial fireworks display, you can launch one particle into the air and then cause the particle to explode in a second shower of light and color.

- **Texture Sheet:** If you want hand-drawn particles, this is for you. You can specify a 2D texture sheet where the animation moves from image to image.

- **Renderer:** Allows you to customize how the particles are shown. Billboards are 2D images that generally face the player. A mesh renderer is done in 3D space and will require more resources.

Taken together, this is an impressive list! You can make particle systems with complex behaviors.

Making Texture Sheets in Photoshop

Photoshop and other graphics editors make it easy to create tiled texture sheets (or *atlases*) for use in particle systems. First, decide how many tiles you want, how large each will be, and how you plan to lay them out. For example, say you want eight tiles to animate through, each 64 × 64 pixels. If arranged in a 4 × 2 grid, your file needs to be 256 × 128. You could also arrange them in a straight line, for a file size of 512 × 64. Create a new file using the correct dimensions.

In Photoshop, choose View > Show > Grid, or press Ctrl+', displaying a regular grid across your work surface. To set the grid up so that each square corresponds to one tile, choose Edit > Preferences > Guides, Grid, and Slices. Under the Grid section, change the Gridline Every field to 64 (for this example) and set the drop-down list to pixels. Change the subdivisions to 1 unless you want extra gridlines within each tile. Click OK to save your changes. See Figure 13.6.

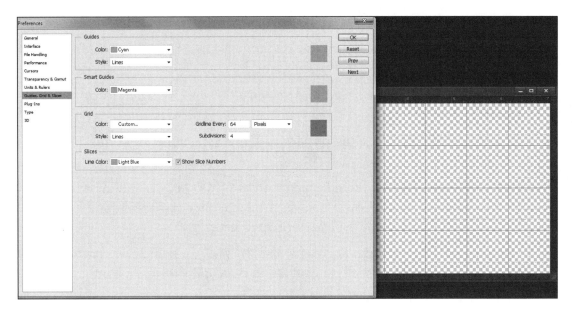

Figure 13.6
Setting up a grid in Photoshop.
Source: Adobe Systems Inc.

Now when you paint your new particle textures, just ensure that each tile stays neatly within each grid line, and save the file in a format that preserves the alpha channel of your particles.

Advanced Particle Systems

These particle systems are good for most jobs you'll run across, but Unity allows them to be combined to greatly expand your particle repertoire.

You are not limited to one set of particles. You can have multiple particle systems working together. You can create additional particle systems, and use the Hierarchy view to make them all children of a single system. When you start, stop, or reset the parent particle system, the child systems also take the action. The combined particle systems can be controlled as one. When you combine particle systems, the results can be impressive. You are limited only by your imagination and your processing power.

An electric burn effect might have an emitter that makes bright pulses of light, another emitter that gives off a plume of smoke, and another emitter that drops sparks. Then, those sparks can have sub-emitters that give off small amounts of smoke. Creative use of sprite sheets on the sparks can make it look like even more sparks are flying, and sprite sheets on the smoke can light up at the right times to give a cloudlike texture to the plume.

A water fountain might launch into the air, giving off a light mist through a sub-emitter. When they hit the plane of the water, they might be replaced with water droplet sprites. A simple billboard placed at the center can give a nearly transparent rainbow as light travels through the mist.

Be careful to watch your total sprite count, as every sprite has a tiny performance cost. Dozens of sprites can be effective. Hundreds of sprites can be visually stunning and complex. Thousands of sprites can bring a system to a crawl.

PARTICLES FOR *WIDGET*

Some aspects of the *Widget* game can definitely make use of particle systems, like Widget's Taser attack, which at the moment consists of only a simple animation. Open your latest Unity scene file and save a new copy of it, naming it Chapter 13. From the companion website, import the contents of the Chapter 13 > Textures folder into the *Widget* project, placing them in the Particles directory of the Assets folder. Make sure that all the particle textures are imported with an alpha-ready compression, like DXT5. Otherwise, they won't show up as expected in the shader.

Pickup Items

The first simple particle system you can make is an attention-grabber for the various pickup items around the scene. Currently, the objects can be a little hard to spot from a distance. A simple sparkle effect can help the players see the objects as Widget rolls along. For this simple sparkle effect, you'll create a particle system:

1. Create a new particle system by choosing GameObject > Create Other > Particle System and naming it something more descriptive, like Attention Sparkles.

2. Create a new material to use with the system. Make a new material in the Particles folder and choose Particles > Additive Shader to assign the shader. Locate the newly imported attention_sparkle_PART texture and assign it to the material.

3. Assign this new sparkle material to the particle system's Renderer module. While you are there, disable the Cast Shadows and Receive Shadows settings.

4. In the Texture Sheet Animation module, change the fields to X = 4 and Y = 2. Because the image is tiled with eight frames, you need to make sure to set the UV field correctly. By default, the Frame over Time setting is a straight line from 0 to 8, which will give a simple animation.

5. Begin tweaking the particle system. To start, set the following properties as follows:

- **Start Size to Between Two Constants:** Change the sizes to 0.1 and 0.3.
- **Start Speed to Between Two Constants:** Change the sizes to 0.5 and 1.5.
- **Max Particles:** Set this to 20.
- **Emission Rate:** Set this to 5 particles per second.
- **Size over Lifetime to Between Two Constants:** Change the sizes to 1 and 1.5.

This will produce a slowly animating sparkle effect that rises into the sky before fading from view, as shown in Figure 13.7. Make a prefab of this finished effect.

Figure 13.7
A sparkle effect attached to a screw pickup point.
Source: Unity Technologies.

Now you need to assign the new effect to your prefabs. Create an instance of the gear and pickup prefabs in the scene (if they do not exist already) and parent the newly created sparkle effect to the pickups, allowing this to break the old prefab connections. Move the sparkle effect so that it rests nicely on top of the pickup items. Reconnect these new object groups to the old prefab by dragging the group from the Hierarchy view to the prefab in the Project view.

All that's left is to run the effect from the pickup script you wrote earlier, because you want to make sure that it starts and stops emitting at the proper times. Open the PickupItems.js script and create a new variable for the emitter at the top of the file:

```
var sparkleEmitter : ParticleSystem;
```

In the `OnTriggerEnter()` function, after where you set the `pickedUp` variable equal to `True`, add a new line to turn off the emitter when the player grabs the item:

```
sparkleEmitter.Stop;
```

Now scroll down the file to the `Reset()` function. Add the following to the bottom of this function:

```
sparkleEmitter.Play;
```

This ensures that the emitter will start playing when the pickup object is instantiated. Back in the pickups prefab, assign your new particle systems to this variable in the Inspector. Save your work and test your new pickups; they should be much more shiny and easier to spot now. Any one of the particle's property fields, like emit, can be changed via scripting, allowing you complete and precise control over every aspect of your system.

Checkpoint Activation

The checkpoint object could also use a particle effect to notify the player which checkpoint is currently active—right now they all look the same. Instead of using a spherical emitter, you'll create a cylindrical emitter that fits the base of the checkpoint using a mesh emitter. To create a cylindrical emitter, follow these steps:

1. Create a new simple cylinder object. To do so, choose Game Object > Create Other > Cylinder. You'll use this mesh as a starting point for the new system. Rescale the cylinder to X = 4, Y = 0, and Z = 4.

2. Delete both the Mesh Renderer and Capsule Collider components from the cylinder. Neither of these is needed for the particle system. This leaves you with just the mesh filter. Now add the Particle System component. The base setup for a mesh emitter is now complete.

3. Create a new material to use with the mesh particle system and name it Station Sparkles. Find the newly imported texture file station_spark_PART.tif and assign it to the material. For this material, also choose Particle > Additive Shader to assign the shader.

4. Assign this new material to the Renderer Material and set up the rest of the properties as follows:
   - **General module:** Set Start Speed to 0 and disable Play on Awake.
   - **Emission module:** Set Rate to 50.

- **Shape module:** Set Shape to Mesh and select the cylinder created in step 1.

- **Velocity over Lifetime module:** Choose Random Between Two Constants, with Y ranging from 0 to 0.5.

- **Size over Lifetime module:** Choose Random Between Two Constants, from 0.1 to 0.6.

- **Texture Sheet Animation module:** Set X to 4 and Y to 4.

- **Renderer module:** Disable Cast Shadows and Receive Shadows.

5. Change any other properties to achieve the look you want.

6. Create a prefab of this new effect, parent it to one of the checkpoint objects in the scene (break the old connections), and then reparent this new checkpoint object to the old CheckPoint prefab to update it with the sparkle effect. Align the sparkle effect so that it sits nicely on the platform, as shown in Figure 13.8.

Figure 13.8
An activated checkpoint.
Source: Unity Technologies.

As with the pickups, you'll also need to update a script to make the particles function as wanted. Open the CheckPoint.js script and add a new variable at the top of the file for your sparkle emitter:

```
var activeEmitter : ParticleSystem;
```

You'll set this to activate only when the player sets a new checkpoint as his current respawn point. Then scroll down to the `BeActive()` function and add the following:

```
activeEmitter.Play;
```

This will start the emitter when the player triggers the checkpoint by rolling over it. Now you just need to turn it off when the player sets a new point as active. In the `BeInactive()` function, add the following:

```
activeEmitter.Stop;
```

That's it. Assign the particle system to the activeEmitter variable in the Inspector. Save your script and test your new systems by putting at least two checkpoint objects down in the scene and rolling between the two. The particle systems will turn on and off depending on whichever one Widget sets as last active.

Widget's Attack

Widget's taser attack is up next for a particle treatment. Applying a one-shot effect whenever the player presses the attack key will provide a bit more much-needed feedback. To create a particle system for Widget's attack, follow these steps:

1. Create a new particle system and name it electricity.

2. Create a new material to use with the particle system. Find the newly imported texture file electricity_PART.tif and assign it to the material. For this material, choose Particle > Additive Shader to assign a shader.

3. Assign this new material to the particle renderer and set up the rest of the properties as follows:

    - **Particle module:** Disable Looping (you can keep this enabled while tweaking, but be sure to turn it off when you're done), set Duration to 1, set Start Lifetime to 0.1, set Start Speed to 0.1, set Start Size as a range between 0.1 and 0.5, and disable Play on Awake.

    - **Emission module:** Set Rate to 50.

    - **Shape module:** Set Shape to Sphere.

    - **Texture Sheet Animation module:** Set X to 4 and Y to 1.

    - **Renderer module:** Disable Cast Shadows and Receive Shadows.

4. Create a prefab of this new effect, parent it to Widget (break the old connections), and then reparent this new checkpoint object to the old Widget prefab to update it with the effect link. Align the effect so that it sits neatly around Widget.

Now you just need to attach the emitter to Widget's attack. Open the Widget_AttackContoller.js file and add a new variable for the emitter:

```
var attackEmitter : ParticleSystem;
```

You need to create a new function to handle the particles instead of just turning the emitter on and off. Create a new function at the bottom of the file:

```
function PlayParticles(){
}
```

Within this function, you'll start and stop the emitter directly, but also give it some time to play the effects. Add the following to the middle of the function body:

```
attackEmitter.Play;
yield WaitForSeconds(attackEmitter.Duration );
attackEmitter.Stop;
```

The function will now wait for the minimum amount of time for the emitter to play before shutting off again. In the `DidAttack()` function above this, add a call to this function beneath the line `yield WaitForSeconds(attackHitTime)`:

```
PlayParticles();
```

Now whenever the player successfully attacks, the one-shot system will trigger. Connect the electricity particle system to the attackEmitter variable in the Inspector and test it. See Figure 13.9.

Figure 13.9
Widget attacks!
Source: Unity Technologies.

Making an explosion for a dying enemy is a little more complicated. You'll need to use two particle systems in tandem to get the right effect—one for the explosion and one for the resulting smoke.

Try creating this pair of particle systems on your own, using the hints that follow. If you get stuck, you can always review the Final Project files from the companion website to see how the sample explosion system is set up.

1. Make a one-shot particle system for the explosion. Use the spark_ PART.tif texture file and make sure that the particles grow in size to simulate the spreading explosion. Try to get the timing of the emitter right so that the particles look like they're being emitted with great force over the course of just one second.

2. Create a smoke effect particle system using the smoke_PART.tif file and choose Particles > Multiply Shader to apply a shader. Remember to make the smoke rise upward and to have the effect last about five seconds long. Play with some of the random force or rotation values to try to get a more billowy look.

3. Make a new prefab with these two systems and name it Explosion. Remember that when a particle system is parented to another particle system, they work together as one. Attach this object to the E_Bunny prefab.

Open the EBunny_Status.js file and make a new variable for your particle effects:

```
var explosion : ParticleSystem;
```

Assign this variable in the Inspector with your new explosion and smoke effect. Remember to align the particles correctly on the Bunny prefab or you'll never see it in action. Then create a new function to handle the effects at the bottom of the file:

```
function PlayEffects(){
}
```

Like with Widget, you'll need to control exactly when each emitter turns on and off. Add the following to the body of this function:

```
explosion.Play;
yield WaitForSeconds(.5);
GameObject.Find("root").GetComponent(SkinnedMeshRenderer).enabled = false;
yield WaitForSeconds(.5);
explosion.Stop;
```

First, you need to start the emitter. After a brief pause, you then turn off the bunny's mesh renderer, making her invisible. This way, her body won't poke through any piece of the resulting explosion. After waiting a bit more, you turn off the fire part of the explosion, wait a bit longer, and then finish off by completing the smoke emitter. Scroll up to the EBunny's `Die()` function and insert a call to the `Play Effects()` function here:

```
[. . .]
Destroy(gameObject.GetComponent(EBunny_AIController));
yield WaitForSeconds(animation["EBunny_Death"].length - 5);

//Play effects goes here
PlayEffects();

//Cache location of dead body for pickups
var itemLocation = gameObject.transform.position;
[. . .]
```

Try testing your new and improved exploding bunny, as shown in Figure 13.10! Create and add more particle effects as you see fit. Possible areas to explore include some simple water splashes around the bridge and a trail renderer for Widget when he uses his boost skill.

Figure 13.10
Gone in a flash.
Source: Unity Technologies.

As you can see, particles are a relatively quick and easy way to add some punch and pizzazz to your game, while also sometimes making it easier to play. Only one last kind of effect is left to add to Widget now: audio.

COMPLETED SCRIPTS

The newly completed and updated scripts are also available on the companion website in the Chapter 13 folder. PickupItems.js appears in Listing 13.1.

Listing 13.1   PickupItems.js

```
//PickupItems: Handles any items lying around the world that Widget can pick up
var itemType : InventoryItem;
var itemAmount = 1;
var sparkleEmitter : ParticleSystem;
private var pickedUp = false;

//When Widget finds an item on the field-------------
function OnTriggerEnter(collider: Collider){
      //Make sure that this is a player hitting the item and not an enemy
      var playerStatus : Widget_Status = Collider.GetComponent(Widget_Status);
      if(playerStatus == null)
           return;
      //Stop it from being picked up twice by accident
      if(pickedUp)
           return;
      //If everything's good, put it in Widget's Inventory
      var widgetInventory = collider.GetComponent(Widget_Inventory);
      widgetInventory.GetItem(itemType, itemAmount);
      pickedUp = true;
      //Stop any FX when picking it up
      sparkleEmitter.Stop;
      //Get rid of it now that it's in the inventory
      Destroy(gameObject);
}

//Make sure the pickup is set up properly with a collider
function Reset (){
      if (collider == null){
           gameObject.AddComponent(SphereCollider);
      }
      collider.isTrigger = true;
      sparkleEmitter.Play;
}
@script AddComponentMenu("Inventory/PickupItems")
```

CheckPoint.js appears in Listing 13.2.

Listing 13.2   CheckPoint.js

```
//Checkpoint.js: Checkpoints in the level--active for
//the last selected one and first for the initial one at startup
//The static declaration makes the isActivePt variable global
//across all instances of this script in the game
static var isActivePt : CheckPoint;
var firstPt : CheckPoint;
var activeEmitter : ParticleSystem;
var playerStatus : Widget_Status;
playerStatus = GameObject.FindWithTag("Player").GetComponent(Widget_Status);

function Start(){
      //Initialize first point
      isActivePt = firstPt;
      if(isActivePt == this){
           BeActive();
      }
}
//When the player encounters a point, this is called
//when the collision occurs
function OnTriggerEnter(){
      //First turn off the old respawn point if this is a
      //newly encountered one
      if(isActivePt != this){
           isActivePt.BeInactive();
           //Then set the new one
           isActivePt = this;
           BeActive();
      }
      playerStatus.AddHealth(playerStatus.maxHealth);
      playerStatus.AddEnergy(playerStatus.maxEnergy);
      //Print("Player stepped on me");
}
//Calls all the FX and audio to make the triggered point
//"activate" visually
function BeActive(){
      activeEmitter.Play;
}
//Calls all the FX and audio to make any old triggered point
//"inactivate" visually
```

```
function BeInactive(){
      activeEmitter.Stop;
}
@script AddComponentMenu("Environment Props/CheckPt")
```

Widget_AttackController.js appears in Listing 13.3.

Listing 13.3   Widget_AttackController.js

```
//Widget_AttackController: Handles the player's attack
//input and deals damage to the targeted enemy
var attackHitTime = 0.2;
var attackTime = 0.5;
var attackPosition = new Vector3 (0, 1, 0);
var attackRadius = 2.0;
var damage= 1.0;
var attackEmitter : ParticleSystem;

//----------------------------------------------------
private var busy = false;
private var ourLocation;
private var enemies : GameObject[] ;
var controller : Widget_Controller;
controller = GetComponent(Widget_Controller);
//Allow the player to attack if he is not busy and
//the Attack button was pressed
function Update (){
      if(!busy && Input.GetButtonDown ("Attack") && controller.IsGrounded()
&& !controller.IsMoving()){
            DidAttack();
            busy = true;
      }
}
function DidAttack (){
      //Play the animation regardless of whether we hit something
      animation.CrossFadeQueued("Taser", 0.1, QueueMode.PlayNow);
      yield WaitForSeconds(attackHitTime);

      //Play effects
      PlayParticles();
      ourLocation = transform.TransformPoint(attackPosition);
      enemies = GameObject.FindGameObjectsWithTag("Enemy");
```

```
        //See if any enemies are within range of the attack
        //This will hit all in range
        for (var enemy : GameObject in enemies){
                var enemyStatus = enemy.GetComponent(EBunny_Status);
                if (enemyStatus == null){
                        continue;
                }
                if (Vector3.Distance(enemy.transform.position, ourLocation) <
attackRadius){
                        //Apply damage for hitting
                        enemyStatus.ApplyDamage(damage);
                }
        }
        yield WaitForSeconds(attackTime - attackHitTime);
        busy = false;
}
function GetClosestEnemy() : GameObject{
        enemies = GameObject.FindGameObjectsWithTag("Enemy");
        var distanceToEnemy = Mathf.Infinity;
        var wantedEnemy;
        for (var enemy : GameObject in enemies){
                newDistanceToEnemy = Vector3.Distance(enemy.transform.position,
transform.position);
                if (newDistanceToEnemy < distanceToEnemy){
                        distanceToEnemy = newDistanceToEnemy;
                        wantedEnemy = enemy;
                }
        }
        return wantedEnemy;
}
function PlayParticles(){
        attackEmitter.Play;
        yield WaitForSeconds(attackEmitter.duration );
        attackEmitter.Stop;
}
@script AddComponentMenu("Player/Widget's Attack Controller")
```

EBunny_Status.js appears in Listing 13.4.

Listing 13.4   EBunny_Status.js

```
//EBunny_Status: Controls the state information of the enemy bunny
var health: float = 10.0;
var energy: float = 10.0;
private var dead = false;
var charImage : Texture2D;
var explosion : ParticleSystem;

//PickupItems held------------------------------------
var numHeldItemsMin = 1;
var numHeldItemsMax = 3;
var pickup1: GameObject;
var pickup2: GameObject;

//State functions------------------------------------
function ApplyDamage(damage: float){
      if (health <= 0)
              return;
      health -= damage;
      animation.Play("EBunny_Hit");

      //Check health and call Die if need to
      if(!dead && health <= 0){
             health = 0; //For GUI
              dead = true;
             Die();
      }
}
function Die (){
      animation.Stop();
      animation.Play("EBunny_Death");
      Destroy(gameObject.GetComponent(EBunny_AIController));
      yield WaitForSeconds(animation["EBunny_Death"].length - 0.5);

      //Play effects
      PlayEffects();

      //Cache location of dead body for pickups
      var itemLocation = gameObject.transform.position;
      //Drop a random number of reward pickups for the player yield
      WaitForSeconds(5);
      var rewardItems = Random.Range(numHeldItemsMin, numHeldItemsMax) + 1;
```

```
        for (var i = 0; i < rewardItems; i++){
              var randomItemLocation = itemLocation;
              randomItemLocation.x += Random.Range(-2, 2);
              randomItemLocation.y += 1; //Keep it off the ground
              randomItemLocation.z += Random.Range(-2, 2);
              if (Random.value > 0.5)
                    Instantiate(pickup1, randomItemLocation,
pickup1.transform.rotation);
                 else
                    Instantiate(pickup2, randomItemLocation,
pickup2.transform.rotation);
        }

      //Remove killed enemy from the scene
      Destroy(gameObject);
}
function IsDead() : boolean{
      return dead;
}
function GetCharImage(): Texture2D{
      return charImage;
}
function PlayEffects(){
        explosion.Play;
        yield WaitForSeconds(.5);
        GameObject.Find("root").GetComponent(SkinnedMeshRenderer).enabled = false;
        yield WaitForSeconds(.5);
        explosion.Stop;
}
@script AddComponentMenu("Enemies/Bunny'sStateManager")
```

CHAPTER 14

ADDING AUDIO AND MUSIC

Sound effects and music can be overlooked during much of a game's development. When the game's audio is done well, players tend not to consciously think about it. Players usually don't say things like "That was a very satisfying click sound." Nonetheless, the small audio details are very important to give the game a distinctive feel. In addition to being one of the most effective ways to set a mood for a level, sounds also provide much needed feedback and information, from weapon firings to interface clicks.

Audio is handled relatively late in a game project. It needs to be attached to objects in the world, to animations, and to events. Composers can write scores and audio technicians can collect great sound samples, but until the objects are created it is difficult to get timings correct and attach them to the game.

Sounds need to provide meaningful information and fit the game world. Finding just the right sound for a footstep or button click can be an arduous task. While training, trial and error, and perseverance are the only ways to find just the right sound, Unity at least makes it easy to put sound into your game once you're ready.

FEEDBACK AND AMBIENCE

One of the more recognizable aspects of game audio is the background music track. Most games play some sort of music during level exploration, battles, or menu selection. If you switch out the background music, you can easily (and relatively cheaply) change the mood of the scene. Dealing with a sad scene? Plop in a solo piano or violin. Need to increase the player's adrenaline? Write or find a song with heavy, percussive beats and short, quippy lines. If you're fairly new to audio, analyze some of your favorite games and movies. Identify the scenes you think are the most successful in mood and tone and study what the audio designer did. Although you may need a fair amount of training and experience to write music, you just need to train your ear to be good at selecting it.

Older games made heavy use of MIDI and sampled sounds. These days, however, more and more games are starting to use live recordings from individual instruments or complete orchestras. For the most part, the live instruments sound better in every way, but using them involves is a slight increase in memory overhead and a significant monetary expense. For the solo developer or hobbyist, MIDI transcriptions and mixes are still the easiest way to go. For information on free MIDI libraries, transcription, and mixing software packages, see Appendix D, "Resources and References." There are a lot of resources for audio on the Internet, and you may even be able to work out a deal with a composer or sound designer who wants to show his work in games and interactive media.

Caution

> When scouring the Internet for background music pieces, be absolutely sure you have the legal rights to use the work in your game. If the license agreement is vague, contact the artist. Most semi-professional and amateur musicians love to have their songs presented to new potential audiences, and some will allow you to do so free if proper credit is given.

Audio cues and sound effects are also highly important to get right when making a game. Play one of your favorite games for five minutes and just note how many different sounds are employed at any given moment. Footsteps on the ground need individual sounds (often of more than one variety for different materials), buttons need clicks, ambient objects like birds and water need noises, collisions need explosions...the list goes on. While a given game may need 20 or so background musical pieces, the same game may require well over 1,000 unique sounds and effects to correctly portray the audio of the levels. Games with recorded text can have several hundred thousand recorded vocal lines. There are tricks you can employ, like pitch bending and remixing, to reuse a single sound multiple times, but in general, be prepared to devote a large amount of time to finding and hooking up sound effects.

For the *Widget* game, a small selection of sound effects and background music is provided for your use. These recordings were made on a Yamaha CVP401 and mixed in Adobe Audition and are free for you to use for your own projects. You can find the music and sound effect files in the companion website in the Chapter 14 folder.

SETTING UP A SIMPLE AUDIO CLIP

Any audio file is imported into Unity as an audio clip. The list of formats is always growing. Supported audio formats include AIF, WAV, MP3, and OGG. Tracker-style formats include MOD, S3M, IT, and XM. By default, Unity does not compress your files, but you may change this through the Inspector.

To start, locate the Chapter 14 folder from the companion website and import the contents of the Audio folder into your project, placing it into the Audio folder there. You should have a BG Tracks folder (containing background music) and a Sound FX folder (with shorter effect clips). You don't need to import the Source folder into your project.

Select any one of the imported audio files while in the Project view to see its import information in the Inspector. Figure 14.1 shows the BG track. The settings are as follows:

Figure 14.1
An imported audio clip.
Source: Unity Technologies.

- **Audio Format:** Selects whether to import the file as compressed or native. Native files are larger but have better sound quality. For shorter files, this is okay, but any lengthier piece of music should be compressed. MP3 files are automatically set as compressed.

- **3D Sound:** Plays this sound in 3D space as positional audio. Both mono and stereo sounds can be played in 3D.

- **Force to Mono:** Plays a stereo sound as mono.

- **Load Type:** The Decompress on Load setting loads the audio clip into working memory once the scene is loaded, which can consume a lot of space but give better performance. The Compressed in Memory setting loads the file and decodes sections as needed, taking less memory but costing in performance. The Stream from Disc setting will load blocks of audio as they are needed. Use this for very large audio files.

- **Hardware Decoding:** Some devices, such as the iPhone and XBox 360, contain specialized hardware that can decode special audio formats with minimal CPU work. If you are targeting that hardware, this option should be enabled.

- **Gapless Looping:** Some devices, like smart phones, may use this feature when sound files must be seamlessly looped. Without this setting, some phones might have a very brief pause at the loop point.

- **Compression:** The amount of compression Unity should apply to the clip. If your audio file is a little on the large size, try increasing the compression ratio. In general, you should look to compress your files until you start to get some audible deterioration. This is especially true if you are targeting a smart phone or a Web player.

A graph of the waveform is also displayed in the Inspector, and you can preview the sound by clicking the black arrow button at the top-right of the Preview pane.

In general, audio in Unity is played by various audio sources, which are picked up by the Audio Listener. You can think of the Audio Listener as a giant microphone that picks up any audio around it. Because Unity does play sound in 3D, sounds placed farther away in the scene will be quieter than those closest to the Audio Listener. Each scene can have only one Audio Listener active at any time.

By default, the main camera is populated with the Audio Listener component. Depending on your game, this may be the perfect spot for it. If you're making a first person–type game, you'll probably want the Audio Listener attached to your player object so 3D sounds correctly positioned. Because the main camera follows Widget around, then it's acceptable to keep the Audio Listener with Widget. If you want to move the Audio Listener, simply select the GameObject you want to attach it to and navigate to Component > Audio > Audio Listener. This component has no properties to set.

Audio sources are used to simulate anything in your world that could emit sound, including birds, running water, falling rocks, and so on. The source controls all the major properties of sound playback, like pitch, volume, and rolloff, and can play any audio clip you have imported into the game.

Ambient Sound Effects

Open your last save of the *Widget* game or open the Chapter 14 Scene file from the companion website. Import the audio clips as described earlier if you haven't yet. You'll give *Widget* a little bit of ambient noise before moving on to more singular sounds.

To add ambient noise, follow these steps:

1. Navigate to the place in your level where you placed the bridge over the river. Create an empty GameObject and place it near the surface of the water. Rename it Water Sound.

2. Add an Audio Source component to the GameObject by choosing Component > Audio > Audio Source. This will also create a little speaker icon at the GameObject's location, making it easier to place. An example of the source is shown in Figure 14.2.

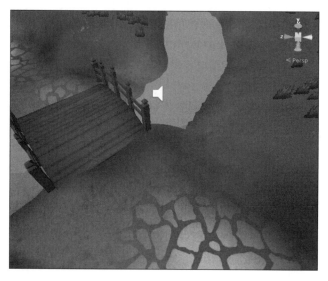

Figure 14.2
The water audio source.
Source: Unity Technologies.

3. Now you need to actually give the source something to play. Either drag and drop the newly imported water.mp3 clip into the audio clip field or select it from the drop-down list. Change the volume to something around 0.5 and select the Loop checkbox to have the sound run continuously. You can leave the other selections as they are.

4. Test the sound in the game by rolling Widget toward the water. The sound should get louder as Widget approaches the bridge and fade out the farther away he gets.

All ambient sound effects can be set up in this way. You can also try parenting these audio sources to moving GameObjects to simulate moving sounds like those made by birds.

Controlling Sounds Through Scripts

Calling sounds with scripts isn't much harder than setting up an audio source, and it does give you a lot more finesse in how you use them. To start, you'll add a hit sound and death sound for Widget, which will give the player some better feedback on the character's health.

First, you need to set up the Widget prefab to play sounds. Select the prefab in the Project view and add an Audio Source component (choose Component > Audio > Audio Source). Don't worry about setting up any of the source properties; you'll do that on the script side. Any GameObject that you want to play sounds must have an Audio Source component, even if it is completely script driven.

Open the Widget_Status.js script and add some new variables to the top of the file. You'll need to make an AudioClip variable for each of the two sounds:

```
//Sound effects------------------------------------
var hitSound: AudioClip;
var deathSound: AudioClip;
```

Because you've already written functions in this script to handle both damage done to Widget and his eventual death, adding the audio functionality is simple. Locate the ApplyDamage() function in this file and add a new if statement to handle the sound. Place the if statement after the health -= damage line:

```
health -= damage;
if(hitSound){
}
```

Now that you've verified that a clip exists and that Widget did in fact get damaged, you just need to play the sound. Inside the `if` statement, add the following:

```
audio.clip = hitSound;
audio.Play();
```

`audio` is a GameObject variable that Unity uses to reference the clip stored in the Audio Source component of that GameObject. Here, you're telling Unity which sound to populate the source with, and then to play it. The death sound will be set up similarly. Locate the `Die()` function in the script and add the following to the top of the function:

```
if(deathSound){
audio.clip = deathSound;
audio.Play();
}
```

Unity will now fill the audio source with a new clip, the death sound, and then play it whenever Widget loses all his hit points. By calling audio clips from scripts, you can easily store and play more than one file per source.

Back in the editor, populate the hitSound field on the Widget prefab with the crash.mp3 sound, and place the taser.mp3 clip into the deathSound field. Test your game by running into one of the bunny enemies or by rolling into the water.

A few other sound effects have been provided for you. Try hooking up similar sounds to the Widget attack controller (a sound to play when Widget uses his attack) and for the bunny's own attacks and death. Figure 14.3 shows the Widget prefab with these two sounds and a third attack sound attached to the attack controller.

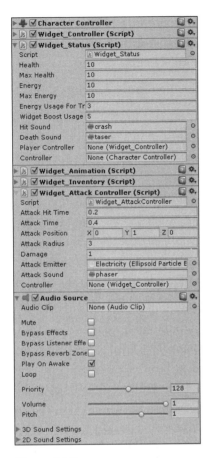

Figure 14.3
The finished Widget prefab.

Source: Unity Technologies.

The AudioSource class has other functions that you may find beneficial when setting up more complex clips. You can programmatically change the pitch and volume, stop or pause a given clip, or determine whether a particular audio clip is playing. Check Appendix B, "Common Classes," for more information on this class.

Adding Background Music

All that's left now is to set up some background music for the menu and main game level. For both of these, you'll set up a new Audio Source object and attach it to the main camera in each scene. You don't want these clips to be located or played in 3D space, as they should be heard regardless of where the player is.

Let's start off with the level music:

1. Create a new empty GameObject and rename it BGMusic. Parent this new object to the main camera in the scene. Give this new object an Audio Source component. You could of course attach an audio source directly to the camera, but as this houses the Audio Listener, it's better to keep the two separate. Reset the position of the BGMusic object to (0,0,0).

2. Locate the BG track file in the Audio folder and populate the BGMusic audio source with it. Select the Loop checkbox and set the Volume to about 0.5. You can also deselect the 3D Sound field on the track's Import properties. Because you're only using this as simple, static music, this functionality isn't needed.

3. Test your game with the new background music in place. Specifically, try to fire all the sound effects you placed to ensure that the different volumes are set correctly. You may want to lower the background music volume to suit your personal taste.

4. The main menu scene is handled in much the same way. Save your work in the Chapter 14 scene file; then open the scene file where you saved your main menu screen from Chapter 11, "Designing the Game's GUI (Graphical User Interface)."

5. Follow the same steps to attach a new Audio Source GameObject to the main camera. Populate the audio source with the BG track and reset the Loop and Volume fields.

The Whole Is Greater Than the Sum of Its Parts

Congratulations! You now know all the basics for making your own games in Unity, from concept to scripts to sound. Take this time to open the Final Project Files on the companion website and import any additional pieces you want. Many more art and GUI pieces have been provided on the website for you to expand your game, or you can go and make your own assets. Make new levels, expand the current one, and just have fun with it.

These are the same parts that are used in making all games, large and small. When you put the pieces together in creative ways, you can create new and creative entertainment for the world to enjoy.

The last chapters go over some basic optimization and debugging techniques in Unity, as well as how to package your game as either a standalone app or a Web game.

COMPLETED SCRIPT

These can be found on the companion website in the Chapter 14 folder, but are included here for reference. Widget_Status.js appears in Listing 14.1.

Listing 14.1   Widget_Status.js (updated)

```
//Widget_Status: Handles Widget's state machine
//Keep track of health, energy, and all the chunky stuff

//Vitals------------------------------------------------
var health: float = 10.0;
var maxHealth: float= 10.0;
var energy: float = 10.0;
var maxEnergy: float = 10.0;
var energyUsageForTransform: float = 3.0;
var widgetBoostUsage :float = 5.0;

//Sound effects----------------------------------------
var hitSound: AudioClip;
var deathSound: AudioClip;

//Cache controllers------------------------------------
var playerController: Widget_Controller;
playerController = GetComponent(Widget_Controller);
var controller : CharacterController;
controller = GetComponent(CharacterController);

//Helper controller functions--------------------------
function ApplyDamage(damage: float){
      health -= damage;

      //Play hit sound if it exists
      if(hitSound){
            audio.clip = hitSound;
            audio.Play();
      }
      //Check health and call Die if need be
      if(health <= 0){
            health = 0; //for GUI
            Die();
      }
}
function AddHealth(boost: float){
      //Add health and set to min of (current health + boost) or health max
      health += boost;
```

```
        if(health >= maxHealth){
                health = maxHealth;
        }
        print("added health: " + health);
}
function AddEnergy(boost: float){
        //Add energy and set to min of (current en + boost) or en max
        energy += boost;
        if(energy >= maxEnergy){
                energy = maxEnergy;
        }
        print("added energy: " + energy);
}
function Die(){
        //Play death sound if it exists
        if(deathSound) {
                audio.clip = deathSound;
                audio.Play();
        }
        print("dead!");
        playerController.isControllable = false;
        animationState = GetComponent(Widget_Animation);
        animationState.PlayDie();
        yield WaitForSeconds(animation["Die"].length -0.2);
        HideCharacter();
        yield WaitForSeconds(1);

        //Restart player at last respawn check point and give max life
        if(CheckPoint.isActivePt){
                controller.transform.position = CheckPoint.isActivePt.transform.position;
                controller.transform.position.y += 0.5;
                //So not to get stuck in the platform itself
         }
        ShowCharacter();
        health = maxHealth;
}
function HideCharacter(){
GameObject.Find("Body").GetComponent(SkinnedMeshRenderer).enabled = false;
        GameObject.Find("Wheels").GetComponent(SkinnedMeshRenderer).enabled = false;
        playerController.isControllable = false;
}
```

```
function ShowCharacter(){
GameObject.Find("Body").GetComponent(SkinnedMeshRenderer).enabled = true;
      GameObject.Find("Wheels").GetComponent(SkinnedMeshRenderer).enabled = true;
      playerController.isControllable = true;
}
@script AddComponentMenu("Player/Widget'sStateManager")
```

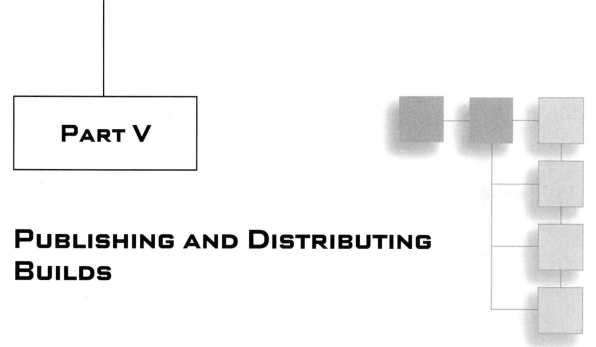

PART V

PUBLISHING AND DISTRIBUTING BUILDS

At this point, your game is fully playable and functioning, but probably shouldn't be shown to others quite yet. First, it could benefit from a quick debugging and optimization pass, ensuring that no little errors linger to trip up players and that everything runs as smoothly as possible. After this, there's only one final thing left to do: to build and save your game as a standalone application so that any and all can enjoy it without being tethered to a computer.

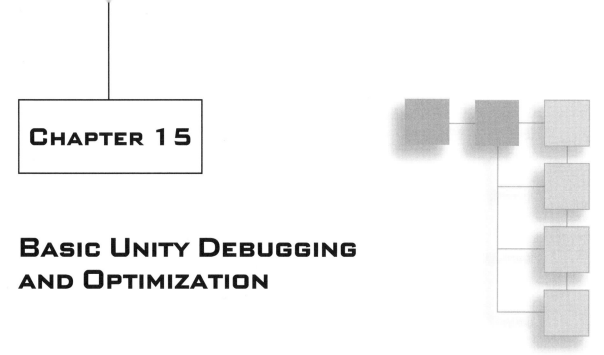

CHAPTER 15

BASIC UNITY DEBUGGING AND OPTIMIZATION

Anyone who's written any kind of software knows the importance of debugging and code optimization. Bugs and errors always creep in—often in completely unexpected and hard-to-test areas)—and code can run slower and slower as more stuff gets thrown in. Most games are pretty complicated pieces of software, and many months are devoted at the end of the project to finding bugs, fixing them, and optimizing the game.

Beyond code, the artwork in a game also needs to be compressed and optimized, both to speed performance and to reduce final file size. You may have the best-looking game ever, but if it doesn't fit on your platform's distributable, no one is going to see it. The new editions of Unity now include many tools and utilities to help developers in their quest against buggy code and bloated artwork.

DEBUGGING IN UNITY

With Unity's code-and-test-as-you-go methodology, it's usually pretty hard to introduce blatant errors into your game: When you click the Play button, you will quickly spot any simple errors in the Console. However, as your game becomes more complex, hidden and infrequent bugs may start to creep into your work. Tracking these down can be a lengthy and time-consuming process. Good tools and coding practices can help, but there's no quick fix or magic solution for easy debugging.

If you are a programmer accustomed to comprehensive debugging functionality available in languages like C++ using tools like Visual Studio, you will quickly discover that the debugging tools available in Unity are relatively limited. Unity's debugging tools are improving with every major release, however.

The Console

You've already done a bit of basic debugging through your work in the Console window. Non-fatal errors that the game runs into are printed here, marked by a red octagonal symbol (see Figure 15.1), and warning messages are displayed with a yellow symbol.

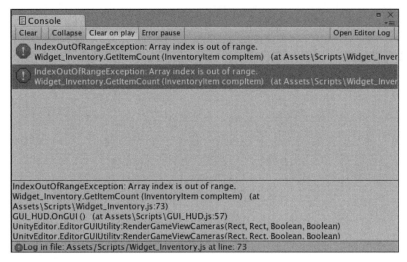

Figure 15.1
An error in the Console window.
Source: Unity Technologies.

The Console tries to narrow down the work of finding the source of the bug for you, listing the script and line number where the error occurred. Unity will also provide you with a brief description of what actually went wrong—in this case, an index for an array is out of range. Although this won't always be the original source of the error, it can help in starting to track it down.

MonoDevelop provides many debugging tools. You can drop breakpoints and watch values as they change, but it is missing some of the more powerful debugging aids programmers are used to. If you're using a third-party coding environment (like Visual Studio) along with tools to bridge the gap between the debugger and Unity, you'll have access to all the debugging functionality you're accustomed to—not just breakpoints, but also things like dump files and memory inspectors. Even so, the Console debugger is going to be your main tool when it comes to tracking down problems. Ample use of print statements and output strings to a log file are among the most reliable ways to track down errors. It's not the prettiest or easiest way to find bugs, but in general, the Console does a good job at locating errors and giving them meaningful labels.

The Log Files

Your game's log files can also provide needed information on what exactly was going on when the bug or crash occurred. Log files are stored in different locations on your computer based on whether the file was created from within the editor or from a standalone game application or Web player. Figure 15.2 shows a sample log file created from within the editor.

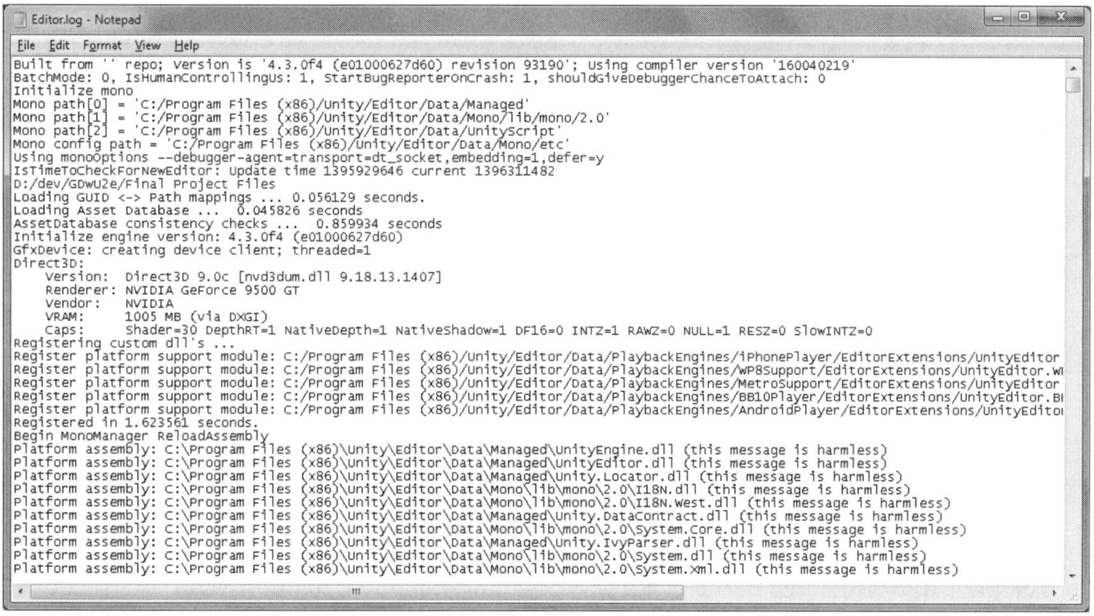

Figure 15.2
The startup information from playing the game in the editor.
Used with permission from Microsoft.

Errors shown in the Console will be printed into the logs each time they occur, with information on the location and type of error found. You can access the editor log file from within Unity on the Console window. Open the Console and then click the Open Editor Log button in the upper-right corner.

If you want to see log files generated from a built game, you'll need to manually find them on your computer. For Mac users, all the logs are stored in one place:

- ~/Library/Logs/Unity/

If you're using a Windows machine, the editor and game logs are stored in two different locations. In Windows XP, they're found here:

- C:\Documents and Settings\Local Settings\temp\UnityWebPlayer\log
- C:\Documents and Settings\UserName\Local Settings\Application Data\Unity\Editor

In Windows Vista, Windows 7, and Windows 8, they're located here:

- C:\Users\UserName\AppData\Local\Temp\Low\UnityWebPlayer\log
- C:\Users\UserName\AppData\Local\Unity\Editor

Note

On Windows machines, the Local Settings folder is hidden by default, so you'll need to enable viewing first. In XP, navigate to Tools > Folder Options and click on the View tab. Under the Advanced Settings section, click Show Hidden Files and Folders to enable it. In Windows Vista, Windows 7, and Windows 8, you can access the Folder Options menu from Organize Folder and Search Options.

The Editor.log file is updated and rewritten each time you play the game in the editor, but Unity does automatically store the previous log file for you in the same location, naming it Editor-prev.log. If you want to save and examine earlier logs, you'll need to save them manually.

Some of these log files can become large and unwieldy, and it can be hard to spot where things worked differently or changed from one version to the next. A neat way to deal with this problem is have the computer do the work for you. Many text editors are equipped with a utility to detect and highlight line changes, making your job a whole lot faster. Notepad++ is an example of a downloadable free text editor capable of highlighting changes, you can find a link in Appendix D, "Resources and References."

OPTIMIZATION

While debugging utilities in Unity may be a little on the light side, the editor does come packed with a multitude of tools and emulators to help with optimization and cleanup. Many of these are fairly new and have been introduced as the engine has grown and developed over the years. With the notable exception of the Profiler, all the optimization tools are available in both Unity Free and Pro.

The Profiler

Available only to users with a Pro license, the Profiler instruments your code, letting you know exactly how the game utilizes your computer's resources and the time it takes to render, animate, or run through code. By default, the Profiler doesn't cause a noticeable delay or lag in your game and has a rather small overhead. If you turn on Deep Profiling, however, all of your code is instrumented and recorded, and this does create a very large and noticeable memory overhead. For some complex games, Deep Profiling may actually not be an option—it is definitely possible to crash Unity and make the editor run out of memory using this approach!

You can access the main Profiler window by choosing Window > Profiler or pressing Ctrl+7. If instead you'd like to just profile specific areas of your game (like a single function), you can use the `BeginSample` and `EndSample` function calls found within the `Profiler` class to do so.

For those with the Pro version, the Profiler provides a nice peek into how your game runs and functions from frame to frame, but it isn't the only option available to you for optimization. For everyone else with the Free license, there are still many things you can do to make your game run faster, smarter, and smaller.

Code Optimization

One of the first areas you can look to optimize is your scripts. Although it may appear at first glance that your code is clean and fast, there are a few tricks you can employ to make it run even better in Unity. A few milliseconds may not sound like much, but you'll see a noticeable jump in frame rate if you can even shave one millisecond off of each function call.

Static Typing

If you've been using JavaScript for your code, go back over it and ensure that you've statically typed all your variables. (Recall from Chapter 6, "Scripting in Unity," that a statically typed variable is one where the type is explicitly given.) While dynamically typed variables may be easier and faster for you to write, they are incredibly slow to run, as Unity has to infer the type every time it uses the variable. This can add up ridiculously quickly.

Sometimes it's simple to see where you've dynamically typed a variable, but it's still easy to miss a few while wading through thousands of lines of code. Luckily, you can quickly test for dynamically typed variables by putting #pragma strict at the top of every script file. This one line will force Unity to disable dynamic typing. When the engine then encounters a variable that isn't statically typed, it will report an error in the Console.

Cache Lookups to Components

As you've done in many of the scripts, caching a link to a GameObject or component can make your game run much faster. Normally, each time a function like GetComponent() is used, Unity has to search through all the objects and components until it finds the one you requested. If you know you'll need a particular object multiple times, create a variable that links to it directly.

```
Function Awake() {
        var controller : CharacterController ;
        controller = GetComponent(CharacterController);
}
```

The variable controller can now be used to reference the component directly instead of having to search for it. Of course, you won't need (or want) to do this every time you use GetComponent(), but if you know you'll be manipulating objects every frame, it's definitely worth creating a cache.

Cull Based on Player Location

The best way to make your code faster is to never call it in the first place. If the player can't see something on the screen, then odds are it doesn't need to be running. You can use techniques to check the distance to the player or use the provided functions OnBecameVisible() and OnBecameInvisible() to do the work for you. These two functions check to see whether the given object is in the field of the camera and can be quickly and easily used to start up and shut down unnecessary commands and actions. Triggers can also be handy ways to tell whether a player is close enough for something to start running. If the player enters a given field of influence, start the script running. When he leaves, shut it down.

Even without the Profiler, there still are a lot of tweaks you can do on your own to make your scripts run faster and more efficiently.

Emulation

Unity offers two emulation utilities to test how your game would run on different hardware: Graphics Emulation and Network Emulation. You access both from the editor's Edit menu.

Graphics Emulation limits the capabilities of your graphics card, disabling features as the list goes down. The list changes based on your target platform. It might list older shader models or simulate graphics of a target handheld platform.

If you're writing custom shaders or use lots of flashy effects, emulation can provide a quick look into how your game would likely perform on hardware of that nature. This is not a replacement for standard compatibility testing, but it does provide a quick approximation of some of the errors you could expect to see.

If your game is destined for the Web player, you can also emulate what kind of Internet connection your player could be using. Network emulation attempts to parody the different kinds of connections (broadband, DSL, dial-up, and so on) by delaying packet information and inflating the ping. For dial-up connections, the developers at Unity even went a step further by introducing dropped packets and variance, creating a truly nasty connection.

Rendering Statistics Page

In addition to the emulation test, there are other aspects of graphics optimization you can explore to make your game run more smoothly. In the Game view, click the Stats button in the upper-right corner. This opens a Statistics page for your game, with information like the number of draw calls and frame rate. As you play your game, the window will update with current information, enabling you to quickly identify problem areas in your levels. Figure 15.3 shows the statistics for the *Widget* game.

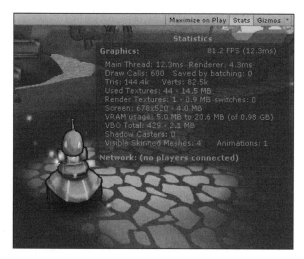

Figure 15.3
Widget's basic stats.
Source: Unity Technologies.

From this, you can see at a glance that the frames per second (FPS) is pretty good, but the game is using a fair number of animations and a large number of draw calls. With this information in hand, targeted optimization can begin. A breakdown of the different read-outs follows:

- **FPS information:** How much time it takes to render and process one frame in milliseconds, and the derived frame rate in seconds.

- **Main Thread and Renderer:** How many milliseconds are being spent in each portion of the program.

- **Draw Calls:** How many total objects are rendered in the scene. Some objects may be counted more than once, as some kinds of lighting will result in multiple draw calls for a single object.

- **Tris and Verts:** The number of triangles and vertices drawn.

- **Used Textures:** The total number of textures drawn that frame, and how much memory is used.

- **Render Textures:** The total number and size of render textures drawn that frame.

- **Screen:** The current screen resolution and memory used.

- **VRAM Usage:** An approximation of how much video memory your game is using. Your total available memory is displayed afterward.

- **VBO Total:** The number of unique meshes that were uploaded to the graphics card, and the memory used.

- **Visible Skinned Meshes:** The number of skinned meshes currently being rendered.

- **Animations:** The number of animations actively playing.

- **Network:** The number of players connected, if any.

With this information always at your fingertips, you can quickly update any art and see immediate feedback on what the changes provide.

Reducing File Size

One of the first ways to optimize your graphics is to critically look at the size of your assets. Textures and audio are two of the main culprits for large game installs, and they should be the first place you look to compress or shorten.

Because Unity processes all your art assets when you import, it's quick and easy to compress or limit the texture sizes used. In most development environments, you would need to go back to your original art, manually resize it, and then reimport it into the engine. In Unity, you can set the Max Texture Size setting in the Inspector for each texture used in your game, as well as change the compression format. Reduce the rendered texture size and increase the compression for all your textures until you begin to see some deterioration in the visuals. As these tweaks do not permanently change anything in your original art files, you can always go back and change the levels again at your convenience.

Ensure that all your audio clips are also compressed and do not contain any unnecessary silence or lead time. If a sound needs to be played multiple times, loop it in the engine and not in the actual file itself. Be cognizant of how your audio clips are stored, especially if you're developing for the Web player.

If you're still having memory issues, look into compressing your imported meshes and animation clips. Compressing meshes will make your game take up less disk space, while compressing animations saves both runtime memory and disk space. Compressing animations too much, however, can lead to jumpy behavior, so always perform small tweaks at first.

Finally, Unity only builds your game with the assets you actually used in your levels. If you have a few assets sitting in your Project folder that you never used, it's okay, they can stay there. Unity removes any unused assets from the project list during the game build, so you don't need to worry about stray pieces of art making your game bigger than it should be.

Other Ways to Optimize Graphics

Compressing and reducing file size are great ways to save memory space for your game's disk footprint, but you'll also need to look into optimizing the graphics while the game is running. The Rendering Statistics window can help you pinpoint particular areas in need of more attention and work.

If you notice a drop in frame rate in an area in your level, check to see how far it goes. Does the drop occur only when a particular object is onscreen? When a certain particle effect is playing? Try to narrow down the cause of your bad performance before you start randomly changing different things.

One cause of bad performance to check for is lighting. Pixel lights look great and can really set the mood of a scene, but they're much more intensive to render than a vertex light. If the light isn't that important, or the objects lit are far away from the player, change the lighting to Force Vertex to start.

Baking in simple light data (like with the terrain lightmaps) is another great way to save performance while not compromising visual quality. If your objects never move and are always illuminated from the same, non-moving source, consider baking the light data into your textures directly. Maya and other 3D graphics packages can make great-looking light bakes quickly and easily.

If you're using generated shadows in your game (not fake ones like the projector blob), check to see if they're the cause of a performance hit. You don't need to cut your shadows out completely, but make sure the quality settings are as low as they can go. Also, look at using hard shadows rather than soft ones. For important objects, like a main character, you can still use a nicer shadow quality, but you can save on performance by using cheaper shadows for less-important things.

Finally, if you have multiple meshes using the same material and shader, consider combining them into one mesh. It's always faster for Unity to render one object than to render many, even if they all share the same texture and have the same number of polygons. This usually isn't something you can easily do on the engine side, but if you need to make drastic performance tweaks, every little bit helps.

With optimization and debugging complete, it's now time to bundle up your game and prepare to show it to the world!

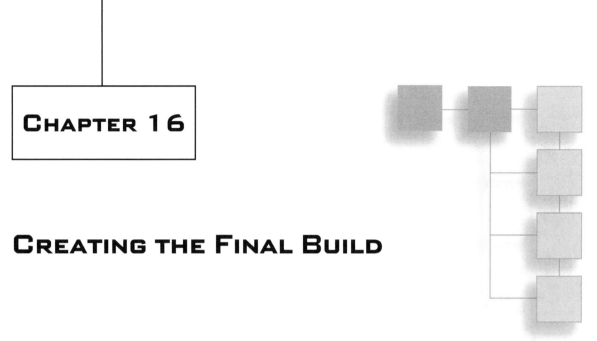

CHAPTER 16

CREATING THE FINAL BUILD

Now that all the hard work is finished, you need to be able to show the world your creation. The basic Unity license allows several deployment options for your game. You can deploy as a standalone app (Windows, Mac, and Linux) or as a Web player. You can deploy for various mobile devices such as Android, iOS, and Blackberry. The Pro version allows you to customize your loading screen, complete with a custom banner, icons, and menus to allow users to change both graphic and input options.

PREPPING FOR THE BUILD

Before you set the build options and select the scenes you want to include in the final game, you need to make sure all the basic player options are set to your satisfaction. Depending on the size of your game, building can take anywhere from a few seconds to hours, so it's usually worthwhile to check that all your basic settings are correct up front rather than have to rebuild a whole project because one text field was wrong.

Setting Up the Player

The basic information for your final game is stored in the Player Settings Manager, which you can access by choosing Edit > Project Settings > Player. Open the Player Settings

Manager to view the various properties in the Inspector, as shown in Figure 16.1. They are as follows:

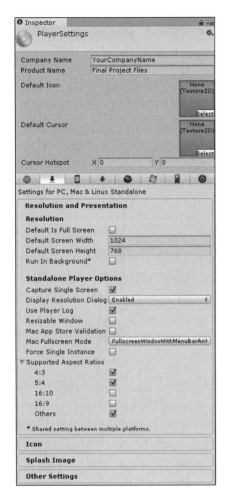

Figure 16.1
The Player Settings Manager.
Source: Unity Technologies.

- **Company Name:** Enter the name of your company or studio. This name will be used by the game install to house the Preferences file.

- **Product Name:** The name of your game! This name will appear in the menu bar and in the Install folder.

- **Default Icon:** The icon to use for your application when shown on desktops, downloaders, and app lists.

- **Default Cursor:** A custom cursor to use for devices that support cursors. You can customize your arrow with a graphic style suitable for your game.

- **Cursor Hotspot:** If you use a custom cursor, the location in the image to use for the mouse hot spot. Traditionally it is in the upper left corner, but you can make a target or other shape that places the hotspot in a custom location.

Then you have the mother lode of option screens. In all of Unity's views, this collection of settings is among the most comprehensive list. From left to right, it has custom settings for the Web player; standalone applications on PC, Mac, and Linux; and clients for iOS (the Apple family of devices), Android, BlackBerry, Windows Store, Windows Phone 8, and Google Native.

Each platform has its own collection of expandable option sets for screen resolutions, icons, splash screens, and other settings that are unique to that environment. You can change the default compression formats, change the OS compatibility to limit access on older devices, optimize for specific devices, and much more.

There's no time like the present, so fill out your name and game name and set the properties to whatever you'd like. Sample icons and a banner image are provided in the Chapter 16 folder. A sample setup for a standalone app of *Widget* is shown in Figure 16.2.

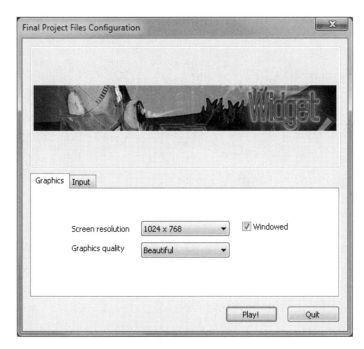

Figure 16.2
The *Widget* settings window shown at launch.
Source: Unity Technologies.

Finally, the `Application` Class

Now you just need to make sure that the main menu is ready to go. Back in Chapter 11, "Designing the Game's GUI (Graphical User Interface)," you set up the basic script to load your game from the Play button. Open the GUI_MainMenu.js script and ensure that the `Application.LoadLevel()` function is loading the correct scene file. Change the name of the scene file to match whichever level you want the application to start with. For example, my main menu will load the Chapter_16 scene file, as it is my most recent version.

The `Application` class houses all the important functions that load your various game levels as well as the basic commands for starting and quitting the game. The class also contains quite a few useful methods for looking up important information on the current state of your application. Is it loading a level? What version of Unity is it using? It running in the editor? Some of the more notable members are described here:

- `levelCount:` This read-only variable returns the total number of levels contained in your game. This is particularly useful if you want to load a random level.

- `isEditor:` This variable returns whether the game is running in the editor. You may find later you only want some things to function while in the editor or have the game disable large features for testing quickly and easily.

- `runInBackground:` You can set whether the game should continue to run if it loses focus.

- `unityVersion:` The version of Unity being used to play the game.

- `Quit:` Call this function to quit the application (like you did in the main menu script). This is ignored if the game is a Web app.

- `LoadLevel:` Load the specified level.

Once you've updated or verified your main menu script, it's time to actually make a build.

Build Settings

To create a build of your game, you need to first specify what levels you want Unity to include. Unity will not just create a mass build of all your project files. Instead, it requires you to pick and choose exactly what scenes are to be included. From your scene selection, it will then only include the needed assets into the build package. Unused assets will not be included or take up any unnecessary space.

To start your build process, choose File > Build Settings or press Ctrl+Shift+B. In the dialog box that appears, you add the scene files you'd like to include and decide which kind of application Unity should make.

To start populating your build, open your Main Menu scene file, and pick your platform. Then click the Add Current button in Build Settings. This will tell Unity you want to include this file in your final game. Next, open your main game level and click the Add Current button again. The Build Settings dialog box should look like Figure 16.3.

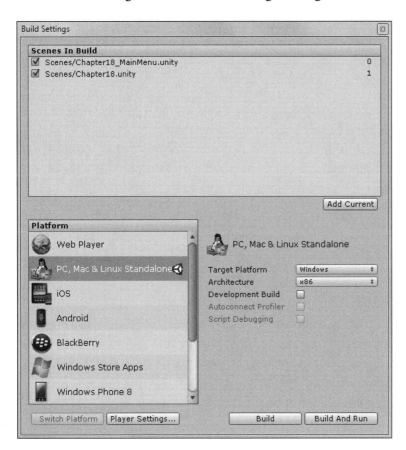

Figure 16.3
The Build Settings dialog box.
Source: Unity Technologies.

You'll notice that Unity assigns an index number to each scene file as you add it, starting at 0, and renumbers them based on each scene's position in the list. If you deselect a checkbox next to a scene file, it won't be loaded in the build. You can also rearrange the scenes in the list by clicking and dragging—an easy fix if you happen to load them out of order. Just remember that whichever scene file is assigned the index value of 0 will always start up your game. Make sure it's the main menu in this case.

Note

Now that your scene files have associated index values in the Build menu, you may find it easier from now on to reference the index number with `Application.LoadLevel()` calls. Instead of having to type a name or change it later, just use the index to load whichever level you want, such as `Application.LoadLevel(1)`.

There are additional options for each platform under Player Settings that you can adjust, but you will generally want to leave these at the defaults unless you have a reason to change them.

The Build Settings information is saved with your project file, and you don't need to redo it each time you want to make a new build. For now, set the game to create as a stand-alone app based on your own computer. Click the Build button to create your game. Unity will prompt you for a filename and save path at this time. You can click Build and Run if you want Unity to also launch the game when it's finished.

Once Unity finishes building, it will kindly open the folder where you saved your game. Double-click it to run your finished game! Go enjoy the fruits of your labor—you've earned it.

OTHER BUILD FEATURES

After you've made your first game or two, you may want to add some new features for dedicated players or package your asset files for use in another project. Perhaps you were hasty in one of your builds, or maybe you want to offer downloadable content (DLC) to your players. Either way, you don't need to create a new build of your game—you can instead have the player load separate asset packs on load.

Asset Bundles

If you have a Unity Pro license, you can use an asset bundle to handle your new additions. There is no limit on the number of different bundles you can associate with a game, and the creation of one is rather simple. From within a script, call the function `BuildPipeline.BuildAssetBundle()`. The argument is an array containing a list of all the additional objects you want to include. Once this is made, you can later load this bundle by calling `AssetBundle.Load()`.

Resource Folders

If you have Unity Basic, you can still create add-ons for your game with resource folders. To do this, simply create a new folder in your Project view and name it Resources. If you want to load an object inside this, simply call `Resources.Load()`.

You may also find asset bundles and resource folders an easy way to load assets at runtime, which can be incredibly useful for a Web game. The app itself is pretty tiny and loads quickly, and then you can stream in only the assets you need, only when you need them.

Packing Up Assets for Later

You can also create asset packages from within your Project view, making it easy to share your assets with another user or save them for later use on a different project. To create a package, simply highlight all the items in the Project view you want to include. Then right-click and select Export Package, as shown in Figure 16.4.

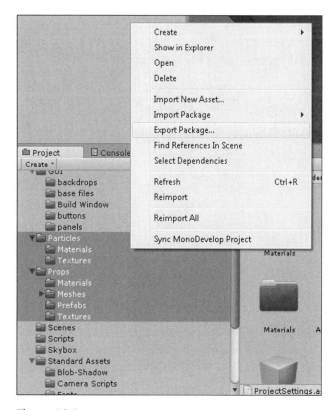

Figure 16.4
Exporting a package.
Source: Unity Technologies.

This opens a dialog box where you can select the individual files you want to include and also decide whether you want to include any dependencies—this is nice if you don't know what the other project already has. Click the Export button and choose a destination for the saved file. Depending on the number and size of the assets selected, this process can take a while. Once you have a package ready to go, you can import it into any project you want by right-clicking in the Project view and selecting Import Package.

THE END OF THE ROAD?

You've now made your first Unity game from start to finish, but it doesn't end here. There are many more advanced features not covered in this book and many changes and tweaks you can make to the *Widget* game alone.

There are several resources in the appendixes to help you continue. Appendix D, "Resources and References," lists some books and websites for extended reading. Appendix C, "Going Forward" discusses some areas of the *Widget* game that you might like to try to improve. *Widget* has some intentional flaws and underdeveloped areas so you can try your new skills in an unguided manner. If you're not ready to start your own project from scratch, it's a good place to continue working on your own.

Unity is an exciting engine that has started to really gain some ground as a competitive option for the hobbyist, student, and professional developer. However, it isn't an engine that makes games. People do. You do. You now have enough knowledge and know-how; go out and make games.

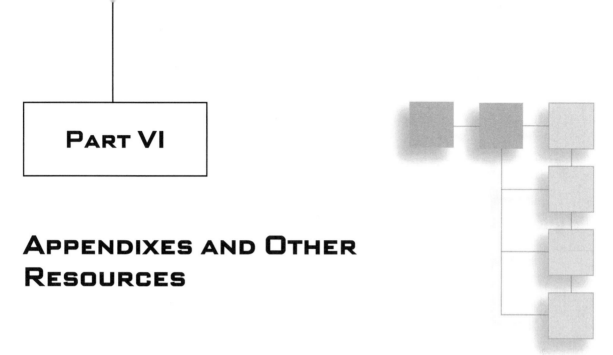

PART VI

APPENDIXES AND OTHER RESOURCES

Here, you'll find all sorts of resources, including shortcuts and hotkeys you might find helpful, a list of common classes you'll likely use as you build your game in Unity, an appendix that provides some extra exercises and examples to try on your own, an appendix with a list of further resources and references should you need them, and finally, a glossary of terms for your reference as you're reading.

Appendix A

Shortcuts and Hotkeys

Table A.1   File Shortcuts

Function	Windows Key	Mac Key
New Scene	Ctrl+N	⌘+N
Open Scene	Ctrl+O	⌘+O
Save Scene	Ctrl+S	⌘+S
Save Scene As	Ctrl+Shift+S	⌘+Shift+S
Build Settings	Ctrl+Shift+B	⌘+Shift+B
Build and Run	Ctrl+B	⌘+B

Table A.2   File Edit Shortcuts

Function	Windows Key	Mac Key
Undo	Ctrl+Z	⌘+Z
Redo	Ctrl+Y	⌘+Shift+Z
Cut	Ctrl+X	⌘+X

(Continued)

Table A.2   File Edit Shortcuts (*Continued*)

Function	Windows Key	Mac Key
Copy	Ctrl+C	⌘+C
Paste	Ctrl+V	⌘+V
Duplicate	Ctrl+D	⌘+D
Delete	Shift+Del	⌘+Delete
Frame Selected	F	F
Find	Ctrl+F	⌘+F
Select All	Ctrl+A	⌘+A
Play	Ctrl+P	⌘+P
Pause	Ctrl+Shift+P	⌘+Shift+P
Step	Ctrl+Alt+P	⌘+Ctrl+P
Load Selection #*	Ctrl+Shift+#*	⌘+Shift+#*
Save Selection #*	Ctrl+Alt+#*	⌘+Ctrl+#*

*# is any number 1–9

Table A.3   File GameObject Shortcuts

Function	Windows Key	Mac Key
Create Empty GameObject	Ctrl+Shift+N	⌘+Shift+N
Move to View	Ctrl+Alt+F	⌘+Ctrl+F
Align with View	Ctrl+Shift+F	Ctrl+Shift+F
Rotate Selected GameObject	E	E
Move Selected GameObject	W	W
Scale Selected GameObject	R	R
Refresh Project List	Ctrl+R	⌘+R
Make Parent	P	P

Table A.4 File Window Shortcuts

Function	Windows Key	Mac Key
Next Window	Ctrl+Tab	⌘+Tab
Previous Window	Ctrl+Shift+Tab	⌘+Shift+Tab
Scene	Ctrl+1	F7
Game	Ctrl+2	F8
Inspector	Ctrl+3	F6
Hierarchy	Ctrl+4	F5
Project	Ctrl+5	F4
Animation	Ctrl+6	F2
Profiler	Ctrl+7	⌘+7
Asset Server	Ctrl+0	⌘+0
Console	Ctrl+Shift+C	⌘+Shift+C

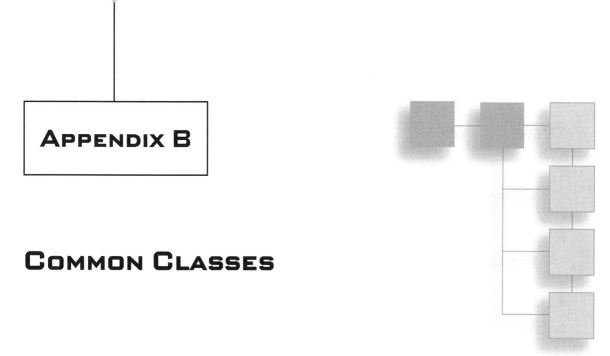

Appendix B

Common Classes

Following is a list of some of the more commonly used classes, with a breakdown of some of their important members.

MonoBehaviour

Every script derives from MonoBehaviour (note the British spelling of "behaviour"). JavaScript automatically derives from this class, whereas C# and Boo must explicitly derive it.

Functions of the MonoBehaviour class are as follows:

- **Update():void:** Called every frame, and is the most often used function to implement game logic and behavior.
- **LateUpdate():void:** Called after all updates have finished running.
- **FixedUpdate():void:** Should be used instead of Update() if physics calculations need to be made.
- **Awake():void:** Called when the script instance is loaded.
- **Start():void:** Called right before any update functions are called for the first time, after Awake().
- **OnTriggerEnter(other: Collider):void:** Called when the collider object other enters the trigger. Pairs with OnTriggerExit().

■ `OnCollisionEnter(collisionInfo: Collision):void`: Called when the collider or rigid body begins touching another collider or rigid body. Pairs with `OnCollisionExit()`.

■ `OnBecameVisible():void`: Called when the renderer becomes visible to any camera. The message being sent to all scripts attached to the renderer. Pairs with `OnBecameInvisible()`.

■ `OnApplicationPause(pause: bool):void`: Message is sent to all GameObjects when the player pauses.

■ `OnApplicationQuit():void`: Message is sent to all GameObjects when the user quits the application.

■ `GetComponent(type: Type):Component`: Returns the component of the specified type if found; returns `null` if not.

■ `SendMessage(functionName: string, value:object=null, options:SendMessageOptions = SendMessageOptions.RequireReceiver):void`: Calls the function named `functionName` on every `MonoBehaviour` attached to the GameObject.

■ `Instantiate(original:Object, position:Vector3, rotation:Quaternion): Object`: Creates an instance of the object `original` and returns the instance. The instanced object is placed at position and then rotated to the given rotation.

■ `Destroy(object:Object, t:float=0.0F):void`: Removes the specified GameObject, component, or asset at the given time from current, if specified.

■ `FindObjectsOfType(type:Type):Object[]`: Returns an array of all active and loaded objects matching the specified type.

■ `DontDestroyOnLoad(target:Object):void`: Ensures that the target object is not automatically destroyed when loading a new scene.

Variables of the `MonoBehaviour` class are as follows:

■ `enabled: bool`: Enabled behaviors are updated every frame.

■ `transform: Transform`: Keyword to reference the `Transform` component attached to the GameObject. Returns `null` if no matching component is found.

■ `audio: AudioSource`: Keyword to reference the `AudioSource` component attached to the GameObject. Returns `null` if no matching component is found.

■ `rigidbody: Rigidbody`: Keyword to reference the `Rigidbody` component attached to the GameObject. Returns `null` if no matching rigid body is found.

- **animation: Animation:** Keyword to reference the `Animation` component attached to the GameObject. Returns `null` if no matching component is found.

- **camera: Camera:** Keyword to reference the `Camera` component attached to the GameObject. Returns `null` if no matching component is found.

- **guiText: GUIText:** Keyword to reference the `GUIText` component attached to the GameObject. Returns `null` if no matching component is found.

- **collider: Collider:** Keyword to reference the `Collider` component attached to the GameObject. Returns `null` if no matching component is found.

- **renderer: Renderer:** Keyword to reference the `Renderer` component attached to the GameObject. Returns `null` if no matching component is found.

- **tag: string:** The given tag of the GameObject.

- **name: string:** The name of the GameObject.

Transform

`Transform` governs the position, rotation, and scale of a GameObject. Every GameObject has a `Transform` component.

Functions of the `Transform` class are as follows:

- **Translate(translation: Vector3, relative:Space = Space.Self):void:** Call to move the transform in the given direction for the specified distance.

- **Rotate(eulerAngles: Vector3, relative:Space = Space.Self):void:** Call to rotate the object by the specified `eulerAngles`.

- **LookAt(target: Transform, worldUp: Vector3= Vector3.up):void:** Call to rotate the transform so that its forward vector points at the target's position.

Variables of the `Transform` class are as follows:

- **position: Vector3:** The location of the object in world space.

- **eulerAngles: Vector3:** The rotation of the object given as Euler angles in degrees.

- **right: Vector3:** The red axis of the transform in world space.

- **up: Vector3:** The green axis of the transform in world space.

- **forward: Vector3:** The blue axis of the transform in world space.

- **rotation: Quaternion:** The rotation of the object in world space given as a quaternion.

Rigidbody

The `Rigidbody` class allows you to control the movement of a GameObject through physics simulation.

Functions of the `Rigidbody` class are as follows:

- `SetDensity(density: float):void`: Sets the mass of the object by assuming a constant density.

- `AddForce(force: Vector3, mode: ForceMode = ForceMode.Force) : void`: Applies a given force to the rigid body. If the force is great enough to overcome its inertia, it will start moving.

- `AddTorque(torque: Vector3, mode:ForceMoce = ForceMode.Force) : void`: Applies a given torque to the rigid body. If the torque is great enough to overcome its inertia, it will start rotating around the torque axis.

- `Sleep():void`: Forces the rigid body to sleep for at least one frame.

Variables of the `Rigidbody` class are as follows:

- `velocity: Vector3`: The velocity vector of the rigid body.

- `drag: float`: The drag of the object—how quickly it slows down.

- `mass: float`: The mass of the rigid body. Usually, this number should be between 0.1 and 10, as values outside these bounds can make the physics simulation unstable.

CharacterController

The `CharacterController` class allows for the easy and straightforward control of an object's movement without having to set up a rigid body. An object with this kind of controller is not affected by forces, will only move with one of the `Move` functions, and will only have its movement obstructed by collisions with other colliders.

Functions of the `CharacterController` class are as follows:

- `SimpleMove(speed: Vector3): bool`: Moves the controller with the given speed in meters/sec. Gravity is automatically applied.

- `Move(motion: Vector3): CollisionFlags`: Moves the controller with the given motion. Any colliders it hits while moving are stored in `CollisionFlags`. Unlike with `SimpleMove`, gravity is not applied.

Variables of the `CharacterController` class are as follows:

- **`isGrounded: bool`:** During the last complete move, was the controller touching the ground?

- **`collisionFlags: CollisionFlags`:** Stores what part of the collider capsule collided with another object during the last move call.

Mathf

`Mathf` is Unity's math library. The basic trig identity and operator functions are not listed here.

Functions of the `Mathf` class are as follows:

- **`Ceil(f: float):float`:** Returns the smallest integer greater than or equal to *f*.

- **`Round(f: float):float`:** Returns the nearest integer to *f*. If *f* ends in .5, the nearest even integer is returned.

- **`Clamp(value: float, min: float, max: float): float`:** Clamps the value between the specified min and max floats.

- **`Lerp(a: float, b: float, time: float): float`:** Interpolates *a* toward *b* by time. Time is clamped automatically between 0 and 1.

- **`PingPong(t: float, max: float): float`:** Swings the value of *t* so that it's never larger than the specified max and never smaller than 0.

- **`DeltaAngle(a: float, b: float): float`:** Calculates the shortest distance between the two specified angles *a* and *b*.

Variables of the `Mathf` class are as follows:

- **`Infinity: float`:** A representation of positive infinity (read-only).

- **`NegativeInfinity: float`:** A representation of negative infinity (read-only).

- **`Deg2Rad: float`:** The degrees to radians conversion constant (read-only). Pairs with Rad2Deg.

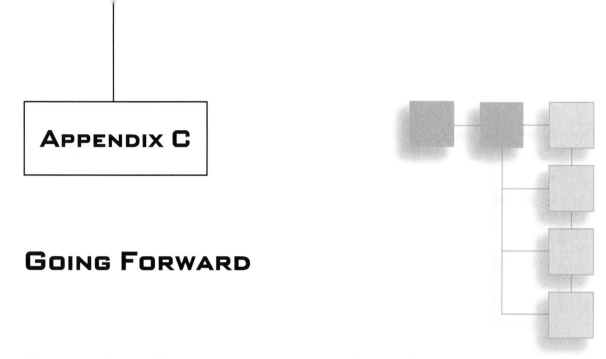

APPENDIX C

GOING FORWARD

This appendix provides some extra exercises and examples to try on your own, all expanding on the skills and knowledge you picked up in the previous chapters. Some of these exercises reference the Design Documents, which are located on the companion website. Many of these require the importation of new assets, which you can find in the Final Project Files and Asset Bundle on the companion website. You can also get creative with primitive GameObjects or use free models you find online to showcase your work.

DESIGN EXERCISES

Consider these design-related exercises to expand on what you've done so far:

- Create a new mechanic in the *Widget* game involving Widget's movement. Think of things he's currently unable to do: double-jump, hover, spin, and so on. Implement the new movement mechanic and hook up the proper input commands.

- Design and lay out a new level for Widget to explore as described in the Design Docs. You can either pick a new level or fully flesh out the Plains one. Extra: Create the portal between the two levels and have Widget load from one to the next. (Don't forget to handle his inventory correctly so it's not deleted between scenes.)

SCRIPTING EXERCISES

Consider these scripting-related exercises to expand on what you've done so far:

- Clean up the camera script so that the camera doesn't pass through objects (like trees). Alternatively, cull large blocky objects so they don't block the camera's view.

- Create a new control schema for the camera that always stays to Widget's back. That way, if the players switch their direction suddenly, the camera moves smoothly to follow them.

- Add a waystation to the forest section of the map (provided in the final assets) and script the scene where the waystation removes the rocks blocking Widget's path, as described in the Design Docs. Use particle systems effectively to hide the deletion of the GameObjects.

- Continue the functionality of the waypoint stores by allowing Widget to buy repair kits and energy packs for gears and screws. Create a way for Widget to purchase a new form (as described in the Design Docs). If a player does not have the right number of items in his inventory, inform him of what he's missing.

- Add some pizzazz to the pickup items by dropping them into the world and having them bounce along the environment until they come to a standstill.

- Implement new attacks and actions for each of Widget's forms, as described in the Design Docs.

- Create a new kind of basic enemy with a different AI: patrolling. Have this new enemy patrol a set path, which he deviates from if the player is spotted. If the enemy loses interest in the player, he should return to his path.

- Create the boss encounter for the Plains area as described in the Design Docs. Have the enemy stay within his bounds and pick between attacking, defending, or doing nothing (giving the player a chance to retaliate). Remember to make the boss drop his unique item, and decide whether the player should get any other kind of reward as well.

- Implement a scoring system, giving the player a better idea of his overall progress. What actions or accomplishments should add to the score? How much? Should anything detract? Would you show the score always or only display it at the end of the game?

ART AND ANIMATION EXERCISES

Consider these exercises related to art and animation to expand on what you've done so far:

- Create a cut scene in Unity depicting Widget's arrival in the forest area. See the Design Docs for a description of the event.

- Create additional animations in Unity for the EBunny enemy.

- Create a cut scene of a camera rollover of the environment—useful for quick introductions to new levels.

- Add more particle effects into the game. For example, add smoke or sparks when two robots fight or collide, a splash of water for when objects hit the river, dust or dirt clouds to follow Widget when he moves, etc.

AUDIO EXERCISES

Consider these sound-related exercises to expand on what you've done so far:

- Add more sound effects to the game—for example, when Widget collects a pickup item, when the user clicks a button, when an enemy enters into range for the first time, or when the EBunny attacks. You could also add more ambient noises.

- Add a new background song into the game when Widget encounters a boss or enemy. Find a pleasing way to merge from the normal background song to the battle theme and then back again once the fight is over.

GUI EXERCISES

Consider these GUI-related exercises to expand on what you've done so far:

- Create a Pause screen that stops the action in the world, halts player input, and hosts a button for quitting or continuing play.

- Create a Game Over screen and define a time when it would appear.

- Implement the interface for a waypoint store screen. How should the waystation's inventory appear? How will Widget's? Will players drag and drop items or click buttons?

- Finish implementing the HUD described in the Design Docs for Widget's forms. Each form button should only appear once it's created in the store.

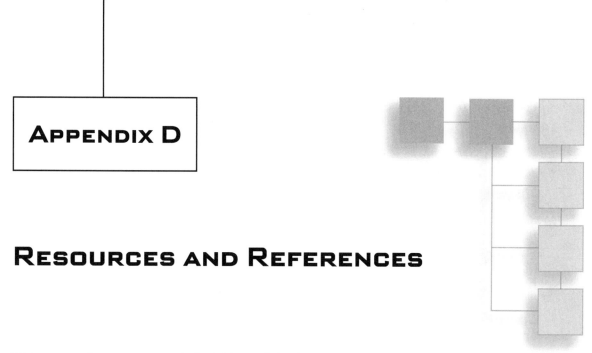

APPENDIX D

RESOURCES AND REFERENCES

This appendix contains a helpful list of further resources or references, should you need them. Included are additional texts, websites, and tool packages, broken down by game discipline.

BOOKS

This section contains a collection of texts for further reading and study, organized by discipline.

For more information on design, see the following:

- *Rules of Play* by Katie Salen and Eric Zimmerman: One of the introductory texts on game design.

- *Challenges for Game Designers* by Brenda Brathwaite and Ian Schreiber: For those interested in expanding their design skills, this book pushes you to develop new skills and processes through a series of fun exercises.

- *A Theory of Fun for Game Design* by Raph Koster: A light but inspiring read.

- *Patterns in Game Design* by Staffan Björk and Jussi Holopainen: Dense with information and intimidating to some, this is a fabulous reference-style book for any designer's shelves.

For more information on art, see the following:

- **Introducing Maya 2011** **by Dariush Derakhshani:** A comprehensive startup guide to computer graphics and Maya 2011.

- **Digital Texturing and Painting** **by Owen Demers:** A great look at how traditional painting techniques can enhance your digital textures.

- **Stop Staring** **by Jason Osipa:** Covers the basics and advanced techniques in human facial animation.

- **Digital Lighting & Rendering** **by Jeremy Birn:** The sister book to Demers', this book is a great start for anyone interested in computer-generated lighting and rendering techniques.

For more information on programming in general, see the following:

- **JavaScript: The Definitive Guide** **by David Flanagan:** For those interested in JavaScript and what it has to offer, this is one of the best texts on the market.

- **Programming Logic and Design, Comprehensive** **by Joyce Farrell:** A more traditional and comprehensive look at logic and programming structure.

- **Essential Mathematics for Games and Interactive Applications** **by James M. Van Verth and Lars M. Bishop:** If you feel your math skills aren't up to snuff, this is the book for you.

- **Game Programming Gems Series**: Not introductory texts, the books in this series are nonetheless among the must-haves for any game developer.

PROGRAMS

This section contains links to downloadable programs you might be interested in. Some are open source and free to use, and others offer free trials before purchase.

Art-related programs include the following:

- **MonoDevelop (monodevelop.com):** A free IDE designed for C# and other .NET languages.

- **Maya (usa.autodesk.com):** A comprehensive tool for 3D modeling, animation, visual effects, and rendering. A free trial is available.

- **Blender (www.blender.org):** A free, open source 3D graphics tool, available for all major operating systems.

- **Cheetah (www.cheetah3d.com):** A 3D modeling and animation suite for Mac OSX.

- **ZBrush (www.pixologic.com):** A modeling suite with a unique approach to sculpting and texturing.

- **GIMP (www.gimp.org):** A free, open source image-manipulation and creation suite.

- **Photoshop (www.adobe.com/products/photoshop):** An industry-standard image-manipulation and creation suite.

Scripting-related programs include the following:

- **MonoDevelop (monodevelop.com):** A free integrated development environment (IDE) designed for C# and other .NET languages.

- **Visual Studio (www.microsoft.com/express):** Microsoft's Visual Studio Express suite is the free IDE version of their popular Visual Studio.

- **emacs (www.gnu.org/software/emacs):** A free, extensible, customizable text editor.

- **UnityDevelop (www.subethaedit.net):** Another free, very lean text editor.

- **Notepad++ (notepad-plus-plus.org):** A free source-code editor and general replacement for the default Notepad application.

SCRIPTING AND GENERAL UNITY HELP

Check out these links for Unity-specific help and guidance:

- **Unity (unity3d.com):** Unity's home page.

- **Unify Community (www.unifycommunity.com):** One of the go-to spots on the Internet for scripting help and support.

- **Unity Answers (answers.unity3d.com):** Ask a questions of Unity vets, see posted responses, and follow hot topics about the engine.

- **Unity Community Forums (forum.unity3d.com):** Sign up for a forum account and get postings.

- **irc.freenode.net:** If you're on IRC, join #unity3d to chat in real time with other users.

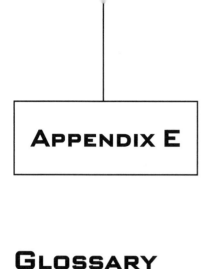

APPENDIX E

GLOSSARY

A

alpha/alpha map/alpha channels   An alpha channel allows an image to appear partially or fully transparent. Areas of the channel that are painted black denote full transparency, whereas areas of the channel painted white denote full opacity. By combining the alpha with the normal color channels, an image can appear to be nonsquare, be semitransparent, or have "holes" cut out of it.

animation layers   In computer animation, the artist can construct his animation data on different layers, which can then be composited together for a final shot. In this way, specific layers can be reused across multiple rigs, allowing the animator to share data and not have to redo his work. Alternatively, a specific layer can be tweaked independently, allowing for greater control. For example, an animated human character may make use of three layers: one for his mouth (for lip synching), one for his facial expressions (for eye blinks, smiles, and twitches), and one for body movement. The artist can then easily change one area without disrupting others.

application programming interface (API)   An API is an interface implemented by one piece of software that allows it to "talk" and interact with another, much like how a mouse allows you to interface directly with the computer. APIs generally consist of a collection of libraries, which contain the data structures and calls used to talk between the two pieces of software, much like how you might use a dual-language dictionary to translate from one spoken language to another.

array   A data structure that consists of a collection of elements in a list, each associated with a special index number denoting its place in the list.

artificial intelligence (AI)   The set of commands that dictates how a given computer-controlled entity behaves. The moniker "intelligence" is a bit misleading, as these commands only explain how something should react in a given situation. The program doesn't actually do any "thinking."

asset   In Unity, an asset is anything you've placed into your game scene or imported into your project. Script files, meshes, textures, GameObjects, and lights are all examples of assets.

B

backlight   In lighting, the backlight is the light source placed behind the target object, generally directly across from the camera. It creates a soft outline and halo around the target object, giving it some definition and allowing it to pop from the background.

behavior (AI script)   A behavior defines how a particular programmed entity (such as an enemy) will behave in a given situation. Usually this takes the form of some kind of environment evaluation followed by a list of what to do if the situation arises. For example, an enemy may have a programmed behavior that tells it to fire its weapon if the player is in sight and within 20 paces. The behavior could be further refined with more conditionals to make it appear as if the enemy takes into account movement speed, obstacles in its path, or anything else in the scene that may be relevant.

billboard   A billboard is a flat (2D) plane upon which an image is displayed or projected. Billboards always turn to face the camera so as not to break the illusion that they are not in fact 3D objects. These are used primarily to replace geometry far away from the player's camera, making the game still look richly populated but not eating up too much memory.

blend shapes   An animation technique that is especially useful for creating different facial expressions. Key expressions (angry, happy, and sad) are created, and then intermediate states are programmatically created by blending the different aspects together.

Boo   An object-oriented programming language using Python-inspired syntax. It is sometimes referred to as a dialect of Python. Boo is compatible with Microsoft .NET and Mono and has been in active use since 2003.

Boolean   A logical data type that can be set as only one of two values: true or false.

built-in array   A statically typed array that runs incredibly quickly in Unity. The type and size of the array must be set at its creation. It trades off the flexibility of a dynamic array for speed.

bump map   A grayscale image used to simulate the appearance of raised texture on a surface, like wrinkles, bumps, or scratches. Dark areas on a bump map correspond to recessed areas, whereas lighter areas appear to push out from the object's surface.

C

C#   Pronounced "C sharp," this is a multi-paradigm programming language developed by Microsoft within the .NET framework. It was later approved as a standard by ECMA and ISO. From its inception, C# was designed to be simple, modern, and generally useful regardless of the task at hand.

cache   In Unity, caching a link to a GameObject in code allows a script to directly access any component of the GameObject without having to locate it in the scene list. If any component is going to be referenced or changed multiple times (especially in a call like Update()), a cache should be used.

capsule collider   A collider in Unity that is shaped like a giant capsule or pill. These are intended to be used for humanoid character collision bounds, as they are fairly good and cheap approximations of a human's head, torso, and legs.

Cartesian   Specifies a point in a given plane by a pair of numerical coordinates, which denote its position along the vertical and horizontal axes. Common Cartesian planes are based on X-Y coordinates and are displayed in the notation (X,Y), where X and Y are replaced by the specific numeral, such as (0,0) or (−1, 5). Cartesian coordinates can also be used to denote other dimensional spaces, simply by appending the new axis in the notation. A 3D space described by the X, Y, and Z axes is noted (X,Y,Z). See Figure E.1.

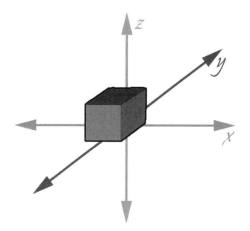

Figure E.1
The Cartesian coordinate system.

character controller   The character controller denotes the component that controls a character in a game that does not make use of rigid body physics. Its properties describe the shape and size of the capsule collider and the specific details regarding its collision with the environment.

character rig   The collection of bones, joints, and interface controls that an animator can use to make a character mesh move. The rig is placed inside the mesh, and then individual vertices are mapped (skinned) to the rig's bones, denoting which bone should move which part of the mesh's body, much like how your own muscles move specific bones. Rigs can be shared across multiple meshes if they're shaped similarly.

child   In a parent-child relationship, the child is an object that is connected to the parent and inherits all of the parent's properties: position, rotation, and scale. The child object may be changed and updated independently of the parent object, but any change made to the parent object propagates to the child object.

collision   The effect described when two objects' bounding areas intersect in the game world.

component   An attachment in Unity to a GameObject that describes a specific property or relationship. Some simple components include audio sources, materials, mesh colliders, and skinned mesh renderers. A component can be independently created, but it can't do anything until it is assigned to a GameObject.

conditional statement/test   Conditional statements in scripting include phrases like "if" and "or," and are used to evaluate a given situation to provide a set response. For example, a simple code for moving an object could read: "If the object is red, then move it right. If the object is green, move it left. If it is any other color, move it up."

control (GUI)   A specific kind of interface element, like a button, text field, or selection group. Controls can be simple, like a button, or complex, such as a combination of multiple control types to make one new hybrid one.

cookies/light cookies   Simple textures or decals applied to a light to make it appear more complex than it is, or to give the illusion that it's shining "through" something. For example, a grid outline could be applied to a spotlight to make it seem as if the light is shining through a window. The grid lines block out the light and make it look like a window pane, when in reality it's just a simple line.

core (of a game)   The basic idea or theme statement behind your game. The core statement sums up everything that your game is about.

co-routine   A program component describing sections of code to be run using multiple different points or conditions for suspending and resuming.

cube map   A method in graphics to map an environment onto a six-sided cube. The cube map can then be applied to a material to create the illusion of a reflection. It would then seem as if the object were reflecting the world around it, when in reality it was just displaying a static image. Cube maps can also be used for skyboxes and for creating global illumination illusions.

curve (animation)   An interpolated curve connects the various keyframes set by an animator, giving the object in question the path it should follow. Curves can be tweaked individually, which can sometimes be easier to deal with than the specific keys.

D

debugging   The act of locating and identifying errors (bugs) in a script and then systematically fixing them.

detail maps   These provide an extra layer of detail as the camera approaches the object in question. These small, finely detailed textures are faded in using a detail shader. These can be effective to show wood grain, sand, grit, or fine brickwork in a texture.

detail mesh (Terrain Engine)   A quick-to-render mesh painted onto a terrain to give it some extra small detail—things like rocks, flowers, or other small objects. Larger objects should be placed by hand, but detail meshes are "painted" on using brush strokes, allowing for the quick placement of multiple meshes at one time.

diffuse   Describes flat, normal color. Diffuse shaders, for example, show only the RGB channels of a texture—no reflection or specular highlights.

DXT compression   A family of lossy texture compression algorithms developed by S3 Graphics, Ltd. These compression algorithms are widely used by the gaming industry and support textures with alpha channels and up to 64-bit color data.

E

emitter   Part of a particle system that projects, or emits, the individual particles into the world. Emitters can have different shapes and can be directional, allowing for the exact placement and size of the particles at hand.

enum   The enum, or enumerated type, is a data type comprised of a set of named values. These names are usually some form of identifier that behaves like a constant in the language. You can think of red, green, and blue as being three named values, or enumerators, of the enumerated type called "colors."

F

feature set   The feature set of a game describes the main ideas or mechanics that make the game unique. The feature set is often used to describe a game to a potential new customer or market, as it conveniently breaks down the core into easy digestible chunks.

feedback (GUI)   Feedback is the part of a GUI system that lets users know what effect, if any, their actions had on a given system. Without feedback, users might never know if a button they clicked did anything or if the system is processing a request. Feedback generally takes the form of switching colors, playing a small sound, or changing screens.

fill light   The fill light in a lighting setup fills the scene with soft ambient light and, in computer graphics, helps give the illusion that light is bouncing off of the surfaces of objects in the scene. Fill lights help smooth the contrast between highlights and shadows and help soften the general look of a scene.

forward kinematics (FK)   A way of animating a model by moving the parent joint first and then subsequent joints afterward. For example, in an FK rig, the shoulder rotation of a human would be set first, followed by the elbow and then the wrist.

frames per second (FPS)   The number of frames the engine computes and renders per second of real time. Most games shoot for a frame rate of over 30 FPS, since the human eye reads frame rates lower than this as flickering.

function   A set of sub-instructions in a script that performs a specific task. Functions can be called (started) from other places in the code, allowing for more complex systems and calculations than a simple linear collection of lines would allow.

G

GameObject   The basic data type in Unity. GameObjects are basically containers for components and do not have any properties or characteristics of their own.

gizmo   A simple bounding box or tool used for manipulating objects in an engine or 3D modeling package. The Scale, Rotation, and Transform tools are all gizmos.

global/static variable   A variable that is accessible in any scope—that is, it is universally available no matter where you are in your scripts. Although variables can be great for accessing important properties (like a main character's health), they can be tedious and difficult to track and can inadvertently introduce bugs.

graphical user interface (GUI)   A type of computer interface that allows users to interact with the system with a collection of pictures and icons rather than by typing commands in a console window. Many games make use of a GUI in some way—displaying health points, showing a map of the area, or giving the user onscreen buttons to click to perform an action.

grass (Terrain Engine)   A terrain object that paints 2D billboards, or textures, onto the terrain. This is particularly useful for things like flowers or grasses. Anything that needs to be displayed in 3D, like a rock, should use a detail mesh.

H

heads up display (HUD)   A display in video games that generally refers to the bits of information displayed on a player's main screen (like current health, lives, or selected attack or item). It takes its name from modern aircraft HUDs. HUD information does not have to be brought up actively by the players (like a menu). It is always visible. Some games, however, do provide an option for players to hide or disable the HUD.

heightmap   A 2D grayscale image from which Unity can interpolate height. Darker areas denote recessed areas (valleys), and lighter, whiter areas denote height (peaks).

I

instance   A copy of a prefab added to a scene. This can be done in the editor by the user directly, or instances can be programmatically created and placed through scripts. Instances share all the properties of the parent prefab.

instantiation   The act of creating an instance at runtime, through scripts.

interpolation   The method by which a complete range of data points is constructed from only a few specified elements, like drawing a curve through a few points on a graph. Interpolations are used extensively in games to create animation curves and to describe how an object should move from one point to the next. See Figure E.2.

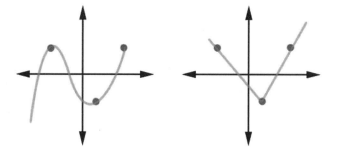

Figure E.2
Two different interpolated graphs based on the same points of data.

inverse kinematics (IK)   A method for animating by moving the child object first and then interpolating the position of the intermediate objects therein. For example, in a human rig, the arm can be set up as an IK system, reaching from the shoulder to the wrist. The animator can grab the wrist and move it to a new location. Doing so will move the elbow and arm segments naturally with the wrist, but the shoulder will remain at a fixed point.

isometric projection   A way to visually represent a 3D space on a 2D plane (like your monitor). Isometric projections are characterized by their particular foreshortening approach, where objects do not get smaller with distance. They do not depict realistic perspective.

J

JavaScript   A language using syntax influenced by C originally developed by Netscape for use in programming websites. Unity's implementation of JavaScript (also sometimes referred to as UnityScript) is about 20 times faster than traditional JavaScript and is the official language of the engine.

JavaScript array   The Array class implemented in JavaScript is a native .NET array. JavaScript arrays are dynamic and allow for resizing, sorting, and all the basic array operations you may be familiar with, but are slower to run and do not show up in the Inspector.

K

key (animation)/keyframe   After positioning his rig into the pose he wants at a specific time, the animator can set a key, thus saving the position, rotation, and scale data for the object at that moment of time. He can then skip a few frames later (multiple frames making up one second of film) and set a new key for the object's next important pose. The computer can then interpolate the data and move the object from one stored pose to the next.

key light   The main source of light in a given lighting setup. The key light often represents the strongest source of light available—something like a giant spot or the sun.

keyword   A special word in Unity that helps you reference specific components more quickly or provides access to needed functions. These are often shortcuts for some of the most used features. For example, instead of having to locate a GameObject's Audio Source component via GetComponent, you can use the predefined keyword "audio" to reference it directly.

L

light   A special GameObject in the Unity engine that creates the illusion of illumination. A light can light other objects either per pixel or per vertex and in the Unity Pro version can cast shadows.

lightmap   A flat texture describing the brightness of specified surfaces, usually as a grayscale image. Useful for static objects, light terrains, and environment pieces. Darker areas of the texture correspond to shadowed areas, whereas lighter areas of the texture indicate places that are receiving light. The brighter the texture area, the brighter the light on the surface.

loop (`for` **and** `while`)   Special programming statements that allow a piece of code to be executed repeatedly. Loops can be finite and iterate over a given set of instructions—say, from X = 0 to X = 10—or be infinitely run until stopped by an outside force.

M

material   Describes the color and specific textural properties of a GameObject. Materials also control how much any given texture is tiled or stretched across an object. Each material is associated with a specific shader and provides access to tweak that shader's particular parameters.

mechanic   A rule in a game. Mechanics describe specifically how something works, from walking to punching to leveling up. Similar and related mechanics are often grouped into systems. For example, you may have a mechanic to describe how a character walks, another for how he runs, and a third for how he swims. All three mechanics make up a movement system.

member variable   Describes any variable defined outside of a function in a script file. Public member variables are then accessible for editing and assignment in the Inspector.

mesh   A collection of vertices, edges, and faces that make up a 3D model.

mesh collider   The most complex collider shape available in Unity. Instead of abstracting the collision boundaries down into a primitive shape (like a sphere or box), a more complex mesh is used. This collider gives the most exact collision detection, but it is slower to use.

mip map   A smaller and smaller version of a texture file, which is swapped in when the textured object gets farther away from the camera. This not only helps increase rendering speed, but also helps reduce artifacts created from aliasing.

Mono   A free, open source project intended to create a set of standard .NET-compatible tools. Unity's game logic runs on Mono.

Musical Instrument Digital Interface (MIDI)   A standardized way to represent music—pitch, volume, vibrato, and so on—in a series of simple messages. Music is stored as a set of coded instructions instead of as an audio waveform. MIDI software can then interpret the instructions and play the song back.

N

normal distribution   Usually associated with the probability density function of the same name, the normal distribution describes the classic bell curve. It approximates the idea that values tend to cluster around the mean, with smaller and smaller amounts of data located at the extremities. Normal distributions are a classic way to implement random functions in game logic. For example, suppose you have an attack that deals a mean damage of 5, with a min of 1 and a max of 9. Rather than just having the script randomly pick a value from 1 to 9, it should instead more often pick a number close to 5 and every now and then pick one closer to 1 or 9.

normal map   Gives the illusion that an object is more finely modeled or detailed than it actually is. Rather than having to sculpt every fold or line on a face (which can take a long time), a normal map is painted and then applied to the model. Much like a heightmap, darker areas on the map recede into the mesh, whereas lighter, whiter areas push out.

null   A null pointer has a value that indicates that it isn't currently referring to an object. (This doesn't necessarily mean zero.)

O

operator   A simple primitive function, like addition (+) or division (/). In scripting, some operators can be used on multiple data types, not just numbers. For example, the addition operator can be used to add two numbers (5 + 3 = 8) or to conjoin two strings ("Hello" + "World" = "Hello World").

optimization   The act of making your game run faster, smoother, and more efficiently. This can include rewriting code to run better, making textures smaller, or changing the quality settings of rendering-intensive processes like casting dynamic shadows.

orthographic   When modeling, an orthographic projection shows the main Cartesian projections of a given object. For example, a modeler often wants an orthographic concept image to work from. The concept artist would then provide a front view, side view, and back view for the modeler. With these three flat views, she can more accurately sculpt a 3D model.

P

parent   In a parent-child relationship, the parent object is the top object in the hierarchy chain. Any changes made to the parent object pass down to all the children, their children, their children's children, and so on. A child object may be changed independently of the parent. *See also* child.

particle   One instanced piece emitted in a particle system. For example, a game may make use of a particle system to describe a set of leaves blowing through a scene. Each individual leaf is a particle in the system.

particle system   The collection of particles and their emitter used to simulate effects in a game, usually things that are hard to render or produce otherwise (like smoke, fire, sparks, and so on). Meshes may also be used as particles in a system, like leaves, snowflakes, or bubbles, and then changed and animated as one mass through the emitter.

performance   How well the computer runs a given application. For example, a game that's running at 10 FPS on the lowest possible graphics settings has bad performance. On the other hand, an application running at 80 FPS with every setting set to the top level has a high performance.

perspective   The collection of ways in which a 3D space is represented on a 2D space, like a 3D world on your flat monitor. Different perspectives are characterized by the way they handle objects getting smaller as they're placed farther from the camera, including stretching the proportions of an individual object along the viewer's line of sight (foreshortening).

pivot point   When rotating an object, the invisible point around which it rotates. Often, this point is located in the exact center of the object, but it can be moved anywhere (including outside the object into empty space) to simulate different effects.

Poisson distribution   A method to describe the probability of an event occurring over a given set of time. These are often bell-shaped in nature and can be skewed to one side or the other. They are related to normal distributions and are another great way to implement the feeling of randomness in game logic.

prefab   A reusable object that can be instanced in the game level. All instances are linked to the original prefab. A change in the original will update automatically to all the instances.

private variable   A variable that cannot be accessed outside of the script in which it is defined and cannot be shown or referenced in the Inspector.

projector   Used in Unity to "project" a given image onto something else. Shadows are often faked with projectors—a black image is projected onto the ground underneath the character, making it appear as if it were actually casting a shadow.

pseudo code   An easy, compact way of describing code so that it can be read by a human and not by a computer. Often, programmers like to start their scripting with pseudo code, as it allows them to get their thoughts in order before actually using programmatic syntax.

R–S

rigid body   In Unity, a rigid body controls an object's position through physics simulation. For example, instead of manually moving an object around a scene, something with a rigid body component will react naturally to gravity (it will fall) and collide or bounce off of other objects it encounters.

scripting environment   A software application that provides extended abilities to facilitate script writing. Common utilities include word completion, syntax highlighting, and a debugger.

shader   Describes the physical properties of your object and how light interacts with it. For example, a simple diffuse shader may be used to describe a piece of old wood, whereas a reflective shader would be used for a shiny piece of metal.

skinned mesh   A mesh that has an animation rig attached to it. Skinning a mesh involves specifying which vertices are controlled by which rig bones.

skybox   A large box (or sometimes hemisphere) placed or projected around a game world, giving the impression of a faraway landscape or sky. Skyboxes in Unity are generally created with cube map projection.

spawn   The live creation of an object in-game, similar to instantiation. In many games, the player character spawns at the beginning of a level and then respawns (revives) at particular locations when he dies.

specular   In Unity, this defines the way light is reflected off a given surface. An object with high specularity is very glassy and reflects a large swath of light. Objects with low specularity aren't as reflective and reflect light in a smaller area.

splat map   An alternate naming convention for textures applied to a terrain. Usually, multiple splat maps are used in conjunction with each other to paint a given terrain, painted at different opacities to give the impression of greater detail.

sprite   A 2D image or animation. Sprites are often used in particle systems, but they can also be used to animate figures in a 2D game. For example, a character in a 2D game would have a sprite for each main pose in a walk animation. The computer would then loop through each sprite to give the illusion that the character was actually moving.

static mesh   Meshes that are not or cannot be animated per vertex. They can be animated as a whole object—that is, translated, scaled, or rotated.

system (of mechanics)   A collection of related mechanics—for example, mechanics defining how to fight using a sword, cast a spell, defend, and use offensive items could be collected into a battle system.

T

terrain   A sculpted mesh that allows you to paint landscapes easily and efficiently. If an outdoor area is needed, terrains are a low-overhead and highly customizable option.

texture   A map applied to the surface of a polygon or mesh, often to provide color or reflection data.

toon shader   Creates the effect of traditional cel shading in pen and paper animation, but in 3D graphic form. These appear to be hand drawn like a comic or cartoon.

tree (Terrain Engine)   Unity's trees are special paintable objects on terrains. Up close to the camera, trees are rendered as full 3D objects, whereas trees in the distance are billboarded. This creates the illusion of dense terrain, yet is much faster to render than had all the trees been 3D models. *See also* billboard.

trigger   A special collider that fires an event when another specified collider enters or leaves its bounding area. Triggers can be tied to physical objects in the scene or be invisible areas seen only in the editor.

true color   A method for displaying and storing a large number of different colors along with their hues and shades. True color can display approximately 16.7 million distinct colors.

U

unit   The unit of measurement across a scene. In Unity, 1 unit equals 1 real-world meter, making it fairly easy to scale objects and judge distances in a realistic manner.

user interface (UI)   A system by which a human interacts with a computer using both hardware and software components. These include elements such as mice, a keyboard, and an onscreen Exit button.

UV map   The flat texture generated by unwrapping a 3D model. UV maps are then painted to create diffuse texture maps and reapplied to the original model. Often, each individual UV on the map is mapped to one vertex on the model.

V

vector   An element that has both a length and a direction component, or magnitude and direction.

vertex   A data structure that defines a unique point in either 2D or 3D space. On a 3D mesh, the vertices describe the actual shape of the object. Edges are drawn between them that are then extrapolated into polygonal faces.

W–X

widget   A GUI element that allows the user to manipulate data or an object onscreen. The Move, Scale, and Rotate tools in Unity are all widgets, as are simpler items like menu buttons.

XML   A standard way to encode documents and contain information in an easy-to-access form. Many games and APIs use XML (short for Extensible Markup Language) documents to store applications and save data.

INDEX